Toward the Postmodern

Philosophy and Literary Theory

Series Editor: Hugh J. Silverman

This series provides full-scale, in-depth assessments of important issues in the context of philosophy and literary theory, as they inscribe themselves in the developing archive of textual studies. It highlights studies that take a philosophical or theoretical position with respect to literature, literary study, and the practice of criticism. The individual volumes focus on semiotics, hermeneutics, post-phenomenology, deconstruction, postmodernism, feminism, cultural criticism, and other new developments in the philosophico-literary debate.

Stephen Barker
Autoaesthetics

Robert Bernasconi
Heidegger in Question

Véronique M. Fóti
*Heidegger and the Poets**

Richard Kearney
Poetics of Modernity

Jean-François Lyotard
*Toward the Postmodern**

Michael Naas
Turning: From Persuasion to Philosophy

Wilhelm S. Wurzer
*Filming and Judgment**

*Available in paperback

Toward the Postmodern

—◆—

Jean-François Lyotard

Edited by
Robert Harvey
and
Mark S. Roberts

Humanities Press
New Jersey

First published 1993 by Humanities Press International, Inc.
Atlantic Highlands, New Jersey 07716

First paperback reprint 1995

Articles originally published in French: *Des dispositifs pulsionnels*;
Dérive à partir de Marx et Freud; *Rudiments païens*
All © Christian Bourgois, Editeur, 1980
English translation © Humanities Press International, Inc., 1993
With the exception of "Oedipe juif," English translation by
permission of Semiotext(e).
"Sur la force des faibles" © Jean-François Lyotard, 1976
"Ce qui est 'de l'art'" © Jean-François Lyotard, 1992
"Retour sur le retour" © Jean-François Lyotard, 1992
"Psychoanalytic Approach" article from *Main Trends in Aesthetics
and the Sciences of Art* © Unesco, 1978
Reproduced with the permission of Unesco.
"A Few Words to Sing"
"The Survivor"
"Prescription"
English texts © Jean-François Lyotard, 1992
English translations © Humanities Press International, Inc., 1993
Sequenza III is reprinted with permission from Universal Edition
(London) Ltd., London, © 1968
All editorial material and apparatus © Humanities Press International, Inc., 1993

Library of Congress Cataloging-in-Publication Data
Lyotard, Jean-François.
    [Essays. English. Selections]
    Toward the postmodern / Jean-François Lyotard ; edited by Robert
Harvey and Mark S. Roberts.
        p.   cm.   — (Philosophy and literary theory)
    Includes bibliographical references and index.
    ISBN 0–391–3890–7 (pbk)
    1. Postmodernism. I. Harvey, Robert, 1951– . II. Roberts,
Mark S. III. Title. IV. Series.
B831.2.L96   1993
194—dc20   92–719
                    CIP

A catalog record for this book is available from the British Library.

Printed in the United States of America

Contents

◆

Note on the Translation	*vii*
Acknowledgments	*ix*
Editors' Introduction	*xii*

PART ONE: THE LIBIDINAL

1. The Psychoanalytic Approach to Artistic and Literary Expression	2
2. On a Figure of Discourse	12
3. Jewish Oedipus	27
4. "A Few Words to Sing"	41

PART TWO: THE PAGAN

5. On the Strength of the Weak	62
6. Humor in Semiotheology	73
7. Futility in Revolution	87
8. Retortion in Theopolitics	115
9. False Flights in Literature	125

PART THREE: THE INTRACTABLE

10. The Survivor   144

11. On What Is "Art"   164

12. Prescription   176

13. Return upon the Return   192

    Notes   207
    Bibliography   223
    Index   245

Note on the Translation

———◆———

The essays composing *Toward the Postmodern* have been translated by both its editors and by several other scholars long familiar with Lyotard's work. As editors, we have ensured terminological consistency and accuracy of expression throughout the volume. Whenever available, standard English translations of works cited by Lyotard have been used, with any variance noted.

In the course of editing the text, we have discovered a number of technical (psychoanalytic, linguistic, philosophical) or polysemic terms employed by Lyotard that might have posed problems. Careful deliberation has been devoted to the following choices:

balayage = scanning
bande = track, strip
capter = to collect
capturer = to harness
charme = lure
découpage = has been left untranslated, has no exact equivalent in English where the borrowed word designates the art of decorating a surface with paper cutouts. To approach Lyotard's intended meaning, the French definitions of *découpage* should be recalled: (1) the act of cutting up; (2) children's cutouts; (3) the division of a scenario into scenes.
dessaisissement = disseizure
détourner = to deviate, to divert, to lead astray
écriture = scripture (holy), writing
événementiel = eventful
instance = agency, insistence (Lacan)
jeux scéniques or *ludi scoenici* = playing out scenes, scene-playing
langagier = language-like
lexique = glossary
rusé = artful

vii

suppôt = instrument
vain = vain

Of course, Lyotard's intention in using these and other terms is always contextual. Thus each meaning can be drawn from a careful reading of his texts. However, for glossaries containing concise and more or less reliable definitions of some typically Lyotardian notions, the reader may refer to Bill Readings's *Introducing Lyotard: Art and Politics* (London and New York: Routledge, 1991) and *The Differend*, trans. by Georges Van Den Abbeele (Minneapolis: University of Minnesota Press, 1988).

Acknowledgments

———◆———

We would first like to thank the translators named below for their prompt work and accurate renderings.

We are indebted especially to Jean-François Lyotard for his inspiration and aid at all stages of the manuscript. Thanks also to David Allison, Geoff Bennington, Rachel Bowlby, Jean-François Chanet, Dick Howard, Hugh J. Silverman, and Victor Tejera, who provided valuable advice and assistance. Finally, we would like to thank Hélène Volat for the exhaustive bibliography.

Permission to reprint and/or translate the contents was granted and is recognized as follows:

"Principales tendances actuelles de l'étude psychanalytique des expressions artistiques et littéraires," *Dérive à partir de Marx et Freud* (1973): 53–77; "The Psychoanalytic Approach to Artistic and Literary Expression" appeared in its original form under the title "Psychoanalytic Approach" in *Main Trends in Aesthetics and the Sciences of Art* (1978); ©UNESCO granted permission to reprint our altered version of this anonymous translation.[†]

"Sur une figure de discours" is from *Des dispositifs pulsionnels* (1973, 1980): 127–47. This text was originally presented at an international symposium on the theory of the text at Urbino, Italy, in July 1972. Original English translation: Mark S. Roberts.[†]

"Oedipe juif" first appeared in *Critique* 26, no. 277 (1970): 530–45, then in *Dérive à partir de Marx et Freud* (1973): 167–88. Susan Hanson's original translation, which we have used here, was first published as "Jewish Oedipus" in *Genre* 10 no. 3 (1977): 395–411, and it reappeared in *Drift-works* (1984): 35–53.[†]

"'A Few Words to Sing': Sequenza III" was written in collaboration with

Dominique Avron, *Musique en jeu* 2 (1971): 28–44 and was republished in *Dérive à partir de Marx et Freud* (1973): 248–71. Original English translation: Leonard R. Lawlor.‡

"Sequenza III" is used by permission of European American Music Distributors Corporation, sole U.S. and Canadian agent for Universal Edition (London) Ltd., London; ©1968 by Universal Edition (London) Ltd., London.

"Sur la force des faibles" first appeared in the *Lyotard* issue of *L'Arc* 64 (1976): 4–12. Original English translation: Fred J. Evans.‡

"Humour en sémiothéologie" first appeared as "Que le signe est hostie, et l'inverse; et comment s'en débarrasser," *Critique* 30, no. 342 (1975): 1111–26, then in *Rudiments païens* (1977): 32–59. Original English translation: Mira Kamdar.†

"Futilité en révolution" first appeared as "Considérations préliminaires à une histoire païenne: Notes sur la déchristianisation," in Gilbert Lascault, ed., *Vers une esthétique sans entrave* (1975): 255–87, then in *Rudiments païens* (1977): 157–212. Original English translation: Kenneth Berri.†

"Rétorsion en théopolitique" first appeared as "Puissance des traces, ou contribution de Ernst Bloch à une histoire païenne," in Gérard Raulet, ed., *Utopie–Marxisme selon Ernst Bloch* (1976): 57–67, then in *Rudiments païens* (1977): 60–80. Original English translation: Mira Kamdar.†

"Faux-fuyant dans la littérature" first appeared as "La Confession coupée" in Georges Raillard, ed., *Butor* (1974): 124–69, then in *Rudiments païens* (1977): 81–114. Original English translation: Robert Harvey.†

"Le Survivant" appeared in Miguel Abensour et al., eds., *Ontologie et politique: Actes du colloque Hannah Arendt*, 257–76 (Paris: Tierce, 1988), then as "Survivant: Arendt" in *Lectures d'enfance* (1991): 59–87. Original English translation: Robert Harvey and Mark S. Roberts.‡

"Ce qui est 'de l'art'" appeared as "Désordre: Valéry" in *Lectures d'enfance* (1991): 109–26. Original English translation: Robert Harvey.‡

"La Prescription" first appeared in *Rue Descartes* (Collège International de Philosophie) 1, no. 2 (1991): 239–54, then as "Prescription: Kafka" in

Lectures d'enfance (1991): 35–56. "Prescription," Christopher Fynsk's English translation, which we use with his permission here, appeared in its original form in *L'Esprit créateur* 31, no. 1 (Spring 1991): 15–31.‡

"Retour sur le retour" was first published in *L'Ecrit du temps* 19 (1988): 3–17, then as "Retour: Joyce" in *Lectures d'enfance* (1991): 11–33. Original English translation: Robert Harvey and Mark S. Roberts.‡

---

† Christian Bourgois, Editeur, granted Humanities Press permission to translate and publish these texts.
‡ Permission to translate and publish was granted by Jean-François Lyotard.

Editors' Introduction

◆

PRELIMINARY CONCERNS

The immediate goal of *Toward the Postmodern* is to provide English-speaking readers with the most illuminating examples of Jean-François Lyotard's aesthetic critique of language, literature, and discourse. Three constituent purposes were of concern to us in preparing this volume: (1) to allow Lyotard's own writings to reveal, in their diachronical organization, a continuing search for original images and for a new language of basic concepts in the philosophy of literature and aesthetics; (2) to present a series of essays reflecting the distinctive preoccupations crucial to the development of Lyotard's thought—essays that demonstrate a certain thematic progression; (3) to remedy the truncated and somewhat inverted view many English-speaking readers have of Lyotard's intellectual trajectory.

Although several of Lyotard's books and two anthologies are now available in English, both the scope and precise chronology of his philosophical preoccupations remain less than clear.[1] Surprisingly, perhaps, to some readers, Lyotard's writings from the late 1960s to his most recent reflections are theoretically quite consistent. Punctuating that time frame, the texts that follow—with their fascinating shifts in style and variations in focus—will serve as a guide for reading and interpreting the evolution of Lyotard's innovative and crucial thinking.

To address our second concern, we have selected essays that are interconnected thematically. While all of the present writings deal with language, discourse, or literature (and most often all three), the three main sections also represent discrete phases in Lyotard's career. Part One, "The Libidinal," featuring a series of articles he wrote in the aftermath of May '68, could be loosely characterized as efforts to wed Marx's political economics with Freud's libido theory. The themes and solutions found in "The Libidinal" also reflect Lyotard's unique approach to the main motivating intellectual concerns of that period. Moreover, because focal points of his distinctive preoccupations appear in this period, and because, as is the case with most philosophers, Lyotard's mature work has been patiently built upon earlier insights, "The Libidinal" entails the ideas elaborated in subsequent sections of *Toward the Postmodern*. There is thus an intrinsic connection between these early works and those selected for Part Two, "The Pagan," which in turn leads to Lyotard's most recent work, found in Part Three, "The Intractable."

Our third concern as editors is to allow Lyotard's own voice to rectify a commonly accepted misunderstanding in the English-speaking world about his main interests and, consequently, the directions and foci of his career. Most modern French philosophers have been introduced to the English-speaking public through translations of their earliest foundational works. This is true of Sartre's *Being and Nothingness* (1956), Merleau-Ponty's *Phenomenology of Perception* (1962), Dufrenne's *Phenomenology of Aesthetic Experience* (1973), Foucault's *Order of Things* (1970), and Derrida's *Speech and Phenomena* (1973), as well as of a number of others. Lyotard, however, became known through the English translation of a highly specialized book written on commission for the Québec government approximately twenty-five years after his first major publication.

The Postmodern Condition: A Report on Knowledge ([1979] 1984) has, more than any other work by Lyotard to the present day, marked its author as a postmodernist, an heir of Wittgenstein's philosophy of language, and a philosopher of science and technology. While *The Postmodern Condition* may have partially characterized Lyotard's concerns in the early 1980s, it neither provides a complete picture of his activities prior to that period nor does it in any way render intelligible the influences from his earlier works that invariably surface in later writings.

Lyotard's public career actually began in the late 1940s, not as a nascent postmodernist or a philosopher of science, but rather as a political activist writing newspaper articles critical of French policy in Algeria.[2] During this period of militancy in the small but influential group, "Socialisme ou barbarie,"[3] he also published a concise critical essay on phenomenology and its shifts through mid-century (*La Phénoménologie* [1954])—critical particularly with regard to the questions of intersubjectivity, history, and historicity. The decade of the 1960s witnessed the disbanding of "Socialisme ou barbarie" and the completion of Lyotard's dissertation in philosophy, which he later transformed into what many will argue is his greatest work to date, *Discours, figure* (1971). Along with *Economie libidinale* (1974), *Discours, figure* served as the basis for an extraordinarily fruitful period featuring some crucial essays in aesthetics, psychoanalysis, and politics. By the mid-1970s, he was already established as one of the major figures in French aesthetics, having written numerous exhibition catalogues, articles, and reviews in the

field—writings that reflected his interest in Merleau-Ponty's phenomenology, Dufrenne's notion of poetic language, and the work of many art
theoreticians, including André Lhote and Pierre Kaufmann. He had also
acquired a reputation as a strident defender of the international artistic
avant-garde.

However, the inflation of critical commentary on *The Postmodern Condition*, and the fashionable debate in which the book found itself engaged,
distracted Lyotard's English-speaking audience from enjoying the broader
dimensions of his project. Conveying a truth that would paradoxically
remain hidden by the very book in which it appeared, a biographical note
appended to the American edition of *The Postmodern Condition* affirmed
that Lyotard "is best known for his studies of aesthetics and of the psycho-
political dimensions of discourses." Indeed, the breadth of Lyotard's en-
gagement with theories and productions of art and the polemical vigor of his
aesthetic critique should, we hope, be evinced by the tour through his career
that the essays arranged here represent. Belatedly, but appropriately, this
tour should, at the same time, recontextualize Lyotard's approach to the
postmodern problematic as an intervening episode that was by no means
determinant of the project as a whole.

STYLES/INTENTIONS

Essential to any consideration of Lyotard's style is a sense of his intellectual
development. *Discours, figure* sets the stage for what was to be known as his
drift in tone and subject matter, prefiguring the motifs of the libidinal, the
pagan, and the intractable. As these writings attest, Lyotard's drift—since
leaving "Socialisme ou barbarie"—may be described as a Marxian-Freudian
one. It is not a drift, however, *away* from Marx and Freud, as has been
argued by many commentators. A sober consideration of the title, *Dérive à
partir de Marx et Freud* (1973) should suggest that Lyotard's committed
study of the two thinkers inspired his drift and that it remains a drift *with*
Marx and Freud—if only weakly so. Only in this way can we envision the
trajectory from various libidinal economies, through pagan histories, to the
intractable problems of language and judgment that he has been confronting
since *Le Différend* (1983). Lyotard never fully breaks with the great harbin-
gers of modernity, but chooses rather to follow abidingly, patiently, gener-
ously the lessons gleaned from their theories and methods to further their
own speculations.

This respect for tradition, moreover, explains Lyotard's hesitance to
dissociate himself entirely from the project of the Enlightenment—a move
perhaps more aptly attributable to many of his contemporaries. While
embracing and renewing the force of eighteenth-century critical philosophy,
he tirelessly labors to dispell the idealistic belief in reason's capacity to

totalize and master knowledge. The task he assigns to critique is a sort of primary mobility that lends voice to repressed minorities by parasitically inhering in and undermining official political events. These minorities function as centers of weakness, within general discourse, often surfacing in the form of wild, uncontrolled artwork: theatricality or representation to the hilt.

Discourse is thus by no means limited to conventionally defined art forms. For Lyotard, artistic creation haunts the political body and, at certain critical moments, breaks away from this collective superego, seeking to unmask the horrors perpetrated by the secular religion of majoritary power. One of the strangest and lengthiest essays here brings this pagan unmasking to life. In a meandering restitution of spontaneous sansculotte street theater wending its way into the hall of the Convention, he constructs a daring indictment of Rousseau's revolutionary progeny for betraying women in the months just prior to the Terror.

Pagan theater, suppressed for parodying the hypocrisy of republican order, extends an investigation whose origins may be perceived in the essay "Jewish Oedipus." The incontrovertible product of our encounter with signs being the act of representation, allegorical as well as real theaters become the habitual stages upon which the whole of Lyotard's aesthetic development is enacted. *Mise-en-scène* stands at the heart of his project: just as the expression's primal scene or stage must be at once understood figuratively and literally, at once past, present, and future, at once joyous game and austere ritual, so must the parodic act described by the *mise-en-scène*. In this regard, *mise-en-scène* evokes both imaginary constructs and positioning in "reality."

Lyotard's conceptualization of the *pagan* (entailing a new calendar—pagan time, pagan history . . . pagan ritual) becomes a new means for him to lend expression to the locus of the "figure"—a sociohistorical universal corresponding to the basic incommensurability ("the event") at the heart of discourse. The pagan is the triumph of the weak, armed with their humor, over the irony of the strong. Framing Lyotard's famous analysis of the postmodern in our time, pagan and libidinal manifestations in art and society will form the foundation of his later concern with the sublime. Similarly, the elements converging in the thematic of "The Intractable" are fundamental to understanding the notion of "differend."

Like general discourse, literary production is not bound to the crafting of narratives and figures (upon which various degrees of decipherment might be imposed): it extends to all mappings of surfaces. In reference to the literary work, Lyotard requires—gently, as always—that the notion of "surface" be understood in the most literal sense. Like Vernet's landscapes, as envisioned by Diderot, the literary event beckons the reader forth, inviting him to move upon surfaces that the artwork both represents and is.

Literary works, whether considered individually or as a group, are, for Lyotard, the mappings of a dystopia. *Dystopia* does not merely describe the imaginary landscape of some individual subject-writing-literature; dystopia is rather a space of subjective dislocation common to all transhistoric individuals and to which the literary craft gives expression.

In the same way that page surfaces, folds, collage effects, and blank spaces serve as fundamental elements of the literary apparatus, silences, coughing, muttering, even the artificial construct of musical notation contribute as much to the transmission of the musical experience as do the notes, melodies, harmonies, rhythms. Yet Lyotard does not take the compositions that he is most interested in—those of John Cage, Henri Pousseur, Mauricio Kagel, Luciano Berio—for expressions of musicality crafted merely for transcending prior ones: they are minor narratives, frail utterances possessing a power equal to that of humor. Through these compositions, music becomes paganism *now*.

Just as Lyotard's literary, pictorial, and musical aesthetics entails a radical rethinking of the spatiality of the text, temporality comes to play an unexpected role. Although he has a reputation for embracing the postmodern, he is hesitant to argue that art possesses the power to displace historical or linear time. The temporal quality of literary and musical works is much more modest: along the lines of Proust's *Remembrance of Things Past*, these artifacts embody the event's aporia—an aporia that all historical time harbors. By requiring not only the mobilization of libidinal energy but its coupling with the activity of reading, the artwork breathes life into the time of the event.

Michel Butor's *Mobile* (1963) is generally viewed as his flight from accepted literary genres. In meditating upon Butor's writings and interviews since the event of *Mobile*, Lyotard detects a yearning for the divine in Butor's attempt to trace a libidinal history, similar to the one imagined in the chapter on the pre-Terror festivals. For such an operation to be possible in the realm of literature, the book must become a body. Lyotard terms this material upon which the artist's desire is revealed "the great conductive skin of anonymous intensities," thus anticipating one of the most striking ethical images of "The Intractable."

Kafka's profoundly troubling story, "In the Penal Colony," provides Lyotard with a most graphic illustration of what he has learned of the law's propensity for prescribing. The prescription is, at a primary level, at the level of Kafka's story, an aesthetization of the law, a literal application of the law's punishment performed as a cursive inscription upon the body of an adult. But the prescription is also, as the word conveys, a writing that takes place *before*—Kafka's allegory of the infant's initiation into language as devastating corporeal punishment inflicted by the "touch" of the adult word. This powerful analysis recalls earlier writings collected here: "A [libidinal] history imagines a body comparable to the one Freud supposes in very young children, a body upon which love and death wander and halt unexpectedly, causing an event."[4]

Many of these essays are circumstantial: the particular problematic analyzed has its origins in Lyotard's chance encounters with critical works with which many readers may not be familiar. In this sense, *Toward the Postmodern* affords a unique glimpse into readings not commonly associated with its author. For example, works by André Lhote and Pierre Kaufmann serve as the basis for "On a Figure of Discourse." Louis Marin's study of Pascal and the Port-Royal Logic inspired the reflection entitled "Humor in Semiotheology." Jean Starobinski's introduction to the French edition of *Hamlet and Oedipus* gave rise to "Jewish Oedipus." "Futility in Revolution" plunges us into the stir caused among historians by Daniel Guérin's *Class Struggle in the First Republic*, carefully considers Mona Ozouf's book on revolutionary festivals during the same period, and confronts (albeit more distantly) contemporary analyses of the Terror from Furet to Soboul. Rife with didactically simple dialogue, "Retortion in Theopolitics" reads like a fable in which a May-'68-generation student has been chosen to sit next to Ernst Bloch in a philosophical eternity. Unable to fathom this turn of posthumous fate, "Bloch" is gradually drawn to the arguments of the young student—arguments that ironically are based on the student's reading of Bloch's *Thomas Münzer*.

Lyotard's writing displays disconcerting shifts in style as well as a propensity for witticisms, aphorisms, metalepses. However, despite an appearance of casualness, he takes meticulous care in selecting and utilizing his terms. Far from deploring this constant play of expression as a flight from clarity, we see it as laden with meaning—a testimonial to Lyotard's confidence in the word, whether written or spoken, to ultimately convey intent. His rationale for a style that shuns the sobriety of traditional written exposition is perhaps best explained in the preface to his recently published *Leçons sur l'analytique du sublime* (1991): "the 'author' would like to have the visible marks of oral teaching be a sort of awkward homage to that so very strange 'profession': one only 'learns philosophy' by learning how to philosophize" (10). *Toward the Postmodern* will have succeeded if it furthers this learning.

ROBERT HARVEY
MARK S. ROBERTS

Part One

◆

THE LIBIDINAL

1

◆

The Psychoanalytic
Approach to Artistic
and Literary Expression

Setting out to evaluate the research in a specific scientific field has proven to be a simple endeavor only in appearance. Indeed, it is impossible to achieve such a project unless the concepts of *expression* and the *psychoanalytic approach* to literary and artistic expressions are defined. Examining the principal approaches in question reveals that the definition and scope of these terms cause divergences between current trends not explicitly revealed by these trends. Rather than producing a pseudoscientific evaluation, it seems more appropriate for us to steer a course through the maze of those current trends, in the wake of the problem created by the terms *expression* and *psychoanalytical approach* to literary and artistic expressions.

1. The question is twofold (yet single) because the problems of expression and of research based on a psychoanalytic interpretation of a literary or plastic artwork share the same basic problematic. It seems possible to construct this problematic in a Freudian sense by contrasting *expression* with *meaning*, and the relationship between expressing and expressed with the relationship between one text and another. The meaning of a statement presupposes the existence of a common code: the language in which it is produced. To understand a text written in a foreign language, once the writing has been deciphered, requires its translation into the reader's native language; understanding a text written in the reader's language gives rise to a commentary or interpretation formulated in the same language (metalanguage).

Expression also calls for interpretation or commentary. But where plastic expression is concerned, it is evident that the work and its spoken or written commentary do not pertain to the same frame of reference. Plastic expression belongs to a space with properties quite different from those appropriate to linguistic space. In the case of literary expression, despite the apparent uniformity of the signifier for both the work and its interpretation (both being articulated discourse), one may postulate that they are profoundly different to the extent that the written work is laden with *figure*. At least three types of figure can be identified, each with its specific place and mode of existence in the work: the image induced in the reader's mind, the trope governing the order of linguistic signifiers, and the form or configuration of the narrative. Because of the presence of figure in literary work, it pertains in part to a space that could be termed topological and it borrows operations from a realm of the signifier that is different from that of the language of communication. This enables it to oppose a certain density to the commentary, comparable with that of a painting or sculpture, in this respect at least.[1]

One might agree that expression is present when the work's signifier cannot be translated into the language that provides the interpretive commentary, that is, the strict meaning. For example, a painting by Van Gogh is not a translation of his descriptive discourse about it in his letters to Theo.[2]

It is obvious that figurative operations reveal the same traits as those used by Freud in locating the unconscious order, that is, "absence of contradiction, primary process (mobility of cathexis), timelessness, and a substitution of psychical reality for external reality."[3] Freud carefully describes the same operations in *Jokes and Their Relation to the Unconscious* (1912), perhaps, as Ehrenzweig observed, the most important text about the psychoanalytic theory of art. It is important because it is the only one in which the operations that form the object (in this case witticisms, but also artworks) are analyzed and related to the workings of the unconscious.[4] Expression is the presence, in the secondary process, in discourse and in realist representation, of operations belonging to the unconscious system. The introduction of such operations always consists in the formation of a figure in one or several of the connotations mentioned earlier. This figure comes from "another scene"[5] than the language-like, pictural, or sculptural one in which it appears. It is the expression of a different kind of meaning, and the meaning it expresses is not present in the work in the same way as is its immediate significance.[6]

The primacy of the figure, an arrangement of an object's parts that cannot be deduced from the laws of the structure to which it belongs,[7] was, as we know, related by Freud to the constitution of the wish. The hallucinatory nature of the image produced is due to "helplessness,"[8] a state in which an overflow of energy finds no outlet in real life and revives the traces of past satisfaction through a process of regression. Hallucination, whether dream-like or not, constitutes the basic datum of art: the manifestation of a nonperceptual reality. This reality, which Freud terms *psychical*, is related to the pleasure principle. It is not subject to the twofold requirement imposed by the reality principle: the association of psychical energy with the linguistic system and "reality-testing" of representations.[9]

But the figure in which the wish is gratified is not limited to the hallucinatory image. This image is itself an expression: it is the fleeting coincidental expression of a more primitive figurative force, the primal fantasy. There are several good reasons to accord the name *figure* to this fantasy: it is not subject to the logic of perception and language; it is a sort of form or configuration that will order the perceptions, speech, and affects of the subject throughout his life; it is the imprint in psychical reality of the wish and of the forbidden, that is, the trace left on the subject by the withdrawal of the signifier, the mark of a lack.[10] For Freud, art must be considered with reference to fantasy.[11] Not only did he attempt a direct demonstration on Leonardo da Vinci and provide an involuntary illustration with Michelangelo's *Moses*, but in his theoretical texts he describes the artist "as a man who evades reality because he cannot reconcile himself to renouncing the satisfaction of impulses, as is demanded by reality from the beginning—a man who in a fantasy life gives free rein to his erotic desires and ambitions."[12] But the artist does not hide his fantasies; he lends them form as real objects and, moreover, renders their representation a source of aesthetic pleasure.[13] According to Freud, the aesthetic object exists for art lovers as well, that is, *in reality*, only because of a similar lack. "The dissatisfaction produced by the substitution of the reality principle for the pleasure principle is itself a part of reality."[14] Thus the artwork finds its place in the gap left free for wish-fulfillment by the withdrawal of the signifier. Freud interprets aesthetic pleasure in economic terms, as a seductive reward [*Verlockungsprämie*], as the permission given the reader or the art lover "to gratify his own fantasies without reproach or shame."[15] The pleasure of art is the same as the pleasure of play: it is announced that *in reality*, reality will be put aside in favor of pleasure. Paul Ricoeur[16] believes that he can build up his hermeneutic interpretation of Freud on the basis of the specific nature of aesthetic pleasure in relation to the libido, as characterized by the term *reward*, that enables released emotion to find its catharsis.

2. We can now understand what Freud meant when he stated that art is a "reconciliation [*Versöhnung*] of the two principles" of pleasure and reality, and in what sense this thesis must be taken as a starting point. Play does not reconcile fantasy and perceptual reality by rendering one immanent in the other; rather it proceeds from the realization of their dissociation, while affirming the rights of the former in the enclaves that it creates in the latter. Art, an offspring of childhood play, is also in no sense a fusion of realities, which in Freud's view must remain forever separate.[17] Admittedly, the artist brings about a much closer interpenetration of the two processes, collecting the elusive in the actual configuration of his play; an artwork, however, let

us repeat, only belongs to reality by reason of the gap opened up by the lack, which (for Freud) rules out any hope that the wish will ever become the actual world, that reality will ever become a game (here we see how the path chosen by Herbert Marcuse[18] conflicts with the spirit of Freud). Above all this is perhaps the point where the anaclisis of art and illness breaks down. The function of art is not to provide a true simulacrum of wish-fulfillment, but to show by the play of its figures which deconstructions should be achieved, in the order of perception and language (that is, in the preconscious field), so that a figure of an unconscious order can be discerned through its very elusiveness (I would not say recognized, since deconstructions in which the figures dwell are themselves obstacles to lucid perception and intelligence): the beating of wings, Nietzsche's doves' feet, and so on. The purpose of art is to reveal the unfulfilled wish to which the artist's impatience and dissatisfaction bear witness. Due recognition must be given to what differentiates the function of the figure in art from its function in dream or symptom. In the expressions of the artwork, the same operations of condensation, displacement, and figuration, which in the dream or symptom have no purpose but to disguise the wish because it is intolerable, are used to set aside the harmonious, the reassuring, the familiar, what Ehrenzweig calls "good form" (that is, the secondary process, the order of the preconscious) in order to expose the ugly, the disquieting, the strange, the formless, which represent the chaos of the unconscious. One merit of Melanie Klein's school was to expose the fundamental purpose of ugliness in great works.[19] Ehrenzweig's analyses, although carried out from a completely different angle (that of depth psychology) and bearing on a different aspect (no longer the relations of objects, but the operations that produce the work), reached the same conclusions with regard to the presence of the horrible ("horrible beauty," as Baudelaire wrote) in aesthetic emotion. The work that results from this approach must be situated beyond the beautiful and the ugly. This is not to say that aesthetic emotion should be identified, as Ehrenzweig suggests, with the emotion produced by the orgasm, in which terror is similarly mixed with pleasure.[20] If this were so, the figure in art could not fulfill the function of catharsis. Freud always firmly postulated this function. Associated with it is the entire enigma of the difference between the symptom and the artwork, between illness and expression.[21]

To identify this difference it is useful to refer to the central figure in Maurice Blanchot's thinking:[22] it will be apparent that these are the meditations of an expert. Orpheus descends into the night of hell to rescue Eurydice on the condition, imposed by Hades and Cora, that he would not look at her until they reached the upper world. However, at the gates of hell, he turns around to look and loses her. A song nevertheless rose from the dismembered body of Orpheus.

What the artist is expressing is the figure of the unconscious (the original fantasy): the figure both of his wish and of his death. He knows that in its bareness this figure cannot be endured, and that if it is to be made manifest, it will be at the cost of first being brought near the light, reconciled with the laws of daylight, remodeled in line with good form and *thingness*. Stop the tale here, and you will find yourself holding the same position on fantasy and art as does Klein's school: the reconciling function of fantasy (even that of adapting to reality), the need for the artist to go into mourning (to not look at Eurydice) for the interiorized object if he wishes to be able to resurrect and exhibit it in the category of the beautiful.[23] But the legend goes on: Orpheus turns around. His desire to *see* the figure overcomes his desire to bring it to the light. Orpheus wants to see in the night, to see night. By trying to see Eurydice, he loses all hope of making her be seen: the figure is that which has no face; it kills the one that looks at it because it fills him with its own night. If the Ego should come to take place where the Id is,[24] it would immediately cease to be Ego. There is no "reversible regression."[25] It was for the sake of this backward look that Orpheus went to fetch Eurydice, and not to create an artwork; the artist did not plunge into the night to put himself in a condition to compose a harmonious song, to reconcile night and day, to become renowned for his art. He went in search of the figural agency, the other of his very work, the unseeable, or death itself. In the artist the desire to see death even at the price of dying is stronger than his desire to create. We must stop looking at the problem of art in terms of creation. And as to the wish to look at the night, a work is never more than the proof of a failure to fulfill it. To contrast an artwork with a symptom, as one would success (or reconciliation, peace, even victory) with failure (or hostility or dualism), is to adopt the same attitude with regard to expression as does academism; it is to tolerate only "art" that is reassuring, that reconciles, that is separate, as exemplified in the semblance of life in official alienation.

Some observations of Klein's school will help us to grasp the purpose of expression, provided they are divorced from the concept of *ego-gratification* or the equilibration of object-relations, in which they are frequently enmeshed. The purpose of expression is neither knowledge nor beauty, but truth. Knowledge and beauty are charms, temptations that attract the poet and the painter, that incite them to soften, to render intelligible, logical, and attractive the rough sketch extracted from the night. They move them to create a work. But truth appears where it is least expected. Its emergence is sufficient to make an artwork, but an artwork will not cause it to emerge. The power of a literary or pictorial expression does not lie in its harmony (nor in the "victory" of the Ego); it is what contains and maintains open and free the field of words, lines, colors, and values, so that truth can figure itself therein. When guilt and fear assail the sick painter, his work closes in; it no longer houses truth; it becomes the stereotyped exteriorization of the hallucinations that haunt him.[26] This type of exteriorization is quite different from expression. Obsession and schizophrenia in themselves no more make it possible to disclose the figure than does health. If Eurydice flings herself in front of Orpheus and obliges him to look at her, there has not been in the subject that desire to see, that transgression of the frontier between day and night, that chink between the eyelids where the figure pauses for a second, leaving behind it a trace that is truth. A work that is forced upon its author does not disclose the trace of fantasy as a force of deconstruction, as a primary process marked by "free cathexis"; rather, it discloses the imprint of a defense mechanism, an unchanging matrix, a work showing anxiety in the face of desire against which all defenses are raised. The truth-bearing power does not derive from the fact that the nameless terror is "overcome," "left behind," "pacified," or "known," but from the fact that the field should be left free for the elusive to leave its trace. Joanna Field is closest to the essential when she states that the voluntary work of the artist is only "to plan the gap, to provide the framework within which the creative forces could have free play," and William Fairbairn is right in recognizing that this effort is identical to that required of the subject by the basic rule of analysis.[27] In this enlarged and sustained vacuum, the primary process can leave a trace of its operations without this trace being instantly ordered and repressed by the secondary process. Disease is not just the irruption of the unconscious; it is both that irruption and a furious struggle against it. Genius, like illness, may sound the same depths in search of the figure, but it does not oppose it: it desires it.

The artist is not a victorious neurotic. It is not true to say that the greatness of his work is in inverse proportion to the intensity of the psychic disorder from which he suffers. Hölderlin's poems of madness, the canvases Van Gogh painted at Arles and Auvers, Antonin Artaud's writings, the inmate of the asylum at Rodez are there to testify to the credibility of the principle that from the depths of madness truth may be uttered. The converse is not true: intensity of internal disorder is not sufficient to produce poetry.[28] It is conceivable, and has been observed, that a single subject may harbor both terror of the nightly figure (along with aberrant fantasies, repeated ceremonials, reliance on a mental straightjacket, the products of this secret terror) and at the same time the wish to share it in the fact and the strength to leave open some terrain for poetic or plastic expression, on which it could leave a trace. No doubt this type of coexistence is unendurable and can drive the subject to the breaking point, to suicide, to repression of the urge for truth (like Rimbaud), or to the vain confusion of the final state.

3. As long as the psychoanalytical approach to literary and artistic expression fails to give due recognition to this urge for truth, this desire to see,

it will be condemned to extending the shameful list of diagnoses of works, of the subject matter of these works, or of their authors.[29] In 1941, Gerhard Kraus counted eighteen diagnoses of Van Gogh since 1920 (they alternated between schizophrenia and epilepsy). Charles Mauron[30] adds his diagnosis: castration trauma. In 1954 Daniel E. Schneider corroborated: "He lives under the constant overpowering threat and masochistic passive homosexual unconscious wish for castration."[31] In a recent article, Marthe Robert[32] also noted the ambivalent feeling toward the father in the clinical picture (the father a priest, religious vocation of the son, replacement of preaching by painting), but finally she cannot resist making her own diagnosis (tendency to narcissistic neurosis with melancholia). In this study, however, the question of building a relationship between the "case" and the "creator" is mooted.

One methodological condition for such a construction should be the establishment of an intelligible relationship between the particular style of the artist under study, that is, the new set of literary or pictorial problems initiated by him as "creator," and the unconscious set of problems associated with his "case." It is of no interest whatever to conjecture whether Van Gogh suffered from narcissistic neurosis, schizophrenia, or epilepsy: first, in the absence of the subject, the psychoanalyst declares a prescriptive dispensation; next, such a conjecture would assume that the secret of the forms produced by the painter or the writer is within the scope of clinical analysis and that clinical discourse is the whole of critical discourse. Even supposing that it were possible, by means of documentary processing (which, moreover, is extremely difficult), to identify those expressive forms that are in significant correlation with symptoms and ultimately with clinical cases, no light would be thrown on the relationship of expression to the neurosis or psychosis.[33]

The painstaking exposure of themes and their unconscious foundations in literary works has been the object of research by Charles Mauron and the psychocritical school. Both from the psychoanalytic angle and from that of the theory of creation, this trend is related to Klein's school, as we have seen. But it includes considerable innovations with regard to literary criticism. Far from purporting to establish immediate correlations between the supposed initial trauma and the manifest content of a given work, it interposes between the two extremes intermediate formations corresponding to superposed layers of forms, the sedimentation of which would, in short, represent the genesis of works in their plurality, originating in a deep-seated matrix. This implies a sort of generative set of fantasies that, in connection with literary figures, would be comparable to generative grammars dealing with the immediate constituents of speech, while avoiding the semiologists' error (in the view of psychoanalysts) of treating figure as if it were speech.

It is impossible here to give an account of Mauron's subtle analyses, which both illustrate and justify his method—a method that can in no way be criticized for being simplistic. The arrangement in tiers or layers of figures, and their internal organization, corresponds to the arrangement of meaning revealed by the analysis: withdrawal (primary repression) by way of deconstruction and freezing in uncontrollable forms. But psychological criticism perhaps omits a fundamental element from the literary work (as from the artistic work): namely, the element of lack or disseizure (Kaufmann). In his analyses of the origin of the "personal myth" and of the figures it gives rise to, Mauron doubtless admits the postulate of a lack of being, of a withdrawal of meaning, that is variously revealed by the authors under study. But this disseizure is then solidified on the fantasmatic scene; it is identified as a figural theme in such a way that an empty space is at play, so to speak, only within the work, in its content. But the question posed by literature, painting, or music to criticism (and inspired by psychoanalysis) concerns the space *in which* the works appear, in which they become possible. Any set of fantasies is due to some disseizure. But its operation also consists in enclosing, in an inaugural and constant figuration, the vertigo that it causes. Thus, it has this sort of lack as its *content-area* (as revealed by Mauron). Artistic or literary work reverses the relation between expression and the area opened up by the withdrawal of meaning. It is not content to exteriorize its deep-seated figures in symptoms. It exposes, if not the set of fantasies itself, at least its traces by making available an open, "deconstructed" space that even goes so far as to distort the laws of language and perception in such a way that the formative operations of the figures of the unconscious and of their traces can, in this unencumbered space, produce other figures, new figures, which can then be either poetic or plastic.

To consider Mallarmé as a man whose unconscious was haunted by the figure of a dead maiden must not stop one from studying the movement that clears a space for this figure in which the play of forms, by multiplying operations of segmentation and combination, can produce new expressions. I would say that unconscious figures, insofar as they are constituted and have the value of fate, the value of meaning born of disseizure, will find in the secondary process as a bound process (linguistic constraints, constraints of connotation of good form, of reality, and so on), an ally that will put all its own constraints at their service. It is by endeavoring to break through these constraints and to prevent their freezing into an ice barrier of established meanings that the artist will consent to what, in the unconscious, is mere disseizure and eliminate any defensive rigidity. That this disseizure should thus be desired (where it is dreaded in morbid exteriorization) is the very essence of inspiration: there lies the principle of its truth-bearing function.

Transgression of the rule constitutes the visible aspect of this work, which may, admittedly, be assimilated to dream-work and in general to the operations of the primary process, but which repeats these operations only by reversing them, inasmuch as it applies them to the very outcome of that process, namely the figures produced by fantasy.[34] Due precisely to this effort at transgression, which is characteristic of the desire to write or paint, the works of Mallarmé, Cézanne, Joyce, or Picasso are associated with the advent of desire that constitutes the history of the West, and that leads it toward an ever-more radical criticism or constraint in poetry or the plastic arts, a criticism that finds its counterpart in revolutionary criticism or economic, social, and political constraints.

Assuredly, "modern art" is particularly revealing in this connection, and it can inspire some thoughts on the validity of the function of catharsis that Freud, after Aristotle, recognized in artistic and literary expression: for that opening-up of a free space in which the operations producing the deepest figures can become manifest, that "let-be" attitude, that dizziness and that active passiveness, are its principal concern. Nevertheless, every great expression has been "modern" in this respect and continues to be so; a particularly valuable proof of this assertion, because it lies at the heart of Freud's work, is to be found in the role played by expressions of the art of tragedy (particularly in Sophocles and Shakespeare) in the very institution of psychoanalysis. This role is neither illustrative nor didactic; in no way can it be considered to pertain to what may be termed "applied psychoanalysis"; nor is it solely heuristic; it is, rather, truly constituent in the sense that it was by reference to the tragic scene where the dramas of Oedipus and of Hamlet take place that Freud was able to assign a place for the coming-together (the "recognition," as Starobinski calls it, echoing Aristotle) of the results of his self-analysis with those of his clinical practice, thus establishing their universal relevance.[35] For the twofold operation to succeed, enabling Freud to situate the patient and himself as analyst, each in relation to the other, it is essential to call on the drama—canonical, so to speak—of unconscious desire in *Oedipus Rex* and of neurosis in *Hamlet*. Still obscure and unrecognized in writings such as "Project for a Scientific Psychology" (1895), all the effort being concentrated on building up a system of knowledge, the Oedipus complex, the universal starting point of psychoanalysis, has never been the subject of a full-length study, perhaps because of the eminent truth-value achieved through its expression in tragedy.[36]

If the scene of tragedy is apt to provide a springboard for the psychoanalytical scene, it is because the inversion has already taken place whereby the space of desire, the primal fantasy space centered on the lack that is basic to it, is represented in the scenic space, which is the space opened up by the desire to see the desire. It is not only through the element of fate in tragedy that it will inspire the theme of psychoanalysis. The position of expression, which calls upon the same disseizure in the artist as in the hero (but a disseizure that is sought after, not merely encountered as in the case of Oedipus, or inhibiting as in the case of Hamlet); this position prefigures the relationship of speech in analysis with the desire that is its object. Is not the twofold rule that compels the subject on the one hand to practice free association, and analyst on the other to listen to the patient's remarks with "[evenly] suspended, poised attention" tantamount to holding open, free of secondary constraints, a region in which the figural forms can reveal their presence? Once this area is freed, the difference between art and analysis is perhaps no greater than that between the desire to see the desire and the desire to give it expression.

Here we see the roles exchange places and how expressive or representative practice serves as an introduction of psychoanalytic practice to itself.

In short, current trends may be broken down as follows:

1.1 Reading a work as an expression of drives (of the author or subject), that is, as a symptom.

1.2 The same reading corrected by introducing a theory of sublimation, which is most often a theory of Ego formation.

1.3 An interpretation of the literary or artistic creation as a process of mourning for the interiorized object and of the exteriorization of fantasy in an empty space.

2.1 A theory of literary or plastic space as the counterpart of unconscious space.

2.2 A reading of the work as a process of spatialization retroacting upon emotional constitutive disseizure—that of the lack of the Other's word.

2.3 A reflection focused on the function of truth in literature and the arts, and on the role that the space in which artworks play can fill in the very constitution of psychoanalysis.[37]

Translator anonymous

2

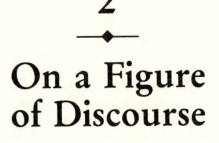

On a Figure
of Discourse

1. What I wish to convey is governed by a work that is neither linguistic, semiological, nor even philosophical, but political, in a sense that is neither institutional (Parliament, elections, parties, and so on) nor even "Marxist" (class struggle, the proletariat, the Party, and so on)—a sense obviously much too close to the first one. It is political in a sense that is "not yet" determined and that perhaps will remain, must always remain, to be determined.

This politics would not concern the determination of institutions—that is, the rules of organization—but the determination of a space for the play of libidinal intensities, affects, and passions. There is nothing *utopic* about it in the current sense of the term. Rather, it is what the world seeks blindly today through practices or experiences of all kinds, whose sole common trait is that they are held to be frivolous.

I hope my discourse will have the intensity of this frivolity—that, for example, it will amuse you.

2. I would like to outline quickly the analysis of a language apparatus, since I am concerned here with the text. Like the political apparatus, the language apparatus at work in the psychoanalytic cure (under the name *therapeutic project*, for example) exhibits the cure's efficacy, its pragmatic character. I analyze this apparatus in the same way that Freud and Lacan describe, prescribe, and imagine it in their own texts on the subject. It is thus not an effective apparatus (for it to be so, one would have to work on tape recordings, which, not coincidentally, raises difficulties), but the apparatus that psychoanalysis desires in its so-called technical, strategic, and tactical texts. It is the machinery that harnesses, channels, and drains libidinal energy as psychoanalysis, since Freud, has desired to assemble it and make it functional. I am compelled to begin by going back to some general points (for which I apologize). This recapitulation, which I believe indispensable in order to situate my point of departure, focuses on the libidinal economy.[1]

3. The word *desire* has two meanings in Freud's work: there is the sense of wish (*Wunsch*) and that of force or energy (Nietzsche's *Wille*). The tenor of Freud's theory varies greatly through the constant intermingling of these two senses. But with the publication in 1920 of *Beyond the Pleasure Principle*, this variation diverges markedly.

4. As long as Freud considers force-desire from a mechanical point of view (as in the *Outline* of 1895, in chapter 7 of *The Interpretation of Dreams*, and up until *Beyond the Pleasure Principle*), he can adjust this concept of force to that of wish, to desire seeking its own fulfillment. This adjustment is made through the theory of dream, fantasm (daydream), and representation. This theory can be described as follows: The quanta of energy (which is the same as desire, insofar as it is force) that cannot be discharged in a specific action with respect to reality become represented on a scene opened up within the psychical apparatus (or is it within the subject?)—a scene opened by this impossibility, by this very lack.

This helps us to understand the theory and the double meaning of the fulfillment of desire: it legitimizes the two senses of the word *desire*. On the one hand, the wish-desire that the subject experiences and cannot satisfy [*Befriedigung*] is realized only in dreams, images, and representations. On the other hand, there is a machine, the psychical apparatus, that receives a charge, an overload of potential, which, because of the interior theater, it is able to release. The theory of the fulfillment of desire imposes a mechanical sense on the hypothesis of force—mechanical to the extent that disorder (that is, the overload) is assumed to come from the outside (the *primal scene* played this role for a long time in Freud's theory). The apparatus of harnessing and draining energy is always presumed to proceed on its own, obeying some finality. This results in a correlation between the collected energy and the capacity of the apparatus, which will be governed by a regulating brain, by a memory, by a language. The model for every mechanical machine is this cybernetic machine; that is, one that is profoundly homogeneous with respect to representations and projects produced by subjects.

5. Freud introduces the concept of the *death instinct* in *Beyond the Pleasure Principle*. This concept by no means signifies (as he himself mistakenly assumed, particularly in *Civilization and Its Discontents*) aggression or sadism. Such an interpretation belongs to the notion of desire as wish [*Wunsch*], as desire felt *by a subject*. The death instinct is simply the idea (as opposed to the concept) that the machine for collecting and draining energy is not a well-regulated mechanical device. In this regard, Freud points to the repetition of acts, situations, discourses, or gestures (nightmares, repetition of failure) that cannot be fulfillments of desire (of "pleasures") in the equivocal sense of the term (the first theory of desire), but that, on the contrary, are associated with the most extreme suffering, the grinding of

the psychical apparatus, and the "subject's" scream. Parallel to the principle of constancy that rules over (regulates) pleasure in its relation with the exterior world ("reality"), there is, Freud claims, a "Nirvana principle," which must be spoken of as a *Will to Power*, a desire related to potential, to might (but not in the vulgar sense), a desire of intensities.

6. The Nirvana principle is a non-principle. It has no unity of reference; even if one claims, as Freud does, that it is the zero, instead of being the constancy of regulation, this still does not explain it: for that matter, it is also infinity. Freud describes the principle in chapter 6 of *The Interpretation of Dreams* and in the article "The Unconscious" (1915); it is a force beyond the rules of negation, of implication, of alternation, of temporal succession; a force that works by means of elementary operations, in fact by means of the sole operation of displacement (*Verschiebung* or *Enstellung*), of which all others, from the economic point of view, are particular cases. In Freud's topographical metaphor, displacement is the same as operation. Separate elements will be aggregated; connected elements will be dissociated; still others will be reversed.

7. We can only speak negatively of this non-principle, of this desire as force that works within extreme intensities (so different is it from the force of labor in capitalism, a form in which this same intensive force is reduced to the quantitative conditions imposed by the law of value). The predominance of language is in effect the predominance of regulation, of the principle of constancy.

Speaking requires the exclusion, among others, of extreme intensities related to phonation (throat rattles, screams, slow monotones, gasping, laughing, sneezing, and so on). It does not require the exclusion of the "body," which is itself an effect of rather regulated order, but the exclusion of unforeseeable displacements of intensity in the phonatory cavity. The regulation of displacements—that is, the regulation of intensities—is, a fortiori, on the other regions of the bodily surface, the principle (the principle of constancy) that, according to linguistics, operates, at least as a model, at all levels of language (syntax, for example) and at all levels of metalanguages (theoretics, logic).

8. Language is, for the modern Western world at least, a region of economy (that is, saving) of force, of the exclusion of intensities. Desire as intensive force does not enter into the scientific (or claiming to be so) consideration of language. The fundamental hypothesis of all science is that its object *is* a system or can be *related* to a system. The object of the desire of every "science," including linguistics and semiotics, is the regulation of displacements, the law: thus the exclusion of libidinal intensities from its object and thus, also, from its discourse.

The operative criterion of science expresses the same desire. The operative character of a scientific statement is reducible to the semantic condition required for a "good" formal system, for its completeness. Every statement of scientific theory satisfies at least one element of the domain of interpretation (for instance, fact). The discourse of science functions as a regulating machine vis-à-vis intensity. Events become the elements of a totality. Freud said time itself, a distinct part of that machine, is a "protective shield."

9. In reality, the death instinct (intensity or drift) should be envisioned as positivity. The slow or lightning-quick displacement of investments is precisely positivity insofar as it escapes the rules of language and is without reason. What is positive in this sense is what is beyond regulated deviations, gaps or borders, or hierarchies. It is the positivity of forgetfulness and/or of conservation without sense or memory. Freud always takes *jouissance* as a model of this intensity. If *jouissance* is positivity, it is because it is the impossible (that is, unthinkable) condensation of the strongest and weakest intensity. This is undoubtedly the model of the anaphora: not only outside the regulation of language but also outside the regulation of the instituted body. Here lies a positivity, an incompossible multiplicity.

10. Why and how is this errant energy harnessed and inscribed in an apparatus or figure?

Why? Because anything that is taken as an object (for example, thing, painting, text, body) is produced. That is, it results from the metamorphosis of energy in one form or another. Every object is composed of energy that is at rest, quiescent, provisionally conserved, inscribed. The apparatus or figure is only a metaphorical operator. It is itself already composed of stabilized, conserved energy. Freud employs the word *investment* in this sense (more in military than financial terms).

How? Three preliminary remarks:

1. The harnessing or inscription of energy is always poorly carried out. It results from the action of the "death instinct."
2. These apparatuses are quite numerous; I will eventually give some examples.
3. First, however, it is necessary to note an important point: they are neither social nor psychical in extension. The same apparatuses can be found operating upon and treating energy on the scale of either an individual or a group. Inversely, they can operate upon both scales at once, since several apparatuses can share the individual and the group.

11. I will briefly demonstrate an apparatus in what is called *painting*. Modern painting and music are perfect examples, because actively operating within them is the dissolution or dilution of apparatuses that govern regions

(one must think of regimes and rules), including the region of "painting," and so on—and thus painting and music make regions appear retroactively (deferred action) as figures, as apparatuses.

Alain Kirili notes that painting and writing must be brought together under the category of inscription and cites Chinese calligraphy as an example. But this is saying too much: the category of inscription simply exceeds the basic opposition between painting and writing. It is also saying too little: pictorial inscription involves color, pigments; it is produced by chromatic inscriptions. Thus there is a binding of the libido with the network of color and of everything onto a support. It is a work of chromatic inscription. Apparatuses form out of such connections, that is, out of those investments or blockages of energy that channel it, assuring its transformation.

The following examples may be cited:

— The hand takes some colored powder and applies it to the lips, to paper.
— One hand holds a stencil; in the palm of the other we place a little powdered rust and then blow.
— A camera lens captures solar energy and records it on film; the eye records the developed photo; the hand reproduces it on a blowup a hundred times larger.
— A hand dips a little brush into nail polish and applies it to the nails of the other hand.
— Two arms lift up a paint can and pour the contents on a canvas laid on the ground.
— A glass is placed between an object and the eye; the chin is locked in a chin strap, which immobilizes the head (the eye). The hand traces the contour of the object on the glass. The tracing is transferred to a canvas (the apparatus of Dürer and Leonardo).

There are an enormous number of apparatuses! The apparatus is the organization of network connections, channeling, regulating the ebb and flow of energy, in all regions.

12. Let us now examine the apparatuses that govern the region of language by taking what Emile Benveniste calls, with regard to French verbal tenses and pronouns, the "*modes of utterance*": historical narrative and discourse.[2]

Benveniste distinguishes historical narrative and discourse as two modes of utterance by virtue of their surface traits: for the narrative, the use of the third person and aorist (weak) tenses (the past definite, the imperfect, the pluperfect, the future perfect: "La lutte commerciale ne *devait* pas *cesser*"). For speeches, the first and second persons are customary, as are the tenses of discourse (present, perfect, and future). These surface traits, moreover, overlap certain aspects and modalities (which are not marked on the surface in French); notably, traits concerning the relation of the subject of the utterance with the subject of what is uttered and the relation of the tense of the utterance with the tense of what is uttered.

For example, in French narrative, *"il apparut"* (the past definite, an aoristic tense) indicates, if we include in its analysis all of its extension in modality and aspect (in the perspectives opened by Antoine Culioli's research):

1. an aspect of the relation speaker/utterance: participation is excluded;
2. an aspect marking the mode of the processes' unfolding: it is punctual;
3. a modality marking the mode of assertion: affirmation;
4. a modality marking certitude or probability: here it is a question of certitude;
5. a usage of the pronominal function: the exclusion of both first and second person.

Here we have a language-like apparatus, that is, an ordering that allows for the binding of libido with language (support, surface of inscription). There is then a production of "effects of meaning," in the acception of affects. This apparatus allows the filtering of numerous possibilities (for example, discourse, theory) and thus the circumscription of a language-like modality (for example, tale, myth, story, novel). This is a metamorphosis of libidinal energy into objects, into quiescent language-like energy, which in their turn will transform into affects, emotions, bodily inscriptions, wars, revolts, literary glosses, semiotics, and so on. The apparatus of narrative is thus a transformer of energy that effectuates the displacements of modalities and the libido's places of inscription.

13. Discourse as libidinal apparatus

Discourse is in itself an apparatus-figure, parallel to the historical narrative (narration and description). It is impossible to claim that any apparatus is more natural than any other, that discourse is more fundamental than any other language-like form. It is also quite impossible to follow Genette on this point, when he writes:

> In truth, discourse has only the purity to preserve, for it is the "natural" mode of language, the most natural and the most universal, receiving by definition all forms; the narrative, on the contrary, is a particular mode, *marked*, defined by a certain number of restrictive exclusions and conditions (refusal of the present tense, of the first person, etc.). Narrative cannot "discourse" without leaving itself.[3]

There is no less exclusion in the discursive utterance than there is in the narrative one, no fewer markings and, consequently, effects of meaning, affects. As an example, here is a news report from the Renault Corporation on the Pierre Overney affair:

These various attempts having thus completely failed, the commandos *surrendered* this afternoon after a methodical attack on the main entrance to the *avenue Emile Zola*. Right when the night shift was being replaced by the morning shift, when there was a great bustle of workers on this avenue, a commando unit of about 80 persons, armed with clubs and lead pipes, *rushed* some guards present at the entrance. Six guards, who were not *armed with* weapons, *were soundly beaten* and injured. It was then that an administrative employee of a security firm, who was in no way officially a security guard and who, however, was made the object of deadly force, *came to* the aid of the endangered guards. Confronted by the mob and unable to break himself or the guards loose, the administrative employee, who was carrying a pistol, *pulled it out* and *fired* into the air. A second shot *was to strike* one of the members of the commando unit who *succumbed* to the wound. The employee voluntarily *turned himself over* to the police. An investigation *is* under way. The injured guards *have been evacuated* to the central infirmary and immediately *sent* to Ambroise Paré Hospital.[4]

We have merely emphasized the markers of narrative and discourse upon the verbal tense.[5]

14. The effects of meaning of the narrative and those of discourse are described, by Benveniste, in terms of their connecting to the subject, to the utterance, and to the present of the utterance. Discourse marks this connection, narrative effaces it. The event cannot be situated on the first person and the tense of the utterance (the present) as axes; the *I* does not speak, the event belongs to another scene where I *can* speak, and what unfolds out there is not within the reach of discourse.

Inversely, what effaces the so-called naturalness or universality of my discourse is the possibility of articulating a process, an event, or a state (in the description) that takes place outside of the speaking subject, that bears no reference to its temporality.

In these effects of meaning, narrative sets up a scene without the theater hall; discourse sets every scene in exteriority; the theater hall and the present of speakers are gone. The scene without hall is perhaps the utopia of myth, of lore. The hall without the scene (in which every event is dissolved into a discourse in the first person) is the assembly, the court. An example of the predominance of this discursive level of articulation is the configuration of the polis insofar as the circle of speakers turn their backs on barbarian exteriority. Discourse is a libidinal apparatus that turns into the event—the intensity, in the region of existing language, which refers it to the sole present of the existing speakers. The discursive text inscribes itself in a record book, in an account book, in public records, though in an inscription that is always reactualizable, potentially re-vivable, eternally present (Husserl), in a journal. Day-to-day discourse, or the present of discourse, passes through every "it's then" of narrative. Responsibility is a visible effect of this apparatus of discourse, a responsibility for the very possibility of speaking. All libidinal energy is collected and maintained not solely in the region of language, but at that impossible point, both fleeting and stable, of the instant of utterance.

The subject is himself an effect of this discursive apparatus. He is the exclusive investment of the utterance's present through the libido, its collecting and its fixation in that highly improbable form that is both infinitely empty and full of potential statements, both inexchangeable in its actuality and fully exchangeable as an instance of speech.

15. But inside the apparatus of that figure that is discourse there are even stranger figures, including psychoanalytic apparatuses ("inside?" this would be to admit the preeminence of discourse as I have just described it, with its presumed responsible subject).

I would like to set apart what might be called the paradox of the psychoanalytic apparatus (which is no less paradoxical, I suggest, than myth or the discourse of legal forensics) from the paradox of faith in Judaic discourse. This paradox may be broken down as follows:

15.1 An exclusive privilege is granted to language (the book, the prohibition against human images) as a region where desire can play (Exod. 20:3 [2nd Commandment]).

15.2 The privilege is granted, at the heart of language, to destination (speaker/listener, locutor/allocutor, I/Thou), that is, to the pronomial functions, I/Thou. In fact, this privilege is granted to the relation of the statement to the utterance.

15.3 It is necessary to note the disregard, central to the preceding aspect, as to what is actually said (and as to that of which one is speaking). Importance is accorded only to the fact of speaking, of "casually talking to" someone. Speech is set up as an object (Exod. 20:19: the people say to Moses: "Speak to us yourself, and we will listen; but do not let God speak to us, or we shall die"). The statement has no value as content, meaning, or information, but rather as a present, a gift sent, whether it is received or not (the covenant is made and the preservation of speech is placed by God in the mouth of Jacob and his progeny: Isa. 59:20, 21).

15.4 Inside this libidinal language of destiny-objectivity lies the great paradox concerning the position of the speakers. In effect, in modern linguistic analysis, "I" is he who speaks, "You" listens to "I" and can in turn speak, say "I." Whereas in the Judaic position, "I" is seized by your speech; "You" is what speaks (first), and "I" is to whom the speech is directed. But you cannot answer. (Job 9:2–3: "Indeed, I know it as you say: how can man be in the right against God? If any were so rash as to challenge him for reasons, one in a thousand would be more than they could answer." This is the translation of the Head Rabbi; the Christian translation reverses the meaning: not being one of a thousand, man cannot respond.) Here we witness a multiplication of screens. The instance of speech recedes, is effaced as a tangible actuality. Actuality becomes potential!

15.5 If one takes into account the third point, language as gift, it follows that the "I" receives the gift of speech, that it is indebted to speech, to *that* speech, to that gift. The sin consists in failing to recognize, in repudiating that debt.

15.6 Finally, the absolute Judaic characteristic is that there is no possible reversal of this relation, that the positions "I" and "You" cannot be exchanged. This absence of reversal is a close approximation of the Jewish God's position. It excludes all mediation (Christ, Hegel), all "Us" who would be "I-and-You." There is no arbiter between "You" and "Me." (Job 9:19–35, especially 32–34: "Yes, I am a man, and he is not; and so no argument, no suit between the two of us is possible. There is no arbiter between us, to lay his hand on both, to stay his rod from me, or keep away his daunting terrors.") It thus excludes any possibility of the debt being wiped out.

We should note the play of the imperative in such speech: the imperative is what directs speech, or more profoundly, as Levinas says, the fact of speech seizes the listener before any of its contents, or anything signified. This seizure arises from the fact that the reversal or the exchange of the instance of speech and of tense is impossible.

16. If commentary on the effect of meaning is necessary, we could take Levinas's reading of *Chabat* 88a–88b, commenting on Exod. 19:17, and the commentaries of the Rabbis:

> *Yes, we will do first, then we will listen*; listening to a voice is *ipso facto* acceptance of the obligation regarding that which speaks. Intelligibility is fidelity to the truth, incorruptible and prior to all human activity; it protects this activity like a cloud which, according to the Talmud, enveloped the Israelites in the desert. . . . The Torah is an order to which the self adheres without having to enter into it, an order outside of being and of choice.[6]

17. Now, the psychoanalytic apparatus:

17.1 Language is the only activity received in the relation. It is a "talking cure." But why *cure*? Breuer, in *Studies on Hysteria* (1895), writes: "Anna O. had given to this procedure the perfectly appropriate and serious name of 'talking cure' and the humorous name of 'chimney sweeping.'" She knew that after having spoken, she would lose her headache and her "energy." Thus it is a work that turns more energy into less energy, the less bound into the more bound.

Freud, in the same text, specifies the nature of this work:

When memories return in the form of pictures our task is in general easier than when they return as thoughts. Hysterical patients, who are as a rule of a "visual" type, do not make such difficulties for the analyst as those with obsessions.

Once a picture has emerged from the patient's memory, we may hear him say that it becomes fragmentary and obscure in proportion as he proceeds with his description of it. *The patient is, as it were, getting rid of it by turning it into words.* We go on to examine the memory picture itself in order to discover the direction in which our work is to proceed. "Look at the picture once more. Has it disappeared?" "Most of it, yes, but I still see the detail." "Then this residue must still mean something. Either you will see something new in addition to it, or something will occur to you in connection with it." When this work has been accomplished, the patient's field of vision is once more free and we can conjure up another picture. On other occasions, however, a picture of this kind will remain obstinately before the patient's inward eye, in spite of his having described it; and this is an indication to me that he still has something important to tell me about the topic of the picture. As soon as this has been done the picture vanishes, like a ghost that has been laid.[7]

The movement of the cure runs from the incommunicable to the communicable, from the inexchangeable to the exchangeable, from the scene without the hall to the hall without the scene. It is a question of collecting and detouring the energetic fluxes, which are blocked (or supposed so) in certain scenes, toward language, thus a question of passing from libidinal to political economy, a question of liquidating high-low intensities through their reabsorption into language. One goes from expenditure to saving. It is a faithful respondent to the Judaic mistrust of the image or the body.

17.2 The desire that energy be dissolved into language inevitably leads analysis to assume that the unconscious is structured like a language:

What I listen for is understanding [says the analyst]. Understanding does not force me to comprehend. What I hear remains no less a discourse, even if it had as little discursivity as an interjection. For an interjection is of the order of language, and not an expressive cry. It is a part of the discourse which does not give way to any other for syntactic effects in that specific language.[8]

It is here that the first sense of *Wo es war, soll ich werden* arises: I *must* put myself in the place of the Id. The substitution of the third person neuter, and probably plural, for the first person singular requires that the third person be a "true" person, that is, a potential speaker. "I" must come there where the Id was. Id can say "I," Id is "You." Similarly, the absence of inflection in the temporal forms inherent in the Id should give way to the deployment of the history of the subject, a narrative situated on the level of articulated discourse:

The desire of the dream is not assumed by the speaking subject: "I" in his speech. Articulated instead of the Other, it is discourse—a discourse that Freud has begun to parse. It is just that the wishes that it constitutes have no optative stress in order to modify the indicative of their formula. What one might see here as a linguistic reference that we call the space of the verb is actually that of realization (the true meaning of *Wunscherfüllung*).[9]

A second complementary implication relevant to this *sollen* will be examined below.

17.3 The analysand's discourse—not being one of either cognition or knowledge—is one of gift, offer, and, consequently, of request. But what is requested? *Nothing.* The request is intransitive. Is this the case for the offering as well? It is an offering of words, and money.

> If I frustrate him [says the analyst], it is because he asks something of me. Precisely, to answer him. He knows, however, that this will only be words, something he could get from anybody. He is not even sure he will be grateful to me; whether they will be good words, still less bad ones. He does not ask me for the spoken words. He asks me . . . owing to the fact that he speaks: his request is intransitive, it does not contain an object.[10]

Intransitivity here is only a matter of transformations of energy. We are dealing with nonsense. The offer and request belong, rather, on the level of uttered discourse and thus to the register of the subject. The "region" of transference is opened by this register, maintaining securely the discharge of libidinal energy in the figure of discourse (I/You and their assumed reversal). In this regard, the psychoanalytic apparatus consists in favoring the offer/request, the offering, the prayer, that is, the affective dimension or the range of energy in the very act of speaking. Transference assumes that every "good" transformation of energy passes through the figure that is discourse.

17.4 But this is not all. The figure, in psychoanalytic usage, is not only that of discourse but also that of faith in the sense of the Judaic paradox. It is the second acception of the previously mentioned *sollen*. Id speaks, but "I" cannot effectively put myself in its place. Id will never be a "You" in the way that the instance of speech is exchanged between "You" and "Me." The analyst does not respond, as Freud stresses in his "Observations on Transference-Love" (1915):

> It is, therefore, just as disastrous for the analysis if the patient's craving for love is gratified as if it is suppressed. The course the analyst must pursue is neither of these; it is one for which there is no model in real life. He must take care not to steer away from the transference-love, or to repulse it or to make it distasteful to the patient; but he must just as resolutely withold any response to it.[11]

Why? Proper technique dictates that a response to the question would allow for a discharge of energy:

> The treatment must be carried out in abstinence. Instead, I shall state it as a fundamental principle that the patient's need and longing should be allowed to persist in her, in order that they may serve as forces impelling her to do work and to make changes, and that we must beware of appeasing those forces by means of surrogates.[12]

This work of displacing investments from the invested region (the body, for example, in hysteria) toward a new region (discourse) is *translaboration*. There is a suspension of *jouissance* in its repetitive insistence. We see that the proper technique is political and economic in that it "puts something to work."

Regarding the proper deontological "ethics" that he also invoked, Freud introduces the "effect of responsibility," already noted concerning Judaism. The motif at first appears medical:

> For him, it is an unavoidable consequence of a medical situation, like the exposure of the patient's body or the imparting of a vital secret. It is therefore plain to him that he must not derive any personal advantage from it. The patient's willingness makes no difference; it merely throws the whole responsibility on the analyst himself.[13]

But the therapeutic is of an entirely different order, one that is essentially Mosaic:

> However highly he may prize love he must prize even more highly the opportunity for helping his patient over a decisive stage in her life. She has to learn from him to overcome the pleasure principle, to give up a satisfaction which lies to hand but is socially not acceptable, in favor of a more distant one, which is perhaps altogether uncertain, but which is both psychologically and socially unimpeachable.[14]

The analyst is without response, irresponsible with regard to the immediate request; he is responsible, however, for another request, one presumably hidden nearby. He can respond, but only to a third party.

One might say that the patient is like the people of Israel. She wants images, answers, *jouissance*, she confuses the "I" and its meaning; she cannot hear Yahweh, because she cannot see him. The psychoanalyst is like Moses: he does not respond to the request of the Israelites; he responds to the command, to the distraint of Yahweh. In the psychoanalytic relation, the analysand says "I" and "You"; the analyst says "You," never "I," at least as vehicle for a gift of affect. This serves as a means of verifying the fact that his level of articulation is no longer that of an exchangeable discourse (which is reputed, at that point, to be illusory); it is instead the distorted, *entsellte*, cleft level of the paradox. In the end, the Id, the unconscious, is Yahweh. It seizes the Israelite-patient before any request, before any cleavage of the "I/You," multiplying the screens, the mediations that efface its presence. It speaks in the imperative, it gives imperiously, and, ultimately, it (dis)seizes.

18. A certain isomorphism between the Judaic apparatus and that of psychoanalysis is pertinent. In both cases, the function of regulation is assured by the same procedures that I described briefly above. This isomorphism has a certain significance for a political libidinal-economy. I have, until now, largely overlooked this concept, but I should raise several points:

1. These processes have an "arbitrary," figural character. They are not grounded in anything other than themselves. They refer back to nothing. Insofar as they are empty, they are not even signifiers. What is important, rather, is their fullness of circumscription: the stable investment of libidinal energy upon a region of language, and within that region on the level of articulation called discourse ("I," "You"), and still further within, on a torsion that introduces the inexchangeability of "I" and "You."

2. It must be affirmed—not by exclusion or set principle—that the positivity of these investments produces the Greek *Couroi* that (in Henri Jeanmaire, Jean-Pierre Vernant, Pierre Vidal-Naquet) is turned away from *Physis* and forms a closed and empty circle that circumscribes the space of the city as a space of discourse, of exchangeable speech, and of a new "effectiveness": rhetoric and politics. What is positive in this figure is the production of new libidinal operators, rather than the effects of meaning, which are always relative to the exteriority chosen in order to describe the apparatus.

If this figural production were to be carefully described (to a much greater extent than I am able to do here), one would be led to completely abandon the historicist-dialectical ideology that identifies reality with a succession of cultural forms engendering one another. This ideology corresponds to the predominance of the narrative apparatus.

3. It is necessary, in particular, to stress the above mentioned so-called torsion at work in the figure I have described. I say "so-called torsion," for in order to affirm a torsion, it would be necessary to grasp the non-twisted. Now, it is true that the irresponsibility of the "You" is a torsion in relation to the figure of an exchangeable discourse (for example, if during a discussion in a conference, governed in principle by the law of exchangeability, a designated speaker [listener] refuses to speak, to become "I"). But the inverse is no less true: the rule of exchangeability (that is, the law of the value of exchange) is altogether twisted in relation to the rules of narrative or the discourse of faith. Imagine, if you will, Moses in conference with the Israelites; imagine the tape recorder (that is, the record, the historical inscription of the discourse) in the analyst's office! We could just as easily say that all of these figures are twisted and that none are; we are here in the

absent singularity of unity, in the generalized relativity of the figural. What is certain is that every apparatus, wherever it may be, because it is viewed from the perspective of an other (for example, the figure of the discourse of science), can only appear twisted, irrational (but there is no rationality). This torsion is, as it were, the emblem in the apparatus of *jouissance*, the trace of an instinctual drift, of death-*jouissance*. In my description of the discourse of faith or of psychoanalysis, the torsion is located in the inexchangeability of the positions I/You.

4. If we wish to translate this twisted apparatus into effects of meaning, it will be necessary to translate the entirety of linguistic modalities and aspects of the discourse of faith into "the localization of the place of *jouissance*." One might say, for example, the following:

— In not responding, the analyst institutes the irreversability; he defers the repetitive discharge of instincts, the *jouissance* of the patient; he imposes the work.

— In the master-slave relationship, the slave is the one who renounces sexual release (risking death) in order to survive; he must work, the discharge is displaced onto the tool; the master attains pleasure (expends).

— In the analyst/analysand relationship, it is apparently the master-analyst who, in forgoing sexual release (abstinence, frustration), forgoes, in fact, the *jouissance* of the hysteric (or of the obsessive personality), forgoes actual consummation, the expenditure of energy into sexuality. Effectively, however, he takes his bearings from another *jouissance*.

— The *jouissance* of the analyst is not only to "love the truth as one loves the sexual object," as André Green proposes, and/or there are several ways of loving a sexual object, and/or there are several acceptions of the word *truth* (this is the difference between psychoanalysis and science). The analyst's *jouissance* consists in being disseized by the voice of the Other; his desire is not to *act* according to the law, responding to the request of the law, since that law is not truly understood (the Other cannot *say* anything to me, he just speaks to me). No, his desire is not merely to will something, or rather, it is to will not to will, to will to be and to remain disseized (*Wille zu Unmacht*). If the analyst does not answer, it is because the request of the patient is for him only an occasion (if not to listen, to understand) to listen to the voice of the Other. What orients the psychoanalytic relationship, from the point of view of the analyst, is his own desire to remain disseized. His disseizure is proof of the Other's power over him and thus his own power over the field of the Other. He is situated like Moses vis-à-vis Israel and Yahweh.

5. One final remark. In the apparatus of psychoanalytic desire, *jouissance*

is lodged, set in place, by listening to the Other as "You." This figure (this localization) makes it appear very close to the apparatus of paranoia, at least as it is described by Freud and Lacan. There is, however, a difference. In paranoiac desire, *jouissance* is lodged, set in place, *is in the place of* the Other as "You." For psychoanalysis, "I" cannot: "I" must not place myself in "You" (since "You" do not speak); in paranoiac delusions, "I" "can" do it. This is a new torsion.

The torsions in psychoanalysis and in paranoia are thus different. But the psychoanalytic localization is not necessarily the best place, nor is its apparatus the most true. Freud himself brings this to our attention in a text where he fearlessly envisions paranoia as a good place to situate the torsion of psychoanalysis. Witness the final passages from "Psychoanalytic Notes upon an Autobiographical Account of a Case of Paranoia (Dementia Paranoides)" (1911):

> Schreber's "rays of God," which are made up of a condensation of the sun's rays, of nerve fibres, and of spermatozoa, are in reality nothing else than a concrete representation of libidinal cathexes; and they thus lend his delusions a striking similarity with our theory. His belief that the world must come to an end because his ego was attracting all the rays to itself, his anxious concern at a later period, during the process of reconstruction, lest God should sever his ray-connection with him—these and many other details of Schreber's delusional formation sound almost like endopsychic perceptions of the processes whose existence I have assumed in these pages as the basis of our explanation of paranoia.[15]

Here comes the vertiginous moment, the loss of references by shifting the apparatus:

> I can nevertheless call a friend and fellow-specialist to witness that I had developed my theory of paranoia before I became acquainted with the contents of Schreber's book. It remains for the future to decide whether there is more delusion in my theory than I should like to admit, or whether there is more truth in Schreber's delusion than other people are as yet prepared to believe.[16]

Obviously, the future will never bring anything of this sort. The relation from one apparatus to the other is never diachronic because it is never discursive.

Translated by Mark S. Roberts

3

---◆---

Jewish Oedipus

In Freud's work, there is a language of knowledge and a truth-work. They keep each other company. The former draws its sustenance from Helmholtz: it manifests itself in the *Project for a Scientific Psychology* (1895), in the relentless elaboration of the topographies. It is constructed in theory, on a plane that would be absent from that of which it speaks. Neither the constant disordering of the system, as the beginning of "Instincts and Their Vicissitudes" (1915) describes, nor the endless closure of the theory, prevents our confronting a linguistic space that is in principle closed. Freud's genius consists in treating these disturbances not as obstacles, but as revelations.

It is in the language of cognition that desire displaces, condenses, suppresses, and subverts regular relations and leaves traces. The trace of desire is not writing, but a transgression of writing, just as the operations by which desire takes possession of the *Traumgedanke* (dream-thought) and converts it into oneiric staging deconstruct the clear residues of daytime discourse and perception. Truth does not speak, *stricto sensu*. Belonging to distance, to the rupture with the thing that discourse requires, it is cognition that speaks. Cognition produces a theory in the space of the possible, delivered from things, and then seeks in things what may serve as a referential model for its discourse, as a field of interpretation. Truth does not carry out this secondary disjunction but, rather, works *within* this disjunction. It leaves its trace on discourse, the fulguration of a slip, a silence, a forbidden metaphor, a portmanteau word, nonsense, a scream. But its effects come from *elsewhere*, signaling their uncanniness in that they do violence to the order (of regulated language) in which they are inscribed. Spoken language, be it that of cognition, serves here to mirror these truth effects. André Green states this quite well in reference to literary works:

> In the long sequence of signifiers whose chain constitutes the work, the unconscious signified rises between two signifiers from the absence in which it is hidden and necessitates the difference between the "natural"

form of discourse and its literary form. Not to express therein what is to be said, but to show, by veiling it, what is to be hidden.[1]

One can, one must draw a riposte to writing's integrism from the other scene's mode of presence in discourse. And this is precisely what André Green does.

The rule of free association and that of suspended attention, Jean Laplanche has recalled, work like a speculum on the language of signification—that is, that of communication and knowledge—with its principles of pertinence and economy.[2] They open language to what, coming from elsewhere, leaves its mark upon it. They keep it from sealing itself up by reclosing and repressing figures of truth. Deconstructive work converges with that of the unconscious by dismantling the bastion of signification. In this surface stretched out between the tedium of words forever dwelling on reasons, the antilogic of meaning will find the screen onto which to trace its figures. Not the figure itself, lost like Eurydice, but the figural, lateral, and peripheral inscriptions, like the sparse strokes Cézanne traced with watercolor in 1905—strokes that seem to come from the other side of the white paper, with which the eye is left to compare and identify the figure whose shards they are: Mont Sainte-Victoire. Standing before the mountain for hours on end, what does Cézanne do? He associates freely, maintaining an evenly suspended, indiscriminate attention to what thing-bound and gestaltist perception force us not to see. He deconstructs an order, a writing; he wants to see the bad form, to see what active, adaptive focalization represses at the periphery of the field: the anamorphoses, curves, obliques, and laterals.

Art is the locus of a double reversal where the space of disseizure, enclosed by all fantasy and upon which it is reclosed as the lack of signifier from which it issues, returns to externally offer itself to that profound figure that may thus inscribe its traces upon it. Or, in other words, the interior space, what escapes reception, which clutches the primordial figure, escapes from it, turns around, returns to invest it, and presents a stage for its operations. The artwork is a symptom insofar as it *is* a set of traces referable in principle to a primal fantasy. It is not a symptom in that it *bears* these traces, that is, exhibits them. The artwork is a trace bearing a trace, a representation that is itself representative. This implies that desire is desired, not so as to articulate or theorize it but to see it. And desire must not even be affirmed to see it, to render it into a work. For it is not true that painting or literature progress in the abstraction [*relevé*] of these figures due to people who "want to make artworks" or "authors"; on the contrary, they have never gained but for the imprudence of those who were ready to sacrifice all past or future works for a glimpse, however fleeting, of the faceless figure.

Theater is dream insofar as it fascinates and comprises a hallucination giving rise to identification. It is also not dream insofar as it is a dream intensified, the scene of the dream set on *its* own stage, the figural space of fantasy installed in its figural space of representation. This in no way means that fantasy or the unconscious process in general is mastered in dramatic creation. The unconscious process is not controllable. Rather, the theater shows that it is our master and that we are disseized. It manifests the misconception of conception, the delusion of those who would seek knowledge of Oedipus. And it *shows* it—that is, as spectators we are effectively disseized in our turn, since theater is a staged scene, simultaneously a fascinating figure and true. As André Green puts it:

> Truth, says Freud at the end of his work, is only attained through its deformations that are not the doing of some counterfeiter, but which are a necessity for all men who want to avoid the displeasure associated with the revelation of the inadmissible. This constraint is the *deformative constraint*. Whence the failure of recognition when the truth arises.[3]

And more distinctly still:

> What can be said of the Oedipus knot is not that it is an inaccessible signified, but a signified that offers itself only in its absence. This absence is not a lack of existence, nor furtive flight from any attempt at seizure. . . . The fantasy, the dream, the symptom, inhabited by *unconscious representation*, speak this absence. An absence that would not be a reflection of death, but death in life itself, in the replication of lack, insofar as it traces and shifts it. The theater accepts the challenge to invoke this absence in the most scandalous way possible, since nowhere does language hold forth the discourse of presence with more ostentation. . . . In the theater absence must be sought lurking in the intensification of repeated speech.[4]

II

In his preface to Ernest Jones's *Hamlet and Oedipus*, Jean Starobinski has collected all the passages concerning Oedipus in Freud's writings and has ascertained that references to Hamlet are accompanied by references to Oedipus, beginning as early as a letter to Fliess dated 15 October 1897.[5] He thus recognizes in these tragic figures a mediating function "between Freud's past and his patient,"[6] a mediation that sustains the following system of analogies: the Ego is like Oedipus; Oedipus was us; Hamlet is Oedipus repeated; Hamlet is the neurotic one.[7]

This group of transformations is what articulates the particular figures through which Freud's desire to see/know is fulfilled. In discovering such a group, I believe that Starobinski not only admirably brings us close to what *truth-work* might be, but also informs us of the capital fact that this work operates through the mediation of the tragic scene. Finally, Starobinski sets us off on an important track: Hamlet's *inability to fulfill* the paternal word as the difference between modernity and the Greek world.

The first of these truth operations is a comparison; the other three are metaphors. They all signify a transport of identity under different proper names. These names appear as masks or as face values, standing for something else. They are faceable figures, announcing another figure, without a face. These figures are organized in depth on the model of a kind of genealogical tree: from Oedipus, placed at the greatest depth, directly issues the displacement of *me to us* and from this group to Hamlet; a second generation issues under Hamlet's governance, a second bearing [*portée*] of displacement, one that will allow the identification of the group me-us in the neurotic and make psychoanalytic practice possible.

How do we justify these displacements and this hierarchy of figures? Where in his work has Freud ever set forth these presuppositions? What theory grounds them? What theory do they ground? These are irrelevant questions. Something, a name, a destiny, can stand for something else without any announcement of the rules of substitution or transformation authorizing this "standing for." We are at the antipodes of science. It is easy for us, following Freud, to recognize in these unforeseen displacements operations of the unconscious process. They take place in non-recognition, in another place. But isn't taking one thing for the other precisely the error, the delusion that these displacements engender? Isn't it mad to take dream-work for truth-work?

III

At precisely this point, the reversal on the dramatic stage intervenes and founds that "stroke of daring" of which Starobinski speaks.[8] To take oneself for Oedipus, if Oedipus were a simple figure, would in effect be dream-work, an unconscious process of identification. But Oedipus is a reversed figure, since Sophocles produces the simple figure of Oedipus, who is, right up to his desire to know, the figure of non-recognition, thus bringing it into view. In staging the text that the prince weaves around, so as to account for the pestilence that attacks Thebes, Sophocles manifests it as an aberration. The errant subject emerges as a hero, as figural fate, with his noisy words, his ignorant knowledge. What pushes him onward, what manifests his errancy, is the presence of traces of truth—a presence that will utter its last word through the mouth of Tiresias. The event of the profound figure of parricide and incest punctuates the drama, leading the errant seeker back again and again in this figure's direction. (I count seven occurrences beginning with the encounter with the oracle of the pestilence and ending with the testimony of the Therapon, lines 1110–1185.)

The errancy is manifested, in the chains of reason that Oedipus invents, by the event of a trace. The text of reason/unreason serves as a mirror upon which a line coming from elsewhere may appear. The figural space, the topological space of transgression in which his fantasy gives him his father to kill and his mother to marry, returns to invest the fantasmatic figure and offer it to our view. Theatrical staging is not the repetition of fantasmatic staging, but its double reversal, its placement in a space possessing the same properties as that of the unconscious. But rather than fantasy setting the stage and ordering the figures that fulfill desire—that is, the desire to see that fantasmatic—Sophocles offers the dramatic space in which it may visibly fulfill its non-recognition and its operations. The properties of the unconscious space that Freud, as we know, has described in paragraph 5 of "The Unconscious" (1915), appear on stage in the form of an event, but an unjustified event that violates the laws of logic and the rules of ethics. No reason is given for its appearance, and the unreason of the reasonable and rational is manifested through it.

Freud's identification with Oedipus is not really an identification. Rather, as Starobinski argues, it is a recognition, neither of a cognitive nor non-cognitive nature, a representation of his own fantasmatic figure in Sophocles's re-presentation of that of Oedipus. There is an infinite power of replication in the figure.[9] For it is itself in its most archaic form—what Freud called "primal fantasy"—already a cleavage, both an unpresentable matrix and a fantasmatic spectacle, both inside and outside. With the theater, the figure's outside, its staging, exhibits traces of the matrix, its inside.

Truth-work consists in leaving the stage free for the figural event, in allowing attention to float equally on all the constituents of the errant one's discourse so that a cry, slip, or silence coming from elsewhere may be heard. Theodor Reik said that the rule of free-floating attention requires the analyst to have a "third ear."[10] Oedipus the king has one eye too many, wrote Hölderlin. The difference between theatrical action and psychoanalytic practice does not lie in the quantity of replication, which is basically the same in each, but in the field of replication. In both cases, the sensory supplement is obtained by a deconstructive excess aimed in the direction of the latent. But in one case, it is to hear, in the other, to see. Freud will leave the realm of Sophocles, or rather Shakespeare, when he attempts to state (the order of hearing) what tragedy shows. This is a return to the text, but not a return to cognition, for Freud has passed through representation's oscillation. He will pass his own discourse of knowledge through it, reversing his text through events comparable to those that punctuate Oedipus's quest: the death instincts, the final event, will mark in the theory the place of facelessness and the unsignifiable, the limit of representation and theory.

IV

But what about Hamlet? Why does he fall into this position of secondary representation, of re-presentation of the oedipal figure? Freud immediately noticed the difference. In his letter to Fliess, which serves as Starobinski's starting point, he diagnoses Hamlet as a hysteric (based on the following symptoms: the expression "Thus conscience does make cowards of us all" [III.i.83];[11] hesitation in avenging his father's death; the feeling of guilt as one who is conscious; the denial of sexuality with Ophelia; a death similar to his father's, which is at the same time a punishment for his own inaction). However, let us leave diagnosis aside and ask ourselves: in the order of representation, what is there in *Hamlet* that is not in *Oedipus*?

There is *unfulfillment*. This can be seen as the psychological dimension of neurosis, or the tragic dimension of thought. Unfulfillment has quite another dimension. Oedipus fulfills his fate of desire; Hamlet's very fate is unfulfillment of desire. This chiasmus extends between what is Greek and what is Jewish, between the tragic and the ethical.

In Greek tragedy traces of a profound figure, by which we are disseized of an origin, may appear. This does not take the form of a reconciliation (despite what Freud said, for example, in "Creative Writers and Daydreaming" (1908), or in the "Formulations on Two Principles of Mental Functioning" (1911) but that of a re-presentation. The field is left "free" for the play of primary process within secondary process. And, to be sure, the former will play *us*! Nevertheless, this disseizure (of the spectator in the tragic) is the game to play (to be played) for the violent eruption of truth. Here discourse has not repressed the figure, but seeks to welcome it. Discourse becomes desire, plays desire. This is what constantly fascinates Freud, and what, as he knows from the very start, will always be kept at a distance.

In Jewish ethics, representation is forbidden. The eye closes and the ear opens to hear the father's word. The image figure is rejected because, as fulfillment of desire and seduction, its truth-function is denied. "Hearing," says Rudolf Bultmann, "is the way to perceive God. . . . Hearing is the fact—abolishing all distance—of knowing oneself as reached, of recognizing the word of he who speaks."[12] Thus one does not *speculate*, nor concern oneself with ontology, as Levinas might say. How hard it is to keep fascination at a distance!

> How does one oppose oneself to the name of God—He who I dare say, never shows himself, nor speaks, who certainly spoke on Mount Sinai, but about whom it has never been known if He spoke for a long time. Nor do we know if He said all He is credited with, or if He didn't limit Himself to the first sentence, to the first word, or even to the first letter of the Decalogue, which, as if by accident, is the unpronounceable *alef*! What are the attributes and promises ascribed to such an enigmatic God worth? What value do all the subtleties and abstractions of the Revelation have alongside the splendid apparition of the earth children who wear the sun as a medallion?[13]

Nevertheless, the ethical subject knows himself to be seized by an Other who has spoken, disseized of an origin. He is "elected" in the "irrecusable election by the Good which is, for the elected, always now and forever fulfilled"; elected in "a filial passivity which is more passive than all passivity." And this passivity

> does not become Eros, since nothing suppresses in this passivity the trace of the Other in its virility so as to reduce the Other to the Same. The an-archic bond between the subject and the Good links up with the outside.[14]

The difference between the Other, the Father who has spoken, the dead voice or the voice of the dead, on the one hand, and on the other, me the Son, Hamlet, is not a revocable difference. And if it is not, it is due to Evil, Divine Grace. Due, as Levinas says, "to the very egoism of the Self posing itself as its own origin."[15] (Oh! Oedipus, race of Laius, race of warriors born directly from the earth, without parents!) If this presumption of autonomy were lacking, disseizure would be ignored, passivity would be of a nature other than the Good: God would be a fact. It is necessary that the son *not fulfill* the word, that no hope of reconciliation, which would make the Other return to the bosom of the Same, be permitted. It is necessary that the son's seizure by the voice be more archaic than his freedom and that his freedom be the sin, the crime, of the impossible reseizure.

> The teaching of the Torah cannot come to the human individual through the effect of a choice: what must be received in order to render free choice possible cannot have been chosen, except after the fact [*après coup*]. In the beginning was chaos. Unless it were an assent other than that which is made after scrutiny and that death threatens an infidelity. . . . Freedom as taught in the Jewish text begins in non-freedom, which—far from being slavery or childhood—is a beyond freedom.[16]

Here there is no reconciliatory dialectic, no philosophical optimism. "The Jews remain particularly insensitive to Jesus. . . . The Bible provides the symbols, but the Talmud does not 'fulfill' the Bible as the New Testament claims to fulfill and also continue the Old."[17]

The ethical rejection affects not only the ontological fulfillment of Christ, but also that of cognition, the Odyssey of knowledge. The latter is denounced as an odyssey of the Self, as desire simply to be tempted, to have been tempted, and to have emerged intact from the "ordeal":

> The tempted Self is still outside, it can listen to the song of the sirens without jeopardizing the return to its island. It can brush against evil, hear it without succumbing to it, test it without being affected by it, try it without living it, take calculated risks.[18]

In the eyes of the Jew this is "the European certain at least of his retreat as subject, secure in his extra-territorial subjectivity, sure of his separation with regard to the Whole."[19]

Let us place this rejection by Levinas alongside a diagnosis by Freud:

The feeling of security with which I follow the hero [of popular novels] through his dangerous adventures is the same as that with which a real hero throws himself into the water to save a drowning man, or exposes himself to the fire of the enemy while storming a battery. It is the very feeling of being a hero which one of our best authors [*Auzengruber*] has so well expressed in the famous phrase, "Nothing can happen to me!" It seems to me, however, that this significant mark of invulnerability very clearly betrays—His Majesty the Ego, the hero of all day-dreams and all novels.[20]

It is precisely to this Same that ingests all Other that Levinas opposes his reading of the *"Chabat" Treatise* (88a and 88b), which is a commentary on Exod. 19:17, and where he finds the following:

Rav Simai taught that, when the Israelites made a covenant *to do* before *hearing*, six hundred thousand angels descended and attached to each Israelite two crowns, one for doing, the other for hearing. . . . Rabbi Eliezer said: "When the Israelites (etc.). . . . First the doing, then the hearing."[21]

Levinas finds the Revelation to be "a Yes more ancient than naive spontaneity," for the Torah is "an order which the self grasps without having to enter into it." Here once again is the voice of the father: "To hear a voice is *ipso facto* to accept the obligation with regard to he who speaks."[22]

But now we understand that just hearing this voice, understanding it, obeying it as a command, submitting to it by overcoming one's egotism—all operations that are mediations, require mediations, lead to processes (to discourses of process, as Kierkegaard said)—are unsuitable. This dead voice, this writing, is not a message, but rather a gift. It is the true present as absence, and this gift consists in the fact that the subject is grasped by it, seized. This leads Levinas to write: "The Torah is given in the light of a face."[23] This voice is a light, and the face, as *Totality and Infinity* has taught us, is what the invisible illuminates, the presence of the absolute Other.[24] "Plato reminds us of the long ordeals of the eye, which wants to fix the sun in its resting place. But the sun is not forever withdrawn from view. The invisible of the Bible is the idea of Good beyond being."[25] In face of the eye's Odyssey, which loops in the sun, there is disseizure without return.

V

The truly fundamental thesis of *Moses and Monotheism* (1939) is not Moses's Egyptian origin. Freud never hides the fact that he absolutely needs this romantic hypothesis about his hero's birth for his construct.[26] It is in fact on the condition that Moses is not Jewish that it will become plausible that the Hebrew people, tired of his domination, put him to death. The essential point for Freud is that Moses was murdered, since through this *Agieren*, this acting-out (the compulsive murder of the father figure, repeating in its non-recognition that of the primal father, thematized in *Totem and Taboo* in 1913) the Jews escape the general movement of the primary murder and the religion of reconciliation, Christianity, which offers the libido its compromise formations. For the Jews, the son does not have to ask for and obtain a reconciliation with the father. There is already an alliance between them, which is a *pre-conciliation*.[27] The alliance is not contractual, since the absolute inequality of the two parties constitutes it. The son is seized by the father's voice, and what this voice gives is neither a heritage nor a mission, nor even less a knowledge; this gift is the commandment that the son may be and remain seized by the father's voice:

GHOST: Adieu, adieu! Hamlet, remember me, [I.v.91]
HAMLET: Now to my word;
        It is, "Adieu, adieu! remember me." [I.v.110–11]

This modality of superiority that compels the son to remain in a position of absolute inequality before the father is what the tragedy of Hamlet stages. We must assuredly agree with Jones that Hamlet's reluctance to avenge his father's murder proceeds from his identification with the murderer and that Claudius, through the king's assassination and his marriage to the widow, occupies the son's place in the triangle of the royal Danish family. But what is important is this *displacement*, because of which Hamlet, unlike Oedipus, does not fulfill his desire. Hamlet seems to come to grips with the oedipal *after* it has manifested itself in the double crime of his uncle. An other has taken both his and his father's place and has exposed the desire in its scandal.

Hamlet's tragedy thus begins after *Oedipus the King*, and the articulation of the figures of the desire to see/know in Freud finds its respondent in that of the figures of desire that Western theater exhibits. The displacement of the son by the uncle introduces, in the order of affects, Hamlet's ambivalence with regard to Cornelius. But what is truly important is that, in the scenic order properly speaking, this displacement is correlative to an essential displacement of the subject in his relation to desire. *Oedipus fulfills his desire in non-recognition; Hamlet fails to fulfill his desire in representation.* The complex function of representation in Shakespearian tragedy must be linked to the dimension of unfulfillment, that is, to the contribution of the properly Judaic. Let us try to establish these two points: we will perhaps be able to understand what the Danish prince adds to the Greek king and why he doubles for him as a figure of desire in the constitution of psychoanalysis.

Let us begin with the function of representation. There is, to be sure, the play within the play, the tragedy of Gonzago, that Hamlet stages to trap his uncle: "the play's the thing / Wherein I'll catch the conscience of the king" (II.ii.612–13). While he indicates to the actors the way to play their parts, Hamlet forcefully defines the function of theater: "the purpose of playing, whose end, both at the first and now, was and is, to hold as 'twere the mirror up to nature" (III.ii.21–23).

Let me once again place next to this mirror of the stage Freud's remarks in his "Recommendations to Physicians Practising Psychoanalysis" (1912): "The doctor should be opaque to his patients, and, like a mirror, should show them nothing but what is shown to him."[28]

Gonzago's tragedy represents Hamlet's, and only a slight displacement—the murderer is the nephew of the victim, not his brother—disguises the crudeness of the repetition/rehearsal. Hamlet counts on the tragic effect of recognition to trip Claudius up. Thus the theater itself serves a function on stage similar to that served by the prophet Tiresias in *Oedipus*. The king of Thebes was an innocent criminal: being unable to recognize it, he had to encounter the truth. But since the end of Olympus, the parricides (fratricides) and the incestuous are no longer innocent; they are "cognizant" of their crime and are able to "recognize" it when it is represented.

The play within the play gives, as it were, the manifest function of representation:

Gonzago———Queen   =   King———Gertrude

　　　　Nephew   Claudius

Its latent function is elsewhere. There is another duplication, another specular presentation in the Shakespearian tragedy, the subject of which is no longer Claudius, but Hamlet himself. There are two families at play on the Shakespearian stage: the Hamlets and the Poloniuses. Here, the oedipal triangle is replicated thus:

Dead King———Gertrude   =   Polonius———Ophelia

　　　　Hamlet   Laertes

Between these two sets lie two major modalities of the relation: that of the spectacle, the mirror with its ambivalence, and that of acting-out. Examining them will allow us to understand the displacement of Ophelia onto the position that Gertrude occupies. We immediately notice that the play barely mentions Polonius's wife, except in one passage, which I leave the reader to judge: Laertes, enraged by his father's death, replies to Claudius, who tries to calm him: "That drop of blood that's calm proclaims me bastard / Cries cuckold to my father, brands the harlot / Even here, between the chaste unsmirched brow / Of my true mother" (IV.v.116–19).

Speaking to Laertes, Hamlet says: "For, by the image of my cause, I see / The portraiture of his . . ." (V.ii.77–78). For Hamlet, Laertes stands as a representation of self: a father to avenge; a woman of his blood rendered "mad," "seduced," to restore to her honor, that is, to her place. Like the prince, Laertes finds himself facing the scandal of desire. But Hamlet probes Laertes as if he were a model: he recognizes himself in the same place but does not affectively identify with him. Laertes, angry and indignant, unhesitatingly fulfills his debt of death and honor. We know why: the father's murderer and Ophelia's seducer is not a man of the family, is not himself a father-figure with which he can identify. Here we encounter the difference that, with repetition, gives (the) representation, a function of recognition in distancing. During the duel with Laertes in act 5, Hamlet declares: "I'll be your foil, Laertes" (V.ii.255). This *foil* is both the sword and the offset ("anything that sets something off by contrast," *Concise Oxford Dictionary*.) "I will be your sword" announces the exchange of swords in the course of battle, the exchange of poison that one of them carries, the exchange of death: "my death will be yours," which is the classic relation with the Double. But it seems to me that "I will be your offset" means "you must fulfill the debt of vengeance, I will not; I will only watch you fulfill it. Instead of acting on the Hamlets' stage, I watch you act on that of the Poloniuses." The representative distance relieves the pressure of the debt. Here one is close to articulating unfulfillment with representation.

But that is not all. The two triangles do not communicate by representation, but by *Agieren*. Hamlet plays an important role on the stage of the Poloniuses: he kills the father and alienates the daughter. This role is exactly symmetrical to the one performed by the uncle, Claudius, on the stage of the Hamlets. But here the mirror (Poloniuses') does not reflect the image: not for one moment does Hamlet view himself as the father's murderer and the woman's seducer. When he intervenes on the Poloniuses' stage, it is as an *other*. And he "knows" it; that is, he maintains his identification with Laertes and continues to know nothing of his identification with Claudius, with the father's murderer:

> Wasn't Hamlet wrong'd Laertes? Never Hamlet:
> If Hamlet from himself be ta'en away,
> And when he's not himself does wrong Laertes,
> Then Hamlet does it not: Hamlet denies it.
> [V.ii.233–37]

How heavy the argumentation of this denial. And the other, the unjust ("Who does it then?") goes unnamed—"his madness" (ibid.).

We, however, know him. The dagger thrust through the drapery (Good Lord!) has pierced Polonius in place of Claudius. The seduction-castration of Ophelia has replaced that to which Hamlet's mother almost fell victim. Hamlet has fulfilled his desire, but outside, on the Poloniuses' stage. This stage is another scene, in that Hamlet doesn't see where he is (in Claudius) and attempts to see himself where he is not (in Laertes). Hamlet's desire is unfulfilled on the royal stage; it is acted-out (*agierte*) on this other scene. The two triangles, then, can be articulated in the following way:

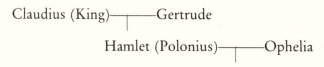

Claudius (King)——Gertrude

Hamlet (Polonius)——Ophelia

Laertes

Whether it is a matter of Gonzago's tragedy or that of the Poloniuses, the function assigned to representation remains one of recognition. The principle is that in the play of desire's figure, the subject in the audience recognizes his fate, recognizes his lack of recognition. This principle, applied by Hamlet upon the stage, induces the expected effect on the spectator, Claudius. But Hamlet, himself a spectator of the other scene (the Poloniuses'), fails to recognize his fate, his nonrecognition. He only sees this negatively, as his own coldness, slowness, inertia; as his own inability to take revenge in the time prescribed, compared to Laertes' precipitous violence. All this scene shows him of himself is his unfulfillment as a son. What it hides from him is precisely his rootedness in the son's position, in "filial passivity."

Before examining this articulation with desire, let me add a further word on the specificity of representation in *Hamlet*.

I have presented theater as the reversal of figural fantasmatic space onto the (formally analogous) space of representation. *Hamlet* responds to this reversal a first time: Shakespeare represents his own fantasmatic space on the stage of the Globe and thus offers it for recognition. The play responds to it a second time: Hamlet, in placing Gonzago on the stage, returns and presents for recognition the oedipal figure that lurks in Claudius. But the third stage (the Poloniuses') does not perform this function. Since it is not representative, it does not act like a mirror: Hamlet's vision as a spectator is occluded once and for all by a blind spot. What this scene offers Hamlet is an alibi. "I am Laertes" (that is, "I am not Claudius"), "I must still fulfill the paternal word" (that is, "I have already not fulfilled it by killing Polonius"). This is a scene produced by a foreclosed parricidal or incestuous compulsion. Hamlet's fate is to be the stage manager, which is to be unable to fulfill the paternal order, to take the place of the father, to remain disseized, irreconcilable. Thus upon the Shakespearian stage next to the Italian stage (Gonzago), which is analogous to the preceding one, there is an entirely other scene (the Poloniuses') where the tragic reversal is itself reversed. This scene is thus a direct exteriorization unelaborated by the double theatrical reversal, the direct externalization of Hamlet's fate. In short, it is a scene that is a symptom. But it is through the Shakespearian cast of these various scenes that *we* in the audience are able to see the blind spot, to see Hamlet not see, and that Freud can begin to perceive what the other scene is—the unconscious—and to point to neurosis as the impossibility of re-presentation.

Now, the other point: the relation between unfulfillment and the complex function of representation. First we must understand this unfulfillment. Oedipus fulfills his desire by taking the place of his father; his desire and his fate coincide. For Hamlet, the father's place is taken and the paternal command is to leave it vacant; this vacancy can only be attained by suppressing the usurper. But the latter is for Hamlet a father figure. The formula of Hamlet's desire is: kill your father. The formula of his fate, of his debt is: kill his simulacrum. He will eventually kill a simulacrum of a simulacrum, Polonius, who is further removed from the father figure than Claudius (as the configuration of the Polonius family indicates, especially the relation Polonius–Ophelia). There is both an unfulfillment of desire and a fulfillment of fate. There is a fulfillment of unfulfillment. This is the configuration of the *Agieren*, that effectuates desire without fulfilling it, outside its scene, on an alibi stage contrived by derivation and without re-presentation.

This is, moreover, precisely the configuration of rejection that, according to Freud, bars the path to anamnesis for the Jews. Just as Hamlet, by killing Polonius on the other stage, will fail to recognize his parricidal desire and remain seized by the task intimated by the voice, the Hebrew people, by killing Moses in a process of acting-out, foregoes recognizing itself as the father's murderer and cuts off the path to reconciliation. This is precisely the path traced by the desire to see, that is; the Christian path that announces the vision of a father at its culmination. "It is not I, Hamlet, who has killed my father (it is Claudius); my father speaks to me, as I am chosen by him; all those appearing as father figures are usurpers: Claudius, Polonius (Hamlet). Knowledge is usurpation of the position of the Word by the self. I am and remain the absolute son, the passivity, which is the Good." Egoism, the heroism of the self whose model is Laertes (and even Claudius as well as Oedipus), is renounced on the manifest level.

If this is indeed the difference between *Oedipus* and *Hamlet*, a difference between the representation of desire fulfilling itself in non-recognition and desire failing to fulfill itself in compulsive representation—a difference between Greek fate (Apollo is not a paternal voice) and Jewish *kerygma*—one can perhaps begin to comprehend the figures disclosed by Starobinski. And we can understand as well what Freud, on a day of anger, wrote to Pastor Pfister, whom he had just violently accused of knowing nothing of the sexual theory of neurosis:

> I can only envy you, from a therapeutic point of view, the possibility of sublimation in religion. But what is fine in religion certainly does not belong to psychoanalysis. It is normal that in therapeutic matters our paths should separate here and so they may remain. Quite in passing, why was psychoanalysis not created by one of all the pious men: why was it for an entirely atheist Jew that one waited?[29]

It was necessary to wait for a Jew because it had to be someone for whom religious reconciliation ("sublimation") was prohibited, for whom art, representation itself, could not serve the Greek function of truth. It was necessary *to wait* because it was essential that this someone belong to the people for whom the beginning is the end of Oedipus and the end of the theater—a people that has renounced the desire to see to an extent that it wants to *do* before it wants to *hear* (because there is still too much seeing in hearing).

And it was necessary that this Jew be an atheist so that the renounced desire to see could change into a desire to know; that the staging, this opening of the secondary space to primary process, could give way to the analogous opening that the double rule of free association and free-floating attention hollows out. But this must occur in discourse alone, with back turned, without looking, even without the third eye, with only the third ear: the ear that wants to hear *what* the voice of the Other says, instead of being seized and disseized. This is the atheism demanded by Freud.

Translated by Susan Hanson

4

"A Few Words to Sing"

COMMUNICATIVE DISCOURSE AND FIGURAL WORK

The function of art and politics is to make people dream, to fulfill their desires (but not to allow their realization), to transform the world, to change life, to offer a stage on which desire (the director) plays out its fantasmatical theatrics. The *operations* common to the dream (or to the symptom), to this art, and to this politics must, therefore, be recovered and made manifest. One such manifestation is *critique*, which must now be applied to art and politics.

Four operations define the dream-work: condensation, displacement, considerations of representability, and secondary revision.[1] The first two must be seen as the fundamental operations of the unconscious; the other two as mixed procedures at the center of which the demands of desire and censorship are respected simultaneously

The following are the characteristics of the unconscious process according to Freud:[2]

1. "[The Unconscious] instinctual impulses are co-ordinate with one another, exist side by side without being influenced by one another, and are exempt from mutual contradiction. . . . There are in this system no negation, no doubt, no degrees of certainty." This implies "judgments" outside the categories of quality (neither affirmative nor negative) and modality (neither assertoric nor hypothetical).

2. "The cathectic intensities [in the Unconscious] are much more mobile." In the *primary process*, in contrast to the secondary process (language, action), energy is not "connected"; it is "free." Displacement and condensation are the characteristic operations of this nonconnection. Thus we cannot identify them with the operations at work in language.

3. "The processes of the system Ucs. are *timeless*; i.e., they are not ordered temporally, are not altered by the passage of time; they have no reference to time at all." Here we find the violation of one of the essential pivots of discourse's organization. In particular, the lack of reference to the

actual time of the speaker (*linguistic time* in Emile Benveniste's terminology) would have as its correlate the elision of the speaking subject.

4. "The Ucs. processes pay just as little regard to *reality*. They are subject to the pleasure principle . . . , [to] the replacement of external by psychical reality." Neither the referent nor the context of unconscious "discourse" can be recognized.

The characteristic that captures all of this, however, is the mobility of cathexes. Mobility signifies that the basic condition of discourse, that is, discontinuity or the existence of *articuli*, is not satisfied by unconscious "discourse." Freud always characterizes the unconscious as work, as an other of discourse, and not as another discourse. Primary and secondary space are broken down as are continuity and discontinuity, the noncon- nected and the connected, the atemporal and the temporal, the asubjective and the subjective, the amodal and the modal, the aqualitative and the qualitative. We use the word *figural* to designate every trace of the primary in the secondary.

In a text, the effects of the unconscious are marked by transgressions of the sort listed above. Even in a plastic representation (a painting), the work of the unconscious deconstructs the rules of design, of value, of chromatic composition, decoration, and subject, and can even go so far as to act critically on the plastic support itself. This means that the characteristics enumerated by Freud apply not only to discourse but also to the representa- tion of reality insofar as it is encoded, that is, written. This holds a fortiori for film, which brings together the characteristics of discourse and those of plastic representation.

It is true that the discourse of music does not refer to a referent in the same way that language does. Nevertheless, music appears as a temporal organiza- tion (diachronic, like speech) of discontinuous elements (*articuli*, the notes) defined, like phonemes, by their place in a system (the scale and rules of harmony). In music the work of the unconscious produces effects of mean- ing by transgressing diverse levels: temporal organization (rhythm, develop- ment), steps between the elements (the scale), discontinuity between the elements (existence of notes), composition of elements out of other ele- ments, sonorous material of so-called musical objects.

Let us reverse the proposition: every transgression of this type is equal to a trace of the primary process; that is, a transgression makes the listener grasp the secondary, the "linguistic," the "written" character of the music to which his ear is attuned and in which this trace is marked. Such transgres- sions then have a critical function, at least as long as they are not in turn connoted, that is, replaced in a new language as a constitutive operation, such as a rhetorical one, although they may be more elementary.

Luciano Berio's place is central regarding this problematic. He belongs to

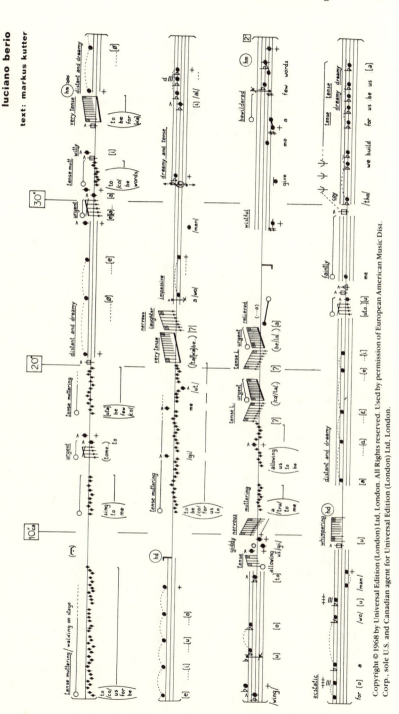

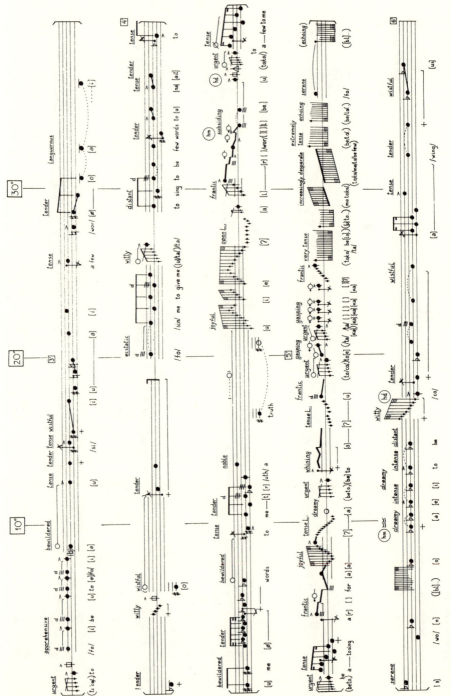

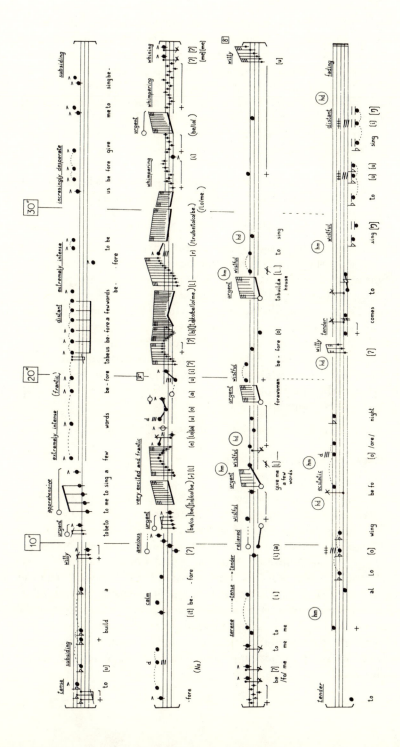

the movement of accelerated deconstruction, which seized upon the princi-ples and levels of musical discourse, not only because he is a "modern musician" (connoted already), but also because he works directly, explicitly, upon the relation between language and music. In *Sequenza III* he is not content with the critical movement (sonorous disorder in the musical order) that we have indicated. He is not even content to oppose language as order against music as disorder. Rather, he reverses the roles, attributing to the musical region a coefficient elevated to a secondary organization, while speech appears shaken to its phonetic roots by the primary process. This reversal of usual roles—the musical object being, in principle, further from the connective model than the linguistic object—deserves reflection. It is necessary to situate it in relation to critical reversal in general.

LANGUAGE, MUSIC, CRITICAL REVERSAL

There is a Western hypothesis concerning the musical object that would claim that it is a quasi discourse. This hypothesis signifies that the sonorous organization must certainly entail (quasi) deviations but that the principles of order remain sufficiently sensible that the listener still recognizes what he is in the process of hearing (discourse). Such a double demand corresponds to the compromise between a system that allows the production of recogniz-able musical "discourses" and the "free play" of transgressive operations in relation to that system. This play, however, does not cease to constitute itself in a second-order system, and the operations do not cease to be connoted there. In short, a rhetoric is formed.

From a descriptive point of view there are three levels:

1. the system (scale, harmony) that allows the production of musical discourse;
2. the transgressive operations; and
3. the rhetorical aspect of these operations.

From the point of view of energy, it is easy to understand that every non-connoted deviation is like an event. It blocks the communication of the musical "discourse." Being unheard of, every deviation necessitates a sup-plementary expenditure of energy so as to be heard and believed. Neverthe-less, if it does not exceed the limits fixed by the rules of the system (the first level), the event is reabsorbed. It becomes situated in the rhetorical field and the affective result is, first, a surprise, followed immediately by a kind of satisfaction. This is comparable to a joke [*mot d'esprit*]: Freud stresses the limits that the deviations of language must respect in order to be witty [*rire d'esprit*]. Similarly, the equilibrium of surprise and satisfaction, of the charge and discharge of the psychical apparatus, makes for a strictly governed musical pleasure.

From a historical point of view, we are tempted to say (leaving the concern of accuracy and specificity to the specialists) that during the classical age musical events (of the second level) remained enclosed in the field authorized by the system (the first level) and could thus be easily connoted in musical rhetoric (the third level). In music, this would occur in a manner similar to what would arise in painting and literature. Up to the period 1860–1880, the various schools leave musical space intact, as do modern painters. No modern painter (the Impressionists included) questions plastic space; nor do novelists question literary space. The break represented by Cézanne, the Cubists, and, especially, the Abstractionists, consists in (and Pierre Francastel has shown this as well) the displacement of plastic space. This break is the end of representation, the end of working the plastic support. The line, value, and color are treated as something in which a scene is recognized, and not as something to be seen itself. The same holds for Mallarmé and the Dada movement in literature. Musicologists would undoubtedly know where the fracture took place in music: Wagner, Schoenberg, Webern?

For someone who is not a musicologist, it appears in any case indisputable that free jazz or electronic music is no longer restricted to simple deviations from accepted rules.[3] These are displaced expressions, in which the primary process operates upon the very language, the system (the first level), of traditional music. In particular, the classical instrument disappears. The classical instrument was, as Gaston Bachelard would say of scientific method, only produced through theory: it was a mediator sublimating sonority and noise into its theoretical "good." A sound is judged as good when it is in its place in the theoretical discourse of music. When so located, even bad sounds can be listened to.

It appears to us impossible to consider this transgressive movement of music (of painting, literature, theater) outside a problematic of desire in its relation to capitalism. Problematic of desire: "art," which has been dead for a century, functioned as the self-reconciliation of the social, the recuperation of affects in a system of exchangeable signs; "art" was a language of the passions. Problematic of capitalism: all signs can be transformed into goods; that is, any object (a vehicle for a number of affects as well as a representative of instinct) can acquire exchange value and can enter into the circuit of capital, and its production can engender surplus value. Here we discover the inexhaustible market offered to the field of desire.

At the end of the nineteenth century, as capitalism spread and was reinforced, it became impossible for an artist to continue to produce art as if the artist's expressions had a value of affective participation and reconciliation. Simply, they either have or do not have an exchange value. And if they do play a role of reconciliation, it is because they function as ideological moments in the circuit of capital. The circulation of affects and instinctual representatives overlap with the circulation of capital. The translatability of artistic signs is no longer defined in terms of shared emotions, but in terms of exchange value. The traces of the unconscious, the marks of desire upon the works of the secondary process, are bought and sold. Desire is or will be collected in the network of capital, that is, in the hyper-rational and hyper-operatory secondary process.

A reversal of art's function is necessary for it to become anti-art. What is at stake is no longer the effect of participation, but that of contestation; no longer the circulation of signs (everywhere smuggled), but their critique as tools of alienation. Critique must itself be constantly recuperated, constantly displaced; it must become primary mobility. Art transports things "elsewhere"; it is the death instinct. The struggle between capital and anti-art is a conflict between, on the one hand, Western neurosis or psychosis in its most severe phase (the phase where libidinal formations are entirely repressed or foreclosed in the discourse of capital) and, on the other, anti-art, concrete music, the production of works seeking to certify the existence of an irreparable alterity in the circuit, seeking to show by traces the presence-absence of meaning irreducible to a linguistic or accountable signification.

DISCOURSE AND "ACCENTS"

The acquisition of articulated language requires the repression of sonorous value. The phonemes that form distinctive units are not vibrations that we must reproduce or recognize while observing their frequency, amplitude, and intensity; they are merely units that allow us to distinguish monemes (or morphemes), that is, meaningful units. A child learns to speak his mother tongue by repressing irrelevant phonetic possibilities. The opposition between primary and secondary can be easily spotted in sonorous material. The sonorous machine of the libidinal body (which manufactures sighs, hiccups, burps, cries, hisses, pants, groans, laughter, raspberries, clicks, interruptions, sobs, and so on, and which manufactures the displacements that become the intensity, the pitch, and the prosody of sentences marked with great emotion), plugged directly into desire's hazardous current, must become independent of desire. The plastic, mobile, non-connected, sonorous cavern must become the phonetic cavity regulated in such a way as to respect relevant deviations.

Berio's *Visage* (1961) describes the battle in which transmittable meaning finds itself encircled, surrounded, penetrated, *mimicked*, by figural expression. Cries not only overlap entirely with the vocal field on which the traces of the affect can work, but they also constitute a material that tends to be organized on the model of discourse. Berio writes that "we can listen to *Visage* as a metaphor of vocal behavior," and that if it "signifies discourse," it does this "essentially at the level of onomatopoeia." The piece "does not present a meaningful discourse, but rather its simulacrum. Only one word is pronounced, the word *parole* which means 'words' in Italian."

How can vocal sounds elicit an effect of pseudospeech? And what is the function of this simulacrum? Vocal sounds can produce this effect in the same way that Saul Steinberg can produce a pseudowriting: by employing phonic (or written) units as material and by assembling them into forms analogous to those that produce, in sonorous space or upon a graphic support, the grouping of distinctive units into meaningful ones. The simulation therefore consists in a double operation. On the one hand, it decomposes linguistic behavior down to its phonic units and even at this level introduces units originating in foreign languages or in non-languages (aphasia). On the other, it envelops this phonic chaos in sonorous and grammatical connections that create an illusion. For example, groups of vocal sounds can be broken up in such a way as to produce quasi words, or they can be placed in a poetics evoking that of some language (Slavic, Turkish). The first of these operations corresponds exactly to oneiric displacement. The phonological units are no longer interpreted as parts of a system, but according to their immediate sonorous value. They are withdrawn from their system, displaced. The second operation consists of a secondary revision aimed at erecting a semblance of order vis-à-vis the chaos left by desire in the preconscious order.

We cannot say that this is onomatopoeia in the strict sense of the term, at least if onomatopoeia means the transfer of the designated thing's sonorous quality to the phonetic organization of the word that signifies it (the equivalent in writing would be calligraphy). What Berio means here by *onomatopoeia* is the presence in discourse, not of the sonority of the thing, but of the sonority *of the affect* that the thing would provoke. If the piercing cry or the sudden muttering refer to things, to situations, if they have a powerful force of reference, if they open around themselves a space of events, it is because they manifest in language itself the presence-absence of primary space under the various types of *Entstellung*, of deconstruction. The explosion of meaningful units, the disorder of combined distinctive units, the simulacrum of découpage and of prosody oblige the listener to restore to the sonorous constituents of language their unwieldy affective charge. Onomatopoeia is here the transfer of affect to simulated "words." The sonority of the affect is the disruption, by the unconscious, of the mother tongue's phonology, and, consequently, of phonetics.

What is closest to the pseudolanguage of *Visage* is the supposed first language that Rousseau imagined in the *Essay on the Origin of Language*. Rousseau placed it in opposition to communicative language, just as music is opposed to painting. To communicate needs, it suffices to show the needed object, and an indicating gesture does the job. Language, however, is human because it transports passions, and therefore needs "accents": "these accents, which thrill us, these tones of voice that cannot fail to be heard, penetrate to the very depths of the heart, carrying there the emotions they wring from us, forcing us in spite of ourselves to feel what we hear."[4] This first language "in its mechanical part . . . would have to correspond to its initial object, presenting to the senses as well as to the understanding the almost inevitable impression of the passion that it seeks to communicate. . . . Most of the root words would be imitative sounds or accents of passion, or effects of sense objects. It would contain many onomatopoeic expressions."[5]

This brings to the fore the function of the simulacrum, which is to display the music assumed at the origin of speech, the music of passions that communicative language represses. According to Rousseau (and perhaps Berio), communicative language is born from the music of passion, which must and can present itself only as a metaphor of itself in communicative language. Figural order is masked and presented in the discursive order.

WORKING ON DISCOURSE

In *Sequenza III*, the "libretto" plays a much more important role than in *Visage*. In *Visage* there is only the word *parole*, while in *Sequenza III* there is a poem by Markus Kutter:

> give me a few words
> for a woman to sing
> a truth allowing us
> to build a house
> without worrying
> before night comes.

This text contains, prior to all musical work, the marks of figural operations. Without claiming to enumerate everything that would determine all the levels of language (language both as a system and as speech), the following may be noted.

1. The Syntactic Level

1.1 The rules of punctuation governing the system of language are not respected (agrammaticality). This produces an ambiguity in regard to the découpage. Several phrases are possible:

a. give me a few words . . . to sing a truth . . .
b. give me a few words . . . to sing, [give me] a truth . . .
c. give me . . . a truth before night comes.
d. give me a few words allowing us . . .

1.2 There is also ambiguity at the level of the phrase: "allowing us" can be understood as "to allow us" or "which allow us." This ambiguity is not agrammatical: it is permitted by the system of language. Although it is precisely the phrase that must reduce ambiguity, this is not the case here.

2. The Semantic Level

2.1 From the point of view of the rules governing lexical selection, a "truth" is not permitted to "construct a house," even in English. We can, strictly, "sing a truth," but only in poems.

2.2 From the contextual point of view, there is an ambiguity in the "us." "Us" can be either "I" + "you" or "I" + "he" (or "she"). Although the addressee, the "you," is not specified here, which is not unusual in literature, we cannot decide whether the truth that allows the construction of the house is to be given to him and to me or to this "woman" and to me.

The text of the libretto is therefore already worked. This work can be understood only as a group of operations of the unconscious process. It consists of the transgression of the rules that assure good communication. Surely the deviations are not very important; they do not extend beyond the meaningful units. And some, like the elision of the subject, are already heavily connoted. In *Circles* (1960), Berio supports his instrumental and vocal elaboration with fragments from e. e. cummings's poems, which themselves contain distortions more extreme than Kutter's. Nevertheless, the function that guides the operations acting upon the text of *Sequenza III*'s libretto resembles the work of *Visage*: to create a figural space of anxiety at the heart of discourse.

The vocal treatment of the text sensibly augments the affective charge of the musical object because it extends the deconstructive operations sketched in the poem. In particular, it applies them to the distinctive units themselves. Yet here we have a semblance of discourse justified by the discrete character of the units. The pseudospoken parts are opposed to the sung parts as the discontinuous is to the continuous. But we see that many of these discrete units (for example, the clicking sound found in the Zulu language) are not standard to English, the language of the text. Some are not found in any language because they are produced by using the hands alone (finger snapping) or in conjunction with the phonological apparatus (hands clapping in front of the mouth, but cupped in order to mute the sound). These elements refer to the expressive power of a body, in which the presence of language is not limited to the phonological apparatus alone. The linguistic term loses its arbitrary character, that is, its discontinuity. Or, at least, it preserves its appearance only. It assumes a function of the sign properly speaking insofar as it refers to an exteriority, that of the libidinal body, which it evokes through its own discontinuity.

Let us take the case of laughter. The expression of affects obeys the rules of good behavior used by "civilized" people. When Berio introduces various sorts of laughter, always identifiable as laughter, even though encoded in the musical score, he does violence to these rules of behavior on several levels.

1. In the course of concerts as we know them, laughter is limited to the audience, to the public side, and shows that the work performed is mediocre or badly played. Placing the laughter on the stage violates the sacred space in which musicians play. This space draws its power of taboo principally from the fact that it resembles, for the quasi totality of concert halls, the space of representation in Italian theater. We see this type of transgression in Stockhausen's *Momente*. The reversal consists in applause inscribed into the beginning of the musical score and interpreted by the musicians. The difference is that the applause is based upon a certain rhythm: a form (*Bildung*) is created. The laughter in the *Sequenza* is not given special attention. By means of its position in the diachronic chain, it fulfills a certain function and assumes a certain form.

2. To score the laughter (and not only the laughter), Berio must transgress the rules of musical writing by inventing a new code. Such transgressions have become commonplace now that compositions make use of electronically produced sounds.

3. He transgresses the rules of interpretation of song: we learn in music conservatories to sustain all sounds by controlling the movements of the diaphragm, that is, the expiration of breath, as much as possible. Now, laughter occasions an exhalation of large quantities of air in a short period of time which requires barely controlled pressure on the diaphragm.

4. Finally and above all, Berio clearly transgresses the rules of behavior, which instruct us that it is not proper to laugh in someone's face, to laugh alone. We do not laugh whenever we want to, without regard for time and place. We repress our howls and giggles. We must not laugh without a reason. The laughter of the *Sequenza* intrudes into propriety as such. It is motivated neither by the signified of the text nor by the musical signifier.

In his brief commentary on the *Sequenza*, Berio writes: "I would like to suggest that behind *Sequenza III* lies the dissimulated memory of Grock, the last great clown." And he recounts that as a child he had Grock for a neighbor, that Grock lived in a bizarre house surrounded by a Japanese garden, that with his classmates he went over the wire fence to steal oranges and tangerines from his neighbor, whom he did not know to be Grock. Only later, at about age eleven, he saw Grock on stage, "not knowing, like everyone else in the audience, whether to laugh or to cry, and tempted to laugh and cry at the same time."

In exchange for the stolen fruit, this *Sequenza* repays to Grock the language of emotions that the eleven-year-old Berio felt to be at once impossible and inevitable, the language the clown had "spoken" in the ledger Berio kept for him, the language of the visible body miming the libidinal body. This is an inevitable language if we surrender body and soul to "seriousness," the secondary, the so-called adult; it is an impossible language, not only because it is unbearable by its affective charge, but also because it is unpronounceable. What seems to appear only sequentially and in isolated intervals in the preconscious and conscious activity is condensed here into an instant: pain and laughter, jubilation and anxiety, anger and tenderness.

"Free" affective energy is indifferent to the rules of propriety and to the prescription not to laugh and cry at the same time. The affective polyvalence of the different vocal sonorities proffered by Cathy Berberian is contracted by means of condensation;[6] it produces a sort of space of emotional simultaneity, which defies the rhetoric of feelings. It therefore tends to suggest what the atemporality of the unconscious processes could be. The score gives no less than sixty-one types of directives for the vocal performance. At the hundredth second and over an interval of three seconds, we find the following cues: "tense laughter," "urgent," "relieved." We notice twenty-one indications of this type between 4'50" and 5'20", that is, over the course of thirty seconds. Berio does not want these indications to result in any sort of representation or pantomime. Rather, they are to determine spontaneously the color, the expression, and the intonation of the voice, not in a conventional fashion, but according to "the emotional code of the interpreter, her vocal suppleness and her own dramaturgy." Explicit care is taken in breaking with customary rhetoric and scenography.

Let us stress the importance of the condensation. *Sequenza* starts in a sort of vocal "in the wings," since the interpreter comes on stage muttering "to/co/us for be" as rapidly as possible. The opening of the work is therefore "offstage," that is, out of earshot, out of place, out of time. Thus Berio's indications at the beginning of the score: "The performer (a singer, an actor or both) appears on stage already muttering as though pursuing an off-stage thought. She stops muttering just before the subsiding of the applause of the public; she resumes after a short silence (at about the eleventh second of the score)."

The "extended muttering" that opens *Sequenza* rests upon a double operation of condensation:

1. condensation bearing upon the major units (morphemes), since the syllables utilized (to, /co/, us, for, be) are already extracted from the poem by the occultation of other syllables:

> "to" (sing/build a house) ("to" is overdetermined);
> "be" (-fore night) /co/ (-mes);

(allowing) "us";
"for" (a woman);

2. condensation bearing upon the small units (phonemes). These syllables must be pronounced as quickly as possible. The interpreter then suppresses every silent interval that permits the successive recognition of select syllables. The rapidity of the utterance, moreover, deforms the phonetic propriety of syllables. We do not hear "to" then "/co/" then "us" then "for," then "be," but "to/co/usforbe." Furthermore, this utterance is repeated. It descends into itself, and it ascends into itself, into ringlets. Thus according to the score, the text, to be *spoken* in the form of a "tense muttering," is written in order to be spoken synchronically:

$$
\left(\begin{array}{c} to \\ /\ co\ / \\ us \\ for \\ be \end{array}\right), \quad \left(\begin{array}{c} sing \\ to \\ me \end{array}\right), \quad \left(\begin{array}{c} to \\ /\ co\ / \\ be \\ words \end{array}\right) \ldots
$$

Berio indicates that the sounds or the words so scored must be repeated rapidly but according to an entirely fortuitous internal order of appearance. This "tense muttering" is taken up again in different material seven times over the course of the first minutes. Then it disappears.

WRITING THE MUSICAL REGION

Faced with work that profoundly disturbs the discursive field, we can only be struck by the dissymmetrical function that song and music fulfill for Berio. Here, in the permutation of expected roles, resides the apparent paradox and undoubtedly the profound motif of *Sequenza*, perhaps the profound motif of his entire work.

There is in principle a strong figural value of continuity, as we have said. What is without beginning and end, without internal articulation, undetermined, appears to be the other of the secondary process, a region of discontinuity and the finite. This opposition governs Rousseau's division of the roles played by indexical and compassionate language. The former arises out of drawing, out of the discontinuity of the line, out of the visible and recognizable form. This is why the former will develop into the latter substitute with the invention and extension of writing. It represses the language of the heart: "the more the words become monotonous, the more the consonants multiply; [. . . as accents fall into disuse . . .] they are replaced by new articulations."[7]

The conflict surrounding the introduction of Italian opera in France belongs to the same problematic.[8] When, for example, Rameau's nephew extravagantly mimicked the work that spoken words and phrases must undergo in the new operatic mode, when he caricatured the predominance of strictly ruled discourse over the language of passions in his uncle's music, he became a representative of the primary process. And when Diderot mimicked with words the nephew's gestured and accented mimicry, this was even more extravagant. We can understand nothing of Diderot apart from this problematic.

To be sure, the properly sung part of *Sequenza III* mimics strictly ruled discourse in the same way as Rameau's nephew did. The final "to sing" projects well beyond what is required for the identification of the words in an economical communication. The multiplication of expressive cues for the sung part, already noted in the "spoken" part, also produces an effect of discontinuity in the linguistic signifier, which results from its subordination to the musical signifier's continuity.

These effects are, however, minimal, and we should even be ready to challenge their force. The traces of the unconscious process (the second level) do not prevail in the musical region of *Sequenza*, but rather in the rhetoric (the third level) by which the sonorous continuum is segmented, distributed, and produced. The numerous and rigorous rules make of song not the region of free movement of energy and affects, but rather that of their incarceration and domestication.

This is obvious in the very form of the work. Henri Pousseur shows, in the concert program, that *Sequenza* is punctuated by a regular oscillation between discourse and song. We can demonstrate this distribution precisely by the following chart, in which the letters "DS" and "DD" designate "deconstructed song" and "deconstructed discourse" respectively:

A. Introduction (1'50"): DD/DS
B. Development (6'10"):
    a. DS (2'30")
    b. DD (1'00")
    c. DS (1'30")
    d. DD (1'10")
C. Conclusion (0'50"): DS

The timetable allows us to emphasize the equilibrium between the diverse parts, with a preponderance of song, albeit of deconstructed song. The découpage into three parts (which we can designate some other way if we think the terms *introduction*, *development*, and *conclusion* are abusive or too connoted) and the binary equilibrium within the development helps us to understand that we are confronted with a very classical form close to that of the sonata and musical rhetoric.

The work is, therefore, carefully balanced. The moments of deconstructed song allow the listener's attention to take up varied positions; the weak dispersion of energy remains highly connected. We fall back into a barely disconcerting music whose regular intervals prove that it is a rather serial composition. We find ourselves on familiar terrain, while the listening is made safe by this melodious and melodic voice. Accidents are rare; the exhalation of breath is sustained for a long period of time; the event is revived within the limits of the variations of pitch and text. The origin of the sound, the "who sings?" and "from where?", is of little concern, in that it resembles the source of any classical *Lied*. We find ourselves in instants of calm compared to the preceding or following moments of tension that introduce the deconstructions of the spoken discourse.

If we study the configuration internal to the areas of song, we may make the same observation. There, too, the deconstructive effect is made sensible more by contrast than directly. Neither the quantity nor the richness of the deviations of spoken or musical discourse produce the deconstructive effect. It is the rigidity of the rules of these discourses, where the rigidly ruled secondary space is constantly affirmed, that enables us to hear the most modest transgressions. For example, the physical time punctuates the score into sections broken at the 10″ mark and fixes its duration absolutely at 8′40″. These strict rules put us at the antipodes of free jazz. And the abundance of cues demonstrates that the interpreter's tempo is no less completely controlled. Finally, the musical distortions themselves, as we have said, appear to us already heavily connoted by means of the *Lied* and the Viennese school and are minimal events.

Sequenza III is no exception. In *Sequenza VII* for oboe (1969), we ascertain a sort of reconstitution of tonal space by a B-natural held by the pipe organ. The entire work is supported by this B. It reappears quite frequently in the oboe part, and the organ continually duplicates it. What role does Berio want it to play? Is it supposed to hold out against the "discourse" of the oboe that is judged to be too deconstructed, too violent? Is the organ pedal supposed to tie together the elements that are too disparate, too "free"? If this is the case, then it would be necessary to admit that there is more timidity here than in *Sequenza III*. Perhaps it is better to say that the B appears as the object par excellence to be deconstructed: the tonic, the foundation of the system of "language" of classical music. Held in abeyance, B operates here for the ear as a remote harmonic, revealing and exposing the basic scheme. By contrast, it sets in relief the deviations of timbre, pitch, and duration; it enhances the play of the oboe. But again, this is done by a very classical and heavily connoted procedure.

The *Sinfonia* (1968) appears to be situated at an even more resolutely "secondary" level. We have the feeling that here Berio returns to a tonal music so close to that of Mahler that, from the rhetorical point of view, they are almost indistinguishable. Has Berio ever deconstructed musical form? Add this one to the tricks that the unconscious plays on us: precisely in reference to *Sinfonia*, Berio suggests that his work be understood as the *Traumdeutung* of this "flux of consciousness" that he takes the scherzo of Mahler's Second Symphony to be. A flux of consciousness is not a dream, and it does not demand a *Deutung*. Rather, it is really a collection of Berio's free associations based upon the Mahlerian "narrative"; that is, it is a material more dreamlike, more "primary," than the narrative. This material, however, is hardly deconstructed, because it is maintained under the strict control of the preconscious, especially if we compare it to dream material. This is a most curious invitation to Freud: to come and take up precisely the place from which he wants to escape, the place of the secondary process. But it also confirms the feeling we are left with after listening to *Sinfonia*.

RECONCILIATION?

In the musical region we have rediscovered the same conflict between expression and discourse that Rousseau described in regard to the "first language." But here this conflict appears wholly otherwise and calls for a wholly other treatment. First and above all, the relation of the elements at work is reversed. The repressed figural order recovers with melody the right to manifest itself entirely by working the discourse. Song allows for a découpage of spoken words or phrases that tears them from the requirements of communicative discourse. The syllables are charged with sonorous and affective value. With the melodic and rhythmic treatment, the sonorous signifier appears capable of throwing the linguistic (secondary) level back again into the expressive (primary) level. The fundamental operation here is the displacement of the intervals and accents.

This, however, is the second point. Passion by right is expressed through song in opera or in the *Lied* only on the condition that passion is measured, written. The deconstruction of spoken words or phrases is balanced by a rhetoric of the melodic theme and of its rhythmic and harmonic accompaniments. The figure disturbing the spoken phrases of the song is thus neutralized by writing the music of song. Here again there is tension between the figural and the textual, but their roles are exchanged. *The musical is more secondary; the spoken more primary.*

All things considered, *Sequenza* appears as a complex whole. It possesses moments of spoken language when the deconstruction is such that communication becomes impossible. Thus moments of the secondary process count precisely as figural moments. It also contains moments of song when the deconstruction is strictly ruled (here discourse is the most recognizable). In this case, figural moments (if it is true that melody, rhythm, harmony serve as expressives) operate as the articulated secondary zone. The cry of Dionysus is where we hear the words of Apollo. And, inversely, the Apollonian harmony is where we hear the Bacchic delirium. Thus a double reversal takes place.

While in the spoken region there is reversal of the figure/discourse relation benefitting the figural, in the sung region the rhetorical becomes dominant. The formula of the first region would be: language does not speak, it is pathos or compassion. That of the second would be: what speaks is music. One must therefore admit that the "classicism" of the musical form assumes a precise role, which is to indicate a displacement—this time a major displacement—in the respective functions of the two regions. The language undone by the cry carries a challenge to communication, to information. It throws into question the ability to exchange linguistic messages; it jams the codes and the networks that guarantee translatability and communicability. Berio writes: "For me, *Visage* also constitutes my tribute to radio, which is the most generous transmitter of useless words." The words have no use, aside from being sung. The words speak only when they sing; without music the words are silent. It is the music that speaks.

Such is at least one possible way of listening to Berio that does not betray the great displacement of roles. Perhaps, however, it is necessary to hear again. If discourse is rendered useless, it is not only because of the intemperate consumerism that modern capitalist society encourages. Berio does not merely target a "civilization" in which everything becomes like a word so as to be exchangeable. If the pulverized phrases and words are adjoined to these areas of song, for which the last "to sing, to sing" represents the model, it is to indicate another fracture. The discourse-cry provokes a strong charge of energy, an accumulation of affective tension, in service to which the song produces economy and peace. Is this reconciliation?

Compare this to Rousseau's description of the presumed first language:

> Since natural sounds are inarticulate, words have few articulations. Interposing some consonants to fill the gaps between vowels would suffice to make them fluid and easy to pronounce. On the other hand, the sounds would be very varied. . . . Since sounds, accents, and number, which are natural, would leave little to articulation, which is conventional, it would be sung rather than spoken. . . . This language . . . would deemphasize grammatical analogy for euphony, number, harmony, and beauty of sounds.[9]

In Rousseau, there is a reconciliation of the primary and the secondary in the fantasy of this natural language, language without *articuli*, language without a father, without castration. In Berio, reconciliation is not possible. The articulated language cuts the universe of the maternal music in two. We do not know how to reconcile the pieces, to sing while speaking. Song is not much more than a pure and simple speech; passion can no more manifest itself than in the infrastructural disorder of words. We are assuredly in something like the eighteenth century, something like the end of a culture. We shall surely change the world and life, but at the price of not being able to revitalize the ideology of reconciliation. Such is the sense of Berio's double reversal, which maintains the *caesura* between the two "languages," just as Freud maintained it between the two processes.

One last word. The isolation of the musical "domain" belongs to the discourse of capitalism. The presentation of the *caesura* between pathos and logos *inside* concert halls accepts the censoring of desire in the distribution of social roles. This keeps deconstruction in its official place. It does not, however, suffice that the event occurs only inside its field; it is now necessary for the field itself to become an event. Without warning, plug *Sequenza III* into the loudspeakers of the University of Nanterre, in the Gare St.-Lazare, in the workshops at Billancourt. By doing so, you will do a service to everyone: to work, to music, to Berio, and to us.

Translated by Leonard R. Lawlor

Part Two

◆

THE PAGAN

5

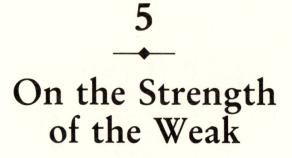

On the Strength
of the Weak

1. CORAX

The title is inspired by a long-standing indignation of the "friends of wisdom" against the artists of the word. Before criticizing their art, before summoning Tisias and Gorgias to appear in court, Plato, through the mouth of Socrates, acknowledges the great orators of the time. It is necessary not to forget, he says, "they [who] observed that probabilities were to be more esteemed than truths; they [who] can make trifles seem more important and important things trifling through the *power of their language* [*rhômê logou*] . . . [must not be forgotten]" (*Phaedrus*, 267a).

Later, Aristotle identifies the small discursive apparatus of which Plato speaks as one of the *commonplaces* of all genres of discourse (political, legal, and ceremonial): it is the ground for magnitudes where one enlarges what is small and diminishes what is large. This is fair oratorical war. But the indignation nonetheless reappears in Aristotle with respect to a closely related procedure attributed to Corax, one of the founders of Sicilian eloquence and the teacher of Gorgias. "My client is accused of brutalities against someone: just look at him, he is weak, puny, this is just not probable." Very well, says Aristotle, the argument rests on a real probability. But if Corax's client is a strapping fellow, he will plead thus: "you can see how robust he is. Isn't that enough to accuse him before the fact? And can you believe that my client would have fallen into the trap? He has avoided a very probable indictment by abstaining from all brutality, and that is why he is innocent."

Shamelessly, says Aristotle, Corax confuses two kinds of probability, the absolute and non-absolute kinds. What is used in the second case is only relative, singular. And the philosopher adds: "This [fallacious procedure of substituting the absolute] is what is meant by *making the worse appear the better cause*. And therein lies the reason why people, rightly, could not abide the training advertised by Protagoras. The thing is a [logical] fraud; the probability concerned is not genuine but spurious, and has no place in any art except [mere] rhetoric and quibbling" (*Rhetoric* 1402a 17ff.).

The *téchnē* of Corax thus consists in a figure of amplification pushed to an extreme. And it is in the use of probabilities that it exceeds what is permitted and ceases to be a *téchnē* in itself. Probability, then, occupies the same position as the arts of discourse and the prudences of life in opposition to theoretical knowledge (science) that deals with truth. But even in the rhetoric of probabilities, as in dialectics, it is necessary to distinguish the pure and the impure, the absolute and the relative, the in-itself and the particular, as one must do also in dialectics. Moreover, Aristotle states, it is exactly the same mistake that is made in dialectics when one argues that the nonexistent *is*, since the nonexistent *is nonexistent*, and that the unknowable can be known, since we can *know* that it is unknown. Here one confuses the same usage of the term taken by itself with the term taken in a particular relation to another term, that is, in these circumstances, with itself.

Against what do the friends of wisdom protest? Against a logical ruse that is also a moral, political, and economical ruse. It consists simply in placing what is given as absolute, as the final word, in relation to itself, and thus placing it in the register of relative and particular things. If probability can serve as the criterion for the judge's verdict, why can't the probability of this usage of probability serve to guide the conduct of the accused? If probability redoubles itself, relates to itself, and anticipates itself, is it any less noble, less valid than "pure" probability?

Aristotle is well aware that a principle of disturbing strength lies at the hand of the weakest defendant—a principle that consists in raising the power of probability (squared, cubed, and so on) and that legitimates the retorsion of any argument (*logos*) if it belongs to the order of probabilities. And what is disturbing about this principle is that the power of a probability "superior" to another power (for example, as $n + 1$ is to n) is not for all that stronger, more pervasive, or "truer." Thus, in these matters, there is no last word, no single criterion, no judge, and no master. The relative, the particular, can be stronger than the absolute or what claims to be absolute.

2. HIPPARCHIA

The field of this still current battle is not only set on the surfaces of language, but, at the same time, on those of living bodies, political societies, economic communities, and age or gender classifications. Through all these, the friends of wisdom—Plato and Aristotle—seek to establish masterful accounts, to fix a non-referable reference, to determine a term that escapes relation and dominates all relations. Before them, the weak tirelessly undo these hierarchies.

The masterful definition of a speaker in the time of Athenian imperialism was: an Athenian citizen who is the son of Athenian parents, receives income from a plot of land, is a male, speaks the Attic language, participates in civic cults, and bears arms. If we look at the composition of the party of the weak, of those whose entire tradition stretches from the Academy to the Lyceum through Thomism to today's university, we have to laugh. For the first Sophists and Cynics are almost exclusively Sicilians and people from Asia Minor. The great adversaries of Platonic Socratism and Aristotelianism, the paradox makers, are provincials from Megara, a vassal city of Athens. Among the Cynics is a woman, Hipparchia, the concubine of Crates, who makes love [se produire] with him in public. The Sophists are nomads, flying professors, traveling from one city to the other to sell their lectures and conferences. Gorgias and Protagoras, very dear, according to their enemies, have been accused of making a fortune in the commerce of words. The Cynics, on the contrary, are poverty itself; but this poverty is no less suspect. It is said that Diogenes was banned from his native city of Sinope for counterfeiting money. His biography presents this admirable formula: "Diogenes who alters morals as he alters money" (Diogenes Laertes VI). Even worse, these inconsistent speakers who fracture the Greek of the masters with their Metic accents go so far as to make their bodies "speak"— for example, by farting—and not at all according to the rules of athletic or warrior competition.

From these particulars, the university composes a veritable clinical table of weak discourses: mercenary, effeminate, adulterated, hysterical.[1] And the university is correct in doing so, for all these tendencies speak against it, against a non-relative place where all discourses come together. One should see clearly that the university can accommodate their discussions, debate their "theses," trap them in the ritual of dialogue, and thus leave the nature of the last word in suspense. Moreover, it sets itself up as the place where this question must be posed, thus as the last place of words, their place par excellence (in the true Aristotelian sense) so to speak.

But the eccentricities of these Cynic madmen, uncultured Megarians, and Sophist clowns will not form a school and thus will not enter this place. They are locked out in the same way that slaves, women, barbarians, and children are barred from citizenship, Hellenic status, and virile homosexuality. But for them this outside is not an outside, because the final place, the last word, the ultimate reference, the absolute simply has no positional value. For them there is no outside, because without an outside, there is no in-itself. The in-itself as supposed interiority immediately falls into exteriority. There is only exteriority, or, more precisely, there is some exteriority.

This can also be said: there are only minorities, there are some minorities. What we call a person is a complex surface made of a multitude of small movements, all minor ones. The same is true of the so-called (universal) concept and the so-called attribution (copula). Minorities without majority. All mastery is usurped and proceeds, as Nietzsche says, from a strange sickness, the belief that there is really something to cure. Decadence is not the multiplication and proliferation of minorities, as the point of view of the last word suggests. Rather, it is mastery, exercised from the point of view of the last word. The so-called remedy *is* the sickness.

It is thus a question of countervaluing margins and the marginal. What the Greek minors say to the contrary, as in Rabelais's great sophistic resurgence, is that there is no margin at all. Only empires, reflecting their borders, frontiers, and marches to conquest, speak of margins.

3. PROTAGORAS

Protagoras exacts his fees from his student, Euathlos. The student protests: "Tell me when I have won a single victory because of you." Protagoras responds: "In any event, I should get the money, the money from my victory if I carry it off, and from yours if you win it" (*Diogenes Laertes*). Of which victory is the professor speaking?

Logical analysis: there is a law, an accord passed between the Sophist and Euathlos, that states: "The money from any victory due to Protagoras will be returned to him." The student claims that there have been no victories and therefore no retribution is due. Protagoras responds: "Pardon me, there is going to be a victory for someone [*ego men an nikeso . . . ean de su*], since there is presently a dispute between us on precisely the question of my fees and only one of us will win. We must therefore apply the law contracted between us to this debate as well. Now if I win it, that will be due to me; and if you win it, that will also be due to me. I must therefore be paid." (Cicero puts Protagoras's reasoning in the mouth of Carneades, *Academica posteriora*, II, 98.)

The power of the paradox consists of including the student-teacher conflict in the class of exterior and inferior conflicts for which the teacher prepares the student or, further, in juxtaposing both student and adversary under the name of Euathlos. If he loses, he will pay like any adversary; but if he wins, he will have to pay in his capacity as student.

A preliminary observation: the master relation is not isolated, nothing protects it from commercial contract relations. This is enough to prevent the institutionalization of a school and the establishment of disciples. For disciples are always minds protected from adversity, kept close to the last word, within the realm of masterly protection. Here adversity cuts across the discipline.

Protagoras's insolence points to something else, which is essentially logical and which one rediscovers elaborated in the work of the Megarians and the early Stoics: *Euathlos the student* and *Euathlos the adversary* are distinct objects of discourse, and that is why it is in no way contradictory to make both the former and latter pay. There is only a paradox from the point of view of one opinion, that of the masters, who want Euathlos to have an identity independent of the circumstances or, at the very least, to have certain essential attributes (for instance, being a student) and others that are accidental (for instance, his status as adversary). Protagoras's paradox simply states that there is no enduring subject under the attributes that we can observe, that no attribute is more important than any other, and that there are as many qualified subjects as situations. Thus Protagoras's logic involves successive evaluations, the destruction of absolutes and substances, and the rejection of all logic by attribution.

Something else to note here is that Protagoras's humor bears a similarity to mercantilism, which made the Greek conservatives, beginning with Plato, very fearful. "You cannot escape the generalized exchange of values: you will not only have to pay for losing, but also for winning—the circulation of capital."

And finally, an idea and a practice of time as diachrony—one thing following the other—is profoundly shaken by the paradox. Protagoras's response to Euathlos anticipates the result of their debate and includes the ulterior result in the current decision: "you can pay me now because I win in both cases." Now the weak, the oppressed, can obtain peculiar results through this figure.

One might say that Protagoras is not exactly the oppressed in this case. What could one be thinking? Euathlos is probably the son of some great family that makes money from its land or from arming warships. Protagoras has only these victories in discourse to live on. He's not even a wage earner; he's an artist.

4. EUBULIDES

Since the beginning, we have been speaking only of one strength: that of inserting the law that weighs heavily on the weak into the register that strength controls, and of the effects that follow. This is only a very minor strength that does not even deserve being accounted for. The *téchnē* of this inclusion is revealed in the Liar's Paradox, attributed to Eubulides of Megara, which Cicero reports in these terms: "If you say that you lie and say so truly, then you lie" (*Academica posteriora* II, 95). The reasoning continues: "but if you say that you lie and that you are lying, then you say so truly, etc."

Here once again we encounter the protest of the Doctors, who set out to refute this diabolical little apparatus. Bertrand Russell is one of the nicest of these mine sweepers, because he does not conceal his game behind meta-physical motives (and rightly so) and because his refutation is given so crudely that it cannot fail to be anything more than it actually is, namely, a decision. We know that this refutation consists in saying that we should distinguish between statements of type 1, which deal with any objects whatsoever, and statements of type 2, which deal with groups of statements of type 1. The paradox of Eubulides, "if you say that you lie and if you say so truly," must be broken up into a statement of type 1, "I lie," and a statement of type 2, "I say truly that," which applies to the group formed by statement 1 whatever might be the truth-value accorded to its propositional variable ("I lie when I say this," "I lie when I say that," and so on).

If one wants to put an end to the vertigo that the paradox engenders, it is necessary, says Russell, to posit in principle that the class of statements of type 2 is not part of the class of statements of type 1 and thus that the truth-value of the latter (the false: *I lie*) cannot modify that of the former (the true: *I say truly that*). Thus one can rescue both the possibility of non-contradiction and mathematics (this being the period of the *Principia Mathematica*), as well as satisfying the expectations of "commonsense logic."

Things are thus made perfectly clear: one must decree the non-inclusion of type 2 in type 1. One will not, however, be able to demonstrate this, since the demonstration requires the non-inclusion itself. This decree is not of a logical order. If, for example, one follows Eubulides, one might ask: of which type is Russell's statement? It is contained in the group formed by the relation (whatever may be the propositional variable) of type 2 statements with type 1 statements. It thus has the property of type 2 statements, since it affirms a truth-value for the group of propositional variables for a statement. But as this latter statement is itself a type 2 statement, Russell's statement will then be a member of the class of its referential statements. This is precisely what it seeks to preclude. If one wishes to avoid this consequence, it will be necessary to introduce a principle of superior rank, positing a type 3 statement (for example, that of Russell) and its disjunction with the type 2; an infinite regress.

In a sense, all this is not very serious. One could create a meta-axiom in order to arrest this regression, acknowledging simply that the truth-values can in fact only be fixed under the condition of this axiom. But in a sense, this *is* quite serious. For this formalism, indeed this artificialism, is just what the masters hide. What happens to their authority if it is not fashioned after an order that is prior to it, if, instead, it decrees itself? What is it that makes Russell's decision more valid than that of some liar? Is their authority purely moral and political? The masters tell us that they save us from the worst. But they decree that the worst is "anarchy," the absence of *arché*.

Before Eubulides, Protagoras held that every representation (*phantasma*) is true (Sextus Empiricus, *Adversus Mathematicus* I). Before Russell, Plato refuted this in the following way: If Protagoras is right, then the statement "every representation is not true" is itself true, since it is a representation. And Plato concluded: "thus the statement 'every representation is true' is false"—a counteruse of the paradox of the weak by a master. But the master's conclusion is off base. For the inclusion of the class of all classes in this latter class, which Plato practices against Protagoras, obviously works against his own conclusion. If it is false that every representation is true, how could we know if Plato's statement is true or false? In truth (!), Protagoras's statement must be understood as the truth not having any contrary. This is what Antisthenes will reiterate.

5. KUNIKA

The body, though obviously not the master body, nor that of the gymnasts, can infiltrate the master discourse, laugh, and make one laugh. One readily sees that *body* is an untrustworthy word, quite capable, like all words, of passing from one side to the other and then to another. So what sort of body is it? Assuredly, the bodies of the weaknesses.

Diogenes Laertes (VI, 6.98) tells of the conversion of Metrocles, a student of the Aristotelian school. He is sick, and one day in the middle of a philosophical discussion some wind escapes him. He is so ashamed that he returns to his home and decides to die of hunger. Crates the Cynic learns of the affair, eats a huge plate of beans, finds Metrocles, and impresses upon him that what would be shameful would be *not* to fart, since that would be contrary to nature. (Incidentally, we see what "nature" can be.) At that point, Metrocles begins to fart at will. Metrocles, cured of the sickness of believing himself sick when his body makes some noise during a master discourse, becomes a Cynic.

When one addresses a supplication to someone, one touches him on the knees. Crates approaches his gymnastics master for this purpose, but he touches him on the buttocks instead. The master is indignant. "Why? says Crates, don't they belong to you just like your knees?" (ibid.). One rightly reads in: belonging to you, a master of the gymnasium.

Hipparchia, the sister of the converted Metrocles, falls in love with Crates. Her distressed parents appeal to Crates to dissuade her from marrying him. Failing this, he then undresses himself in front of her (and, I suppose, in front of them as well), and says to her: this is all your husband possesses. She espouses his cause so well that they make love in public (ibid.).

Diogenes eats in the agora, to everyone's dismay. He refutes this scandal in the following way: "If there is nothing bad about eating, then there is nothing bad about eating in public. Now, there is nothing bad about eating; thus there is nothing bad about eating in public." He masturbates in public, with this for his sole excuse: "Ah, if only one could calm one's hunger like that by rubbing one's stomach!" (ibid.). This is an expedient for the poor. But this poverty reveals some elementary syntheses, ones that the overly rich discourse cannot begin to exhaust.

In the syllogism of the meal in the street, one recognizes the same hypothetical and deictic form that the Megarians and then the Stoics develop. The use of the deictic in the minor premise, often masked (*now there is nothing wrong with eating; now it is daylight*) has recourse to the sensible body: at the moment that I speak, I am hungry. It also has recourse to the synthesis of subjects, those of speech and need, that the masters intend to render impractical, except through their mediation: those who are hungry are silent, those who speak aren't hungry, and we alone, we masters, can articulate the two groups in a hierarchical society, in a hierarchical body.

Another impoverished synthesis in this weak philosophy: when one denies movement in front of Diogenes, he gets up and walks away (ibid.). Isn't this the refutation of the Eleatic paradox, the Achilles of Zeno's paradox of the arrow? Rather than a refutation, it is a displacement of the problem: movement (the synthesis par excellence), being inconceivable, involves not a concept, but rather will. The cynical body organizes perspectives, which is the source of its poor strength, and thus escapes the masters' law, *mimesis*. It turns its back on the animal-machine and the automatons, which are the enslaved bodies dreamed of by the masters.

It is thus not the setting into play of the body proper in its propriety and appropriation that lends strength to the weak. On the contrary, it is the masters who believe that the body is a controllable machine, and that is why they unhesitatingly push its expropriation as far as possible so as to enslave it. They torture it, amputate it alive, humiliate it in sexual practices, and wear it out in labor and death camps. The enfeeblement to which they reduce the body, often to the point of death, reveals an improper body—a body with bits broken into tiny, ephemeral syntheses, which are nonetheless sufficient to show that the power to unify the body is not in the masters' hands and that they usurp it.

This is what Diogenes says when, as a prisoner of pirates, he is auctioned to bidders at the slave market in Crete. The auctioneer shouts to him, "And you, Diogenes, what do you know how to do?" Diogenes responds, "I know how to command, so sell me to Xeniades over there, he has need of a master" (ibid.). The body's impropriety has the same effect as the discourse of the rhetor or medical treatment (Gorgias's *Pharmakon* 82b), in that it renders what is weak strong.

In his experience of sickness and decay, Nietzsche (*Ecce Homo*) depends entirely on this power of obtaining the clearest vision, the most refined tact and skill in spiritual matters, while migraines, nausea, and eye inflammations expropriate his organism and plunge it into a disgust for life. Health emerges in the midst of sickness, not as a desire for a cure, a demand for security, or a recovery, but rather because what passes for the enfeeblement of natural vigor reveals other forces and perspectives, which hide the resounding success of the organism.

6. POROS

Perhaps this revival of the weak body in the midst of the sleek, hard muscles of virile homosexuals (with whom Diogenes continuously banters, since they are the ideal of the community of masters) bears some relation to decadence, or, more precisely, to the emergence of the feminine—a washout in a political society of men. Feminine humor with regard to politics, citizenship, the civic cults of obvious gods, and the masculine effort to construct a history of the strong feelings over the weakness of small passions is perceived and classified by men, occupied with business, as the inability and stupidity of women. When it reappears in the preoccupations of the city, in a thousand forms—the art of seductive speech, poetry, rhetoric, bizarre theologies honoring the hypocrisy and perversity of the divine, stage presentations that adore the pathos rather than the impassiveness of the gods— the citizens then scream "decadence" and fabricate laws, systems, and utopias as remedies to prevent this return.

The remedies are all marked by the same stamp: there is non-being; meaning is absent; let us work toward its advent. So be it: we are in the chaos of sickness; let us conquer the fullness of good health. Two simple examples of this nihilist tradition in the struggle against nihilism: the function assigned to death in both erotic desire and in the authority of speech.

In the story that Plato recounts of Eros's birth (*Symposium*, 203b ff.), it is necessary to pay attention to the qualities that Eros inherited from his father. Poros is the opposite of an aporia, he is the passage, "there are always means to bring something about." And what are the epithets that qualify his son, Love (Eros)? *Epiboulos*, a poacher constantly setting traps for the fair and good; *andreios*, courageous; *itês*, bold, enterprising; *syntonos*, tense and intense; *thêreutês*, a mighty hunger, always weaving some intrigue or other (*tinas mêchanas*); *phronêseôs epithumêtês kai porimos*, keen in the pursuit of wisdom, fertile in resources, a philosopher at all times; *deinos goês*, wonderful sorcerer; *kai pharmekeus*, healer; and *kai sophistês*, sophist. And, Plato adds, he lives and dies in the same day and resurrects himself by well-performed tricks.

Better than anyone, our friends of the *half-breed* call attention to the semantic field marked off by these words. Particularly, that Love is sophistic, dwelling in a space of hunts and pursuits, not in safe places, in a time of metamorphoses, not continuities; and that his logic is that of paradoxes and machinations, not reasons. Prudence and boldness are given to him instead of morality. Like Nietzsche, he is most alive when he is most dead; his pharmacy consists in Phoenix. Thus situated, Eros is the opposite of a master; he is the cousin of the Sophists, Cynics, and Megarians, the cousin of the little ones, of those who live from one day to the next, with inexhaustible strength, *andreia*, and virtue to always be able to turn around (this theme of turning, of the strophe, was itself part of the semantic field considered).

What does the master add to this portrait? Precisely what is needed to disfigure it. And this disfiguration has been the concern of Western ethics, logic, and politics for over two thousand years. Plato adds lack to the portrait. Eros's mother is Poverty, he says, who profits from Poros's drunkenness in order to become pregnant. Women are poverty in the master's discourse. And they make the little calculations in order to be heavy with child.

There is a perfectly masterly idea. This mad Sophist who doesn't care about reasons or ends, who is only passionate about means, and whose entire strength, like that of the weak, consists in setting traps where by definition the balance of disfavorable forces can be reversed, must lack something, claim the friends of wisdom. Otherwise, he simply would not embody wisdom. Thus, here is poverty: Plato invents the desire for immortality as the spur for Love (ibid. 207a ff.). This consummate art, all these techniques, bright and lively inventions, despairs and gaieties, will have to be subordinated to the lack of life, to the fear of death. It will be necessary to declare that what Love wants is to procreate, to make children so as to perpetuate himself and thus attain immortality rather than what he loves. Philosophical love is substituted for sophistic love, and Plato for Protagoras.

In eliminating the flow of affects, woman is situated in the poverty through which, people say, we must pass to attain timeless truth. The dialectic is thus born where woman, like Hegel's slave, plays the beautiful and evil role in a cultural process that is an altogether masterly affair.

A second example: Protagoras, great setter of traps, is accused of impiety and atheism and banned from all of Greece, according to Flavius Philostratus. He might have said that it was "impossible for him to know if the gods exist or not or to conceive of their appearance." Instead, he simply flees. It is interesting to imagine the old tracker being tracked from city to city during those last years. It is quite possible that some of his works were burned.

Socrates finds himself in the same fix, condemned for impiety and corruption of youth. But to a friend of wisdom, death has a different meaning: it can bear witness, which is an idea that never dawned on Protagoras. The Sophist does not place himself above the laws of the city, but under them. Socrates's irony, so provocative during his trial (*Apology*), rests on the masters' contempt for opinions. He only asks to die because he has already forseen this important idea, that is, to die for a cause will attest to his truthfulness and reinforce his credibility. It is hard to imagine the Sophists or Cynics as martyrs. The martyr says: it is true because I die for it; my truth is not of this world. (Thus the grumblers on all sides have found that May '68 lacked enough deaths to look true.) The masters truly love martyrs, including those among their adversaries. But Protagoras's flight brings to mind that of young Horace: it is not merely a matter of saving one's own life, but the possibility of "turning around" and of turning the situation around.

Translated by Fred J. Evans

6

---◆---

Humor in Semiotheology

A SEMIOTICIAN BECOMES ALARMED

To take 450 pages to reflect upon the Port-Royal *Logic* and Pascal's *Pensées* is one of the most academic occupations possible in these times.[1] But (in case you didn't know it) being out-of-date is a modern art! Moreover, one must be outrageously outdated, meaning one must take (or accept) such a distance from what's in the air that it becomes possible to detect or to reveal elements imperceptible to those who breathe it. So be it.

Louis Marin's *Critique of Discourse* minutely dismantles the representative model at work in the Port-Royal *Logic*. This flattening is implemented from the inside, where the antilogic named "Pascal" lurks. Marin's thesis is that the eucharistic utterance "This is my body" forms both the scenario and the scenographic schema of the representative model of the sign. It both belongs to this model and, in the "Pascalian" version or critique, escapes it and is utterable only within an order other than that of representative signs. The eucharistic utterance founds the representative theory of the sign because it affirms, with an affirmation anterior to all negation,[2] that the sign and its reference (here, its signification) can be substituted one for the other: a "coalescence of meaning and reference"[3] in which only a truth can be effected. Very well. In what way can these refinements in linguistic analysis and theology, obtained at the cost of such a classically rigorous style, such obstinate pursuit (one so enamored with what is hidden in the Port-Royal retreat), such an asceticism (itself so Jansenist) in the author's evident vitality—in what way can all this work and all this devotion to old books be modern?

This is a book on the decadence of discourse. A very talented semiotician sets out, following his own path, in the direction of a region misunderstood by semiotics, toward the blank spaces indicating deserts in the cartography of signs.[4] He hears what is pronounced there and understands that it is the dogma of Transubstantiation, itself undecidable within the order of signs. He discovers that semiotics, at least representative semiotics, garners

73

support from the theological affirmation that bodies are meaning and that meaning is corporeal. At the least, his claim to sober scientificity is thereby disrupted. But he also casts doubt upon the fundamental utterance that substantiates religion and philosophy. He follows this path in the company of "Pascal." (Nietzsche, too, had this fellow traveler.) They all end up at the limits of semiotics and the Platonico-Christian theology that underlies it. They thus end up in the vicinity of incredulity, of "libertinage." Speeding up and exacerbating the process of the decadence of discourse would ultimately lead to no longer believing even in the grammar of things. The reader will not be able to tell, after 450 pages, if Louis Marin has gone that far. But the question is raised everywhere, and that is how outrageously out-of-date Marin is.

THE REDUPLICATION OF SEMIOTIC THEATER

From the elements that words are to their combinations in judgments, Port-Royal comprises and elaborates discourse according to the model of representation. Three-quarters of Marin's book is devoted to the analysis of this model. The richness of its erudition, the precision of its conceptualization, and the subtlety of its interpretation make *The Critique of Discourse* quite simply a great classic on the matter of representation. But to understand this, one needs simply to put oneself in Marin's hands. So let us put that aside and turn to this: if one proposes to critique discourse as conceived in this manner, is it not necessary to place oneself somewhere beyond representation? And what is this outpost from which the representative masquerade can be denounced? The place of this outpost will determine the form and the nature of the critique.

The first outpost claims to situate itself in pure exteriority. Odds are that it will remain slave to the apparatus it is confronting, for it is the nature of this apparatus to turn back upon itself indefinitely and to draw within itself the exteriority from which it is critiqued. This dirty trick has been played on most religious, philosophical, political, and aesthetic "oppositions" in the course of Western history: each time these oppositions invoke an Other in the discourses and practices they attack, they are not careful to notice that this Other is, in its construction, implied in the organization of the opposing side and that they themselves are at least party to the Other's theatricality (if not to its theater) even before they begin to dismantle representation. Ruse always turns back on itself.

If you attack the theory of the sign with the "Pascal" included in the logic of Port-Royal, if "Pascal" can be thus placed outside, it will not be long before you see the representative organization reconstitute itself under the names of philosophy of will and philosophy of desire, under the categories of concupiscence and charity. Eventually these categories must in turn be locked up, secured by an inaugural sign, by an authority capable of signing the new scenography (that of the heart), and it must be circumscribed in the enclave of a new drama judged to be more true than that of knowledge. Another truth is still truth. Signs of affect will still be signs. Their logic may try as hard as it likes to turn itself into an ethic disdainful of the logic of words and of powers: logic will turn back on itself.

This is what occurs when Pascal reproaches the Judaic reading of the Old Testament for failing to satisfy his demand for a totalization of meaning:

> Thus, to understand Scripture, we must have a meaning in which all the contrary passages are reconciled. . . . Every author has a meaning in which all the contradictory passages agree, or he has no meaning at all. We cannot affirm the latter of Scripture and the prophets: they undoubtedly are full of good sense. We must then seek for a meaning which reconciles all discrepancies.
>
> The true meaning, then, is not that of the Jews; but in Jesus Christ all the contradictions are reconciled.[5]

While Judaism is denounced as ruse, the correct outposting is defined by the very Hegelian property of a "place of meaning," as Marin puts it, which would be the place of all meanings, including incompatible ones. Under the name of Jesus, therefore, the empire of the theater is reformed so that totalization might include contradiction, but so that the scenographic point will be no less exclusive or fixed than in the one being critiqued. Marin observes: "Jesus Christ . . . , is the only proper name that introduces, as an index, being as text and text as being," and he goes on to say: "Jesus Christ is the sign."[6] It is by this name alone, a double name—*Jesus* being the name of a man and *Christ* or *Messiah* being the name of God—that the greatest "discrepancy" or difference is placed at the center of the system of all signs. Let this center be understood as the plot of all representative scenography.

Immediately the question arises: Why make this sign the first one? In the name of what should this scenography be taken for the ultimate one, and the name of Jesus for the last word? What prevents "Jesus Christ" from being placed, in turn, in a theater, and no longer at the original point of its organization? What prevents one from making this opposition the sign of another opposition, which then becomes the most original? This is what, for example, a Marxist reading of Christian (in this case Jansenist) ideology will do. It is a point of view, or an outpost, that Marin himself does not mind occupying on occasion, one which only fulfills the reduplicative power of the model. Let us examine an important example.

THE CIRCLE OF MISTRUST

Throughout the book is the question of the Eucharist, of the place in the theory of signs to which it is appropriate to assign the sacramental utterance:

"This is my body." In Arnauld and Nicole's text, this utterance is cited only as an example (though more frequently in the last edition [1683]), when the polemic with the Protestants over the dogma of the real presence of God in the sacred bread was at its height. But it is never cited otherwise than as one example, among others, of a sign or of a judgment.

In spite of the modality of this occurrence, Marin, I repeat, maintains the thesis that the eucharistic utterance really occupies the place of substratum—a theological substratum—in the representative theory of discourse. He takes exception with the critical reversal in the anti-text, the "Pascal," that inhabits the *Logic* and in the displacements that mark successive editions of it. However, it is in the confidence placed in the critical import of reversal, and therefore in mistrust, that we find something like Marxism. One aspect of this Marxism is the historical critique that seeks to establish the document—in this case, the *Logic*—but only problematizes it further. Another aspect, even if the transition is unnoticeable, is the critique that, taking into account the problems raised by erudition, no longer aims to establish the text but to overturn its content.

"The precise crossing point at which theology and linguistics are converted one into the other is the Catholic utterance," writes Marin.[7] He goes on to term the occlusion of the utterance "ideological" since it produces representation. The utterance only appears in the theoretical theater as the product of an independent scenography. Marin's critique, following a certain Pascal, is a considerable reversal, in the Marxist sense, since it consists of reestablishing the utterance in its privileged position point in relation to which the entire theater of signs orders itself.

> It was therefore necessary that, in the *Logic*, the eucharistic utterance make language appear to be the particular problem of a more general one; but it was necessary at the same time to cut off the positioning of this problem from its origin or, more precisely, to include the origin as one simple element illustrating the problem whose appearance the origin itself had made possible.[8]

Marin proposes lending the term *ideological circle* to a relation between two notions (in this case, that of the signs of language and of the Eucharist) where neither of the two can be supposed without having recourse to the other, but where one (in this case, that of language) can seem to be independent of the other, an "ideological circle."

But what of this expression, "it is necessary," this necessity for one notion to mask the other, for the sacrament to hide in knowledge, for logical discourse to occlude theological affirmation without totally succeeding? Why must the truth of the *Logic* conceal itself? Let us examine the principles of the investigation and of the reversal: Why, Nietzsche asked, is it better to mistrust what is given than to trust it?

A REMARK ON THE SEMIOTIC MODEL IN THE MARXIST CRITIQUE OF CAPITAL

An aside. Here is a question that is very modern in its outdatedness: the logic of the reversal Marin proposes is no different from the one Marx inflicts upon capital. Capital is also a pseudoproducer reduced by Marx's critique to the product of labor, which capital occludes on its stage as a particular case of the sign in general: the commodity. In both cases, this ideological inversion is righted. And the following remark can be applied just as well to capital as to the *Logic*:

> . . . in a philosophy closed off by the ideology of representation, language [= money] poses no problem, except in those points where signs [= commodities] cease to be representations [= values] in order to become forces [= labor].[9]

Let us note that, once the righting of ideological inversion has been accomplished, the use of the commodity force of labor is endowed with a field of operation no less exclusive than that of the eucharistic utterance. This utterance institutes the thing within the sign and, by an original act of speech emanating from the perfect speaker (whom Marin names the "logothete"),[10] proposes the substitutional ability of one for the other. It is thus that the forgings of signification (which necessitate identity, resemblance, adequation, or conformity between the thing and its representation in discourse) come to be guaranteed.

In the same way, Marxist analysis, by reversing the ideology of the commodity, reveals a unique case of use, since without it the system could not survive, yet it is constant and thus possesses logothetic import. And if it is true that all value proceeds from this use, (for example, labor), then let us call this import "axiothetic." In the Port-Royal *Logic*, if realities can give rise to signs and signs to realization (to meaning, since the signified and the referent are not differentiated), it is because their "coalescence" is assured in the sacramental *act*. In capital, if use can give rise to values and values to use (to economic meaning, since in capital the signified of a value, the valued [*valu*] of its worth [*valant*], is the same as the use it lends to a thing), this substitutional ability depends entirely upon the act of labor. Or, more precisely, it depends upon a use, that of labor power, because this act consists of transforming a given into a product, and, therefore, on the one hand, of bringing the raw exteriority into the social interiority, and, on the other, of externalizing in the form of communicable realities an internal ability to produce them.

As with Christ, labor power is on both sides at once: the gift of meaning as force and the passion of reality as labor. And, like Christ, it is necessary— Marx said so in 1844 and repeated it in 1857–58—to go to the extreme of passion in order that the gift-giving force be revealed with the critique insinuating itself within the movement of exhausting this difference. The critique must place itself there because the foundation consists only of this difference, this inequality, which is exactly what Pascal's (and Marin's) critique asserts concerning Jesus. Moreover, since the critique is nothing but the process of capital itself in its own misunderstanding, it suffices to gather together the aberrant traits running through the *Logic* in order to fracture the edifice of representation masking the true logothete. Marin is to Jansenist logic what Marx is to the logic of capital. But Marx does it through Hegel, while Marin does it through Pascal.

SEVERAL SCENOGRAPHIES, ONE PHILOSOPHY, PHILOSOPHY ITSELF

Let us return to the question at hand: Why is it *necessary* for theological, infrastructural (and even perhaps extrastructural) affirmation to hide in the theater of logical or economic signs? Or: What is the reason—if there is one—for this ruse?

Once we agree to remain within the area circumscribed by the theatrical model, we can move in any direction. We could attribute a reason pertaining to political economy to the theological ruse, itself the reason for the logical ruse. On two very stimulating pages,[11] perhaps difficult to reconcile with his guiding approach (of which incompatibility is a part, just as there are heterogenous orders in the Pascalian perspective), Marin suggests that "Jansenist" ideology is, point for point, the inversion of the language-like and political "economy" that reigns at the court: the silent prayer as counterpoint to boasting flattery; eucharistic communion as antidote to the favors parcelled out by the king. And he adds in a note: "The all too rapid allusion we have made to the structure of state power during the personal reign of Louis XIV should, in turn, lead to another category of signs, that are both signs and material for exchange: gold, money, etc." Mercantilism and its complement, the functioning of the court, would thus be the external theater that the Hermits' theory of representation and ascetic practice take up even while turning it upside down. "A circuit of power from which the 'Jansenists' find themselves excluded: the one they produce, by inverting it, in their own religious ideology."[12]

According to this reading, the reason would pertain to political economy, the theory would be the artful expression of it, and, if the latter is the inversion of the former, this is because the "Jansenists" are "excluded" from the circuit of power. But is this exclusion a fact or a result of their vocation? Do they exclude themselves out of passion or because it benefits them to do so? According to this problematic, that of ideology, it is not enough to say: "Here is what is hidden behind appearances." We must explain how and why the appearance is produced, how and why its scenography and scenario are constructed; not only the appearance of reason in general, but also of the particular reason of appearance, which is the effacement of reason. For my part, I would rather express it this way: social exclusion does not explain ideological reversal. Rather, social exclusion is the tautological doublet of this reversal in Marin's critical scenography.

We could also assign, inversely, a theological reason to the economic one, along the lines of what Hegel does in the *Philosophy of Right* (Part 3, section 2). In the question of ruse's reason, the advantage of a "Hegel" is that he always has an answer ready and that answer is always a good one: in and of itself, Reason ruses. There are other versions: God's ruse in making himself man, the ruse of the intelligible appearing sensible, of Being being, all of which are classics in philosophical discourses and all of which are the same.

Can we decide in which direction to proceed? Will it be toward the economic or the theological? The inverse? Or something else? It doesn't really matter. We are caught up in a chain of theaters like a chain of department stores where the question as to which is the parent is foolish. The Other invoked in order to explain appearance immediately reconstitutes itself as focus for a new representative organization. By imagining the life of the senses as a theater, Plato is led to weave endless metaphors, approaching the highest level of the intelligible: the Idea of Virtue is a sun, the soul has an eye, and so on. The same could be said of the Lacanian schema of the unconscious, which is a topography of the cave: a' as a shadow on the wall, a the ego identified by its ability to see, A as the scenario writer ruling over the sequences of objects passing behind the little wall, and S as the scenographer setting up the organization of representation in the cave as a retreat from presence. (In this, Lacan is the last great living French philosopher: that the Other would give rise to representation through discourse is the masterful utterance upon which philosophy continues to promote itself.)

Do we need more examples? Once they have established labor as the axiothete of the capitalist system of values, what do Marx and Marxists do? They circumscribe a new theater where this force is called upon: a political theater where the hero—the proletariat, as Brecht said—is the name this force takes and the character it adopts. But this hero, in turn, is seized by doubts about the representation: like the force of labor with respect to the capitalist system, the proletariat can only exist in Marxist politics as external, in absentia. The party emerges from a proletariat no longer representable on the social stage, but rather having to be represented on the political stage. The distance that allows substitution (and not the substitutism that explains the distance, as the Trotskyists believed) grows once more between the thing and its representation. And here, again, a fundamental, "politicothetic" utterance is needed to guarantee the "coalescence" of Party and proletariat: for example, a Leninist word whose Jacobinism need not be denounced since it has a basis found in the *Republic*'s cave.

The Humor of Ordinary People, the Irony of the Great

Another denunciation—which probably does not deserve to be called critical—of the representative ruse is possible. This denunciation would more likely be classified under humor and irony.[13] "Pascal" is no less interested in this one than in criticism itself. Instead of beginning by placing ourselves outside representation, we maintain our position there, saying nothing else is possible. And it is just as well that this should be so, as Pascal writes concerning opinions and customs, thereby restoring their full cautionary value to the manners various people take on in social situations and to the prestige they grant to power and knowledge. In this case, one must follow in the manner of ordinary people: "Sane opinions of the people."

But "Pascal" only proceeds up to a certain point: "There is truth in their opinions, but not to the extent they imagine." Ordinary people judge authorities of force and of word to be well founded, when in fact they rest entirely upon themselves as if they were facts. This is as true of the science of geometricians as of the activities of politicians. With singular penetration, Marin plays into the congruence between the two opuscules "De l'esprit géométrique" and "Sur la condition des grands." It is therefore necessary to act like the people (there is nothing better to do than what is done) but also to adhere to an order that surpasses the order of representations, which, at the same time, acts nowhere else but within them: the order of Jesus. It is necessary, therefore, to behave as if representations were true but also "to have a thought in reserve," a thought that is not a principle or an axiom but a force, the gentle force that exceeds discourse and the lead of representations, without going outside them. Here, Jesus is not the rubric of another law, but only the proper name of a paradox.

From this paradox, two usages that separate irony from humor are cleaved apart: the first takes as its pretext the specificity of this order (the heart) to turn all laws in derision. It thus re-engages the movement of externalization of the decisive agency and foreshadows, once more, the hope of something beyond representation. There is romantic, mystical, and psychoanalytic irony in Pascal. But there is also humor: if he too invokes the power of the heart, it is because he suspects its presence to be everywhere possible, in every role on the world's stage and in every situation. Irony is never announced, either in a semiotics of this scene or in an anti-semiotics of its supposed transcendence. It is never sanctioned by a school, a church, or any faculty of wise men. Irony is therefore to be invented, to be encountered step by step and without our being able to take inventory of it. It cannot be appropriated from any angle, even as the negation of all power and knowledge. While irony is a nihilism of signification, humor maintains itself in the affirmation of tensions.

Such are the stakes for Pascal yesterday and for Marin today. Such are the stakes every time: if we assume discourse belongs to the orders of knowledge and power, shall we critique it from the point of view of a truth that remains unclear because it is external to it? Or rather, by pointing out its weaknesses—as Kierkegaard does with Hegel—shall we ironically discredit it with a transcendence that must remain unutterable? Or, finally, will we stand by ordinary people until the end, living and thinking day by day, assured of nothing because mastering nothing, yet invoking no higher authority, be it the Law or the Name, to leave behind "insignificant" realities, to devalue them into representatives of other more noble, more real things or into pure entities totally devoid of sense? Like ordinary people, shall we concern ourselves only with affirming these forces where there is no sign to indicate them, where there is no master to establish the signs? Shall we neither say that the representation is insincere, the scenario pure fiction, the actors mere histrions, nor that the spectators are asleep, chained up, crazy; that we have come to announce what is missing from the representation and the rest, making marks with whatever we find at hand, distinctive marks each time like so many proper names, like distracted, neglected tensions? The weapon on the side of ordinary people is ruse, the only machine capable of making the weakest the strongest. Ruse has humor as its accomplice.

And so, there are three positions: the critical, the ironic, the humorous. In Marin, as in Pascal, the three strands are intertwined. Is this because no ruse can present itself for what it is, but must instead insinuate its way in? Still too easy? Disdain is not always a sure thing and machination can still consist of showing itself.

TO LAUGH IS NOT TO MOCK

We are back to Jesus once again—no longer the Great Totalizer of the True Place of meaning, but the Name of an insignificant and obscure force. However, this is again one of truth's ruses: a truth concealing itself in opinion.

> When it was necessary that he appear, he concealed himself even more by covering himself with humanity. He was much more recognizable when he was invisible than when he made himself visible. And finally, since truth lives in common opinions, when he wanted to fulfill the promise to dwell among men until his last coming, he chose to dwell there in the strangest and most obscure secret he could.[14]

The obscurity of bread conforms with that of the common people and conforms with the general concealment of God that extends even to the smallest things. "As Jesus Christ remained unknown among men, so His truth remains among common opinions without external difference. Thus the Eucharist among ordinary bread."[15] These signs, eclipsed by the brilliance of princely and scholarly semiotics, become ridiculed nonsense and customs judged too coarse when compared to learned discourses and noble policies.

The luster of the latter depends upon a meta-opinion assuring them they hold the correct point of view concerning acts and words. The humor-irony of Pascal (as that of the people and of Marin) arises in observing that this point moves and in suggesting that, by moving, it becomes arbitrary. "The whole Pascalian critique," writes the ex-semiotician, "consists of putting representation's fixed point of view into motion."[16] One can see where this gets Pascal in Chapter 4 of *Pensée* 155: "A town and a stretch of country, when seen from afar, are a town and a stretch of country; but as we draw near we see houses, trees, tiles, leaves, grass, ants, the legs of ants, and so on to infinity. All of it is included in the term 'country.'"[17] Or in *Pensée* 114: "I must do as the artists, stand at a distance, but not too far. How far, then? Guess."[18]

Will we be able to guess? We would have to be diviners. Long ago, the Sophists and the Cynics (but they resurface in Pascal and Marin through Pyrrho and Montaigne) used to say this about the vain discourses of the master philosophers. In the use of words and business, no metalanguage, no distance is established or correct in and of itself. Instead, there is an infinite number of possible distances that, from conventional measure, approach the smallest and the greatest. There is no yardstick, no metron: the gods are ungraspable, the point of view of a god unassignable. But if there is no sure measure, are we then thrown into the dizziness of infinities? Is our alternative either a fictitiously anchored wisdom or mute truth and madness? Nay, does truth's fiction render us mad? And therefore incapable of words or acts? Wise men, princes, and their descendants of today, politicians, defy us with this threat: "if (whatever your feelings on the subject) you don't accept as correct our fixed point of view, you are mad—and vainly so—for you will not change the things you claim to mock. Useless you will be—but loquacious, thus dangerous."

To begin with, humor does not mock, irony does. Irony says: "your laws of discourse, of the state, your customs and casuistries are unimportant. A correct distance there no doubt is, but it is a guarded secret: we do not know what it is. All we can do is act according to its will, which is to elevate it and adore it, and take up arms against those who do not." Pascal quotes Tertullian in the eleventh "Provincial Letter": "it is the Truth properly that has a right to laugh, because she is cheerful, and to make sport of her enemies, because she is sure of the victory."[19] Irony is the laughter of the great over what is vain, of God himself laughing over Adam for having believed it possible to become like Him.

Humor says: "there is no correct point of view, neither the things of this world nor its discourses form a tableau—or if they do, it is only by the arbitrary decision of the beholder, be he prince or scholar." Let us exhibit this arbitrariness, not to ridicule it, but rather to grasp it as imbued with a logic, a space, and a time that are not those of a representative tableau, a logic of singularities, a space of proximities (of infinities), a time of moments. Humor does not invoke a truth more universal than that of the masters; it does not even struggle in the name of the majority by incriminating the masters for being a minority. Humor wants rather to have this recognized: *there are only minorities.*

This proposition, however, out of place in its candor, is enough to dissipate the prestige of the tableau and to undo the representative enclosure. This proposition is enough, and yet it is not. It nonetheless works like this: to laugh when the pope says "God speaks through my decrees," or when the Party says "I am the mouthpiece of the proletariat" is to point out the ruse at the very site of its outpost and without having to go to another outpost to do it. This is what the gods of antiquity did when one of them claimed to be the only true god, as Klossowski reminds us in *The Baphomet.*[20]

To Name Is to Set in Perspective

Does Pascal go that far?[21] He gets close when, in "De l'esprit géométrique," he debates the question of nominal definitions. Marin shows perfectly how the thesis of nominal definition, though borrowed—as they themselves admit—by Arnauld and Nicole from Pascal, plays exactly the opposite role in the *Logic* than it plays in the opuscule. For these logicians, nominal definition has an essential value because it combines the word, what it designates, and what it signifies. But it is also useless—"men naturally having the same idea . . . about very simple things"—and, moreover, it would be impossible: how could one put the singular word that it produces into circulation if this common reason that could lend it the same signification for everyone did not exist beforehand?

Pascal, on the contrary, shows it to be at once arbitrary and inevitable, something to be induced by irony and humor intertwined. The nominal definition is inevitable because it stops the *regressus ad infinitum* implied in the act of defining. However, it does not stop it by becoming the definition of a thing, since of these there is no definition unless one succumbs once again to the vanity of wise men. It puts a stop to the dissolution of discourse in the infinity of displacements by stopping the view at a point. And this point is arbitrary: "We do with the latest principles that appear to reason what we do with material things when we declare a point indivisible where we cannot see beyond it, even though it is by its nature infinitely divisible."[22] Nominal definition is a designation, but designation, far from being an adequation of sign to thing, is, like perspective (in the sense of optical perspective, *but also in Nietzsche's sense*), a "decision" that causes the sign and its referent to exist together. An object is infinitely divisible "by nature," but this nature is neither common reason nor even the very first custom that renders institutions popular and scholarly. It is the unseizability of things, the indecidability of criteria, the inaccessibility of God speaking, and, therefore, the vanity of scholarly discourse.

PASCAL, A CYNIC?

Is Pascal ironic or humorous about nominal definition? He is hesitant, and everyone knows where. But before we recall it here, a word on the theme itself. It's an old battle, even older than nominalism. The battle was engaged long ago by Antisthenes, the first Cynic. Judged by what remains of his work in the writings of his opponents (essentially in Aristotle's *Metaphysics* [1024b, 27–34, and 1043b, 4–14 and 23–32]), Antisthenes goes right to the extremities of the thesis: there is no definition of things as such, only nominal ones; all definitional propositions are deictic (such as, "This is Socrates"); and judgments in general are not of attributive or event-like form (such as, "Socrates the musician" equals "Socrates is giving himself over to the Muses"). Given this, there is no possible contradiction between two speakers, since either they are talking about the same thing and they have to use the same words or, if their utterances differ, it is because they are designating different things. We find traces of this observation in Pascal. And there is also no possibility of error in spite of what was just stated since, if one of the speakers calls a man a woman, it is because he is talking about another object, which, since he is talking about it, is *no less real* than the one at hand. There is no error because there is no non-being. Being is what is named; all nomination is the institution of a "perspective," that is, of being.

A peculiar logic, stubbornly attentive to the "elementary" acts of language, taking them to be so many perspectives or decisions on things, never as adequations of an object whose being, moreover, one might know. Aristotle mocks this as a logic of juxtapositions: nothing is more exact. Pascalian *diversities* are close at hand.

Is Pascal afraid of losing magisterial authority over truth? What "threatens" the Pascalian position is the same affirmation repressed under the names of skepticism, cynicism, nominalism, pragmatism, empiricism— (Nietzschean) "perspectivism": no intelligibility (either real or conceived) is, in general, definable. There is no thought. For a judgment to be true, a metalanguage must authorize it. But there is no master to proffer this metadiscourse. Antisthenes hands matters over at this point to certain Megarians, to whom the Liar's Paradox was imputed. It only takes a Liar's Paradox to laugh at the masters' discourse, and even the wager of believers, as fatuous, and to laugh at certain Sophists who declare that saying anything about the gods is impossible: anything about them and, even less, anything in their place. Such is Greek humor: if the gods were liars, then . . . guess.

DON'T MUNCH ON THE HOLY BREAD

What keeps Pascal from going too far in this direction is Christianity, a certain Christianity. The word of Jesus is not a metalanguage for Pascal. Or, if it is, it is at least a displaced one: Jesus does not speak the discourse of knowledge, and he does not found it. He lets it follow its own device: he lets it flow toward nominalism. Jesus says nothing to authorize the discourse of scholars: as a child at the temple, he jeers at the learned—the little one mocking grownups. He says: "This is my body." (One can but recall here the very beautiful analyses Louis Marin gives of the eucharistic proposition.) This is, it seems, a perfectly cynical speech act. But here is where is lodged the little yet immense divergence. For Antisthenes, there are as many de-nominations as acts of language: none is privileged, none is exclusive—they are all of equal rank. There is no need to be God or a powerful being in some order of kindness for the utterance to have a performative value, just as for Nietzsche, performance, or perspectivization, and "will" are one and the same thing. In Pascal, as at Port-Royal, Jesus' utterance is that of a sacrament, assuring the coalescence of the thing and the sign (their contemporaneity), escaping, as a founding word, the aporias of words yet to be founded, but whose status is unique, exclusive, and universal.

After all, anyone can say—pointing at his trowel, his arm, his pen or the woman he loves—"This is my body." Pascal would allow this, but on condition that in saying so, the person but repeats the founding utterance. It is still acceptable that he find his power of realization in another reserve of strength, in a heart not his own. But it must be one that is assignable, and Jesus Christ's is. It is understood that the sacrament rails at laws, but we do not laugh at the sacrament. Humor says: "I rail at any master who doesn't know how to laugh at himself." Irony leads to joy, but not to this kind of gaiety. I understood the difference one day when, at the altar, in a state of sin, I munched on the Host. Tasteless. The tooth that grinds and mashes up is bestiality, stupidity (*bêtise*), but also perspective. Teeth bite into metalan-guage and into the metasilence of the heart.

THEOLOGY OF DESIRE

In "Pascal," there is obviously an energetics by which one can escape the inconsistencies of semiotics: that of the Port-Royal logicians and others. Louis Marin exposes it forcefully. Speaking of the theory of the Ego:

> Pascalian semantics takes us back in the final analysis to an energetics, to a distribution of force in the signs it traces and where, at the same time, it becomes immobile and disappears."[23]

Or, on the more weighty theory of what is true:

> Even truth itself—"true truth"—is transmuted into a value of desire. . . . Since true judgment and false judgment are articulated in opposite propositions insofar as their content is concerned, but are contained in the *same manner* by their relation to the subjects who utter them, truth will find itself merged with falsehood."[24]

How is this desire conceived? Marin states clearly that it is an alterity and a transcendence suspended from an Other:

> The true, before being simply and purely true, is always already a figure and it is as such that it is, in the final analysis, true. The solution, which is transcendent and consecrates the exteriority of all the elements of discourse, consists of considering this figure as that of another desire. It is not the figure of the ego and of its concupiscence, but that which grace configures in the ego.[25]

Is this then an energetics? It is in fact meaning that, under the lexicon (the metaphor, says Marin)[26] of energies, returns as that which knowledge lacks. The Other is the zero that collects and attracts to itself the energy at work in discourses and in acts. Why zero? Because it is itself undecidable and its truth effects are undiscernible, as not only Pascal but also Port-Royal know: "Truth will find itself merged with falsehood." But it is also zero because it is established, revealed, and, moreover, its figurative effects—undiscernible—are nevertheless localizable like those of the arithmetic operator ($= 0$), or its brother ($= \infty$). This is what allows Marin to write that "infinite distance [is] characteristic of desire as force."[27] This desire therefore contains all the traits of the sign as representation. God speaks; we are ignorant of his language; his word is therefore zero or the equivalent of our infinities. Desire is this mark: the mark of the great signifier over our signifiers. After Lacan, Marin accepts the reversal of terms of general linguistic theory: in their figures, our words and our phrases will become signified by desire, by the effects of the discourse of the Other. Do we evade semiotics with this reversal? We are getting back into it. Such is the despair of irony, nourishing, as it does, the false modesty of the logician (or the psychoanalyst).

By invoking desire, we have as yet said nothing. There is, of course, lack, which Diotimes was already teaching to a credulous Socrates as *Penia*. And lack was enough for representation to preserve all its rights. Representation will only become more nostalgic, more mystical: a rich tradition, in the West, of the negative theology of desire. But humor proceeds from an Eros that is all *Poros*: nothing but a means as *mean*, as a logic without aporia and a politics without utopia. This desire calls for gods much more intriguing than the one who proclaimed himself to be the truth and divinations without sin.

Translated by Mira Kamdar

7

---◆---

Futility in Revolution

Ave, ave, ave Maria.
(Song of the March 22nd Movement).

To my companion in merry May.

THE MONSTROUS BODY OF THE REPUBLIC

"In '93, love appeared as it is: the brother of death."[1] With this statement, Michelet draws attention to no small matter: not only (or not at all) that Danton, Vergniaud, and the like allowed themselves to be led to the scaffold out of an indifference to the *res publica*, but that this indifference was related to their passion for a woman. Prior to any psychology of great or ordinary individuals, what is at play in the intensity of autumn 1793 is the intersection of life and death instincts "upon the body" (as Freud would say) of the First Republic and their mutual dissimulation within one another. The autumn of 1793 compels anyone who is even remotely interested in this historical moment to ask himself at least one question: what is desired in politics anyway?

To answer such a question, it is impossible to trust the analysis of public addresses. If we are to learn anything from history, it involves both unlearning any faith in the agency of meaning and increasing our suspicions. All revolutionary factions declared their desire for happiness—Saint-Just's words come to mind. But outdoing him was the program of the "enraged women" [*les femmes enragées*], those harshest opponents of the Robespierrists, the female Republican Revolutionary citizens: "It is our desire that there not be one single unhappy person in the Republic." The same goes for equality, for liberty, and so on.

Not only men, but signifieds, too, conspire and become suspect. What the Terror wants is to arrest the meaning of words once and for all: a method required by the desire for truth. There must be an organism of meaning

87

harbored in words, and the Jacobin insists that he can seize it and keep it prisoner, then force its appearance. He wishes to secure the exclusive use of that organism, that is, its utterance, for himself, and he denounces as lie, betrayal, or shameful impropriety (we would call it ideology), the presence of "his" words in the mouths of his adversaries. In this sense, power consists of holding performative authority (the speech act). It consists of the capacity to make the signified appear referentially: "in reality." Not only "We declare war" and there is war, but also "Married couples may divorce under certain conditions," and they do, or "Religious services may be freely practiced," and this is so, but above all "Those who speak like ultra-Leftists are reactionary agents," and the proof is that they are guillotined. This is a *productive* power in that it decisively determines reality.

Michelet sees all this clearly in his 1869 preface to the book on the Terror when he situates the position of Robespierre's words in these terms:

> A prodigious act of Jacobin faith. They denied the sun at midday. And this was believed. The medieval affirmation of Catholic dogma ("This bread is not Bread, it is God.") is no more forceful. We return to the old centuries of barbaric credulity. *No reality is real compared to Robespierre's word.* Such is the robust faith of the new Jacobins.[2]

The mystery of the Eucharist, as analyzed by Louis Marin,[3] indicates nothing less than the essence of terroristic power: a statement based on two deictics creating a strange tautology of utterance, maintaining its universal validity.

There is no performative without the exclusion of several speakers from the authority to "perform." Even when the explicit goal of political struggle is to grant freedom of speech (that is, performative power) to everyone, thereby constituting the Republic as a single performing body and bringing to realization everything it says by the simple fact of its utterance, jealousy nonetheless develops in relation to the effective performative position, and terror is used against any ambition to attain it.

What is this terroristic appropriative desire? How can it be articulated with the desire for a body of unified parts that is also unified in its words and acts? Is such an articulation even possible? The sansculottes' struggle for equality and happiness (or death, an alternative that seems to define republican politics) consists of the following: either performative power is lent to the entire social body, or else this body must disappear. But the crazy thing about this articulation is that it is not, or not only, disjunctive. In the clamor raised by this alternative, another figure is hidden: the incoherent and simultaneous affirmation of happiness and death. In the reconciled body announced by political discourses at the conclusion of bitter struggles is embedded the body presently dislocated by the jealousy and death-dealing terror that one part exerts over the other. This part is merely a body of death, since it only exists from and within the fragmentation of the former, from and within the struggle of its fragments, for instance, the Estates, classes, sexes, generations.

Corresponding to the language-like juxtaposition of a unified semantic body and a performative activity that is terroristic by exclusion, the political body is a monster[4] composed of a unified organism and a plurality of drives that are incompatible both with it and with each other. This body is not deformed insofar as its existence would violate some natural form. It is monstrous because it occupies a plurality of spaces, which one might imagine roughly as follows: a totality driven to unify itself, it is organized as a volume, like an enormous three-dimensional object with a center and a perimeter that circumscribes auditorium and stage (nation and Assembly, neighborhood and section), distinguishing between external and internal (France and the foreign, the Republic and its enemies).

However, to the extent that the "body" is dislocated by the divergent drives that course through (or rather constitute) all of its surfaces, regardless of the aforementioned limits, this "body" spreads itself out like a boundless surface in a two-dimensional space comparable to that of a Möbius strip on which, as we know, it is vain to try and distinguish front from back, much less to determine a volume. Here, then, is the monstrosity we may imagine: a spatial power that is at least binary with one element defining a two-dimensional expanse, the other a three-dimensional space. Thus we have an object controlled simultaneously by at least two groups of operative axioms that are, in principle, incompatible.

Such were love and death in 1793. Dialectical arrangements (even Hegel's) fail to render the object they form. They are but language games, practiced on a unified semantic body and presupposing that unity as the unity of language. If they tolerate death instincts, it is only as *Moment* in the history of this body in the sense that they narrate it. This Christian, Hegelian model (which is still that of Lacan) becomes increasingly revealing since it takes death simply as a means of realizing liberty or truth. But the monster is not dialectic. Monster-time—if there is such a thing—does not synchronize or make commensurable the time of natural bodies that they "should" have been with that of centrifugal forces that "prevent" them from being so. If the body of the Republic in the autumn of 1793 is a monster, it lives on in many other times that are both contemporary with each other and yet entirely asynchronous. It is more striking to isolate them than it is to gather them together into one narrative.

PRINCELY HISTORY

The same goes for history and politics. History writes itself only as the narrative of a body, the account of its production and avatars. Politics announces itself only as the desire for this body, and as social strife always itself expressed as the struggle for another, more organic society. Some of the strongest intensities are inevitably presented by the historian as surface events, contingencies (the cost of attaining true necessity), and by the politician as errors stripped of any real importance or as traps attributable to some enemy's Machiavellianism, smudges to be erased. When a historian or a politician considers them, it is, at best, because he sees in them confirmations of the hypothesis he is constructing on the "course of history."

On the contrary, a libidinal history begins by focusing on these oddities. It does so not to decipher them as symptoms, but rather to experience them and transmit their intensities, which the common historian fails to recognize. Such a history imagines a body comparable to the one Freud supposes in very young children, a body upon which love and death wander and halt unexpectedly, causing an event. The two instinctual orders of synthesis and dislocation are at work on that body, not in conflict with, but concealing each other. Repeating Freud's thesis that the effects of unification originate in Eros and the effects of dislocation in the death instincts is not enough: the inverse is no less true, and therein lies the dissimulation. The regulation of these intensities and their folding back onto a single center indeed appears to derive from Eros, but this centripetal activity may also harbor a death-dealing desire to block, cement up, and asphyxiate anything that impedes it. Listen to Robespierre addressing the dechristianizers. The same words harbor intensive movements of altogether opposite directions and are transit points for currents of both love and hate.

When Robespierre sets the guillotine into motion in the name of the Republic's safety, it is without doubt due to a very "erotic" passion for the organic unity of the social body, but it is also through the opposite desire to blow it to pieces, even if this means that he will himself perish. In his final speech of 8 Thermidor, we must understand the terrifying recourse to *vagueness* not so much as a true principle of government, but rather as the proposal for a general disorganization of the social body through the impossibility of fixing meanings that are decidedly hypocritical: "There must necessarily be something vague about penal law, because the conspirators' current character is one of concealment and hypocrisy; therefore justice must be able to seize them in all their forms." Michelet lends full destructive force to this compulsion to reach the top when he writes: "The vilified guillotine seemed to become mad, working randomly. . . . It seems that Robespierre, in his spiralling suspicion, would ultimately have arrested and sent himself to the guillotine."[5] A principle of generalized dissimulation strikes all the pieces of the social body: neither man nor institution is fixed any longer in its own identity. The Jacobin eye succumbs to dizziness, to the vertigo of centralism itself, just as Hegelian totality is threatened by the dispersion of total skepticism.

But the opposite deserves no less attention: how can we distinguish the death-dealing centrifugal thrust in the antireligious fervor that swept the country in the autumn and winter of 1793 from the self-preservation and unitary self-defense against foreign agents and factional erosion? Oblivious to these dissimulations, history, like politics, seems to require a single vantage point, an area of synthesis, a head or an eye that can encompass the diversity of movements within the unification of a single mass: a synthesizing eye, but also an evil eye that strikes dead anything that does not enter its field of vision.

A libidinal history refuses to indulge this complacency of knowledge and princely power. At the very least it must apply to its "corpus" (note the term) the principle of generalized relativity that implies that *there is no privileged standpoint* for deciphering organizations of energy. We may object that relativity only applies to phenomena based on scales far removed from human perception and memory. But does the libido working on history remain on a human scale? Must the res gestae be situated within the so-called framework of a priori human sensibility? After all, what is a "human scale"? As for the forms, these are a priori only for a Kantian reason. History is at least as monstrous as the universe, and probably more so, if we attribute to it what we refuse to the physical world, a principle of dissimilation.

To return to a (very approximate) linguistic terminology, historical discourse institutes the same exclusions as political discourse; that is, it serves the constitution of a performative power. The historian declares who Robespierre is, just as Robespierre declared who the people were and were not. The objection may be raised that the first declaration is not a speech act because it lacks a position of power capable of forcing the object into conformity with discourse. But this objection discounts academic power, which commands the belief of a public of readers (generally students) on whose heads the blade of examination will fall if their discourse does not conform to that of the definer of reality. In rejecting instinctual processes that he deems deviant, superficial, irrelevant, ancillary, or contingent, this reality-definer destroys no less information (be it only by omission) than does the Jacobin politician when the latter rejects as conspiracy, treason, plotting, or at least irresponsibility anything in the information he receives that might force him to modify what he declares to be reality.

We must ask ourselves, then, what is desired, what is the status of desire, not only in politics, but also in historical study, since a continuity exists between the two. If it is true that all interest at the end of this century necessarily turns toward a politics freed from power, we would do well to sketch out a libidinal history and be quite content in achieving such a task.

PAGAN HISTORY

This libidinal history is above all a pagan history. The paganism I have in mind implies not only a multiplicity of gods or a lofty indifference to the question of exclusivity in the performative speech-act ("All the gods [of antiquity] died laughing uncontrollably when they heard one of their number proclaim himself the one and only god").[6] This paganism includes that singular activity that the Roman gods demanded be rendered unto them in addition to the reverence of regular worship: the seemingly incoherent activity of playing out scenes (*ludi scoenici*), the derisive honor of parody. Thus it includes not only the cult of a multiplicity of functions, each of which would be assigned uniquely and consistently to a particular deity and realized in established rituals, but also the theatrical fulfillment of fortuitous "situations"—encounters that any divinity may have "either with another divinity or with a mortal creature,"[7] and that openly belie the exclusive and edifying function that state religion tends to assign it. Pierre Klossowski writes: "The playing out of scenes reserved for deities a sphere where they would display themselves in the sovereign and purely gratuitous *jouissance* of these gods instead of just in their salutary actions toward civil society."[8]

The theme of wasteful intensities acquired through parody, mirroring (by Freud's admission) the unexpected and incessant movements of instincts on the libidinal body of Rome, must be equated with the paganism of a history and politics that I am investigating. We must examine the coexistence of state-regulated cults, culminating in the centuries-long exclusionary centralism of Christian Caesarism, with what Marcus Terentius Varro[9] called a theatrical theology—an inventiveness in parodies and merry, immoral, and cruel games where desires unleash their power of metamorphosis in order to nourish the erotic and death-dealing imagination attributed to the gods. This coexistence, which is essential to the paganism taught by Nietzsche and Klossowski, is also what best attests to the monstrosity of the social body of which a pagan history (not to mention politics) deserves consideration. What we find in the *ludi scoenici* is but the instinctual principle of dissimilation.

Are these abstract considerations? Are they inapplicable to a history? A fortiori to a politics? On the contrary, the point of view of exclusivity leads inevitably to abstraction and to terror. The least agitation on the social body and its monstrosity (its paganism) reveals itself: July 1936, May '68. This is why these phases of turbulence always seem inexplicable and even suspicious to the historian or politician whose exclusive unifying standpoint cannot appreciate (or repress) them except through geological or medical metaphors, which transform them into cataclysms, eruptions, torrential movements, or illnesses affecting a social organism otherwise considered normal.

This also applies to the dechristianization movement in France during the autumn and winter of 1793. Although obvious, the simultaneous emergence of paganism and of the consequential monstrosity of the Republic's body becomes the object of an immense denial, as much on the part of politicians as on the part of historians of the Revolution—even when they are on the extreme Left. What fascinates the "pagan" historian about this crisis is that it is not only a political and social battle (within the established framework of explicit powers or in the still voiceless field of economic interests), but also that acts of violence are enforced in an apparently displaced manner. These acts are divergent in relation to the political domain and are always presented in the form of parodies and by playing out scenes. From them derive disquieting festivities that break down the barrier—essential to the totalizing point of view—between reality and fiction. The improvised scenography of the sansculottes' games disorganizes the well-ordered ritual of Jacobin assemblies and official festivals. Concurrently, the theatrical institution, throughout these historic *journées*, manifests the instinctual processes that operate centrally within the representational function, while suggesting the study of a libidinal economy of spectacle. Sansculottism is not inclined to dreaming, nor is the stage its oneiric or utopian space. One does not go to the theater for a change of scenery: the scene in the streets (a "political" scene) extends into the auditorium and occasionally onto the stage itself. The oppositions making up representation (especially that between spectator and actor) lose a large part of their validity.

In this double displacement of the political and theatrical toward the "scenic," we perceive the libidinal work of pagan gaming. As Michelet suggested in his own way, by more closely examining the position of femininity in these displacements, we might advance the farthest in the exploration of their paganism. For, by ancient tradition, women are excluded from the performative political function; they are not part of the sovereign state; their intervention into public affairs is a revolution within the Revolution that cannot fail to provoke scandal and inspire new *mises-en-scène* destined to quell the Revolution as well as to make it more provocative. These very excesses attest to the fact that the *ludi scoenici* are connected not so much with the female sex, but rather with that monstrosity par excellence: desexualization—if it be true that beyond desexualization, any question of identity becomes absurd.

SEVERAL WAYS OF DEVIATING THE DECHRISTIANIZING MOVEMENT

When they go to describe the dechristianization movement at the end of 1793, the pens of all politicians, historians, Caesars, and Brutuses become possessed by the same figure: the metaphor of disruption. Their disavowal of that movement is embedded in a negative rhetoric: their incapacity to affirm it is the opposite of the power they confer upon themselves to declaim history. But the encounter of sansculotte paganism with historical discourse is the encounter of force with power.

At the Convention on 22 November 1793, Representative Forestier called this movement "a volcanic eruption of truth held captive too long." Danton (on the 26th, at the Assembly) and Robespierre (on the 28th, before the Jacobins) affirmed it to be "a torrent." "An explosion," "a torrent which nothing can resist," writes Dartigoeyte, a representative on mission in the Gers department on 1 January 1794. After Thermidor, Boissy d'Anglas explains that the movement was "madness and furor," that "the priestly institution was struck down by the scandal of an orgy, by the furor of fanaticism itself." And, although in favor of the movement, Edgar Quinet resorts to the same metaphor: "Masses which were still semi-barbarian sought tumultuously to break with the sacerdotal tutelage of the Ancien Régime."

For Daniel Guérin (from whom these quotations were borrowed)[10] the dechristianizing movement is one of the Revolution's essential moments. This confirms Guérin's thesis of a permanent revolution. If this is so, then it is precisely in *exceeding* the course of a bourgeois revolution that this movement proves that a proletarian revolution was originally at work from within:

> Here we not only reach the limits of dechristianization, but the fundamental drama of the Revolution. In the religious sphere, as in so many others, the force that motivated class struggle, the dynamics of mass movement exceeded the framework of the bourgeois revolution and led the Revolution somewhat beyond the objectives set by the revolutionary bourgeoisie. The popular torrent carried the dechristianizers somewhat further than they had forseen. They had only wished to create a diversion.[11]

In this last point, Guérin's thesis is similar to that of Michelet writing on the September moderation of Chaumette and the Commune:

> Several representatives maintained that if another outlet were not opened for the Revolution, if political moderation were not compensated for by religious audacity, to embark on political eliminations was a great risk. These representatives waged terror on things and not on people.[12]

Thus the Commune, Chaumette, and some on the Mountain and in the sections feared Jacobin terror and extremism in religious matters as masks of their own political moderation: "This movement of terror (in the government) was directly opposed to the interests of the religious movements for which Chaumette was working."[13] From one interpretation to the next there is quite an inversion of roles. Force in motion, evil terror, is, for Michelet, that of despotic Robespierrism, which will ultimately become Bonapartism.[14] For Guérin, this is a good violence that comes from the proletarian avant-garde incarnated by the *enragés*, for whom the Commune and Chaumette are the social traitors and Robespierre the bourgeois executioner.

But in both interpretations, the scenography is identical: it is already the scenography that Robespierre employs in November to situate the popular antireligious movement and, in December and January, to combat it. Just read the portrait of the ultra-revolutionary (who, of course, for him is a false revolutionary) sketched by "the Incorruptible" in his report of 5 February 1794 ("on the principles of political ethics which must guide the national Convention in the internal administration of the Republic") and presented under the auspices of the Committee of Public Safety. Quite an eloquent portrait indeed[15] (although somewhat pedantic), it is inspired by the irrationality of the adversary's elusiveness, which assumes that the *enragés* and the Hébertists are the creations of "Prussian, English, Austrian, even Moscovite committees . . . in the service of the same master" as the Royalists.

> Preaching atheism is only a way of absolving superstition and indicting philosophy; the war declared on divinity is only a diversion for royalty. . . . [The dechristianizers] ignore the Austrians in order to make war on the devout. . . . In the name of philosophy, they are carrying out a counterrevolutionary plot.[16]

In his 5 December 1793 "Response" to the kings' manifestos, Robespierre was already practicing the same amalgam of a dechristianizing extreme Leftism with a Royalist Rightism: "The French people and their representatives respect the freedom of all religious practice and proscribe none of them. . . . They condemn the extravagance of philosophism as superstitious folly, travesties, and fanatical pantomimes." This famous speech will serve later to deprive the Hébertists of the Mountain's support, announcing their elimination while giving comfort to the church and throne.

Thus in all three positions (Robespierre's, Michelet's, Guérin's), an identical axiomatic is at work: the dechristianizers create a diversion in a direction (the right one) toward which the social body, true to its nature, was already moving: I (the speaker) proclaim this direction. It therefore exists. *Anything* that does not bring my words to realization is equally suspect. I (Robespierre) am the voice of the nation and of virtue, therefore the dechristianizers are Royalists and immorality itself. Romme, Clootz, and I (Michelet) who mourn them, are the affirmative truth of the Revolution, we are the people who demand "a religion of equal justice for all" and "unprivileged property extended to all." (Robespierre is thus the perpetuation of tyranny and the herald of Bonapartism; the violence and acts of the dechristianizing movement are merely reactions to the Jacobin terror.) Roux, Varlet, Leclerc, Rose Lacombe bear witness to the fever that shakes the social body, and they speak its truth, for it is sick with the class struggle; thus dechristianization is only a displacement of this illness, a false remedy administered by Chaumette and his ilk (Guérin).

All of this is fairly clear. We can argue about the details, but the procedure remains the same—with all three, we remain in the same camp. However great our admiration for Guérin's book, it presents the same performative terrorism (contracted by contact with Trotskyism). Moreover, he makes no mystery of this:

> Robespierre and Michelet were right about everything except where the object of the diversion is concerned. . . . The antireligious campaign was a compensation for moderation on the political level. Above all, it compensated for moderation on the economic and social level. By launching the masses in an assault on heaven, the plebeians hoped to distract them as much as possible from formidable earthly preoccupations and undesirable materialistic questions such as the high cost of living and food. Once the movement had been diverted in this way, they expected to retain mastery of it and make it serve their own goals, that is, the growth of their influence and the satisfaction of their political ambitions.[17]

The same procedure influences Robespierre's thoughts; the difference lies only in the actors—the roles and their dramatic effects are the same. It is not surprising that on this occasion, Guérin recognizes a certain "craftiness" in Robespierre.

PAGANISM VERSUS NIHILISM

The dechristianizing movement is always viewed as nihilistic rather than pagan. If it took place where it did, it must have been in place of something else, and this other, hidden thing, repressed into exteriority, is what everyone will take for the truly real. The religious movement must hide and yet be activated by the intrigues and plots of kings and priests or else of the bourgeois and the Hébertists. This movement cannot possibly have its own reason. Its impulse must come from elsewhere. In short, it must be no more than a sign. Surely for Guérin, nihilism is not this blunt; its stage director not just the bourgeois enemy: "The enterprise had been set in motion artificially, from on high. But its promotors had no idea to what extent it corresponded to the deepest feeling of the popular vanguard. What was a diversion became an uprising."[18]

How are we to interpret this second argument: the deep feeling of the people? Does it mean that it was fundamentally pagan? No, Guérin will say that it is only anticlerical, explaining that the decline of the dechristianizing movement at the end of winter 1793 is due to its failure to "attack the materialist roots of religion."[19] It is too deep for the bourgeoisie, not enough so for a socialist revolution: always marginalized, never just as it is. In turn, religion, through its "material roots," is seen only negatively, as the effect of a lack, a lack of happiness.[20] Here nihilistic thought becomes redoubled through the movements of *too much* and *not enough*, of *not yet* and *already no longer*. The historian himself, confined to his performative speech, measures progress and decline by the yardstick of his truth. His nihilism goes hand in hand with the exclusivity of the position he attributes to speech: the destruction of religion did not take place as it would have if the proletariat had been more developed, that is, if capitalism had been in a more advanced stage. For I say unto you, religion is merely the effect of a lack, and only socialism, by removing the lack, will be able to abolish religion.

No one knows if socialism can suppress the unhappiness said to be at the origin of religious belief. It is certain, however, that this affirmation still implies belief, since it consists of placing the same faith in socialism (in absentia) that is judged as misdirected when it is addressed to a god (in absentia). This (Marxist) politics and this (Jacobin) history, while not dependent on the religion they denounce, surely remain accountable to the same nihilism implied in that religion. We might now attempt to understand the antireligious agitation of 1793 differently. The first step would be to refrain from connecting it to an absent unity, whether it be the Republic or socialism.

To begin with, there is not one, but many dechristianizing movements: the one that is carried out in the official services of the new religion, and, coextensive with, indeed at the heart of this first one, all those events playing themselves out in local improvisations, communal festivals, the remarkable demonstrations of the sansculotte sections of Paris, none of which can be reduced to a single unit of meaning. These movements are neither coordinated nor oriented toward the constitution of a new, greater, more harmonious unity, toward the formation of a new politico-socio-cultural totality: they are roving and fugitive.

These unofficial movements have no future, and the proof is in their rapid decline. This ephemeral character appears to legitimize the resistance of historians and politicians: the antireligious disturbances will not lead to a stable institution and thus will not be committed to memory. They are at most a minor episode within a much longer affair that leads, a century later, to the separation of church and state. But above all, even in their own context, they remain somewhat aberrant, incoherent, inconsequential. The same section of Paris that burns ecclesiastical effects with great derisive pomp before the Assembly in November 1793 will request freedom of religious practice in December. And the same villages will return to their priest the church that three months earlier they had made the headquarters of their sansculotte section. According to what chronology are we then to inscribe these movements, upon what institutional ledger, what established calendar? Historians, devoted to collating facts, have some difficulty incorporating this data into their project. Guérin needs a two-stage dialectical machine to pull it off. Michelet, quite disturbed, loses his eloquence. Leftist bourgeois historians speak of official rules and solemn festivals. We, here, must seek the help and emulate the patience of a Maurice Agulhon investigating the origins and avatars of the Marianne effigy if we are to bring out the elements of Mediterranean and Dionysian paganism in the anti-Christian games at the end of 1793.[21]

PAGANISM IN ITS METHOD

But there is once more a methodological difficulty. The Phrygian cap, the iconography of the Liberty processions (chariots drawn by lions or leopards, surrounded by youths and cupids, decorated with myrtle boughs, accompanied by drums and wind instruments), familiar address [*tu* instead of *vous*—Trans.], collective songs, the abundance of female figures symbolizing Republican virtues—if, by means of these significant examples, we were to endeavor to demonstrate that the anti-Christian movements are in many respects related to the chthonic cults of antiquity, the question of the time in which these movements inscribe themselves and of their chronology must be posed. Here we may take two equally deceptive directions.

We could persist in delineating their genealogy—for example, by tracing the Phrygian cap from the ancient Near East to 1789 Paris, where it lands on Louis XVI's head; by pointing out its use in Rome, where the master placed it on the slave he was about to free, and its political consecration by Brutus and his accomplices after the assassination of Caesar; how it was worn in the Middle Ages; its political use by Dutch and American revolutionaries, then in France in the Faubourg Saint-Antoine after 1789, by the Brissotins in 1792. But while of iconographic interest, such a genealogy would neither explain the appearance of the above-mentioned indices in the atheistic or anticlerical sansculotte movement nor the function they serve in the crisis with which I am concerned. The exact date of this crisis cannot be located on the altogether vague calendar of a genealogy of signs.

Another possibility, however, would be to renounce these legacies by generations and avail ourselves of permanent symbols, linking the resurgence of signs to the effects of a few archetypes; for example, the return of Gaea in popular festivals. But, far from the temporality of instincts, this would lend credence as Jung and Neumann have done, to a very suspect notion of eternity derived from affective contents.

It is equally vain to try to locate a past in these movements without future. They do not possess the temporality of "politics" (understood as an accounting of interests and strengths of opposing parties or as a determination by one party of the means of triumphing over the others). Nor do they belong to a collective unconscious whose contents would be atemporal. And if a genealogy and a typology of signs exists, it would not determine their actualization either. If I am tempted to assimilate them into the Roman *ludi scoenici* and the nocturnal cults of ancient Greece, it is not to explain them according to political history, iconographical history, or history of the collective unconscious. It is rather to reveal deep within all these histories, as well as the signs that are the object of their inquiry, the outpouring of strange intensities that these histories cannot account for. And if these histories cannot account for those signs, it is indeed because the antireligious movements of 1793 have meaning neither within signifying orders nor in the usual historical time-space, but, rather, acquire their form (which is what interests me) from an instinctual force, and because the time-space where they are produced is not that of politico-economic calculation, but that of a libidinal scanning.

Thus, the paganism I have in mind could not be that of instituted ancient religions, even Dionysian ones. Rather, this paganism resides in an infiltration—at the surface of the social body—of areas left open to imaginations and to so-called disordered, useless, dangerous, and singular concrete enterprises: areas left open to the instincts. This occurs at the core of the political and religious institutions themselves—the organization of which we have lost even the slightest notion, since it is precisely what today's thinking and politics ignore or reject. The "houses of vice" whose institution Sade called for in "Français, encore un effort"[22] and perhaps Restif de la Bretonne's "Parthenions" belong to this predisposition. They might at least form one of its poles. In relation to this course of dissimulation and dissimilation, we may understand the extent to which Fourier's program (the project to elide political and economic society in its entirety into a space of carefully controlled games) must necessarily weaken their "scene-making" force.[23]

By dechristianizing, the sansculottes destroy much more than the church or religion. They destroy the "religious" (and, thereby, the history-making) function of the political institution. This function is not only embodied in the immense apparatus issuing from Imperial Catholic Rome, where Caesar and God came to be associated, but also the tradition wherein politics is serious business to be entrusted to those in responsible positions (priests)—a matter of the future, a matter of reconciled totality. For a very short time, if calculated in political chronology (but forever in the unconscious time of "there is [or, there was] once upon a time" and where *once upon a time* suffices for those who encounter that *once*), the sansculottes opened a time-space of meetings, laughter, and anxieties in which the edifice of institutions, weighty issues, and guarantees began tottering.

The time-space I am invoking is no *truer* than the other, and I am not claiming that, with the parodic demonstrations of anti-Christianism, revolutionary reality reveals itself in person. Rather than by emerging, I repeat, this time-space exists within the other through infiltration and dissimulation. The sansculottes were always very traditional politicians and thus Catholics. But the parodic turn taken by their demonstrations suffices to suggest that in this perpetuation of Caesarism, which will actually give rise to the Napoleonic Empire, there lies a very different kind of madness, a violent mobility, a power of invention without reference to a center.

And now for the facts? Let me suggest some of them, fully aware that I am exposing myself to historical quibbling.

THE REVOLUTIONARY FESTIVAL

At the risk of quibbling, however, allow me a parenthesis of apparent pedantry. This study had been completed for over two years when Mona Ozouf's book on the revolutionary festival was published.[24] In it readers will find thousands of previously unpublished pieces of information gathered from primary sources and indispensable to a representation of the festivals. Not without ridicule (but above all not without inconsequence, after what I have said here) could I measure my meager essay against that scholarly compendium. Two other differences, however, add to this imbalance. One is related to the choice of corpus—ten years of Revolution in Ozouf's case, six months of dechristianization in mine—and the other is a difference in strategy. Being a historian, Ozouf wants to *know* what the revolutionary festival is; I am interested in what it is about anti-Christian festivals that *eludes* the historico-political concept. Nonetheless, I shall take the liberty of collecting a few arguments from Ozouf's book that might shore up my fantasies.

Ozouf recognizes in these festivals an "overabundance of meaning"[25] exceeding the quite nihilistic functions of "remedy" or "expedient" to which F.–A. Aulard or A. Mathiez (centralist minds par excellence) would limit their perceptions. I am delighted with this assessment, even if instead of imputing the festivals to a surplus of signification, I am satisfied to detect, in particular aspects of certain festivals, traces of nonsense (as Bloch might say) in the most noble sense of the word. Similarly, Ozouf believes, contrary to Daniel Guérin, that we must associate the "parodic scenes" and "burlesque simulacra" of the winter of 1793–1794 with neither a "specific political event," "defined political intentions," nor a "specific mode of expression of the revolutionary masses."[26] This lends support to my idea that the anti-Christian movements do not derive from recognized historico-political motifs.

Moreover, when Ozouf examines the resurgence in the revolutionary festival in general of signs from antiquity, she does so suspecting (quite legitimately) that "schoolboy memories" and "models of greatness" are at the foundation of the explanations historians habitually give for them. Instead, she emphasizes the "riddle of the overwhelming choice in favor of Antiquity."[27] In retrospect, I believe that my refusal to delineate genealogies of these signs beginning with the ancients is somewhat confirmed.

At one point Ozouf affirms that she has solved the so-called riddle by showing that Sparta, Athens, and Rome were not imitable models for the revolutionaries. Rather, they were the proper names for legislative acts and emblems of political societies dedicated to the instituting function, where individuals have not allowed institutions to elude their grasp and fall into disuse and decadence (in this sense, the revolutionary festival refers to them because of the "instituting" characteristic of this festival).[28] But even in this, despite the reserve I felt for the instituting/instituted operative pair used by Ozouf, I still believe that I am justified, at least by the idea of time implied by the historian's critique, to maintain that the resurgences of ancient customs in the dechristianizers' festivals derive not solely from remembering, but also from forgetting.

However, the point at which Ozouf's work contradicts me is when, allowing herself to be caught up in the declarative vocation of historical discourse, she attributes to the revolutionary festival the very performative function of opening a new era for a new society, which she claims is accounted for by a "transfer of the sacred onto political and social values." The festivals would thus be initiations into a future memory.

And where the contradiction I must endure is heightened to the level of repudiation is when Ozouf, not satisfied with analyzing this function as a historian of mentalities, leaps ahead to conclude with a *declarative* regarding the status not only of the definition of the revolutionary festival, but also of the political and social body, that is, with a political *performance* assigning her own reality to the object of discourse. She writes in her concluding pages that this "transfer of the sacred," in other words (if I am not mistaken) the passing of sovereign authority from the Christian prince to the populace of citizens, "was now [in 1799] accomplished, thus defining a new legitimacy and a hitherto inviolable patrimony"—accomplished to such an extent that it seems impossible to argue that the revolutionary festival "may have failed" in its role as ceremony inaugurating a new era: "the revolutionary festival is exactly what it was meant to be: the beginning of new times."[29]

This conclusion plays tricks on the ears of an old minoritarian and sansculotte historian: it simply takes for reality the Jacobin desire that time actually be measured from the constitutive act of the Republic. This may well have been the intention, conscious or not, governing the organization of the official festivals. But the Jacobin desire is one thing, and its efficacy another. In fact, this desire collides with many other elements, on all flanks, during the Revolution, as well as during the nineteenth century and the beginning of the twentieth. Nor has its legitimacy or "inviolable patrimony" remained uncontested. The body of the Republic has not been a harmoniously designed edifice, nor has its era been that of well-organized festivals held at regular intervals. There has been nothing more sporadic and disrupted than the extent and the duration of the republican monster.

Would this also characterize the "wild" festivals or the uncontrolled aspects of the festivals, especially during the crisis of dechristianization? According to Ozouf, spontaneous parodies and burlesques meant: Let's persevere, the Revolution *is not over*.[30] But in the solemnity of the festival initiating a new era, the opposite idea (which our historian recognizes perfectly well) has currency: the revolution is over, the moment of passage is complete. Only the conspiracy of the Ancien Régime against the new can stir up impulses that no longer appear to right thinkers as revolutionary but instead as archaic and dangerous.

Therefore we must ultimately decide if the revolution is over or not, if the new era has already or not yet begun, if the instituter is free or not in relation to old institutions. The revolutionary festivals are certainly moved by this question, but they do not answer it unanimously, or they fail to answer it at all. And this is why they derive neither from a single concept nor from a single time. The historian's method prescribes the direction of an answer for them; in other words, it *makes decisions* for the social body.

PARODIES

Officially, dechristianization opens the way to solemn ceremonies such as the Festival of Reason on 10 November 1793 in Notre-Dame (redecorated for the occasion) and the Festival of the Supreme Being on 8 June 1794 in the Champ de Mars. Great artists (David, Gossec, Chénier) stage these bleak festivities designed to inaugurate and commemorate the new civic religion, the *theologia civilis*, as Varro called it. They are but the arid results of a short-lived, rationalist thought, the semiotic exercises of diligent pupils. In these ceremonies, preromantic Nature is placed in the service of the new popes. By common consensus, everyone is bored. Within sight of these sinister celebrations is the gaiety of the sansculotte *parodies*. In the Paris sections, in addition to the bonfires stoked with pious works, the marriage of priests, the planting of liberty trees, the closing of churches or their occupation by the section inhabitants, the sending of sacristy treasures to the Convention (based on the principle that the value of relics does not stem from the bit of bone deposited in the reliquary, but from the metal of which the latter is made and from which the government must mint coins in order to purchase arms against kings and priests), the dances in churches, the mocking of catechisms, and the invitation to children to recite parodies of them—in addition to all this, and more significant than these, there are some strange processions before the Convention.

Here is the 12 November description of the Gravilliers section (the section of Jacques Roux, who had been incarcerated at Saint–Pélagie prison for the past two months by the Committee of Public Safety for Paris while nine of his partisans were to be sent by the section to La Force prison two weeks later):

> At its head marches a band of men dressed in sacerdotal and pontifical robes. The music intones *La Carmagnole* and *Marlborough s'en va-t-en guerre*. Banners and crosses are carried in and, the moment the dais enters, the melody of *Ah! le bel oiseau* is heard. All at once, the citizens of this section strip off their disguises and beneath these veils of fanaticism we see the defenders of the fatherland emerge, dressed in the national uniform.[31]

Le Moniteur also describes the impressive procession of the Unité section on 20 November with the entire treasure of Saint-Germain-des-Prés carried on backs and stretchers:

> At its head marches a platoon of the armed forces. Then come the drums, followed by artillery men clothed in sacerdotal vestments and a group of women dressed in white with tricolor sashes. After them comes an endless row of men arranged in two lines and covered with dalmatics, chasubles, and copes. . . . Then, carried along on stretchers, are chalices, ciboria, suns, candelabra, gold and silver plates, a superb reliquary, a cross set with precious stones and a thousand other implements of superstitious practices. . . . After this, musicians intone the revolutionary hymn: we behold all the citizens dressed in priestly garments, dancing to the sounds of *Ça ira*, *La Carmagnole*, *Veillons au salut de l'Empire*, etc.[32]

Even though we do not always have documentation on them as we do for the Assembly, we must imagine these processions actually unfolding in the streets of Paris, along with whatever the provinces and the countryside could come up with. Guérin is one exception to this lack of documentation who, in giving us Dommanget's description, conveys the sense of general scandal. Dommanget writes: "One could see patriots decked out in surplices, chasubles, and copes, goading each other on to destruction with curses, vulgar expressions, and singing or dancing in the debris." He adds, "Childish pranks, ironic saturnalia, masquerades, violent, yet puerile demonstrations."[33] We should interpret these excellent characterizations affirmatively. With great insight, Guérin stresses the revolutionary force of this laughter. It is, in fact, the ancient gods' laughter at the claim that one of them has become unique. In itself, it is a perfectly dechristianized, pre-Christian laughter, that of a horizontal, nonedifying gaiety. If you believe you hear in this laughter an anger still subordinated to the religion whose object it is, then it is because the explanation of what is called the later failure of the anti-Christian movement is yet to come. This is nihilism once again: what happens is listened to through the sound of what will happen—a future anterior nihilism.

These masquerades are truly pagan games. In them, the movement's total success is immediately revealed. The dissimulation of meaning is immediately complete. Who are these savages? Those who now disguise themselves in the magnificent fetishized spoils of their Catholic masters? Or those who wore them to worship them just prior to these events? In a sense, the sansculottes turn themselves into the ethnologists of the great barbarians under the Roman hierarchy. But their ethnology is not Western; it is, rather, pagan. They offer neither theory nor description of Catholicism, but instead parody it, believing they understand it and can make it well enough understood if they can reveal it as a game in its incomprehensible arbitrariness. They expose to public spectacle and uncontrollable laughter what was offered previously for meditation and worship. And this is performed not through criticism, but through mime. The scene-producing game has insinuated itself into what was once ritual: truly Catholic processions enter the Convention only to be transformed into republican parades.

This affair can have quite far-reaching effects, which is why it unnerves right-thinkers of all breeds. When the citizens of Gravilliers remove their chasubles, what do we see? Naked men? No, soldiers—thus, more uniforms. What does Robespierre, beholding these metamorphoses with consternation, say to himself (he being the man of self-identity)? He thinks that what they do with the Catholic uniform, they may also do with the republican one. He thinks that if the church has become a theater, it is clear that the Chamber of Representatives could become one as well. He thinks that metamorphoses might be endless. Thus he realizes he lacks the foundation that every politician needs: the gullibility of the people in the galleries, the authority of the personalities at the tribunal. Dancing and laughing, the sansculotte eludes all powers. And these powers, in turn, can do nothing but wait for the sansculotte to stop so they can take him in hand again and have him reenter the order of politico-religious theatricality. Parody means the impotence of powers, since parody is power conferring authority upon itself. The sansculottes abandon prayer while dancing in religious costume. Across the social "body," libidinal energies are no longer collected and attached to an absent agency, inhibited by waiting or by the reply from a supposed keeper of meaning. These energies are expended, here and now, without regard for consequences or signification.

When it calls for the Festival of Reason to be celebrated on 10 November in Notre-Dame (whose altar will have been veiled by a curtain), the Commune believes it has conquered the church. Instead, it has merely confirmed the temple as the privileged place of representation. It is a simple theatrical and scenographic installation. By bringing their performance of dechristianization to the Convention, the sansculottes, on the other hand, suggest that the Assembly of the People itself may be a theater and a temple, and that if it is not, it is because of the use they make of it. In a dissolution of the first theatrical boundary, the processions cross the streets and appear inside just as they were outdoors. The second boundary, separating hall from stage, is eliminated when the delegated citizens, in the midnight hours, sit on the representatives' benches and speak in their place. Thus it happens that the barriers between exterior and interior, between spectators and actors, between representatives and the represented are broken down. Adventure and encounter advance as possibilities right up to the stage of political worship.

THEATER, DEATH

A study of theater during this period would "confirm" my pagan reading by showing not only that those subjects which closely touch upon the revolutionary situation are successful, but also that the relation between hall and stage is completely displaced.[34] Abbot Maury, a defrocked priest, will come to play himself in an anticlerical drama. A spectator will leap onto the stage, screaming that a suspicious character be arrested at once. An actor will begin to get wary of the sansculottes because of the type of role in which he is cast. The audience often imposes changes in the scenario in the midst of a performance. The strength of pagan laughter is to be found at the origin of Sylvain Maréchal's big success of that theater season, *Le Jugement dernier des rois*.[35] The title is in itself rather parodic, and the play presents all the crowned heads of Europe (including the pope) exiled to an island by a triumphant European sansculotte movement. These crowned heads bicker with each other, come to blows over food,. and are finally engulfed by a volcanic eruption. (What a parody of the metaphor of disruption!) What is remarkable here is that this fantasy of a collective exile of sovereigns displaying their parasitic imbecility had been formulated programmatically by Maréchal in 1788 in a political pamphlet that was suppressed at the time by the royal police.[36] The fantasy appears once again, in 1791, as the object of an unwavering proposal addressed to the Assembly.[37] Once again fiction becomes indiscernible from reality. This is certainly how the audience at the Théâtre de la République understands it: their emotional reaction is so strong at the play's opening performance (the day after Marie-Antoinette's execution) that it turns them, as one newspaper wrote, into "a legion of tyrannicides ready to throw themselves on the leonine species known as kings."[38]

A cleavage between seriousness (politics) and futility (culture) does not exist: dramatic representations have as much repercussion as political speeches. And these consequences scan freely over every part of the social body, which academic practices, and the organization of powers busily separate and compartmentalize in the name of order and clarity. The mixing of genres is the rule of instincts. This mix is not "romantic," but derives instead from the "theology of the theater," which enters into all activities precisely because it does not represent them in a separate theatrical space but rather mimics them right where they are, wherever that might be. And it is understood that the result of this mimicry is not catharsis or some ordinary purging of passions, but an effect of intensification: the sansculottes trust only instinctual forces in order to triumph. It is thus that, having been treated as a space for stage-playing, the battlefield at Valmy rendered the well-known efficient results. We must stop letting ourselves be abused by the phraseology of Reason. When Robespierre or even Chaumette pronounce *Reason*, the word affirms order and power. When it is used by Maréchal or Leclerc (the "atheists"), it elicits the excitation of forces and the ruin of powers. This should teach us to judge words not by their meaning, but by their effect.

I do not mean to suggest that there are two paganisms intermingled in the Terror: one from Roman antiquity, invoked by the legislators and the orators as a model of justice and republican virtue, and the other the paganism I am hoping to evince, which would somehow be more "Dionysian." The official use of Roman customs and labels is not at all pagan: it is already Catholicism—the church as state and vice versa. As proof, we may mention how easily former churches are converted into republican temples and former priests into new politicians, and finally, under Napoleon, the ease with which the reconstitution of "young" imperial Rome takes place. The allusion to Rome, evident in most of the *acts of denomination* carried out by the revolutionary powers until the end of the Empire, is only (and could not be anything but) a metaphor, that is, a comparison between past and present in which the present is erased. Republican and Imperial Rome is simply an excuse for representative religiosity that persists and consolidates its position until the founding of the Empire. This is the repetition that Marx said was always comical in history. And such is the "transfer of sacredness." Not a single metaphor is created by the sansculottes in the autumn of 1793. On the contrary, they create *metamorphoses*. Far from representing ancient Rome, they actualize, in parodies and games (and without referring them to some past), the emotions that are the substance of the political body.

As in Rome, these masquerades include death. The gaiety of the citizens in the Gravilliers and Unité sections explodes in the midst of the guillotine, civil war in the Vendée, and war at France's borders. Death commands no respect as a solemn event; it is considered part of the infinite course of metamorphoses. (Sade might, in this light, be the best sansculotte philosopher, with his assertion that destruction is a fact of nature and his description of Nature as a metamorphic force that implies the dissolution of existing forms.) This is most certainly also a pagan attitude, but one in which it will be necessary to dissociate an antiquity of cult worship from one of games. In the Nièvre, Chaumette and Fouché had decreed on 10 October that this axiom be inscribed at the entrance to all cemeteries: *Death is an eternal sleep.* In the notes for his final speech (8 Thermidor), what does Robespierre say?

> No, Chaumette. No, Fouché. Death is not an eternal sleep. Citizens, erase this impious maxim throwing a veil of mourning over Nature and insulting death from the tombs. Engrave there these words instead: *Death is the beginning of immortality.*

But which death? Clearly it is a death by martyrdom to virtue, death by unconditional conformity to truth. Robespierre again, the same day:

> If I must conceal these truths, let the hemlock be brought to me. . . . Some time ago I promised to leave a formidable testament to the oppressors of the people. I shall publish that testament forthwith in the independent spirit appropriate to the situation in which I have placed myself: to them I bequeath terrible truth and death.[39]

Freud would say something like this: the Ego (Robespierre's) does the work of mourning the loss of his body, recovering and preserving itself as an inalienable love-object, independent of the lost body, in the immortality of truth. This is a stoicism of virility equivalent to the concept of power as it will be inscribed in the Hegelian dialectic of master and slave: a hero is a dead soldier.

In contradistinction to, or rather at the very center of, this philosophical stoicism stands the stoicism of theatricality and *adiaphora*, mingled with the skepticism and epicureanism in popular morality at the decline of pagan Rome. Its formulation would not be *my life for the truth*, but *truth knows no opposite*. I imagine the sansculottes (and without a doubt many revolutionaries bound for the scaffold) no longer dying a personal martyrdom like Robespierre and the paranoid, but dying in the conviction of belonging to a powerful revolution of anonymous forces unable to proceed without the metamorphosis of bodies. Representative Lequinio explained to Rochefort on 10 November (in the Temple of Liberty, it must be confessed) that after death, the body

> rots, is decomposed, and returns . . . to the various elements which were grouped together in composing it; it will strive to form other beings—worms, fish, plants, and a thousand other different bodies. . . . There will be nothing left of us but the disparate molecules that used to form us and the memory of our past existence.[40]

This is the discourse of a true atomist for whom death could never represent a profession of faith, nor, for that matter, life a magisterium. The scene of this discourse's enactment is not a temple, even if it were to be called Nature: sansculotte Nature is limitless, its very borders are merely a transitory collection of atoms, whether they be those of the body itself or those of the social body. Bodies are really only ephemeral localizations of intensities. We will not die as tragic heroes, but in the certainty that the fantasy of divinities (or the chance encounter of atoms) also "wished" this parody of sacrifice. Robespierre said: "It is crime's terror that produces the security of innocence." Sansculotte innocence does not need the protection of a terrorist power: it is not *that* childhood that parents believe they are policing, it is the childhood of a polymorphous "body" traversed or traced over by what amount to acephalous instincts. But of course this innocence never appears except in the form of the Other, the form that offers a pretext for adult powers. Epicurus hidden inside Brutus.

THE REPRESSION OF WOMEN

Discerning sansculotte paganism is most difficult, yet perhaps most decisive, in femininity. That is where dissimulation plays itself out to the fullest. I stress this relative discernibility of paganism in femininity (and not in women) because it is hardly necessary to emphasize the extent to which antifeminism reigned in the popular and lower middle classes of the period. It seems appropriate, then, that whatever we now call women's liberation was then called *libertinage* and was, in general, equivalent to aristocratic immorality. The corruption of morals was the doing of courtesans and nobles: any high-ranking woman was presumed to be a harlot. To the Jacobin mind, a woman involved in public affairs, which was often the case among the nobility in the Ancien Régime, must necessarily become a prostitute. A woman resorting to the stratagem inherent in political service implies the strategic use of her mind and body, seduction, therefore debauchery. In October 1789, Olympe de Gouges complained (in presenting to the Assembly her program of complete equality between men and women) of the "nocturnal administration" of women and of the fact that they "rule mysteriously with a despotic hand." *Les Liaisons dangereuses* figures along with *Tom Jones* among the works that the Revolutionary Committee of the Mountain takes note of during an inventory of a peddler's trunk seized during a house search at the end of January 1794.[41]

Confronted with what is customarily referred to as the problem of prostitution, the question of free unions and of the right of concubines and unwed mothers to receive the same public support as spouses and legal mothers, Jacobinism always adopts the most narrowly conservative solution.[42] In response to a request by Théroigne de Méricourt that women have a consultative vote in the district Assembly of the Club, a strange resolution made by the Cordeliers between 20 and 25 February 1790 recalls that women do indeed, like men, possess a soul and an intelligence (the Council of Mâcon had already decided this at the end of the sixth century) and that the female sex is certainly free to make any proposal in the interest of society, but that, in the end, the Assembly of the Cordeliers is unable to admit Théroigne to the district meeting armed with a consultative vote.[43]

Since everything is more violent by 1793, the element of paganism in the question of women is more readily apparent. Following incidents provoked by the invasion of the Republican Revolutionary Women's Club, located in the ossuary of Saint-Eustache church, by nearby market women from Les Halles, the women from the People's Society in the Bon Conseil section proceed to the Convention to complain about this club, accusing those women of reducing the entire neighborhood to chaos by forcing other women to wear cockades, red caps, and trousers as they themselves do. The Convention requests a report on the club from the Committee of General Security. The very next day it is a fait accompli: Amar reads the report, whose arguments not only conclude with the suppression of all women's clubs and societies, but, as Stephens remarks, "have determined what will later become the official relations between the sexes throughout the country." The committee raises two questions: (1) Are women capable of exercising political rights and of taking an active part in the affairs of government? (2) When assembled in political associations, are they capable of deliberating? The committee then replies in the negative to both questions. Woman's nature is such that she is unfit for political responsibilities, which require a certain equanimity of which she is incapable. Moreover, a woman's appearance in public is pernicious to her reputation. This is why the best service she can offer the Republic is to be a good influence on her husband and raise their children to love freedom.[44]

After this altogether Rousseauvian report, the Assembly unanimously votes (with the exception of one voice, Charlier's) to prohibit any women's association. The Republican Revolutionary Women try to resist. Rose Lacombe leads delegations to the Assembly, to the Council of the Commune. They are received with anger and hatred. "Off with the red cap on women" is the cry from the galleries of the Assembly. In the midst of a great uproar in the Commune on 17 November, Chaumette accuses the "viragos" of being "paid by foreign powers" and hits upon the words of the perfect male chauvinist:

Since when are women allowed to abjure their sex and become men? Since when has decency allowed women to abandon the pious duties of their households, their children's cradles, to enter the public arena, the tribune of disputation ... to fulfill the obligations that nature has relegated to men alone?[45]

Jacobinism energetically sets the faithful and consoling matron, the Roman lady at her hearth, against the Amazon (in ancient iconography the Phrygian cap is *this* woman's customary attribute).[46] For Jacobinism, the political woman is a spy and a harlot. This is because she injects a flagrant contradiction into the set pattern of the social body: she shows that the sexes are not *functions*, that the roles played by men may also be assumed by women, and that therefore there is a transitivity of energies and efficiencies that is indifferent to sexual positions. Thus they reveal the essence of masculine power: performative exclusion. Sylvain Maréchal makes this unabashed assumption in his journal: "Lady citizens! Ho! Are we not your natural representatives, your lawful chargés d'affaires? Can we have any interests separate from yours? Are you not others of ourselves?"[47] For women, he reiterates in a crystal-clear definition of their confinement, "their household is their universe; to them, their husband is all mankind; the rest of the world is unknown to them."[48]

This very reactionary context of feminist material represses but also attests to a "return" of paganism. Here, too, simplifications are to be avoided. It is the period of "goddesses." And it will be said that nothing is less pagan (in my understanding of it), nothing more religious than to sublimate women's situations and actions in the familial and political domains into theological and cultural themes. But it is not only a matter of sublimation. It is true that, in Rome, the matron is deprived of political rights, and that the cults of the most honored female divinities celebrated there seem to be celebrated "in compensation for" this confinement. Still, in Rome, scenes are performed where women play no less a part than men, where the question of their equality is, so to speak, surpassed where the fundamentally dissimilatory characteristics of the instincts is recognized, through many rituals, in its transsexual scope. The programs of many official festivals, from those of very selective, small circles (like the one formed by the *Fratres Arvales*) to the altogether popular rejoicings (the Saturnalia or the *Nonae Caprotinae*), include the most unprogrammed, fantastic, and intrepid acts initiated by the participants.

The goddesses of the Revolution may be situated between the two usual poles: the virgin and the whore, figures diametrically opposed, yet very close to each other. These are figures of girls sharing a common sterility: exempt from reproduction and maternity. Those like Minerva at Notre-Dame (under the name of Reason) may take a position within the circle of men and civic religion. Surrounded by philosophers, that Minerva is dressed in white, her body passionless, her gaze wise, her movements decent.

Michelet tells us that the men of the Commune hesitated when setting the scenario for the Festival of Reason on 10 November:

> On the 7th, a statue was being considered, but people objected: a permanent symbol might be reminiscent of the Virgin and lead to renewed idolatry. They favored an image less fixed, something animated and alive which changed with each holiday and did not give rise to superstition.[49]

This question of the goddess's mobility is decisive. Michelet suggests that it may be understood as humanistic. If they are not made of stone, then these divinities will be women who serve only to represent to the social body the virtues it seeks to adopt. It will be observed that mobile goddesses do not allow for the public's idolatrous identification with the image. They force the image to move, to become conscious of what it is, and what it must become. It is not too farfetched to see in Michelet's observation an anticipation of the Brechtian aesthetic of distanciation: this mobility on stage is critical; it returns the members of the audience to their "real" scene, to social and political activities.

But from the outset, the girl who incarnated Reason at Notre-Dame was immobilized by many restrictions. First, she had to be of good reputation. Fouché strongly advises the provinces: "Choose, for so august a part, persons whose character would lend respectibility to their beauty, the severity of whose morals would repel license and fill mens' hearts with feelings of honesty and purity."[50] Thus what might have become a scene-playing, a freely pagan enterprise, ended up subordinated to the matronly ethic. Often it was honorable wives who filled these roles (mothers as goddesses). They could not be actresses since these were customarily held to be libertines. So sterility, and the corporeal independence it implies, and which likens these unfettered women to masculine figures, frightened the organizers of the service.

The "choreography" prescribed for the goddess in Notre-Dame was so restrained that everyone became exasperated. We know that "Reason" emerged from a temple of philosophy to make her way to a grassy hillock where she sat down surrounded by busts of Voltaire, Rousseau, Montesquieu, and Franklin. She listened to hymns by Chénier and Gossec. Then, returning to her temple, she stopped before entering, turned around, and "bestowed the gentlest of smiles on the spectators."[51] Michelet comments: "a chaste ceremony, sad, arid, boring"; reasoning disciplining reason, a monitored virgin, surrounded by thinkers (of whom some are masters of enlightened misogyny), crippled by edifying music.

THE "FEMININE (IN OTHER WORDS, PAGAN) PRINCIPLE"

We can see from these festivals how Jacobin sensitivity goes hand in hand with the repression of instinctual violence: the goddess's path and that of her gaze never exceed the reassuring space of a strictly functional service. Thus restricted mobility makes the scene of real games compatible with the Jacobin barrier erected everywhere against women's movements, a Rousseauvian politics.

Moreover, this mobility, when developed, is not critical, but instinctual. Its model is found in the 6 October 1789 march on Versailles and the king. All observers agree that there is nothing critical about this procession. But representative apparatuses undergo a tremendous upheaval: the great stage of Versailles, where, for over a century, the glittering spectacle of despotism was played out, is deserted and closed. The space of political gaming has been shifted to Paris, to become the surface not only of somber representations, but also of "playing out scenes": where the chance occurrence of anonymous inspirations continues to threaten the order of institutions, including revolutionary ones.

This passage to playing out scenes had been a sort of passive impulse, the sudden destruction of the power of the gaze, an entirely "feminine" power, independent of controlled representational order. Four years later, the eye of the Jacobin stage director fears the return of this very power and seeks to neutralize it. This is the mobility that the official festivals will eventually throttle, that of the monstrous body of the Republic. The goddesses Reason and Liberty, cap on head and lance in hand, merely represent the instincts, immobilized: such are the limits to which "sensitivity" is tolerated.

When the Republican Revolutionary Women don the red cap, clench the pike, and slip on men's trousers, when they march from Saint-Eustache to Les Halles to force the shrews (the conservative market women manipulated first by the Royalists, then by the Jacobins) into wearing the tricolor cockade, which had been decreed obligatory for all, what comes to light is not a feminine power but the strength of a new displacement. As such, it is the scene of men, the scene no longer of the despot, but of citizens, yet still the same scene, a political scene distinct from and dominating domestic passions (just as in Greece) a dramatic scene offered for respectful contemplation—this scene that is at risk of being energetically shifted. The citizens' theater is brought down to earth, clearing a space where there is no longer *one* political body that, although divided, remains the business of *one* sex. Instead, it is a polymorphous space where the passions are not represented, but effected.

That is what Chaumette cries out (for there is quite a clamor!) to women on 7 November at the Commune. "Your despotism is the only despotism we cannot destroy, since it is founded on love, and consequently on human nature. In the name of human nature, stay as you are."[52] Remain as mute, faithful, and consoling spectators of the social and political tragedy we are performing; your irruption is unnatural—a bacchanal.

If women are to be sent back to their households, we must discriminate between who is married and who is not. Following the incident of 23 July 1793 at the Opéra Comique, precipitated by a blunder in an announcement in which the names of actresses were preceded by the title of *mademoiselle* instead of *citoyenne*, the *Journal des Spectacles* complained immediately:

> Is it not true that the words *citoyen* and *citoyenne* that have been proposed as replacements for former titles of address are insufficient? When some-one says *citoyenne* Saint Aubin, *citoyenne* Desforges, what indicates to me that one is married and the other not? This is, however, what I am apprised of when I hear someone use *Madame* for the first and *Made-moiselle* for the second. . . . I shall not discuss the political question of whether or not the title of *citoyen* may belong equally to all men, but I shall say that that of *citoyenne* could not possibly be appropriate for all women.[53]

What does this gentleman want? To be informed of the status of the rights of his sex over the other. The destruction of signs of the gap between married and unmarried women creates disorder.

People are a fortiori even more scandalized by the issue of informal address that ignores the gap between the sexes even more. "Used as it is today," writes Bouin in June 1794,

> it has a very bad effect on the Revolution by giving us the impression of returning to a state of crudeness and rusticity . . . since it is used by a large number of civil servants with a harsh and brutal tone which offends, humiliates, and alienates hearts instead of winning them over to the current order of things. This pernicious effect is particularly apparent upon women in whom familiar address is in all cases hardly appropriate, scarcely courteous, and barely moral.[54]

The only woman with whom a man may use familiar address without knowing her is a woman who can be bought.

So, when "goddesses" are improvised from time to time in popular assemblies, cabarets, theaters, and street gatherings, not only "counterrev-olutionary" opinion,[55] but the Jacobin and sansculotte opinions as well, formulate the equation: "goddess," therefore public woman, therefore prostitute. We have only to recall Flaubert depicting the invasion of the Tuileries on 24 February 1848: "In the antechamber, standing like a statue of Liberty on a pile of clothing, was a prostitute, immobile, her eyes wide open, terrifying."[56] Such is the phantom of wild, nocturnal, "unchained" woman whom the powers that be (and Jacobins first of all) try to eradicate. The model evidently belongs to the tradition of the Liberalia and above all to the most excessive Bacchanalia that, in Rome, surpassed the official homage paid to the god of wine and sex: a hallucinating maenad tetanized by *jouissance*.

The militant women are taken for such furies.

Opposing the Rousseauvian and quite classical idea that women do not belong to the body of citizens, but that they form another vague, ill-defined, and disturbing body that is to be found outside or beneath the former, the feminist movement cannot avoid falling into the trap set by men: identification with virile power. But beyond this claim, what the unique presence of women in the dechristianization movements of 1793–1794 does reveal, as a polymorphous presence located on the side of sublimated models as well as on the side of the most devalued mobilities, is not so much (or not only) the emancipation of one sex oppressed by the other, but an attempt (here again with no apparent development) to transsexualize the social body, and thus to paganize it.

We know that after the coup d'état of 2 December 1851, the Republicans formed secret societies, one of which was called *La Marianne*. The Royalists referred to the Republic by this name, borrowed from Marivaux's novel, to designate, so they thought, a fast and versatile young woman. In reality, as Leo Spitzer writes, "the subject of *La Vie de Marianne* is not so much the narrative of the individual life of an intrepid young girl, as it is the *glorification of the feminine principle in human thought* revealing itself in life and in literature.[57] This "feminine principle" closely resembles my pagan principle.

Translated by Kenneth Berri

8

◆

Retortion in Theopolitics

Once, in a dream, an angel appeared to a young student of theory (fiction). "Next to whom will I be seated up there?" the dreamer asked the angel. "You will be seated next to Ernst Bloch from Tübingen," and the angel disappeared. So, the youth began searching for this Bloch. He was told that Bloch was a Marxist, a millenarian Christian, an idealist, a hasidic Jew, a historian of ideas, a fairly edifying thinker, the last great nihilist, and the Thomas Münzer of the bureaucratic era. The dreamer collected information. He frequented those modern houses of prayer called university libraries. He concluded after reading a few books that the master was of major, doctoral importance. No need to do like Rabbi Raphael of Belz, who went to the outskirts of town, at sunset, in the middle of the Sabbath, to meet some unknown person, some Isaac Leib Peretz, a drunkard and twice a sinner, only to discover later that he was a saint—the ways of the Lord, praised be His name, are indeed twisted. No, Ernst Bloch seemed to him to be in good standing as far as recognized intelligence and wisdom go. He appeared to be a doctor *honoris causa*, which is why the youth began to worry: "Will I, young student of fiction that I am, really be sitting next to that great philosopher up there? Truly God, I must say, you have some very strange ideas!"

What happened next in the story was that, after pronouncing these words, he collapsed unconscious before the door of the library. What follows relates the youth's thoughts as he lay unconscious. These thoughts seem to have been guided by the following precept: "It is characteristic of hasidism that the masters on whom life depends are hidden, *perhaps even from their own eyes*. They might know they are 'great,' but they don't feel it."[1] The conclusion of these thoughts, if it may be called one, was that this character- istic of dissimulation did not belong to the tzaddik, nor to his master, praised

115

be his name, but to the pagan power of tensions. This is how the student discovered that Doktor Bloch, an extreme nihilistic wise man, was a great affirmative *Narr*, and that it was for this reason the angel wanted him to sit next to Bloch. At least this is what the student supposed. His reasoning follows.

HOPE

He began by railing against the unity of the subject and the dialectical temporality that seemed to him to frame and support the idea of hope. A very academic idea, thought the young thinker, that would be well received by Hegel. Hope is the movement by which the *Noch nicht* appears in the present of the subject, opens it up, exceeds it, and gathers it up in anticipation of something else: a very Hegelian move. "In the end, there remains the subject of need, even when he finds himself—himself and his work— infinitely objectified; he is the driver [*der Treiber*] of historical contradictions."[2] To see the spirit as *Trieb* is no problem for Hegel. The common source for Hegel and Bloch is Jacob Boehme:

> At the heart of negation, Boehme perceives a desire, an emotional drive, an inclination born essentially of a deficiency; desire responds to negation, the negative element is the deficiency manifesting itself in desire, or, to use Boehme's terminology, in hunger.[3]

But to us late-twentieth-century students, this desire still seems to be only a ruse of reason: spirit's ultimate trap for capturing history, the concrete. To us, this so-called concrete only seems to be what is missing from the spirit: what the spirit cares about, the concrete of philosophers. We see this desire as the spirit disguised as flesh, some Jesus or other; once again, a timid accommodation of the Hegelian dialectic, whose uneasy reading is not only possible but required—and not in addition to a quietistic reading, but within one. Hope is just the margin required for the system not to be closed, the distance between the in-itself-for-us and the for-itself. But for us late-twentieth-century capitalized ones, this small gap seems not to be a corrective measure (and seems even less to be a reversal applied to the system), but rather the game intrinsic to its laxism. When Bloch writes[4] that uneasiness (*Unzufriedenheit*) is to drives what hope is to science, does not the parallelism of the two orders itself reveal how the second merely copies the first? Thus the ressentiment of our Parisian student expresses itself. Yet Bloch adds that *Unzufriedenheit* is negativity, whereas *Hoffnung* is positivity. What follows is the youth's hypothesis.

Give hope free reign. Let it slide beyond the "positivity of the negative" toward affirmation. Understand it as the affirmation of what is affirmed.

Understand this science as a gay science. Hope would be the striving toward other powers. A power to grasp not only as *Macht*, but as *Potenz*: spaces to the first, second, fourth, n^{th} power. Affirmative "hope" would be the impulse to multiply the figures of "things" to such an extent that things disappear, along with the pretense of a unitary explanation of them.

The important thing becomes the qualitative extension, the tension in the "states of things" that come about—a tension foreign to any intention. "The representation of the capacity for self-mastery" would be intentional hope, that of the spirit.[5] However, a tensor is at work dissimulated in this hope, and its action, owing nothing to the represented or to belonging, owes everything to an excess of forces, just like the *Schreck* or *Schrack*, the fourth origin according to Boehme, which is a deep nihilistic fear, but, at the same time, "the flash, the flashing manifestation of the Yes."[6]

Can we come to understand this? Can we come to understand hope as a drive hidden within what is edifying? The hope that arises wholly from the *too much* appears modestly (Isaac Leib Peretz) or magnificently (Ernst Bloch) as an effect of poverty animated by a *too little*. It is not a dialectic at play between the *Ja* of the first and the *Nicht* or the *Noch nicht* of the second, but rather *sometimes* a sort of unforeseeable, gracious retortion. Rabbi Yehiel Mikhal of Zlothso, a master of extreme poverty, suggests this in answer to the question: "How can you say every day in prayer 'Blessed be you, Lord, who provides for all needs,' when you lack everything?" The rabbi's answer: "What I need the most is poverty, and that is precisely what is given to me."[7] Precisely where *you* feel lack, Yehiel Mikhal perceives overabundance. But he is not even master of this, not even the master of "his" poverty. He is not a Job who has reached the end of his revolt (a ridiculous assumption), but one who has reached the intimacy of what motivates his distress—power.

On this hope composed of supertensions, affirmative jealousy, *invidia*, could be articulated. Inside the figures of control, of property, and of possessiveness used by ethics to denounce it, we might uncover and honor a libidinal jealousy, independent of the Ego and of its identifications, a libidinal jealousy alien to rights, to the violence of appropriation, and, therefore, to guilt. But this jealousy would be a simple will to power, an irresistible irrigation by the drives of zones of lesser intensity. This affirmative jealousy would be the reverse of Blochian hope. Like the prayer of the tzaddik of Zlothso, the jealousy the Lord feels with regard to Israel is based on an *encroachment* without negativity: the weaker one, Jacob, attracts the stronger and thereby risks becoming the stronger himself. This is why the Man without a Name who wrestles for a whole night with Jacob has to use a ruse, by striking him in the thigh, in order to get the better of him. And this is why Jacob is called Israel, the powerful Jouster, he who jousted against heavenly and human forces and who remained strong (Gen. 32:25). Hope is the name carried by the affection of the less intense for the more intense, and jealousy, the name of the empire the weaker holds over the stronger. Hope is Israel naming the Unnameable. Jealousy is God naming Jacob (or Luther overpowering Münzer?).

Hope would be this: as far as drives go, yes, something happens: events happen. However, an event consists of a relationship between forces that, when accounted for and leading to a predictable directional and dynamic result, can nevertheless be diverted so that the weaker can become the stronger. Such is, according to Bloch, "the unburdened man":

> Nothing outside of himself inhibits him. The child is innocent and only possesses the aptitude for sin. We can extirpate the will to sin from him. But *we have turned the situation around*; accumulated evil loses all its strength the moment we break with it.[8]

At this point, let us recognize *retortion*, an eminent figure from libidinal "history." That Bloch presents it under the guise of freedom of will is the price of the subterfuge that intensities and passions must assume in order to become accredited by philosophy.[9] This same Doktor Bloch invites us, not to decipher this dissimulation, but to *cipher* it, to maintain it with its burden of opacity. He does so in the anecdote entitled "The Hole of the Present,"[10] where, in the following manner, he teaches us about the retortion of the unreal future into a past that is presently fulfilled: a beggar is asked to make a wish; he says he would like to be king; but, once he is made king, he is conquered by his enemies, flees, and in the end finds himself to be the person now telling the story (of what is past), which he had first presented as what his wish would bring him. What does this beggar-king teach us? Not only that the narrator and the hero of the story are one and the same and that reality and desire form a continuum, but, above all, that the time of desire is open to every kind of twist: the royal past presenting itself as an illustrious future, and the unfortunate future (of this past) as the immediate past of present mendacity. A person begins by aspiring to the throne and ends up just hoping for a new shirt.

Thus the Blochian *Noch nicht* escapes the dialectical mechanics. If the *Noch nicht* indicates that the past and the present, like the future, are not yet, it is not that they ever have to get there through a curatorial accumulation and assignation, but rather that they are *not yet past, future, or present*. It is the instinctive that is *noch nicht aufgehoben*, not yet brought out, taken up again, repeated, and taken back in the babble of the philosophical owl, not yet distributed over the temporal axes of reasonable narratives (where the *Noch nicht* will take up residence at the future's pole), not yet constituted as temporal signification; a *Noch* that precisely does not inscribe itself in the diagram of the time of consciousness or of the mind; a "still yet" that is not that of Augustine or Husserl; rather the *already yet* of the beggar-king's anecdote: two antonyms and two antitemporals (*antichrones*) are blended together in an opportune moment.

HUMOR

The student of fiction says to himself, "We will gladly place humor, too, on the side of affirmations." At the beginning of *Thomas Münzer* we read: "Let those who use the world be as if they were not, for the figure of the world is transitory" (1 Cor. 7:31). This is the very formula of nihilism and of the Christian defense against it: has the edifying Doktor who wishes to turn us away from life returned to us? Saint Paul speaks of women when the Corinthian community asks: Should we allow them or not? The apostle: "*ho kairos sunéstalménos estin*," meaning *tempus breve est* (time is short). But *kairos* is neither *chronos* nor *aiôn*. Saint Paul suggests that it implies the right moment (note that it is this same *kairos* on which Gorgias built the whole effectiveness of Sophist discourse). This right or opportune moment is constricted, rare, short, fleeting. And therefore, Saint Paul says, save as much as possible of the energy the flesh inevitably expends. As for the rest, save all "*to loipon*" affects—save this for everything that remains outside of *kairos*, which should alone call forth the libido. And furthermore, "let he who has a woman be as if without, he who weeps as he who weeps not, he who enjoys as he who enjoys not, he who buys as he who possesses not, he who uses this world as he who does not, etc." Thus *kairos*, on the one hand, and the meantime, on the other; the moment, and the rest of time. For the rest of the time, do *as if . . . not*, *hôs mè, als ob . . . nicht*; stock up reserves of energy. In his *Proclamation to Brethren Plotters of Mansfeld*. Münzer invokes Matt. 25 (the Parable of the Ten Bridesmaids and the Parable of the Talents): he who has shall receive; he who has not shall be deprived. The same precept, it seems: stock up reserves of oil, of money for the right moment—the instant when the husband, the master arrives.

None of this is really very humorous. On the contrary, it seems rather prudent, capitalizing. The young student says: "The way I understand the Epistle and the Parable is as financial advice for the advantageous investment of affects and interests." This is the principle on which papal Rome will sell indulgences. After all, to enjoy without enjoying, to buy without possessing anything, to use without using, are these not the definition of capital as asceticism against nihilism, as Christianity pursued in a different way within political economy? Doesn't its irony deceive when it ironizes this world from the point of view of another, when it ironizes this wealth, this accumulation from the point of view of that other wealth, capital, when it ironizes the time of insignificant presence (consumption) from the point of view of the omnitemporality of the signifying absence (accumulation)? Fed by this irony, a romanticism is possible in capital, as in Christian life.

Is this not also the irony of *vanitas* impelling Münzer's Anabaptist movement, the movement that moves Bloch's pen? Does hope for another kingdom not imply the devaluation of that kingdom? Does hope not annihilate the definitions and values of this lowly world for the sake of the other world it envisions? Is work not itself laughable, like all usury, like all usage, at the cost of the unusable capital called hope?

Bloch can be read in this way. So can Münzer and Tertullian, that is, as leftists: nihilists grounded on a guaranteed Beyond. "But," the schoolboy says to himself, swooning, "we post–'68 revolutionaries cannot be candid apologists any more than the post–'56 'Marxist' Bloch. No more than he, can we speak as if we knew the secret of the right moment or as if the energy of the 'leap' were within our power." What in fact spares Bloch from somber irony is humor: the impossibility of gaining a foothold in the beyond and of exploiting it, theoretically and practically. The irony of *hôs mè* states: "What is is as if it were not." Hope states: "What is not is as if it were." But the true brother of affirmative hope is humor, which denounces all fraternization with irony by stating: "Indeed, *even* what is not is as if it were, and in this way, there is no nothingness and no 'remainder.' Everything is or nothing is—it is as you choose. The question remaining is that if something could happen, if the relationship of forces could be twisted back, as my sister Hope hopes it will, no one knows when this might happen."

Through hope, the weaker is rendered into the stronger (as through that rhetorical figure Aristotle denounces). Through humor (in opposition to irony), the weaker, wily enough to not demand more strength, confesses to a sort of "passivity." He cultivates a "stock of surprise: the miniscule . . . , those small emblems that barely pierce." He consents to letting himself be surprised by "some excess which nothing external motivates."[11] He confesses his inability to determine the favorable moment, the instant when this excess will pierce daily existence. He admits his lack of empowerment before intensities. But this admission, which would still be nihilist if it were accompanied by recrimination, is also very affirmative, like hope itself, fully instinctual and in consonance with the logic of drives, since the humorous declaration of lack of empowerment is by itself already a trap. Let us call it *the subterfuge of the weak force*, laid before the powers that be and whose resilience derives from the fact that the powerful are jealous of the weak.

It is thus that humor manifests its indifference to capitalization and also to the composition of energies that tends to expend itself. The important thing is to be *ein innerlicher Narr*,[12] an idiot inside, a sort of unbeliever, empty, weak of spirit, inane: a body ready to perfectly lead the impromptu excess, should that time come. This humor is that of the will to power: lack of empowerment only drives one to despair in times of accumulation. In times of *kairoi*, it is accompanied by unbridled gaiety, at the opposite pole from Lutheran resignation (which offers all the signs of dispair before the *Umsonst*): "To he who demands a sign with audacity, vehemence and zeal, God will not refuse it," Münzer says.[13] And becoming more and more subtle, the young scholar says to himself: "No need to *reconcile* this impatience with the patience of humor."

TRACE

So there is a semiotics to the old master, but one that is quite insensitive to semantic structures and groupings. It is a semiotics of intensities, if two synonymous words may be used together. It is a politics. It hinges entirely on a dissimulation: traces are harnessed in signs, tensors in intelligibles, "strokes of will" in repeatable mechanisms, "figures" (*chiffres*) of the future in "schematics" of the dead past.[14] But the first of these pairs is independent of the second. Bloch, relying on the paradox of the "independent prisoner," turns his back on Freudian theory. ("It wouldn't be too difficult," the excellent student says to himself, "to show that psychoanalytic practice, at least to the extent that it is governed by the 'evenly suspended ear,' has what it takes to sustain a semiotics of forces.") Let us leave that aside for now. What could those strokes that make traces be, if not elements of a discursive system, if not signifying by their very structure? How and of what are they traces? Does not every trace indicate an absence? We modern students have already become masters at these games of absence and signification, masters of faith in the "seriousness" of the letter.

So, concerning Münzer, Bloch already (that is, immediately) turns the problem around: How can significant signs leads us *to will*? How can studying the Scriptures alone give rise to hope, to an aptitude for intensities? Luther is subservient to the letter. He believes in infallible criteria: first, Scripture, because it is revealed; and second, even if the meaning of Scripture is not beyond question, the power to heal, which proves, in principle, that God is on the side of his interpreter.[15] Bloch's hatred for Luther (equal to Münzer's) is directed at the despotism of the established (that is, dead) sign. That hatred is another facet of sacred, humorous anger that, while laughing, strives for the undecidable. "The Word of God is our witness," Luther cries to the prophets of Zwickau, whom he hosts at Wittenberg in March 1520, "show me yours!" And Markus Stübner says: "Wait a bit, brother Martin, we'll show the world our sign!" This is an answer by way of the future, the *Noch nicht*, which already supposes a certain negligence concerning the problem of "bearing witness," concerning the problem of the right to speak, as well as concerning the infamous question: "In *whose name* do you act?"

The so-called prophetic sign (a tensor) obviously cannot be the letter: "The Divine cannot itself be found within any affirmation or word from past centuries, because Revelation is still unfolding," the prophets of Zwickau say. It is not yet finished. And Münzer says: "The voice of the Holy Spirit is in me like the terrible rushing sound of innumerable streams of water [*der grausame Brausen vieler Wasserströme*]. I know more about it than if I had gobbled up a hundred thousand Bibles [*als wenn eines Hunderttausend Bibel gefressen hatte*]."[16] Münzer's is the insatiable Rabelaisian, Nietzschean appetite for intensities, the vertigo of a hundred thousand swallowed Bibles, the laughter of countless *kairoi*.

The letter inaugurates a story, a diachrony where, in principle, the narrative of its incarnation and the astutely complementary one of redemption of the flesh is recounted. But prophecy, with its humor, its hope, and its rage, does not belong to this unfolding of the already in a foreseeable not yet. Whereas Augustinianism ("laicized" or not)[17] capitalizes on signs, prophecy displaces them, shakes them up, solicits them, then rejects them: "To hell with God if he doesn't put himself at my disposal as he did for Abraham and the Prophets."[18] To hell with signs if within them there is no trace. To hell with the scriptures if they provide no opportunity to will for power.

SECT

Is it a diabolical and paranoid claim to subordinate meaning to the affective states of an individual? To brush aside this objection, the learned professor (using *Thomas Münzer* as his basis) wrote the craziest and strongest pages existing, not only on political organization, but on the exploration of the historical body—pages where he opposes sects of traces to the church of signs.[19] Churches are merely made up of many Egos, which is why their beliefs are syncretic and unity is formed around the despotic deposit of the divine utterance. But sects are trans-individual. They only exist as a fleeting knot that will ties with itself. And if names mark them (beginning with the sect of Thomas Münzer), these names are not those of their leaders. They are the *collective proper names* that the sects take on themselves or that they are given. Their unity does not arise from a center or from a law. It results from a simple congruence of many drives rousing many bodies and transforming them into a precarious anonymous fraternity. The sect does not constitute a temporal subject of history, but rather an anonymity within the "history" of opportunities. What causes signs to become traces and to flout God (as what happened in Münster) is not the megalomania of one person, but the violence of a desire for one moment condoned by a multiplicity of bodies that become brothers through this violence.

At this point, it was Ernst Bloch's turn to express surprise that a young student of theory (fiction) had been imposed on him as his neighbor for eternity. In calling himself both Marxist and sectarian, it seemed to him that he had succeeded in displeasing all the moderns: the *clerical Marxists* who, as Europe witnessed in '68, hate all sects, and the *sectarians* who despise the communist church, not to mention the *liberals* who fear both. "What French student, necessarily molded by one or several of these three groups, could bear this conglomeration?" the old tzaddik wondered. "Is providing me with such a neighbor supposed to condemn me to the hell of his recriminations?"

Despair not (answered the student, who in his fainting spell had begun to understand the decree of the angel). Your wisdom has remained hidden from your own eyes, beneath surfaces that provide or have provided a foothold for the edification or the nihilism of philosophers, theologians, moralists, and politicians of decadence. I believe I now understand that from within your work, beneath its estimable surfaces and indeed in spite of them, arises an inestimable force. I was placed next to you in order to make this resonate, and so we could help each other turn back decadence. What is your Marxism? *Omnia sint communia*, which I understand to mean: Let us not worry about propriety—what is called divine is nothing more than the great conductive skin of anonymous intensities. Very well, this is what we fought for and are still fighting for, we the students of theory (fiction). And what is your sectarianism? *Ne pariatur vis*, which translates as: *Strength is jealous*, and the commune of energies can thus only be a minority.

In a passage from your *Münzer* (alas, following for once Engels), under the guise of explaining that the failure in Mülhausen was due to the immaturity of the peasants in 1525, you make an appalling observation: "They aspire to share the land . . . ; they wished for an Empire of humble peasants with no nobility or princes."[20] In this, you were anticipating fifty years of workers' movement experience: we used to say we believed the Empire had been crushed or "Lutheranized" because of the immaturity of (according to our taste) objective or subjective conditions. But today we are beginning to suspect that "they" aspired or aspire to a share in social securities; that they wanted or want an empire of the socially insured, stripped of foremen or bosses. Immaturity does not exist because history does not consist of something (men, productive forces) that becomes adult. In each instance, instead, the empire is everywhere as an alternative to the sect, an alternative present in all social bodies including proletarian ones. The empire is the slackening of hope and of the letter's despotism. So, because of all this, I take my place next to you, so that together we may hear the dreadful question common sense poses today: If everything is shared, why the sect? And if the sect is necessary, how will everything be shared? And, in fact, is a *communist plot* not a monster? Something like a *politics of intensities*?

Such is the question, our question, but your question too: the question of paganism. Whatever you may say, you help us to see that at stake in the small or large spasms that traces are is another space, another logic, another history than those to which Platonism and Judaism together have sought and still seek (under the authority of Jacobinism, Leninism, Trotskyism, Maoism, and liberalism) to consign these spasms and so neutralize them. When you call these doctrines apocalypsism, millenarianism, or prophetism, you still concede too much to philosophy, that is, to the empire. It's not enough to claim that the opportunism of Clement of Alexandria or the servility of Eusebius of Caesarea find their (anticipated) critique in the intransigence of the later works of Tertullian, just as Luther finds his despair in the prophetic violence of Münzer. For critique is part of religion and part of the empire. The church and the party welcome our critique, and not merely through concession: critique is the negative moment in their hermeneutics and pedagogy forming the texture of what they call history. It happened that the prophet Bloch was not tolerated by the Stalinist church. But in some other time (that of Moses) or in some other place (the Italian Communist party), he would have been tolerated by such a church, even a Marxist one. What is important is that neither Ernst Bloch's nor Thomas Münzer's effectiveness may be detected by its relationship to a center alone, even if that center is antagonistic. This effectiveness also derives from altogether independent traces.

The logic and space-time of these traces elude the categories of the center. They belong to paganism: to theatrical theology, polytheism, sensualism; to the sophistics of *kairos*; to *virtù* without a judge. And you present it perfectly, you who go back from Münzer to the paganism of Tauchelm and descend from Münzer again to that of Jean de Leyde in Münster.[21] You, who construct a composite drawing of the anchorite by superimposing an image of Protagoras onto that of Augustine.[22] You who, above all, stress *a contrario* how close paganism is to the Münzerian (and, may I to add, Blochian) experience when you must establish no less than three criteria to try to separate the Baptist inspiration from what you dare call the "false enthusiasm" of Dionysus.[23] I repeat, it is the prophetic enthusiasm that we find suspect today. Today, we know that all piety, of the Judeo-Christian type at least, is pregnant with a church. Today, we gladly credit Münzer, not with having enriched and continued to enrich our capital of hope, but with being the name of a singular trace to which we acquiesce, as you did. It is only in the space-time and in the logic of traces that decadence can be turned back.

With this peroration, the youth regained consciousness. Everyone thought he would do well to read Bloch.

Translated by Mira Kamdar

9

False Flights in Literature

A project would consist in discussing the perversion of the book. Michel Butor's entire work, especially since *Mobile*,[1] must be associated with the work of hundreds of biblioclasts like Dieter Roth, Bruno Lemenuel, Michel Vachey, Humbertus Gojowczyk, the John Cage of *Silence* and *A Year from Monday*, or all those who want to write in space, like Sonia Delaunay with her great scroll in Blaise Cendrars's *Prose of the Trans-Siberian*.[2] These associations are important from the point of view of intensities. What happens when you biblioclasts start treating the surface of inscription, a surface that is precisely what is repressed in writing, especially since the advent of industrial printing?

And to dramatize matters, Butor is an old friend of Klossowski, and Klossowski says: "my syntax is Roberte's skin." *My syntax*, and not the support for my writing or its eventual printing. And *Roberte's skin* is the skin enclosing the volume of a discrete body carrying a proper name. Now isn't what Klossowski expresses here perversion? The hardness, the tension of grammar and glossary operate like the production of a screen stretched to the breaking point. This screen closes upon itself into a voluminous body— the body *of* Roberte—and this body can be connected to a subject who will inhabit its interior. Thus any fixed variation of grammar, of glossary will produce a sign, a shiver, a passing of intensity upon the body proper of the victim. This fixed variation is not necessarily aggression or rather Sadian experimentation: it allows *all* experimentations, for grammatical skin gives change for any patches that are clipped out of it, living change, almost. Setting the stage for what he calls the instrument [*suppôt*], the internal volume of the subject, is it not true that Klossowski's syntactic tension paves the way to all perversion? Does it not do so since it constitutes the supposed body, the imaginary body that will serve as reference for a vain use—a use that destroys intense emotions?

Moreover, speaking in a literary manner (and totally contrary to what Butor does), does this tension not call for the occlusion of the book's material support, of its pages, and therefore for the maintenance of literature and its laws? You biblioclasts cannot make collages-montages out of Sade's texts. Like Klossowski, Sade requires the alternation between cold theoretical discourse and the *tableau vivant*. The book indiscriminately serves as a vehicle for both. It is not itself a libidinal object: it is the procurer, the "go-between"[3] for passions and reasons. How would devastating intensities remain if the laws of the book were corrupted, undone; if the readable arrested the gaze? The work upon the support, the loosening of syntax and glossary (apparent . . . apparent) eliminates the very possibility of imagining an instrument [*suppôt*]. In fact, we cannot even imagine a story, the reference to an individual, to a law, that could undergo the abomination of libidinal experimentation or become its accomplice: victim, prostitute, libertine. Thus we are destined to be not in the coldness (yet too intense) of the discourse and pamphlets of *Philosophy in the Bedroom*, but rather, apparently, in a sort of thermal indifference, in the grayness of extinguished or sublimated passions.

The book's perversion then has two meanings:

1. The book is deviated from its effaced function as messenger; emphasis is placed on contact and the support ensuring contact; the entire tradition of rubbing out the conditions of (pictorial or literary) creation or production, and thus also, and at the same time, of the so-called referential (Jakobson) function of discourse (as well as of the image), are at least put into question, if not interrupted. The book-object surges forth as a surface that hides, designates, and even signifies nothing. This surface begins to have worth in an altogether different way. There is thus an initial perversion in the deviation of the book's function or in the displacement of its diverse functions.

2. The book itself becomes the victim or the accomplice of the libidinal operations that, instead of being inscribed in absentia upon the reference of a narrative, upon its diegesis, upon an imaginary body (even the body of the story), are carried out upon the pages, the typography, the spaces, the page composition, and the organization of the volume. All this will be displaced, stirred up, put into movement, almost set to flight, so as to allow for strange and extremely refined intensities that emanate from the encounters of marks (letters and their bodies, spacings, typographical justifications, sentences, words) on the skin of the book. The "volume" ceases to be thick: its surface is no longer there to open up an "inner" space, a theater, Roberte's body. It is but one piece of a single, immense surface extending well beyond the pages of the book, to the fingers that leaf through it, to the optic nerves that decipher it, to the tympanum that vibrates at hearing it read, to the paths upon which it is carried.

The instrument, or the body proper, is no longer Roberte's body, but only a fragment of that great skin to which the writer (Butor, Vachey) subjects unpleasurable caresses, torments, abominations, and pleasures of all kind. But what is it? What body? Whose body? Who, or rather what, feels pain and pleasure from this concrete poetry? What in Mondrian's or Rothko's abstract painting? What in Henri Pousseur's or Mauricio Kagel's music? Does this question still mean anything? Is it not, precisely, the function of this apparatus of abstraction (or concretion—it's the same) that takes the support (and no longer the represented) for its libidinal object *to eliminate the question of the subject* of desire, to elude pain and *jouissance*, to forsake them in what those who fancy themselves as tough call "formalism." With the disappearance of Roberte's body, Octave's is elided also. And then where is there room for coming [*où est-ce que ça jouit?*]?

The extent to which this is a problem of representation is, once again, readily apparent, except for the fact that the problem should be expressed in terms of libidinal energy. And also the study has gone off in a bit different (shall we say preparatory?) direction.

THE CUT CONFESSION

A book-loving antique dealer named Eckerlein discovered a little volume entitled *The Cut Confession* (last edition: 1739), "confected by the Reverend Father Christophe Leuterbreuver," a Franciscan. Its full title is: *The Cut Confession or The Easy Method for Preparing Oneself for Particular and General Confessions*. On page 44, the Franciscan friar provides these details concerning the utilization of this object:

> We have already said that in order to make use of the following examination, one must mark the sins one has committed by taking a small knife or even a pin and scraping the ends of the lines corresponding to one's sins, each of which are enclosed between two black lines, and cut at the end of the line. Once the entire Examination is read through, it is of those sins which rise up out of the line which one must accuse oneself.

This is enough to make us think that here is the first object-book, here is the first mobile printed object, here is the first open work, the first collage-book. It is surely not the first example of all these. There are, however, some interesting points here: the obvious use of scissors and paste on the page, the combinatory choice left to the sinner or "reader" to organize the strips of words according to the level of his pathos, the cancellation of one combination once it is confessed, and the return to an earlier state. Thus there is a noticeable erasure whose value lies in an exoneration of sins, a redemption, as well as an endless confession, endless *poetry*, complete enumeration, through listing, of every sin that can be committed; that is, an accounting of principal intensities. In each of these points you recognize a theme, or rather an instrumental practice, familiar to Michel Butor.

In addition, the Franciscan addresses a meditation to the penitent sinner consisting of a valorization of the state of penitence with respect to that of innocence. Here is the argument:

> [A] converted sinner is, in any case, more estimable because he is more rare. But if I further say to you, as proof of this truth, that penitence is much more unpleasant than innocence, may I not hope that you will enter into my feeling! With innocence there is, in fact, neither movement nor change (and I compare it to rest and inaction), whereas penitence marks a difference in the state of grace as prodigious as that, in nature, between the weight of a large stone and the lightness of an atom. And do not get it into your head that I am holding up a paradox to you, for it will be found that nothing is more similar than these two differences when it be pondered that a sinner is meaner and harder than a stone, and that, when he has become penitent, he is lighter than an atom.

If penitence is wonderful, it is because it is an alteration in scale, perhaps even an altered state: that of something big into an atom, from the molar to the molecular, from heavy to light fluid, from sadness to joy, from fall (Niagara) to ascent. It is thus *extreme mobility in place*, a nearly mad, incomprehensible voyage that affords pleasure and gaiety together.

Now, this itinerary going nowhere, this nearly vain gaiety deriving solely from an alteration leading from the state of being European to that of being Egyptian, from that of man to that of primate, from white man to Indian, from Parisian to suburbanite or provincial, this gaiety through lightness and miniaturization, this extreme mobility in place, is obviously at the heart of Michel Butor's work, where it is, as in *The Cut Confession*, associated with a sort of redemption.

Thus Butor's work is a "cut confession," an instrument confected by a powerful redemptive organization (for example, the Franciscan *order*: "*I am a mendicant monk*," a *church*). This instrument proceeds from an accounting of all libidinal events. It helps you biblioclasts to survey your body of suffering and of *jouissance*. It is a guide that will help you to transform your indignation at the scandal of your own obscurity into a luminous empire, as Butor tells Georges Charbonnier:

> Ideally, of course, each one of us would rediscover the empire of words, the totality of that empire would become visible to us once more, we could stroll inside that empire, become once again luminous, altogether luminous. And a luminous empire of words implies that all reality would be luminous and that, consequently, we would know what we want.[4]

Imagine if you wrote "sins" [*maux*] instead of "words" [*mots*] how all the little strips would be raised on end; all the sins confessed; all the words to confess them found, known; all the regions of desire discovered, explored, restored to a cartography.

So the empire has become luminous; that is, there is now an empire where before there was only unworthy and scandalous obscurity, inanity such that its elements could only be toted up in the nearly monstrous form of a list ("nearly monstrous" because it is not yet what speaks, not yet an utterance). *List* derives from a Germanic word (*lista*) meaning *edge* or *band*. The list is the luminous imperial system's edging: an impossible place (an edge is unthinkable: it is that by means of which one thinks) where what the empire will compose and what the confessor will cause to speak are held in reserve. The list is the edge where the intelligent empire runs up against stupidity. With all the little strips raised on end, you have become an atom of lightness. But, make no mistake, you are under surveillance so you may be synthesized into molecules, organisms, works; into an empire, a celestial Jerusalem; into an *other* city in which desires are put in order, harmonized, and become Fourierist.

Where is the perversion of this adventure of the cut? On the contrary, is it not *conversion*, repentance, edification, apprenticeship, *Bildung* instead? For the very reason that it prohibits any crossing toward an opaque body of Roberte, any projection or any transference, isn't all this work on the support of writing profoundly edifying, didactic?

> There is most certainly a progression within the work. Inside any work whatsoever, the mode of reading is subject to a progression. Every work is didactic in this regard. Every well-made work is a work made to help us read it, in which things are arranged in such a way as to enable us to read it more and more.[5]

PAIN AND REDEMPTION

One must not, however, be taken in by such pedagogical simplicity. Butor must be understood in terms of the category of duplicity. There is a *pain*. In the "beginning"—that is, all the time one is writing (all the time) there is a pain.

> The fact of writing is, for me, a positive equivalent of suicide, that is, a close relationship exists between death and inspiration. I write so that I won't die, so that I won't cause myself to die. A writer speaks to us from the other side of death.[6]

All right! Is there some way one may determine or qualify this event of death, this encounter? Yes: in answer to Charbonnier, here are Butor's words, beautiful words, for which Charbonnier gives him the cue:

M. B.: There are, in fact, moments where one feels like fading away, moments in which the spectacle of society and the world around us seems sufficiently beautiful for us to be inclined . . . we, you understand, who are a place, a piece that plays . . .

G. C.: That plays in excess!

M. C.: Yes, we have the impression of being a piece in excess. That's where the temptation to suicide comes in. But out of all this, writing allows us to regain a grip.[7]

The pain is obviously being in excess, extraneous, vain, stupid. Klossowski, as you know, ends up naming what Nietzsche called superhuman beings in precisely this way: "extraneous humans." This expression designates those who accept and wish for their inanity and their own dispossession, only because they always find that the "world" is beautiful enough as it is, and that we need only to affirm it. (But is this really the world? Or is it something else altogether: a surface scanned by fluxes from without? Is not to utter "the world" to anticipate the cure we already seek?) In any case, here, in a flash of great pain, Butor senses himself to be this extraneous man. Note, however, that this flash is constant, that is, constant threat and anguish. And he does not tolerate this (in fact intolerable) excess: he writes it, "regains a grip" on it:

> As soon as I start writing, I reverse the situation. And I say, "Yes, this world is beautiful. Yes, this society has all sorts of qualities. But it is not beautiful *enough*." And we will always have all sorts of reasons for not finding the spectacle around us sufficiently beautiful to keep us quiet. It is not sufficiently beautiful.[8]

The pain is thus the inanity, the bestiality of *jouissance* and of the death that it carries with it. The therapy consists in the reversal of the relationship of forces: the power of I in place of the strength of Id.

You may say no, not power, but instrument for redemption: Christ rather than Caesar. Indeed all instrumentality, the nearly mad dimension of it may be found in Butor. He is shocked by the paucity of means before the dark continent; he wants recourse, heavy-handed means; he wants to capitalize on the means of knowing how to articulate the obscure. Michel Vachey said that "the negative blows its horn"[9] in Butor's work. The negative occupies precisely the place of the instrument's category, the means (of production)— what Hegel, in an early text (the Jena *Realphilosophie I*), called *die Mitte*, the medium, the place of mediation. This is a power in conflict with itself, said Hegel, and such is the power of the means [*die Mitte*]. Now, the primary figure of the medium [*Mitte*] is the name: "to grant a name is the right of majesty," says Hegel. But in its singularity, this name is destined to perish: "*language eliminates the singular proferred name.*" Through language we leave singularity, involving it in a network of ungraspable, impalpable, perpetual deferral. We move toward the universal. The same applies to the other figures of the medium: the work and the instrument. Like memory, they are powers of annihilation, but of restrained annihilation: work destroys its material as it destroys the need at its inception, while preserving them in this nothing that is the tool (the zero).

Thus we escape pain and death through extraneousness, excess, inanity, and headless stupidity by becoming a good "stiff," a conservative "stiff," a technological museum of the world and of pathos. The project becomes one of putting the pathetic in place of singular pathos, transforming the fullness of great pain as stupidity or madness under the grand domination and power of the intelligible (Butor says so: "either I write or else it's the psychiatric hospital for me"). The "luminous empire of words" comes to raise up all the areas of the libido, dismembered, atomized, cut up, and shattered as they are. Heading off in search of these words in pieces, pieces broken even into smaller bits, these scraps, no matter how far off they are, and accounting for them, then composing them to make "the world" more beautiful—rearranging it, reproducing it—turning himself into the means of production and of reproduction for the more beautiful to come, capitalizing, but in order to give, Butor is the philanthropic banker of language, the Carnegie of words.

Thus we may clearly see that all this work of flattening, then of recomposing through meticulously composed and in no way fortuitous collages, is *an enterprise of redemption*, as was the Roman empire with Caesarism-Papism. And this is manifest in the découpage and surgery (performed upon fields of words, colors, anatomies, typographies, durations), the general deboning of bodies (institutions, cultures), the delineation of inventories, repertories, enumerations of all objects and speech instruments (which amount to the same thing). This delineation is something like that of boxes that are not mystery houses but the shop-windows of ethnographic museums or exploratoriums, sometimes reminiscent of the little mythologies of a Boltanski.

TEMPTATION

Levinas speaks of the temptation of temptation. With Butor there is a whole style of temptation; I would even go as far as to say that his is *the very style of temptation*. It consists in advancing as far as possible into sin (and sin is self-pluralizing or, worse than that, it is amnesiac singularity). It is to want something just once and then to want it over and over again. Temptation is thus advancement as far as possible into headless singularity, to cut up and dissociate its things and elements, words and elements of words. To lose our head? No, not quite. It is having the wherewithal to lose it: letting it lose itself only to recover it, to save it. Once again we have the dialectic of sin and penitence. What could be more beautiful than a penitent sinner? Certainly not an innocent. It is necessary and right that there be no innocent one.

If taken together, all Butor's books are a great *Cut Confession* in which the ecclesiastic draws up the inventory, the repertory of all sins; then just imagine him probing all possibilities, scrutinizing loins and heads, deploying and stretching out the libidinal band where everything can be invested, turning himself into a sinner in mind, and maybe even in practice (as long as he maintains in mind all reserve), experimenting everywhere, upon all surfaces, regions, positions, times of desire in order to draw up the inventory and obtain the admission. "One says: 'In the end I'll force you to confess.'"[10] Not that what is admitted to is "evil" (for nothing is evil), but because something better exists. And that something is to utter, to reconstruct this clutter, this chaos, this vain death, this horrible excess in a confession. All the cutting and découpage is, thus, far from constituting an abandonment to stupidity, to magnificent headlessness, to the will to power, affirmation, and dispossession, the vain desire of intensities. Using the cutter becomes an edifying, that is, nihilist activity: "the world" was not well tailored; let's re-tailor it; let's make it more aesthetic. Let's take it in without adding a lining [*redoublons-le sans le doubler*], but by setting it free from its double in the meantime.

In the beautiful text, *Intervalle*, Butor writes:

And yet, if it be true that there have been other times, other places, a few moments that have allowed one to expect something else, if it be true that even now there are, fleetingly, other times and other places, is there truly today a single region whose view is not hindered by obscurity or the stench of some cross? In their darkness, messages continue to move along nerves, blood continues to circulate through arteries and veins, nearly immobile muscles (traversed, except for the labial and ocular muscles, only by convulsions) continue to cloak and conceal from their flesh the memento which, within each of our bodies, tirelessly and vainly murmurs to our ears (deafened by silent life) the teachings of defunct nature [*nature morte*], our inner hanging victim, our stifled double, continues to release from its atrocity, news continues to expect its readers, and inventions their beneficiaries.[11]

The present is horrible but it secretes its own overturning.

If this little work makes it, distantly, to happier times . . . , it will be because it contributed, in some way, to the abolishment of this horrible today (yes, horrible, in spite of its good moments, in spite of the continual promises of its worst moments, or by virtue of them), because it protected you against its return, as so many other works protect us against the return of the even more horrible yesterday: the glands of the present moment tirelessly distilling a few drops of paradise. In the bathyscaphe of these words, you will plunge into our night of expectancy, you will drink of its aged alcohol that will lend you courage in your own night which we find so luminous. In the intervals between my paragraphs, I make out your expressions of pity.[12]

To write is to plot the overturning of the horrible present. "I believed, yes, I believed that (infinitesimally, of course) the destiny of the world depended on the fact that I write. And I confess that when I am in the deepest recesses of the prisonhouse of my writing, I always believe this."[13] Apparently far from Butor, true paganism, if it ever really existed, contains no notion of any double to free, any mask to remove. "In constituting his characters, every writer throws off masks that have accumulated over his face. The writer seeks his own nakedness."[14] If difference is what repeats itself, then it is not in the current sense of repetition, that of the same. The double, of course, is still the same; even the improved double is the same with new features, as the oak is essentially the same as the acorn. In true paganism, even plurality does not exist: just singularities, proper names, and lots of masks that mask nothing, but that do indicate intensities.

In Butor, as in the case of the Franciscan friar, mobility is collected into an advent. Transparency, which is an extreme case of mobility, is also collected, conquered. Secondary school students said to Butor, in a discussion following a reading of *Niagara*,[15] that at first they were shocked, but then quickly noticed that there was some unity to it. And when one of the young students asked Butor, "Why does one hear crying and groans?" Butor, in substance, answered: "Niagara is a fall; it is suffering, sin, paradise lost—I must also place that in my composition, have it in my register."

Thus we see the function of labor: shattering and enumeration as approaches to sinful atomism, as temptation; composition and (mathematical) organization as relief, redemption, advent. None of this, however, is in the work's themes, but rather in its productive procedures—that is, perversion and conversion.

ENCOUNTER WITH ENCOUNTER

Let us start out again from pain, from *jouissance*-death. It appears as a theme in *Passage de Milan*[16] in the form of Angèle's death. It is an equivocal scene, over in a flash, a sort of primal scene, an impossible accident, sexual attack. Here is what Butor says to Charbonnier about it:

> There aren't many deaths in my books: it's difficult for me to kill my characters. But I killed [Angèle] without any great regret. Why so? Because in a way she incarnated all the festivity possible in that apartment building. But for me, in order to reach a true festivity, it was necessary to leave that building. Also that young girl's death is a sort of great erasure: you see, it's a big X, a big white or black line (whichever you prefer); it's the cross, the cross formed by the kite's shadow [*l'ombre du milan*], the X

that comes and obliterates everything. Perhaps her death is not sufficiently justified, but that's unimportant since her death must, in a way, come from outside. Once she is dead, this whole world (which, in a way, is my whole childhood) is obliterated. Once that's done, this world must be studied and then one must depart and do something else.[17]

The killing of a young girl is thus necessary in order to begin writing and to leave for Egypt (Louis, the witness who is in love with her, flees there), for another festivity. Angèle's death opens up the Indian space.

But this "Indian space" is neither nature nor a true exteriority: where a theater is possible, there is no nature, there are only cultures. Angèle's death destroys Roberte's skin. It is not life—the other festivity—that is encountered in Egypt, but, once again, death. It consists in the other death complementing Angèle's death, a naked space—yet still a worked space, a networked space, another side of the same surface. We can thus not be Egyptian or Indian; we cannot be a woman, but must be an ethnologist. And ethnology is duplicity, perversion in the sense of duplicity: to save "savagery" threatened by dissolution and to abolish it even further by saving it, by lending order to it:

> as I began to become Egyptian myself, sufficiently steeped in these dissonances to find that I too was faced with an imperious need to attenuate them, to introduce a little order and clarity in the menacing confusion, to become a little better acquainted with the terrain where there was a devastation taking place in which I myself had a hand ineluctably,
>
> the need, consequently, to situate correctly in relation to one another the dissociated elements whose shreds were all I could see in Minya.[18]

Thus Egypt is yet to be written, the dark continent to be transformed into an empire of words.

The same pain of dispossession, of uselessness, the same anguish of vain *jouissance* is encountered once again on the Egyptian surface and will motivate the same compulsion for expropriation [*emprise*], for empire. The Minya hashish experience:

> but as far as I'm concerned, I know very well that as soon as these effects began to wear off, what immediately invaded me was a feeling of discontent and frustration, because I should have been able to experience this beauty, this emotion, even without the power of this weed,
>
> (I was in the middle of the Valley at night, we were returning on foot to Minya), but it was impossible for me to judge to what extent exactly,
>
> because that beauty, as a consequence, far from having been given to me as I had had the illusion it was, all of a sudden had been denied me, whereas I could have attained it,
>
> because I was obliged to mark those few hours, despite their radiance, which endures even today, with a symbol of doubt, just as one marks an uncertain passage in a text with an obelus.[19]

There is thus no place where one might dispense with lending order. Dangerous rites where young girls die are everywhere; everywhere are unbearable intensities *to save*. There is no place (*where* [*où*] is reduced to *either* [*ou*]); illustrations refer only back to themselves. There are no things themselves any more than there are any individuals themselves.

What is thus encountered? What is encountered is the encounter. Such is the function of surface networks, the secret concerning the valorization of the plastic or graphic support, the promotion of the skin to the rank of ultimate agency. Networks are not there merely to lend order, but to allow self-referential fleeting encounters to occur. There are only cities, and this is the theme of the *Aleph* interview. The world is a city, the city is a book, the book is a world-city;[20] a city insofar as it is an incompossible coexistence of heterogeneous spaces-times: a city as intolerable unconscious. And then the flight begins—the voyage as flight before encounters. The flight takes place toward the vanishing point at the end of the railroad tracks, the air terminal hallways, the typographical lines, Mondrian's rectangles, Schoenberg's serial technique, the cannons in Bach's *Musical Offering*. Flight, the flight along mountain paths of Nijinsky gone mad. Aimless flight. A dead girl in a dirty Parisian tenement in the outer districts—thus a short, intolerable pain; a both sleezy and exalted intensity; a cross between a sadistic crime and an appalling accident; an encounter become event; and then, suddenly, "Louis," that is, "Butor," off on the voyage-flight to encounter all that can be encountered.

This voyage-flight is the voyage that encounters nothing, nothing but encounters. It goes nowhere, yet nothing and no one can stop it. It is not even a route. It is the agitation both consecutive to and contemporaneous with pain, and it conveys pain so as to try and bind it. These networks are traces of pain. And at the same time, they form the net in which we seek to trap it, to bind, calm, distract, divert it, to form it: *Bildung*. Butor-Meister's years as apprentice. But this apprenticeship is interminable: a mendicant monk he is, and one prone to false flights (that lovely expression!). Nothing is meant by the fact that the narrative agency who is the presumed subject (is it Butor?) learns from this apprenticeship about the ways of the world-book opened by means of an inane pain. And it should mean nothing in particular or in general. The narrative agency learns the dissolution of things and subjects by itself. It learns its own pain and its own *jouissance*.

That is why "I hate Paris" and "I flee from it" means *I love Paris* and *I return to it*.

TRANSPORTS

Here we must blunder forward. In Butor's work there is an enormous deployment of culture in which he himself sometimes believes. This culture can make him seem like a mandarin; it can induce people to say that he is becoming a classic, an immortal in his own time, and give rise to this pretension to the position of magister. Now to limit ourselves to this deployment is to fall into its trap (and this happens as often to Butor himself as it does to us who read him). Butor sometimes takes himself and has himself taken for the presumed knowing subject, or for what amounts to the same thing, the *luminous continent* (which is nevertheless to be illuminated). But I tell you this: just as he hates and flees a Paris that he returns to, he hates and flees the locus of university knowledge while at the same time teaching in universities all over the world, and he hates and flees literature much more than most writers, while continuing to write. Profound hatred and flight, both in love with what they fear: temptation.

It is thus not really an edifying *Bildung*; it isn't even the object of Butor's work. Yet in affirming this, I must run counter to practically all Butor's consistently edifying statements: art as craftwork, bread on the table for a hundred years, work as hard labor, saving the world, and making it more transparent; and the whole technology of the artwork, the immense bricolage-découpage-collage, how he works, the finished product.[21] And, more generally, as the character is affirmed and identified with the narrative agency (who believes he is "unveiling himself"), there is a sort of self-identification, a strange monumentalization of that thing he knows better than any other to be impossible: a writer.

This successful apprenticeship, this knowledge and know-how, this mastery, this appropriation is precisely that of what Butor speaks, or rather, that which he cannot do otherwise than to speak and carry out. There is something like that imperious and imperial dimension of composition in Schoenberg's sense: the power of the director of stage, sounds, words, and colors, stretched to the limit.

This could foster an initial suspicion. As with Schoenberg, power affirmed in this manner, with this obviousness, this provocative transparency, shuns the established order. This is the overarching theme, the critical and provocative function of Butor's work. But it is not critical in the sense that he becomes the "critic" of great writers in order to criticize what he himself does in light of their works. Rather, this function is critical in the sense that the découpage, collage, and montage of fragments taken from the world-book act immediately as critique upon received arrangements (book and world are received) and as exhibition of the work of writing itself. This composer's power persists, but as enormity—outside the norm. The whole course of his work is but a succession of breaks with received literary models. Butor himself says: "my books are critical objects." However, I wonder if that's really where the essence lies. Or is this rather Schoenberg's ambiguity as revealed by Adorno, the ambiguity of Breton's surrealism as revealed by Artaud.

I think the important thing is not critique, at least not *text*ructive critique. What is important is substitution, the series of displacements that reveal the great equivalences: libidinal locus → earth → book. The resulting surface is not a locus, but rather (already like the Parisian tenement) a city of insane organs functioning outside the regime, a one-sided strip upon which libidinal intensities travel. Butor's displacements are transports engendering this strip and its intolerable pain-*jouissance*. These displacements reveal the fact that the strip includes, may include, or rather *adjoins*[22] all spaces-times: not only that of the rape and death of a beloved girl, but also other incompossibilities every bit as intolerable encountered in Egypt, in the United States, in *Remembrance of Things Past*, between Mondrian and Rothko, and so on.

Thus the strength of the voyage is not really critique, but flight, scanning, wild plotting, the engendering of a single surface: Angèle's skin, a tenement, the land of Egypt, English weather/time, a train to Rome, the grid of America . . .[23]

CAESARISMS

As another point of departure, let us once again use the death of Angèle. It is a Caesarean death—Butor's political nucleus. It produces a Caesar—Butor is a Caesar—and Kyril Ryjik says that *Caesar is dual*. There is the disseized Caesar who has taken flight upon the libidinal body rediscovered in Egypt, the Caesar who, there in Egypt, reencounters what he had fled illicitly once outside the primal belly: *jouissance* and death, supreme pain. This is a frightened Caesar, hunted and fleeing upon the surface of a land that is like a Möbius strip all crumpled, invaginated, full of folds, provincial investments, streams without depth—Rubicons and Brittanys, Niagaras and Koreas. This is the aleatory Caesar. But there is also the awesome Caesar of the *Commentaries*, of the *mens*, of the spirit that claims to be in society with itself, Shakespeare's Caesar whom Brutus must kill, the composing Caesar who wishes to project that terror, that Caesarian he carries inside in the form of powerful contrivances for domination—instruments, forms, imperial expropriations.

From this we get cuttings spread out everywhere: découpages, crafted and mobile postcards, collages and montages, the world refigured as emperor, and the interminable imperial-imperialist succession, which—beginning with Caesar, through the popes, old Vienna, the City of London, and the Berlin of the last Reich—leads us to Washington, the center of all empires, and to Butor's admirable description of it in *Mobile*.[24] From one obelisk to another . . . That description of Washington is admirable precisely because it is carried out as if between the two Caesars: the one Caesar who, crazed with painful *jouissance*, has taken flight, is the Indian who gazes with intractable humor (a Jewish, Czech, Kafkaesque humor, the humor of he who is crushed and overwhelmed by the law, of the Indian creating the impossible ethnology of the white ethnologists), that Indian who gazes at the criss-crossed monument centered upon him and formed by the intersection of lines described by White House–Jefferson and the Capitol–Lincoln. Caesar the dispossessed, the fugitive, admirably describes the Eternal Rome of Caesar the owner and the master; the outlaw describes the legislator who exiles him. And yet the two are one and the same.

The angel-like quality in Fourier: a *white* relationship from which spring all the others . . . And, simultaneously, Fourier's imperialism and what Butor says about it: a *steadfast* prince was needed—Caesar. Angèle's death announces that supreme folly, the conquest of Egypt which is, no doubt, the essence of the political. Egypt is the dark continent. Freud said that the Wolf Man's unconscious was like Egypt: all civilizations impossibly coexist there, no investment is renounced. Fantastic paradox, paragram. Caesar the Younger is the libidinal paragraphy, almost an *anti*graphy. One page by Butor is this paragraphy, this mumbling, these incompossible and tearing (or cutting) intensities, the Vachey strain of biblioclasm. Caesar the emperor (Butor the writer, the composer) strives to unify this. He desires the unity of these places, their assembling and religion. The strategist, the despot, he who wants death (Angèle's death, his own death, the Indians' death) to bear fruit, wishes to make these places confess, to fold back everything upon some great zero point at the center of Rome or Washington that the vanquished Egyptians and Indians meant to say but have not yet said; to make them speak. That is why the question, from Caesar's point of view, is not to dare speak or to dare make someone speak, but rather to know how to speak and to know how to make someone speak:

M. B.: There is a dual scandal, a dual indignation. An indignation that comes from what I see. I see that there is something that should be spoken about, but is not. If things are deep enough in importance, one may come to the point of saying that if it is not spoken about, then it is because we don't know how. Something is missing.

G. C.: "We don't know how" or "we don't dare"?

M. B.: Some things we don't dare to talk about, but what is worse is what we don't know *how* to talk about.[25]

The confessor, the inquisitor, who, like Father Leuterbreuver in *The Cut Confession*, will be the provider, the prompter of the words and the grammar necessary for it to speak. And the instrument for speaking?—dictionary + torture = school.

RELIEF AND RETRACTION

Butor's voyage is thus the very voyage of libidinal duplicity—flight and conquest. Flight, physical features, liquid and sonorous volumes, and perhaps even generalized relativity, the absence of a central observation point, of a Washingtonian obelisk from which all this movement could be thought, weighed, measured. And then, vertigo: the possibility of a delirium caused by the loss of referents (if, of course, relativity is understood in this way). If it is understood this way, then forging on to singularity is necessary, of abandoning the plurality of atomized crowds, the plurality of leaders of the masses. We must indeed forge on to the proper name, not to the sign of something, but the sign as a transfer of singular intensities, priceless and without value, strength of pain and of gaiety that dispenses with its insertion into any network, any structure, any grid (that is, any police-state), in order to confess its meaning. This strength has nothing to confess and no meaning because it *has* nothing. It can only be affirmed as a tensor, an intensity, a sudden, random, *lost* incandescence. The flight leads toward that region pointed to in the "Little Liturgies" of *Illustrations III*. In this regard one should wonder whether Vachey's or Dieter Roth's cutter or Gojowczyk's burnings are not allusions that are yet too strong to order. In music, Dieter Schnebel's *Atemstücke* rather than Pousseur's works comes to mind, or else, of course, those big happenings by John Cage and David Tudor like *Mural Plus Rain Forest*.

Will Butor-Caesar of Egypt now take that route? Will he get rid of the imperial, papal, Jesuit, constructivist, and Bolshevik tradition? Will he switch from Schoenberg to Cage, that very poor and brilliant student of Schoenberg? I would like to examine a couple of texts from *Illustrations III* in which I think I perceive this movement. These are "Little Liturgies," as Butor puts it in his table of contents, "to hasten the arrival of Jacques Herold's great transparency"—here is "the ventral mirror":

> In the middle of a thick crowd whose elements are squeezed up against one another (the Paris subway at six o'clock in the evening is recommended, but trains or buses in Tokyo will do), attentively observe a woman's belly, imagine her skin, her genitals, shrink down to the appropriate dimensions, place yourself inside her uterus, communicate with her through the placenta which she has formed, reverse the current of time, relive within her the orgasm of your origin, make her young again, go back through the phases of her childhood, of her birth, place yourself within her mother's uterus, go back through the phases of her childhood, of her birth, and so on back to primitive man, back to primitive vertebrates, back to the unreachable beginnings of the world,
> or else (if you are a woman, this is probably what you would do first): attentively observe a man's belly, imagine his skin, his genitals, shrink down to the appropriate dimensions, place yourself inside one of his testicles, accelerate the course of time, flow into the belly of his wife, embrace the ovule, grow, be born his son, grow up, go through puberty, fall in love, tremble with desire, flow with him into the belly of another

woman, be born the grandson of the man you observe, grow up, and so on in the endless consumption of the centuries.

While making love, pursue the two voyages simultaneously, Every detail realized increases the vivacity.[26]

And here is the "Little Liturgy" entitled "the cerebral grotto":

During a mountain excursion, select a boulder whose parts shall be identified with those of your own body (anatomical knowledge will be of great help here: future transparency being dependent on detail in this operation). Now take a knife to chisel in the location of the mouth, separate the stone lips, insert the blade between your teeth, try to un- clench the lips while clenching those kept in your former head. Retract the latter, making it sink into the shoulders, sliding along the inside of the arm, traversing the skin of the palm, into the blade, blending with the sharp edge. Once it penetrates the opening, the whole opening is illumin- ated by applause. All the rest of the anterior body follows like an arm turned inside out. Finally comfortable in your own head, animate, by manipulation, the crystals which each command a specific region, verify and correct their placement; move on, using slight vibrations, from pro- jection to bas-relief, make it rise like dough in an oven; then, as high relief, break loose, leaving behind a new skin of stone, indiscernible from the old one. Take up the trail again.[27]

These texts are not without Caesarisms: *every detail realized*, *increases*, and yet *vivacity*, take up the trail, shrink down, *retract . . .*

And, moreover, there is voyage of conquest. Everybody knows this Butor of the conquest: he's the one studied by colloquia, Butorologists, structural- ists, and thesis writers; he's the one who is the subject of the baccalaureat exams. But this is also Fourier's Butor because, in any event, Fourier is only the Caesar-Imperator of libidinal politics. The interview for *Aleph* in 1967, upon his return from Israel, is perhaps clearest with regard to the conquering voyage. Traveling is done with maps, guides, programs, like a general (I recall Borges's story about the emperor who draws up a map of the empire so exact that it overlays it in its every point and the whole country devotes itself to maintaining the map). To travel, documentation is gathered, a system of nets, a poetic machine is woven:

I went about things a bit like an electronic calculator. It would have been very useful if I had had at my disposal a machine! I had to do a machine's work myself, for purely poetic ends.

For me, the earth is like a great dictionary in which there are certain fundamental words: the cities.[28]

The earth is ready for conquest and production, for a dictionary is not a surface of intensities, but the already bureaucratic survey of intensities. It is not the event, but its recording; not the suffering from *jouissif* murder and rape, but its survey (*Aufhebung*! sublation: Egyptian bureaucrat or Roman pontiff's term) . . . just as *The Cut Confession* already places its enumeration, its catalogue of sins between the sinner and the space opened by the narration of the revelation. The earth is ready for conquest, for the use of the great modeling game. The earth, that is language, all languages (and, on the subject of languages, there is always the same hesitation—"Ah, to know them all"; "A good thing, not to know them; rather to know how to play with their very opacity"—to render clarity from their obscurity).

The earth is not a book that would already speak: it is a dictionary—the arrangements remain to be made. It's Napoleon: the institution of codes. We have here the position of the political not as tragedy (as Napoleon wished it to be believed), but as paranoia, as the madness of replacing God or being at his side, the madness of making the world over much more beautifully, of saving it, of cutting it out in another fashion, of arranging it much better. The earth as dictionary, as magazine, as catalogue of what is put into a magazine, as list. And then, after having hatefully forced to confess, to disgorge everything hidden in these lists, with a softly unctuous hatred, once everything is carefully explored, comes the fabrication of beautiful and balanced Fourierist finished products. "But up until now I have not dared to do that. Because up until now I still seek to provide a finished product. Moreover, I already had enough difficulties with the finished product!"[29] Like God, Caesar's body is a finished product; the flight is infinite, but the imperial institution seeks its finitude, its circumscription, its limit. Thus what mendicant Caesar flees, the emperor Caesar will find again on the borders he has erected around his conquests. Once again he will find the threat, the death that appears to come from outside; once again the task of pushing forth this limit, of stretching the border, of beginning to fly forth again in the direction of dark continents: the temptation of Egyptian hashish, of Cleopatra, the regaining of one's grip through imperial writing, and so on in an interminable writing, in an insatiable imperialism that is precisely a fine flight disguised as power.

There is ambiguity in the cutting of *The Cut Confession*. It is the first mobile-book, thus a voyager in its own materiality, but it is the nth edifying, sedentarizing work: it is modern insofar as it is a fluid flight, papist insofar as it is redemptive. This is the ambiguity of perversion itself: the perversion of childhood, errant polymorphy, any erotic plottings whatever upon the libidinal surface, aleatory itineraries of desire; the prostitutive perversion (the Jesuit is a prostitute) of harnessing this errantry and submitting it to an exploitation benefitting some big pimp, or big merchant,[30] benefitting the Caesar-Pope of intensity trafficking. With Caesar, guilt is brought down upon intensities, and thus the displacement of innocence into temptation, into redeemed sin.

By perverting the book at the level of its surface, by making its very surface the support for tracings of intensities, we are heading in the direction of infantile polymorphy. Here, it is against Klossowski that Butor plays, against he who wants to know only of the other perversion: that of the banker of *jouissance*. Inanity of what is written at the surface, disappearance of a reference (*Illustrations*). All that is left are skins and vain spaces.

Only thing is, we compose that skin. We tattoo it in a very classical manner; we sew it back together; we increase its possibilities and the combinations of its possibilities. We become its fashion designer. Then no encounter, with its factual violence, may be encountered. I do not claim that this never happens: if that were the case, no one could write about Butor. Of course this encounter of disseizing intensity occurs: the beauty of the two or three "Little Liturgies," of one or two passages in *Intervalle*, whole pages of *Mobile*. . . . But, in the end, one is compelled to say to oneself: this reaffirmation of pain and *jouissance* is not really there for that, for that flash of beauty. It was put there to match something or another, to occupy a moment in an itinerary. There is a structure. I must discover and grasp it; this organization is everything. (And so on.) That is the second (imperial Jesuit) sense of perversion: these intensities, these sins in which you believe yourself immersed, this bread you eat, these games you enjoy—all of this is composed; it's still God and Emperor stuff; it goes to God-Caesar and it must return to him; it's an effect of despotism. You are deprived of your infantile perversion. The perversion is now that of the master, the educator, the confessor, the composer. You no longer have a right to your childhood; you are guided; you are the victim and the accomplice. Butor's desire is, in any case, to guide you. My wish (that is, my desire) is that he never succeed, that he give infinite/unfinished products, that pain and *jouissance* surface, that he rid himself of glory and despotism, and me, the friendliest of his enemies, along with them.

Translated by Robert Harvey

Part Three

◆

THE INTRACTABLE

10

The Survivor

I shall begin by recalling a few commonplaces—some well-known, others less so—relative to the very principle of what can be considered under a title such as "the survivor." This is necessary in order to clarify how I am approaching the thought of Hannah Arendt. The word *survivor* implies that an entity that is dead or ought to be is still alive. The concept of this "still," a reprieve, a stay of death, brings with it a problematic of time—not just any problematic of time, but one of its relation to the question of the being and non-being of what is. More precisely, of a time in which the entity is in relation with its beginning and its end, in relation with the enigma in which the entity comes to its being as entity and then leaves this being. It is therefore necessarily a double enigma, in that time is twice in relation with "its" non-being: it appears and disappears. But since when the entity is not, it also does not possess "its" non-being (since non-being is non-relation), the enigma to which I refer is that of a relation with what has no relation, that is, with an absolute.

A familiar observation, I dare say. Now to try to be less familiar, we must ask ourselves with respect to which agency the survivor survives. The survivor always survives a death, but the death of what life?

Hegel says that death is the life of the spirit. In phenomenology, spirit does not survive death; it is the sublation of immediate life, and thus spirit is both this life as (past) death *and* life revived and reliving. Spirit lives insofar as it is dead at the very moment that *it was* itself. Constitutively it is in mourning, in Freud's sense of the term. This implies that it is lost to itself insofar as, originally invested in a formation, it objectified that formation in order to know it, insofar as that formation then dies and represents death, and, finally, insofar as by these very facts, spirit returns into itself (narcissism of mourning) through a new formation. Spirit *is* only objectified or invested (this is what an entity is), and the new objectification comprises, contains, conserves the former one, but now fashioned according to the mode of the *no longer*. This mode is that of necessity, or of the third person.

144

The previous formation is no longer alive, the entity that I was can no longer say "I." At this point, I can only speak of it as "it," in the third person. It cannot be other than what it has been (this is its necessity): it is in the state of having been ("being-been," writes Heidegger). Hegel solves this problem with a "we" consisting of him (me formerly) *and* me (now). Such a mysterious *and*.

Let survival be understood (according to this thinking in which nothing is lost) as being yet, as continuing to be, according to modes of power (possibility, ability, eventuality): *event* (something indeterminate still happens, when in fact we should be no longer, not be capable, not be able to stand it any longer.

The Hegelian sublation is that of one mode by another. In a sense, it expresses for thought the paradoxical constitution of the instant: it is not *t*, but always *dt*. Heidegger's *being-been* implies in its determination both that it is no longer and thus could not be other, and that it is the power (the derivative) of another instant (the "following" instant), at which point the being-been will give itself as no longer being.

The mathematical and phenomenological formulation of the instant *dt* thus furnishes an intelligence of survival. What is is alive. Yet, because it contains its own not yet, it is already dead. Time thus provides, at least for the spirit, the foundation of its idea of survival, in the philosophical problematic of spirit or consciousness. In a sense, Husserl's *Retention* holds the whole secret of survival. In the philosophy of ordinary language, time would be considered merely the play of modalities: for example, to *no longer* be capable and to be capable of this *no longer*; impossibility and the possibility of this impossibility.

This time is that of consciousness or spirit, and this survival is its absolute security, just as its death is insured—insured in that it is always a *belle mort*, because it is "retained" in the "we" composed of the now me and the former me.

One question, however, is whether something is not forgotten in this turning back on the no longer, something that therefore does not survive, a remainder that does not remain. What seems as though it must necessarily be lost is the presence then of what is now past. What is now necessary, unchangeable, was, then, contingent. What now has no more power (no more potential), was then power or potential. There is a mortal sadness of the very thing that is retained and transmitted; the sadness of Minerva's owl, of what is bound. The tradition of what was then experienced in the present is its betrayal. The past is betrayed by the simple fact that the present it was is made absent. It lacks a certain mode, the tone of the quick, the lively, even as it is recalled.

In epistemological terms, this can be referred to as its contingency, what Arendt, referring to Kant, calls "desolate contingency." *Desolate* because it is absolutely resistant to the necessitating, universalizing binding through cause and effect. But desolate also in that the singular ontological savor (that taste) of being-there can only be lost to ordinary memory. (Does this savor ever take place? Is it not merely essential that it took place? Does this savor not merely result from the fact of remembering? Is it anything but a result of lack, the result of what memory misses in remembering? Is not every photograph, even a recent one, essentially faded?) The betrayal of the living consists in its being handed over by the survivor. This betrayal is necessary in order for some trace of the old, necessarily altered, "rehashed" present to persist. The witness is always a poor witness, a traitor. But he does, after all, still bear witness.

The question is thus posed within the framework of a philosophy of the subject or of spirit—in a phenomenology. It is the question of the synthesis of time in Augustine, Descartes, Kant, Hegel, Heidegger—the question also of the subject.

We must now observe that if, within this problematic, the life of spirit is designated as a survival, then what is stressed is absence, or that which is lost in what is preserved. The world is gray for Minerva's owl. It is a disaster for Walter Benjamin's Angel, who is pushed backwards into the future by the wind of the past. The Angel sees only disaster in the past, just as the owl is blind to the color of life. The Angel sees the past only as "dis-astered" present. The astral is the tone of the lively. So, the question returns: Was the past really as former present, a disaster? or is it its re-view that dis-asters it? Hegel would affirm the latter; Benjamin, the former. And this makes a difference—all the difference—between the speculative and the post-speculative. In Hegel, mourning gets accomplished; in Benjamin it becomes impossible.

This impossibility of mourning the past presence (and reapplying its force, through new object, to the present self) is called melancholia. If it is not the impossibility of mourning, it is at least a stress placed on the irrevocable loss of presence, that is, on the death of what was there. And along these lines, even what is present now may be sensed as already doomed to no longer being there, becoming the object of a "preventive" melancholia. Is the apparently so lively not already dead?

Birth itself, the beginning, is reckoned, through melancholia, as an illusion. What comes to life—the instant as event, emerging from nothingness—is already doomed to return to nothingness. The only *being*-in-truth is not here. This inversion of appearances can give rise to metaphysics. The eternal present, the living present, is always absent. Being is not entity. This melancholia (which, since Platonism, has been called "Western"—for what reason I do not know) can be found in all thinking when it comes up against its failure, which is also possibility, temporality, modality.

Shunning all entities while remaining melancholic and keeping watch over the perpetual retreat of true being appears to be the way for thought not to betray presence. Series of entities, instants, and instances simply unfold innumerable false births—so many disappearances of the true. Present moments join the ranks of the "unemployed" of presence. A man says to a woman: "No, I don't want a child: he'll just be one more to add to the unemployed." This man expresses melancholia, a lack of faith in the being of being-there. He senses that the transmission, the handing-over of life is the betrayal of truth (which is other than life—"elsewhere"), and he does not want to betray. As for the authentic mode of presence (and who knows what *that* is?), every entity is a survivor.

I will now invert the stress on disappearance. Melancholia omits the other enigma in the relation of the soul with non-being or being: the enigma of appearance. Rather than nothing, being gives entities, instants, objects. Since being appears in "objects," it gets forgotten. Yet it *gives* objects, something *happens*. Expressions like "yet" are concessions to melancholia. But by conceding, of course, I am impugning; or, rather, I am emphasizing the impugnment that exists in melancholia. What melancholia impugns is the fact that there is "nonetheless" something rather than nothing, that this is why there is birth and death, even if the terms are inverted, even if one thinks of every birth as a death, and death as birth into truth.

The impugnment of melancholia or the refutation of nihilism consists solely in this humble question: If the truth is that there is truly nothing, how is it that there appears to be something? Or: Why does truth lie, why does death find itself deferred in birth and life? Even if we agree with the Freud of *Beyond the Pleasure Principle* that the difference between life and death is only one of rhythm (death hurries while life delays), why are there two rhythms? In the thermodynamic terms that Freud inherits from Fechner, why is there differentiation, complexification (neg-entropy), if the physical truth consists in moving to the most probable, simple, undifferentiated state, which is the death of the system (entropy)? This is, of course, only taking one step backward in order to take two forward. But why is it necessary to take two forward? The Freudian hypothesis of Eros is in keeping with the second law of thermodynamics. It still presupposes that complexity is only a simplification in suspense, that life is only a survival.

The fact remains that in examining the enigma of the *sur*-vival, of this *sus*-pense, Freud could never conceive of anything other than an event, whatever the name of that event—and there have been many, for example, the event of sexed reproduction in the history of living things. And in individual ontogenesis, the echo of sexual difference is the event whose savagery the whole life of the individual is unconsciously devoted to "regulating."

But what is this event if we strip it of its scientific or cognitive denomination? It is the enigma of there being a relation with what has no relation; that is, in knowing that it is born and dies, the soul (aptly named) bears witness to the fact that there is not only what is (what it is) but the other of what is. Of course this relation does not take place when it takes place, it has taken place and it *will* take place. Thus, it *will have taken place* all at once, appeared too late, disappeared too soon. And this is because my birth is always only recounted by others, and my death told to me in the stories of the death of others, my stories and others' stories. The relationship with others is, therefore, essential to this relation with the nothingness of its being that is reported to me (whence I come and where I am going), and also essential to the presence of the absence of which the relationship with others (this presence of absence) comes back to me. Essential, too, is the *fabula* to which the pulsation of beginning and end lends rhythm.

I must insist that, if being or nothingness is not the whole of truth, if the event is not entirely a lure, then I declare that the sense of "survival" can be inverted. Complexities, organizations, or orders can be formed, in which a power of arrangement or fashioning is affirmed, or, as Arendt says, the enigmatic faculty of beginning is exercised—a survival that can become truth as well, and alleged life can become the dead survival of that birth. Is this truth a truth of reason? What will be right and will have triumphed over any beginning, any *initium*, is the end and the end of ends, the annihilation of ends. The reason one can *have* or *give* can only reduce the most complex polynomials into the $a = a$ of equality without remainder. This reason will, in the end, deduce and reduce. But something must have raised the question. Perhaps it will be necessary to go to the depths of the last man's nihilism, the man who knows the "banality of evil," who suffers or administers it, or both, to find some *joy* (I am deliberately using Pascal's word, the word of the spirituals), the dark joy of a request made stronger for its being more improbable, and thus more threatened by annihilation and more openly confronted by the truth of nothingness.

In saying this, I do not intend to fall back into the restorative thought of a Hegel. I would simply say, without further explanation, that this thinking about life as enigma of beginning is acceptable only if it is a matter of a scruple, but neither of remission nor of any challenge. The scruple of an *as if*, in which case the mind thrust into the ordeal of nihilism, onto the road to despair and skepticism (which is permanent), knowing that there is nothing to do or say, no valid entity, no entity even which *is*, acts, all the same, as though there were one.

In no way is the effect of this clause cynicism. Cynicism remains derivative of nihilism and perseveres, through its activism, in the melancholia of "nothing is worth it." The effect is neither a *ludic* metaphysics, that is, in which a corpse dons the colors of life in a grimacing and macabre irresponsibility, nor an "artistic" metaphysics of will and values.

The effect is childhood that knows all about *as if*, all about the pain of impotence and the complaint of being too small, of being there late (compared to others) and (as to its strength) of having arrived early, prematurely—childhood that knows all about broken promises, bitter disappointments, failings, and abandonment, but which also knows all about dreaming, memory, question, invention, obstinacy, listening to the heart, love, and real openness to stories. Childhood is the state of the soul inhabited by something to which no answer is ever given. It is led in its undertakings by an arrogant loyalty to this unknown guest to which it feels itself a hostage. Antigone's childhood. I understand childhood here as obedience to a debt (which we can call a debt of life, of time, of event; a debt of being there in spite of everything), a debt for which only the persistent feeling of respect can save the adult from being no more than a survivor, a creature living on reprieve from annihilation.

It is true that one quickly learns that death will forbid paying off the debt, that it will always come too soon, and this alone can make one sink into melancholia or into that wickedness of trying to be the last one to die, as analyzed by Elias Canetti.[1] (I mean even that wickedness required by the will to bear witness, to survive so as to recount.) But childhood consists in the fact of being and acting *as if* one could nonetheless pay off the enigma of being there, as if one could draw interest on the inheritance of birth, of the complex, of the event, not in order to enjoy it, but to transmit it, so that it might be put off, passed on [*remis*]. The drawing of interest on the inheritance of birth thus depends on its constitutive poverty and misery; it is, in other words, like a debt of beginning, the debt of a handing-over (tradition) and of a tradition of the debt. Even the belief that the debt of birth will be paid off by the event of death, that the soul received will be returned, does not stand up to the harshness of a childhood without pity. Its *as if* blocks all righteousness.

How is Hannah Arendt's thought implicated in these few remarks? I am certainly not a judge, as she would have said, to decide this question. Not only because I have not sufficiently dwelt in her work, but because the time I have spent there, although allowing me to recognize something very close to what little I have referred to under the term *survival*, leaves me uncertain nonetheless as to whether I am faithful to her thought. I see three motifs as places to mark that uncertainty: the motifs of birth, tradition, and judgment. These really only constitute one motif, obviously, and I shall not manage to disentangle them properly.

The first motif, birth, concerns precisely the debt that I have just discussed—a debt to the non-being from which an individual has issued and of which childhood (not having asked for anything) is the altogether involuntary witness. It is well known that there is an ontological and historical melancholia at the heart of Arendt's thought. What I have outlined here (with the almost laughably scientific word: entropy) about the truth of non-being as ineluctable death is sometimes modalized by Arendt in related terms. For example, in this passage on "Unpredictability and the Power of the Promise":

> And to a certain extent this is true. If left to themselves, human affairs can only follow the law of mortality, which is the most certain and the only reliable law of a life spent between birth and death. It is the faculty of action that interfaces with this law because it interrupts the inexorable course of daily life, which in its turn, as we saw, interrupted and interfered with the cycle of the biological life process. The life span of man running toward death would inevitably carry everything human to ruin and destruction if it were not for the faculty of interrupting it and beginning something new, a faculty which is inherent in action like an ever-present reminder that men, though they must die, are not born in order to die but in order to begin. Yet just as, from the standpoint of nature, the rectilinear movement of man's life-span between birth and death looks like a peculiar deviation from the common natural rule of cyclical movement, thus action, seen from the viewpoint of the automatic processes which seem to determine the course of the world, looks like a miracle. In the language of natural science, it is the "infinite improbability which occurs regularly." . . .
> The miracle that saves the world, the realm of human affairs, from its normal, "natural" ruin is ultimately the fact of natality, in which the faculty of action is ontologically rooted. It is, in other words, the birth of new men and the *new beginning*, the action they are capable of by virtue of being born. Only the full experience of this capacity can bestow upon human affairs faith and hope, those two essential characteristics of human existence which Greek antiquity ignored altogether, discounting the keeping of faith as a very uncommon and not too important virtue and counting hope among the evils of illusion in Pandora's box. It is this faith in and hope for the world that found perhaps its most glorious and most succinct expression in the few words with which the Gospels announced their "glad tidings": "A child has been born unto us."[2]

For the moment, let me select the following formulations: "law of mortality," "inexorable course of daily life," the "rectilinear" movement of human life, like a "peculiar deviation from the common natural rule," which is cyclical, the "miracle" of action, "infinite improbability" compared with the "automatic processes" that rule the course of the world. All these terms refer, I think, without having to twist them to conform to a general principle of deadening, to the idea of a natural drift that compels all entities toward the more probable, where they dissipate.

Arendt then opposes to this melancholic principle what she calls "action," which, in the ineluctable and natural ruin, would interrupt, begin something new, and be improbable, giving substance to faith and hope.

Let me note that the turn taken by Arendt's thinking here is explicitly humanistic: "men, though they must die, are not born in order to die but in order to begin." I would say that this is a resolutely anthropologized reading of the solution to the third conflict in Kant's Antinomy of Reason, the one that will rule over the deduction of a reality of freedom in the *Second Critique*—much more anthropological than Kant's transcendental lesson. And of course my reservation bears on this uncritical consent given the concept of a humanity of men defined as a vocation to begin something new. No doubt the Kant of the *Third Critique* reaches an analogous conclusion, but one that hangs on the *as if* clause, which modalizes the regulatory idea of a nature working for the benefit of freedom. Where Arendt is a realist, Kant is an analogist, that is, "childish."

What seems more interesting to me is the role Arendt assigns in the economy of this negative entropy to the "fact of natality." In the text I have quoted, she states that the faculty of action is "ontologically rooted" in the fact of natality. How are we to understand this? As the "birth of new men," she writes, as the "new beginning," and finally in the news, the glad tidings, that "a child has been born unto us."

Here I would more than agree: a child is continuously born to us. Birth is not merely the biological fact of parturition, but, under cover and on discovery of this fact, the event of a possible radical alteration in the course compelling things to repeat the same. Childhood is the name of this faculty, in that it brings to the world of being the astonishment of what, for a moment, is nothing yet—of what *is already* without yet being *something*. I say this birth is incessant because it beats the measureless rhythm of a recurrent "survival." This "survival" does not prolong a life that is already dead; it initiates, in the death of what was there, the miracle of what is not yet there, of what is not yet identified.

And yet even in this ontological glimpse of a birth that defies the law of the return of the same, in which we can hear something consonant with what I have called *childhood*, I hesitate in my agreement. I said that we must emancipate the idea of a life as beginning, and not merely as survival, from the triumphalism of a challenge or the conviction of a remission. The passage quoted from *The Human Condition* grants to what Arendt calls the principle of natality and to the initiatory force of action the virtue of a redemption—a virtue I would call *protective*. Often it appears to me to govern the economy or the strategy of Arendt's thinking, through its detours, repentances, and hesitations, and to limit the scope of that thinking. Here is the passage I omitted from what I quoted before:

> Action is, in fact, the one miracle-working faculty of man, as Jesus of Nazareth, whose insights into this faculty can be compared in their originality and unprecedentedness with Socrates' insights into the possibilities of thought, must have known very well when he likened the power to forgive to the more general power of performing miracles, putting both on the same level and within the reach of man.[3]

This passage refers to the previous section of the same book, "Irreversibility and the Power to Forgive." Forgiving, *aphienai*, unbinding and letting go, are understood by Arendt precisely as interruptions of the irreversible chain of effects of action itself in which action can only repeat itself mortally. Forgiving is a re-mittance, a new deal of the cards, what makes a cut in the consequence of necessities and begins; pardon versus abandon. The grandeur of Jesus—with respect to any tradition, be it Roman, oriental, or Jewish—is heightened by the fact of his teaching, by word and deed, and by the fact that it is within the power of the son of man to pardon offenses. What offends is always simply what is as having-been. The miracle of Jesus is that he is an event in the order of necessity. The good tidings that a child is born to us announce, in truth, that with Jesus it is birth that is born here and now, and that the offense of being there—in the world of entities—can be pardoned. Exercised here and now, the pardon whose birth is announced by the good tidings is itself only the birth of the new, the crack of the not yet in the doleful world of the always-the-same. Thus pardoned, according to Arendt, "action" (power to begin) carries with it the promise of its emancipation from necessity returning its effect to the nothingness of the same.

I do not claim that this humanistic, salvationist thinking is Arendt's last word. The text dates from 1958, ten years after the first German edition of "Die Verborgene Tradition"[4] and seven years after the first American edition of *The Origins of Totalitarianism*[5]—works that include the first meditations on the impossible "Jewish" condition. This condition, as we know, reserves for God alone the power to forgive, that is, to begin anew, and refuses the futile temptation of a restorative humanism. If I take as examples the four figures of this condition as Arendt analyzes them in 1948, the "Schlemihl" from Heinrich Heine's *Melodies*, Bernard Lazare's "pariah," Charlie Chaplin's "suspect," and the "K" from Kafka's *Castle* (named by Arendt "the man of goodwill"), I can see nothing—or almost nothing—comparable to the faith and hope promised by the good news of birth in *The Human Condition*. Only the reading of *The Castle* (and I deplore this fact) seems inclined towards a certain optimism: by obstinately remaining in the village, K (in her reading) becomes the witness (though not accepted as such) to the fact that a debt remains unpaid in the order that the castle imposes on the common people. But to my knowledge, this debt, according to Arendt, is not the debt whose creditor is non-being, in the modality of its miracle, birth, or its threat, death. What the castle owes to the village is not the right to judge, to begin, but the right for every man "to have 'a home, a position, real work to do,' to marry and 'to become a member of the community.'"[6] Optimism is not Christ-like, but political. All these words would have to be overcharged with a somewhat arbitrary ontological connotation in order to make the elementary rights of "public man" express what Benjamin might have called the dependence of "action" on the event (*The Human Condition*). The village certainly survives the absence of these rights, but the enjoyment of these rights could itself be no more than a survival compared with "natality." I merely wish to state that even if it were democratic, this community would not escape the threat of banal entropy.

There is probably more "birth" in this sense in Heine's notion of the "Schlemihl," as raised by Arendt, but its tenor is so popular, not to say populist, and so poetic, in the sense of the comical paganism of Rabbi Faibusch (Phoebus Apollo), that I would not want to confuse this *gaiety* with the *joy* of which we were speaking. Yes, there is birth there, but birth to the presence "of such universal things as the sun, music, trees and children."[7] Hence the poetic life of Heine's people ("there is no poet without a people," Arendt repeats—what about Paul Celan?), the public life of Kafka's democratic citizen (oh, how often "revisited"); nothing in these figures is reminiscent of the inverted figure of survival to which I alluded: birth and the child as an interruption in the ineluctable process of deadening. A people's culture, democratic organization: are these not also possible modes of perpetuating identity? Possible figures for inert survival?

It is rather in an earlier text like "We Refugees," reprinted in *The Jew as Pariah* (1978), that something of the thinking of interruption returns.[8] It returns really without excuse, and at the very moment when the community of pardon in the person of its pope, Pius XII, will have "forgotten" to pardon. Here Arendt makes no mistake when she sees, in the fate dealt upon Rolf Hochhuth's *The Deputy*[9] in 1964, the response to one who has just been influenced by her *Eichmann in Jerusalem*.[10] For there is no refuge offered to these refugees, not even that of assimilation, whether poetic or civil, to the people of their land of asylum, which is to say no inscription into a premodern (pagan) or modern (republican) tradition—or, least of all, into a Christian one. It is impossible to survive like this in Europe (she writes in 1943, at the moment that the *Judenfrage* is about to find its Final Solution), because "the outlawing of the Jewish people in Europe has been followed closely by the outlawing of most European nations."[11] So that the refugees "we" are represent "the avant-garde of these peoples," and Jewish history thus ceases to be separate from that of nations.

We can see at what an appalling cost the interminable hesitation between tradition and assimilation finds its "solution," if I dare use this now-accursed term. This text, "We Refugees," has something terrible about it, and its content and tone contain a dreadful bitterness. Arendt mocks the Jews who are doctors in Berlin and freeloaders [*Schnorrer*] in Paris, whose spokesman says: "We have been good Germans in Germany and therefore we shall be good Frenchmen in France,"[12] who no longer succeed in being successful, in assimilating to the bourgeoisie. They have to flee too fast, things move too fast. And anyway, as she said in *Rahel Varnhagen*,[13] Jews cannot assimilate without assimilating anti-Semitism too. As for their own tradition, it cannot be maintained. The shtetl and the ghettoes are burned, and the communities expelled, deported, or massacred. But more than this, the very principle of an installation probably does not conform to the strange tradition in which the kings and the political men will always have been denounced by the Prophets in the name of a Word which de-installs. The Jews do not constitute a people in the sense of a nation. They are without nature, without land. They are linked only by the law of the book and the debt of an alliance and a promise.

Arendt does not make this explicit in "Die Verborgene Tradition," but her eulogy of Bernard Lazare's pariah in another text authorizes me to express it for her here. For if in 1943 she can see in Jews the "avant-garde" (terrible word) of a Europe persecuted by Nazism, and if she can hope in desperation for their inscription into modern history, it is precisely because they are not a natural or national people and because they prefigure a state of being-together to which all European peoples are and will be committed by the totalitarian disaster—a being-together without roots—that behaves according to judgment alone, without any established criterion, the last resource of the survivor. There is no necessity, no *being-needy*, that could in principle deprive the mind of the ability to distinguish between good and evil. The diaspora, persecution, the Shoah, all these accelerated modes of dispatching into nothingness, leave the soul without the support of a tradition; they leave to its desolation only the responsibility of saying yes or no to abjection, only the childhood of the mind, which is the ability to judge. The reminder of a promise of alliance, and thus a reminder of birth, may be heard, stammering feebly, in the night of a young Elie Wiesel, in his supplication, "Why have you forsaken me? Does it mean that you do not exist?"

In the end, Arendt will obviously seek this mind in an embryonic state in Kant's "Analytic of Aesthetic Judgment." Even if she does not see it this way, the fact is that each time, singularly, what is at stake in this reflective judgment is the birth of a subject and thus of a community, but only of a promised birth. With the beautiful, it is pure happiness, the miracle of promise; but with the sublime, it is its impossibility, the imminent threat of non-being. The beautiful is an event of birth; the sublime, one of death.

In the seminars of 1970, Arendt was not preoccupied with the analytic of the sublime, through which, however, there reverberate the horrors of abandonment. The reason, I think, is that the desire to protect and to be protected against the unbearable is stronger in this case than the persistent intrepidness of her enquiry.

Problem of survival: every mind is the child of its parents and survives them. Arendt's mother never abandoned her, and she never abandoned her mother. What mind can declare itself free from defense mechanisms, from forgetful resistance to a total melancholia? One writes because one's attempt at suicide has failed. Arendt says a great deal about Jewish suicide in "We Refugees."

Let us recall that the last Jewish survivors in the caverns of Jotapata besieged by Nero's troops in A.D. 67 discussed whether they had the right to commit suicide. Josephus, the leader, the traitor, and the survivor favored the "solution" (precisely so) that each should kill the other in turn, and be killed by the next. This very Josephus managed to come out last in the drawing of lots and negotiated his fate with the Romans. He then wrote *The Jewish War*. Arendt writes in her *Eichmann in Jerusalem*: "There will always be a survivor to tell the tale."[14] How does she know? How do we know? Because of the Shoah, which is an almost perfect *Vernichtung* in that it would not have taken much more for there to have been no one left to tell of it. And the witnesses who speak are horrified at having been chosen by the evil of survival to tell it.

We should also recall that *we* write and think in a state of relative peace, without having to listen for the doorbell at 6 A.M., without the immediate, constant threat of the most abject of annihilations. Protection against abandonment loses some of its urgency with the thought that persecution is held at bay. Thinking can advance a little more in the direction of catastrophe, the sublime, and non-being, because no one today, with the exception of a few terrorists, "refuses [to the thinker] the right to share the earth," as did those like Eichmann.[15] Rather than "share the earth," I would prefer to speak of the right to *share the story*, the birth and death of the improbable: of sharing judgment. Regarding the refusal of this sharing, this abandonment, who can pardon it? Who can set it right [*remettre*]? And does not Arendt's gesture of protection derive from her intellectual proximity (greater than ours today) to the horror engendered by this refusal?

To return to tradition, it is always threatened with being merely a survival. Through tradition, a state of complexity, a state of textual corpuses is maintained from one generation to another (at least). As a result, children lodge their complaints and take their responsibilities on the basis of a sophisticated and well-founded arrangement of knowledge, know-how, opinions, or of being-together in the most general sense. Here I would refer to the fine pages in *Between Past and Future*[16] on Roman *auctoritas* as foundation, tradition, and religion. As tradition is enriched, as it gains authority, so children are born less and less from nothing—less naked. They may even lose the feeling of non-being, ensured as they are of being inscribed within a continuity overarching deaths and births, that is, any relation to nothingness, to what is without relation. Yet, even in the most "augmented," authorized, and "linking" tradition, the enigma of a something to which there is no response must continue to inhabit the mind secretly (the question of "why me?"), the enigma of the singularity of birth, which cannot be shared, like that of death. The persistence of this enigma can make the mind accessible to something that is prior to the world of culture and tradition, keep it in a state of childhood, that is, unprepared.

Only in preserving the possibility that this enigma may come to mind can tradition be other than the placidly implacable survival of what is already there, and death be inflicted upon the improbability of being born. But by the same token, if its possibility is preserved, uncertainty, whether melancholic or wondrous, persists through the generations to disturb the hold of tradition and of the consensus that feeds off it.

I would like, in short, to situate certain aspects of totalitarianism, as analyzed by Arendt, in relation to this problematic of a tradition of the beginning. In *Between Past and Future* (1961, 1968), the organization of the totalitarian system, already explored in *The Origins of Totalitarianism* (1973), is compared to the structure of an onion. Authoritarianism organizes power in a pyramid, whereas tyranny suspends it with equal indifference over everyone. Arendt notes that the totalitarian onion has the following property: examined from the center, where the leader resides, each stratum appears more "realistic," less "radical," in proportion to its distance from the center. Seen from outside (from "reality"), on the other hand, each stratum looks more committed, more militant, "harder" than the strata whose surfaces precede it. (Esoterism/exoterism: Is the Pythagorean distinction between the *mathematikoi* and the *politikoi* [with respect to their initiation into doctrinal radicality] authoritarian? or is it already totalitarian?)

My questioning here concerns the "realism" of the analysis and, in general, of Arendt's thought.

She writes: "The onion structure enables the system, by its organization, to be resistant to the shock with which it is threatened by the factuality of the real world";[17] "resistant to," in other words, sheltered from. This is a system that deadens events and confrontation. Totalitarianism is thus a vast "counterexcitation" organism, in Freud's sense of the term. But I think that we must then understand "factuality" not so much in the sense of the fact established by the historian (as described by Arendt in the chapter "Truth and Politics" that she added to the later editions of *Between Past and Future* after the uproar provoked by her *Eichmann in Jerusalem*), but rather by accenting what she herself stresses at the end of this chapter, as "what one cannot change."[18]

Hypothetically, politics could change reality; totalitarian politics could change it totally: whence the onion, a system of complete (two-way) filtering of the real, with the aim of transforming reality into ideology or culture. Bearing Freud and what I consider essential in mind, the reality that needs filtering is not so-called brute fact (in Clemenceau's sense: no one can or will ever be able to say that Belgium invaded Germany in August 1914), but its degree of anxiety, its quality of attraction and repulsion, its force of excitation. This quality of the fact does not stem from its established factuality, but from its eluding repression and crossing the strata of the protective onion. The "real" should be understood as *the fact* of desire and not as *a fact* established in the referential field of a cognitive discourse. For the so-called real fact only possesses this power of anxiety because it has an ally at the center of the onion. This ally is the something to which the mind remains hostage and to which there is no respondent (in Freud's terms, no representative), with which it has no (narrational) relationship. It is the "presence" of nothingness, of birth and death, and of indivisible singularity. So much so, that defense against what is called external reality is only necessary insofar as it can awaken this "truth" deemed internal, this something that, more than anything else, cannot be changed or exchanged. The categories of external and internal are practically useless here. When I say "external reality" can awaken inner truth, the metaphor of awakening (so dear to Proust) places me in a space-time that cannot be divided up or clearly decided, that is "outside" or "before" the scene, in the double sense of the theatrical scene and the time of a short story, whether fantasized or not. *Before* and *outside* are misnomers. Simply stated, the découpage of places and moments does not take place or have its moment when it is a question of the [Heideggerian] Thing. Hitler, burrowed down in the center of his onion, is no less exposed to the Thing than a humble Swabian student on the outside. The self is always naked with regard to birth and death and so also to difference, sexual or ontological. But the leader wants to forget and make others forget the terrible nakedness constituting childhood. Thus, for such a powerful instrument of foreclosure, of forgetting, as totalitarianism to be fabricated, the Thing must appear extremely threatening, the relation of desire to the real must be one of extreme defenselessness. That is where the origin of totalitarianism is to be found.

Yet, in reading *The Origins of Totalitarianism*, one comes across—to my knowledge—few indications of this "origin" of totalitarianism. The description is essentially an external one, from a historico-political point of view. Even terror is analyzed mainly in terms of its use, as the means of breaking with the preceding legality. But the following observation is an exception: "The *need* for terror is born of the fear that with the birth of each human being a new beginning might raise and make heard its voice in the world."[19] Yet "fear" seems to me to express little, and the remark conserves a certain tone of advocating a high birthrate.

This objectivation and realism, predominant in the 1951 text, certainly in no way detract from the importance of the analysis. But they do limit its significance for us. For if it is true that the totalitarian tendency has to be grafted onto a heightening of anxiety unequaled in the cultural, political, and philosophical history of the West, then the defeat of the totalitarian regimes alone will doubtless have been insufficient to exhaust the source of totalitarianism's spirit.

I would point to three paths opened to the resurgence, to the survival of this spirit after the political totalitarianism analyzed by Arendt. She shows that, in order to realize the system of total domination, there is no need to have recourse to the *Volk* and that Himmler's power was due to his knowing that "the masses of coordinated philistines provided much better material and were capable of even greater crimes than so-called professional criminals, provided only that these crimes were well organized and assumed the appearance of routine jobs." What Himmler understands, she adds, is that "most people are neither bohemians, fanatics, adventurers, sex maniacs, crackpots, nor social failures, but first and foremost job holders and good family men."[20] In other words, they are ordinary folk who don't want to understand anything about the relation to nothingness and the debt of childhood, and who "distract" themselves from these things by keeping busy. Now this state of mind, which refuses the debt, seems to me just as true, in fact more so, for developed societies at the end of this century as for the Europe in crisis of the 1930s. The massification and activation of the forces of thinking, their exclusive devotion nowadays to what is called "active living," are more completely accomplished than then. And so is what Arendt calls "loneliness," since there is no need of an onion for that.

I will now proceed to a second persistent seed of totalitarianism today, what Ernst Jünger called total mobilization:

> In the interpretation of totalitarianism, all laws have become laws of movement. When the Nazis talked about the law of nature or when the Bolsheviks talk about the law of history, neither nature nor history is any

longer the stabilizing source of authority for the actions of mortal men; they are movements in themselves.

. . . Terror is the realization of the law of movement; its chief aim is to make it possible for the force of Nature or of History to race freely through mankind, unhindered by any spontaneous human action. As such, terror seeks to "stabilize" men in order to liberate the forces of nature or history. It is this movement which singles out the foes of mankind against whom terror is let loose, and no free action of either opposition or sympathy can be permitted to interfere with the elimination of the "objective enemy" of History or Nature, of the class or the race. . . .

Terror as the execution of a law of movement whose ultimate goal is not the welfare of men or the interest of one man but the fabrication of mankind eliminates individuals for the sake of the species, sacrifices the "parts" for the sake of the "whole." The suprahuman force of Nature or History has its own beginning and its own end, so that it can be hindered only by the new beginning and the individual and which the life of each man actually is.[21]

Several decades after Hitler and Stalin, the contemporary system surely no longer invokes history and nature in order to leave behind legality and the capacity to judge. It does not have to tear up treaties and contracts or exterminate lives. The principle rendering humans superfluous as juridical, moral, and particular persons (Catherine Chalier) inhabits the very "acts" of administrated life (Theodor Adorno), creating a void in the minds it administers. This principle is called development. It is an entity no less abstract or anonymous than nature or history, and it maximizes the effect described by Arendt: setting things in motion totally and mobilizing energies. Neither political organization layered like an onion nor the use of terror to break up legality and the debt of birth are indispensable to it. On the contrary, as Jünger knew by 1930, in democratic forms and in the constant adaptation of laws to attain greater well-being, the "law" of development finds both a means and a mask even more powerful (because more acceptable to "philistines") than totalitarian organization. Crude propaganda is discreet in democratic forms: it gives way to the inoffensive rhetoric of the media. And worldwide expansion occurs not through war, but through technological, scientific, and economic competition. The historical names for this Mr. Nice Guy totalitarianism are no longer Stalingrad or Normandy (much less Auschwitz), but Wall Street's Dow Jones Average and the Tokyo's Nikkei Index.

We all share the ideology (but is it an ideology?) that we must, at any cost, develop and complexify in order to survive. The enemy is not human, but rather, entropic. Entropy is at the terminus of what remains of human history, in the form of the explosion of the sun into a black nova in four-and-a-half-billion years. Development is the reply to this immense challenge. And it alone is just, since it is necessary for survival. The faculties of judgment, imagination, and paying homage to birth again are more solicited than suffocated in this process, but solicited in the suffocating busyness of performativity; a busy survival. We should at least, on the basis of this diagnosis, look again at the question of ideology. Development is ideological not because it is out of control in relation to the reality of things, but because it forecloses the anxiety of birth and death as an ontological enigma.

A last observation on the same lines: one inevitable effect of totalitarianism is that children are not allowed enough time for childhood, in the ontological sense in which I have been using the word. On "The Crisis in Education," Arendt writes:

> The more completely modern society discards the distinction between what is private and what is public . . . , the more . . . it introduces between the private and the public a social sphere in which the private is made public and vice versa, the harder it makes things for its children, who by nature require the security of concealment in order to mature undisturbed.[22]

I interpret this formulation as follows: the contemporary system maintains the totalitarian principle of the multiplication of interfaces, but nowadays as network, not as an onion. The "institutions" (school and family) where childhood securely sheltered its insecurity, its questions without answers, while learning adult answers and their inadequacy, where the fate of tradition vis-à-vis anxiety was in play, are destroyed by the contemporary system (it is enough for it to deflect their ends). And they are destroyed because the system places childhood in immediate contact with its demands, which are its responses to anxiety. Childhood has to immediately take its place in the communicational networks that have replaced the onion's strata, to function there as efficiently as possible, that is, to become the carrier of the messages that are circulated there and optimize their information. No time to challenge the old-timers or tradition; on the contrary, save time, to avoid the return of what has to be forgotten—the squatter within the soul. "Let the dead bury the dead" is today understood as the abandonment of the body to administration by undertakers or to medical schools. One either gets rid of dead bodies or makes them serve development.

As for children, so for the dead . . . always. They are the two aspects, in the tradition itself, capable of appealing to the intransmissible.

Arendt recalls the two enemies that the character in Kafka's parable fight simultaneously: "He has two antagonists: the first presses him from behind, from the origin. The second blocks the road ahead. He gives battle to both."²³ It is not just a question of the past and the future, but also of death and birth. What Arendt fails to state, however, is that if the dead here press upon, oppress the soul, and if the children block its escape, it is because they all weigh upon it with the force of what already is what it is. The past is saturated with its consequences and the future with its programs. The castle imposes the reign of its administered time on the soul's time.

There remains the interstice, without extension, which is the instant of judgment, reading, learning, and writing, of "growing up undisturbed," for the child (who only blocks off the future if it is integrated too fast into what the constituted social offers it). It is also—for the tradition that pushes its way up from the depths of time with all the weightiness of the already judged—the time of being questioned. Between children already dead, in a hurry to be (that is, to become "mature" adults), and yet-still-living-corpses—the two groups that survive—thought, in a hurry to get there, "to be there," struggles to bar access to its truth, to its condition of being hostage to something that has not been and will not be, but to which it must bear witness. It renders this witnessing in that it "judges." For it judges from nowhere, and in the name of nothing and no one, past or future, testifying by this that at the heart of necessitating and necessitous immanence, an obedience to what is unbound can be justified.

The temporal state of urgency, decision, effectuation, demanding unfailing adhesion of one instant to the next, corresponds to the multiplication of mediating layers or media networks in spatial totalitarian organization. Freud said that, in the end, time, too—sequential time—must be conceived of as a "protective shield." This would be a time of the complete, of the dense—saturated, and sufficient to the point of satiety—stripped of any modality of possibility (past or future); in short, total in its seriality. Thus non-being is excluded from it, as are inquietude and angst, and, to be sure, the faculty of judgment.

It is the effects of this saturation, I imagine, that indicate to Arendt that man without qualities, Eichmann in Jerusalem, and which she calls the "banality of evil." The totalization of time by the homogenization of *times*, by their banalization, banishes the *Urteilen*, the distinction between what is good and what is evil. It is evil because it eliminates the ability to discern between good and evil. At the end of *The Origins of Totalitarianism*, Arendt calls this state "loneliness," the opposite of solitude.²⁴ It is simply the complementary inverse of the massing of singularities: the massing of time. It is a *new* evil. The old evil requires that, in what is still experienced as the relation to non-being, privilege reverts to disappearance and death, and thus to the melancholic or criminal idea of survival. Similarly, the old good, according to the same inquietude, is the admission of and respect for a debt of appearance or infancy, and one that is judged without any criterion. Nazism does not only say "Thou shalt kill," but also, "Let them disappear so that we may appear." But what is extinguished by our contemporary totalitarianism is the very inquietude of appearance and disappearance.

Massification and survival, mobilization and saturation, and foreclosure are obtained more efficiently by an organization through communicational networks than by totalitarian politics. I know how brutal this diagnosis is. I know that development is inseparable from the society of tradition. I am aware of the advantages of democracy: that is provides more opportunities for judgment than Nazism and allows us not to tremble at the sound of the doorbell at dawn.

But, even so, I still wonder whether "birth" (the ability to judge, the vocation to begin) makes "administered life" just a survival in comparison with the true life of the soul. I wonder if, from this still possible miracle, we can expect any alternative to the system.

One example among others. In the proliferation of initiatives and civil institutions, particularly in the United States, Arendt saw a sort of protection or resistance against the threat of the totalitarianism of the nation-state, that is, against the forgetting of non-being. In the conflict and crisis surrounding the busing of black and white schoolchildren, she supports resistance on the part of families, and local activities against the application at all costs of federal laws designed to assure the integration of school populations. From civil society's capacity to spontaneously come up with organizational modes protecting individual or local concrete freedoms (especially important here because they concern childhood) against a law decreed from afar (as indeed is often the case in the United States, most notably in the 1960s and 1970s), Arendt hears the echo of a power for judging concretely, radically, without theory or criterion, a power that is mutually shared. This is the "common sense" or good sense whose basis she finds in Kant's *Third Critique*. I repeat that this conclusion is only at the cost of an abusively sociologizing reading of Kant's *sensus communis*. Kant's text undoubtedly lends itself to this, since it is not stripped of anthropology in the way that a transcendental analysis would have required. But I do not want to get into a philosophical discussion of Kant's last seminars; I just wonder what this reading of "good sense" still owes to the ideology of workers' councils to which the 1956 Hungarian revolution and, before that, through Heinrich Blücher, the experience of the Spartacus movement lent a sort of authorization.

I say this as someone who, like others, including some much better than I, let myself be taken in by the movement at the time. The interpretation of the Hungarian Councils in these terms can certainly not be recused. What *can* be recused is the possibility of concluding from this that what has been called the self-management of being-together (wrongly named, I think, because it is a sort of *Sebstbehauptung*) could of itself constitute a political or social alternative to totalitarianism, of whatever type. With the destruction of totalitarian systems and their replacement by "permissive" neototalitarianism (or, rather, possibilist neototalitarianism, since the slogan "anything is possible," which Arendt picks up from David Rousset and which is essential to these organizations, underscores this side of the question now more than ever), the very idea of an alternative is extinguished, and with it, that of a revolution.

Birth or infancy, beginning, and finally the ability to judge, surely remain, but in loneliness. Without ideology we could not transfer to the possibility of spontaneous, local initiatives—which are in any case useful for the institution of the contemporary system, that is, the democratic one—the hope that was once placed in workers' councilism as the means of organizing the struggles of the oppressed. The transfer of the forms of revolutionary resistance to the free exercise of citizenship within the frame of democratic laws is still too protective a transfer, and in this sense ideological. It is a surviving.

In a reality that is principally turned toward the survival of complexities in the physical world, the other survival, the openness to non-being (under whatever name) is a debt that persists, in which Pascalian joy and Kafkaesque melancholia take refuge. But they do so in solitary fashion, in the desert filled with loneliness. And the question of community, of being-together, can and must be posed, at this point, from the perspective of this state of the soul's loci.

Translated by Robert Harvey and Mark S. Roberts

11

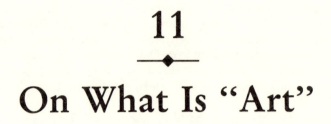

On What Is "Art"

My intent will be to defend the thesis whereby the sentence "This is art" is consistent by its very inconsistency.

I shall begin by analyzing the sentence's properties. It is simple to show that the sentence is not consistent (in the ordinary logical and epistemological sense) when taken literally, without concern for the connotations that the history of modern art attaches to art's "creation" and "reception" (what Paul Valéry terms, respectively, "production" and "consumption").

I shall then attempt to show that one's motives for detecting the inconsistency in the sentence "This is art" are quite possibly traits characteristic of the reflexive status in the artistic operation (for example, writing) and of its reception (for example, reading). In this second step I will tacitly seek help from Kant, but also, especially, from Valéry (even though his angle may seem altogether different).

Finally, it would be appropriate to draw from these brief analyses a few observations relative to disorder and order, nothingness and the witnessing of nothingness, singularity and consensus. These observations will only be provisionally sketched.

1. INCONSISTENCY

Here, I use the term *consistency* for the properties expected of a sentence claiming to state what is true or false. I use the term *cognitive* simply for this family of sentences claiming to state that something (obviously) is true or false. I do so knowing, like everyone else, that this claim is not the same as to verify or falsify a mathematical statement or, let us say, a "physical" one (that is, one possessing a referent reputed to be real, which is not the case for mathematics). I will limit myself here to taking a cognitive physical utterance for a term of comparison by supposing that the sentence "This is art" applies to a real object (referent).

"This is art" appears, at the very least, to be a partial determination if not a definition (defined as a complete description). The sentence attributes a predicate ("art") to a propositional subject ("this"). (This could be expressed otherwise, for example, as Noam Chomsky's noun phrase ["this"] and verb phrase ["is art"]. Linguistically this would be more interesting, but, for that very reason, less enlightening logically or epistemologically. It could also be expressed in Frege-Russell notation.) What is usually called knowledge resides in this attribution of a predicate to a subject. Knowledge is the recognition that an object (referent), named by the propositional subject, belongs to the class named by the predicate. The object named "this" belongs to the class "what is art."

There are, in the vocabulary of *The Differend*,[1] three operations that appear to me indispensable to cognition and recognition. I will not bother to expand upon the problematic that led me to these conclusions: suffice it to say that, considered within a language-like perspective, it is the very problematic of the possibility of knowing a *reality*.

In order for a sentence to be cognitive, that is, capable of indicating the truth or falsity of what is signifies concerning its referent:

1. It must first be endowed with meaning. In other words, it must connect one term with another, and this connection must take place by means of connective (Kant called them synthetic) operators that are reputed to be rational, or at least reasonable. These are the operators that Aristotle, and Kant after him, called categories. In modern logic (which is extensional), the symbol of inclusion ($\supset$) designates the connection of one term with another; the nature of this connection is specified in the play of symbols of quantity, quality, and relationship (parentheses, equals signs, and so on). The existential "this" belongs to the universal class of "what is art."

2. The second (properly physical) condition for a cognition is that the logically conceived sentence must be confronted with "reality." Practically speaking, this means that cases must be presented that appear to verify the meaning of the sentence in question (or at least to falsify the sentence that contradicts it).

I stress the term *case*, and here is how we find it glossed in contemporary logic: "*there is* a certain *x*" and this *x* belongs to *y* (for example, it belongs to what is art). This *there is* obviously eludes the capacity for signification. It belongs to the capacity for showing or indicating. It presupposes that "something" particular is given, here and now, to the locutor (and to the allocutor, who must be able to ascertain that there is, really, this).

The cognitive procedure thus demands that deictics ("here," "now," "this," "that," "I," "you," and so on) be used. In the sentence under question, *this* is precisely such a deictic.

3. For the third condition, you may notice, the deictic "this" only refers to a "there is something" to the extent that it is currently indicated by the current sentence.

The question of this current moment needs to be studied in depth. It is enough, for now, to say that this moment is the *in actu* or the *actu* of performance artists; the *in situ* or the *situ* of performance arts. This raises difficult problems concerning space-time, or, more precisely, concerning not the time in which the sentence is localized, but the time which is marked by the sentence—a marking often effected by the sentence's presence alone and sometimes by its presentation. When we find the term *now* (or any of the deictics adjacent to this term: "here," "you," and so on) in a sentence, it indicates the instant that is contemporaneous with the time in which the current sentence takes place; contemporaneous, but measured (if I may express it this way) from the time of this sentence. To say "today" (a case analogous to "now") is not the same as saying "2 February 1989." In the latter case, the measurement of time is carried out by means of a calendar (years, months, days).

A calendar is an evenly divided grid of proper nouns that allows us to indicate all of the "nows" in a solar year by making them independent of their current designation. When I say "2 February 1989," I am not saying that it is "now" or yesterday or tomorrow. And if it happens that it is in fact "now," the indication of this "now" by its date detaches it from the current moment of the deictic sentence and fixes it on a grid of proper nouns whose interrelationships are ordered in a fixed manner independent of the deictics.

Like all proper nouns, dates are and only are designations (that is, they have no meaning). But, unlike deictics, the designators that dates are fall under the category of what Saul Kripke terms "rigid designators," which I understand to mean that the designated is only designated (and not signified), but that it is identical to itself no matter what the current sentence designating it is.

Thus proper nouns keep their designative value from one sentence to another and from one speaker to another.

Each of the nouns and symbols used by science are such rigid designators and thus proper nouns. Examples of these nouns would be those designating units of length, intensity, weight, mass, and velocity.

Without this "rigidity" in designation, it could not be proved that *this* (a simple deictic) confirms the assertion that *x is y* or that "this is art." For we must be able to place "this" in a world (a grid, for the calendar, but this goes for all tables of designative regularities) of nouns independent of "performances" (sentences insofar as they are current), in order to be certain that both the current sentence P_0 and the *later* sentence P_1 still have the same referent.

It is now obvious what makes the sentence "This is art" inconsistent. To be precise:

1. It is not inconsistent because it presupposes the class of "objects that are art." Recognition must take place: a logically inclusive relationship must

be established between the object under examination and a class to which it is reckoned to belong. This class is thus defined beforehand. We may accept that from this point of view the sentence is consistent, provided that the class of "what is art" be known.

When the receiver (the public) protests that "this is not art," he is holding to an explicit or implicit definition of the class of "what is art."

He cannot be accused of being wrong unless we accept that the definition of this class may change, or, in a case of major importance, if we accept that the "this" in question can contribute to a modification in the definition of this class.

In themselves, neither of these presuppositions (neither a modification of art's definition nor a modifying role played by a certain "this") leads to an inconsistency. A model analogous (but only analogous) to this modification and this modifier may be readily located in the history and epistemology of science. In science, the definition of classes (what is electric, what is dense, what is interactive, and so on) may be enlarged as well. In science, too, it is "this," a designated (and also, of course, named, that is, communicable) reality that may be the modifier of it. This is called discovery and/or invention.

2. Where inconsistency with respect to our sentence's truth or falsity intervenes is in that it lacks the name of "this." It is inconsistent, in this sense, because it is incomplete. It should be linked to another sentence like "The Venus de Milo [name] or the Large Glass [name] is *this* [deictic], and this is art." Without the so-called proper nomination, that is, the exclusive nomination that localizes "this" on a grid of regularities (for example, the nominal catalogue of works belonging to the class of what is art), we do not know *what* we are talking about when we say, simply, "this." Nothing ensures that the speaker of the sentence P_0 (mine) indicates by "this" the same referent as his allocutor. And if they carry on a conversation with each of them, in turn, from sentence to sentence, becoming the locutor and then the allocutor, they will never know if it is of the same referent that they are speaking.

3. Yet this defect is only such within the framework of the exigencies of a cognitive sentence (one whose purpose is to tell the truth concerning a referent). My thinking (following many others) is that the question as to whether this is or is not art (assuming that "this" is named) can only be settled cognitively to the extent that "this" (under its name) is submitted as an object to know or recognize, that is, as a referent either belonging to or not belonging to the class of "what is art."

Under this supposition, "this" (under its name) is submitted as a thing (and this positional operator is called "modality")—that is, as a material object, a "physical" object in the sense discussed above, a "sensible" object if one prefers—to be classified in a set.

Now, there is no doubt that artworks may thus be taken as things to be recognized and placed in known and defined sets. A major portion of literary and art criticism is engaged in this project. This is also the main concern of museum curators and librarians.

Let us examine what Valéry has to say about this procedure in his *Introduction to Poetics*:

There remains the artwork itself, insofar as it is a sensible thing. This is a third consideration quite different from the previous two.

We thus look upon an artwork as an *object*, purely as an object, that is, without adding any part of ourself to it than that which can be applied without distinction to all objects. This is an attitude marked rather distinctly by the absence of any production of value.

What can we do with this object which, this time, can do nothing with us? We surely can do something. We can measure it according to its spatial or temporal nature; we can count the words in a text or the syllables in a line of poetry; we can note that such-and-such a book was published at such-and-such a time, that the composition of some painting is a copy of some other, that a hemistich of Lamartine's may be found in St. Thomas, and that some page of Victor Hugo's belongs, as early as 1645, to an obscure Father Francis. We can point out that such-and-such a reasoning is a paralogism, that this sonnet is incorrect, that the rendering of this subject's arm defies anatomy, and that some use of words is bizarre. All of this is the result of operations which one may assimilate to purely material ones, since they are reducible to superpositions of the artwork (or fragments thereof) to some model.

This treatment of works of the mind does not distinguish them from all other possible works: it places and maintains them at the rank of things imposing a *definable* existence upon them. Here is the point to be remembered:

Everything that we can define is immediately distinguishable from the producing mind and stands in opposition to it. In the same stroke, the mind turns it into the equivalent of a material upon which or an instrument by which it can perform.

The mind thus places that for which it has determined a definition outside its reach and, in this, it shows that it knows itself and only trusts what is not it.[2]

Valéry suggests that the definitional (which is also referential) procedure stands in opposition to what he calls the "producing mind," that is, the mind insofar as it "creates" (to use that old term), and that opposition, according to Valéry, is as present in the "consumer" (the receiver) as in the producer (the writer, the artist).

To the extent that the mind is concerned with art (or, rather, with making art), that it is so little motivated by definition, reference, or conceptual determination, Valéry further suggests in this passage, if it comes to suppose or to apprehend artworks as things, to place them "outside its reach," it is because "it knows itself," because "it only trusts what is not it."

To put it another way, "this" is directed to the cognition of things because "this" is neither a known nor a knowable nor even a recognizable thing to the mind that "produced" "this." Moreover, we may yet ask ourselves whether "what is art" is only established precisely at the instant when "production" (or what Valéry also calls "poetics"—I would say "writing") ceases and makes way for classification.

2. CONSISTENCY

My punctual and awkward recourse to Valéry already causes us to enter the area of consistencies attributable to our inconsistent sentence.

That sentence, "This is art," is not, I repeat, consistent from a cognitive point of view. It therefore is not even classifiable within the sort of critique that Valéry represents in the above text. The unnamed "this" is the point at which it fails vis-à-vis cognitive consistency. And it is beginning with this point that I will ascend once again toward its "poetic" or written consistency.

1. To accomplish this anabasis, I will seek help once again from Valéry, for the insistence of "this" in our sentence appears entirely congruent with the stress Valéry puts on what he calls *act* or *in-act*. I have remarked that a deictic only refers to an element of situation (for example, a person, time, space, object) by placing it in relation to the actuality of the sentence in which that deictic itself appears, in other words, in relation to the current or in-act sentence. On this point, Valéry writes:

> Everything that I have said thus far can be reduced to these few words: *the work of the mind exists only in-act*. Outside of this act, what remains is but an object with no particular relationship with the mind. Bring the statue that you admire to a people sufficiently different from ours: it will be but an insignificant stone; a Parthenon but a small marble quarry. And when a poet's text is used as a collection of grammatical difficulties or examples, it immediately ceases to be a *work of the mind*, since the use to which it is put is altogether foreign to the conditions of its origin, and since a consumption value that would give this work a sense is denied it. (40; italics in original)

It is pointless to belabor what is clearly understood here: this (passably enigmatic) *act* or *in-act*, this act *of the mind* (a no less obscure entity that is properly "the work of the mind") is (negatively) circumscribed at the outset as what is not the artwork as object or thing. The artwork as act is not the artwork as object.

As object, the artwork is named and signified or signifiable. Conditions are placed on it; it is governed by rules of cognitive belonging to either one or several sets.

The mind that recognizes or strives to recognize it ("Is it art?") is not the mind, the poetic mind that makes it. The poetic mind is only in-act, that is, here and now: the mind has neither permanent sights nor a permanent grip on it, because the mind does not possess a defined and constant identity for it.

Valéry expresses it even better in the following passage which may be considered a definition of undefinable actuality or presence:

> However clear, obvious, strong or beautiful is the spiritual event that concludes our expectation, that completes our thought or raises our doubt, nothing is yet irrevocable. Here, the next moment has absolute power over the product of the preceding one. This is because the mind, reduced to its substance alone, does not have the finite at its disposal and is absolutely incapable of linking itself to itself. (48)

According to Valéry, the state of the poetic mind affects the consumer as well as the producer. That poetic state is not, properly speaking, a state, but a mode of temporality remarkable for its discontinuity and discreteness. It is a sort of spasm in which what has been done does not govern what is yet to be done. "The mind . . . is absolutely incapable of linking itself to itself." Neither the linkages, nor the connections between one word and another, nor the connections between one part of a visual or sonorous figure to another are fixed, and, at each moment, there is a "decision" to be made as to how to create linkages. Forming a form (for there will be, in the end, a form) is not bound to a project.

2. The use of the terms *expectation* and *doubt* should be noted in the above passage from Valéry. I have argued that a "decision" had to be made. In the uncertainty in which the disconnection of moments throws the mind—a disconnection that is, thus, a proliferation of possible linkages between one moment and the next—the mind waits for a decision. A decision one waits for is not a decision one makes.

The *act* or the *in-act* thus takes on a meaning that is not immediately a temporal one, but one of *exis*, of being-there, or perhaps even of *ethos*, of availability. Let's say a manner of being, of being with respect to time, of course, but, for this reason, of a manner of being with respect to the linkage. (And I stress that this is not a manner of being with respect to being.) And it is assuredly not a manner of being with respect to the object (even a future, anticipated, or projected object): there is no object in this *exis* or *ethos*.

What the writer, composer, painter, or filmmaker (or even the reader, listener, or spectator) waits for is for "it to come along." What is waited for is the event of the "decision" that serves as act for and end to the infinity of possibles. It should be recalled that: "the mind, reduced to its substance alone, does not have the finite at its disposal." It desires or waits for it, but does not have it at its disposal. The mind will not complete the form.

For it is the case that the mind is nondefinitiveness and the non-ending of linkages, indetermination, and what Valéry, in short, calls disorder:

> Wherever the mind is at stake, everything is at stake. Everything is disorder and any reaction against disorder is of the same nature, for disorder is, further, the condition of its own fecundity: it harbors that promise since its fecundity is contingent upon the unexpected rather than the expected, and upon that of which we are ignorant (and because we are ignorant of it) rather than what we know. (59–60)

This disorder is also the mind's "freedom." Others have referred to free association or *aura*.

The act that decides is not an *action* in the strict sense of the term—it is an event. Valéry writes: "clear, obvious, strong . . . beautiful is the spiritual *event* that concludes our expectation."

We may "lower the degree of freedom in the system of the mind" (strange system), but, Valéry adds,

> as for the rest, I mean as for the modifications and substitutions that this constraint leaves open, we simply wait for what we desire to be produced. For we can do nothing but wait for it. *We have no means by which to reach precisely what it is within us that we wish to obtain.* (49; italics in original)

I believe I recognize in this "freedom" or this "disorder" what I, for my part, call possibility; a disseizure.

"Instability, incoherence, inconsequence constitute," writes Valéry, "the most common regime [of the mind when it gives itself over to] its substance alone" (46).

3. Yet this is a disseizure and a passibility in expectation of their end result. Something is wished for in this expectation. Not something from the regime of voluntary action in which it is "I" who wishes. Something is wished that is not "I," something that is not the completed object, which immediately turns into the simple referent of possible cognitions or interpretations.

These are cognitions or interpretations that only pay indirect homage to inexplicable indetermination through an indefinite proliferation of their determinations and explanations: in one sense, this is or is not art; in some other sense also, this is or is not art. Commentary would be interminable and, more important, futile (incapable of accumulating a patrimony, a capital of clear judgments). This is an eminent difference between the history of commentary on poetic works and that on natural effects.

What, then, is wished for at the heart of uncertainty, in the proliferation of imaginary possibilities? What is desired? Simply the event of an end. In a sense, a death. Yet is it a death of what is simply possible, or a death in order to give birth to the artwork?

Here we must introduce the necessarily concomitant *topos* of the expectation of the act at the heart of disorder, the *topos* of fatigue.

Valéry discerns two kinds of fatigue through art and poetics:

If I link myself to the page that I must write or to the page I wish to understand, I enter, in both cases, into a phase of lesser freedom. But in the two cases, my freedom may have two opposite appearances. My very task may urge me to pursue my freedom and, far from experiencing it as a displeasure, as a divergence from my mind's most natural course, I might give myself over entirely to it, advancing with so much life in the way paved by my design that the feeling of fatigue is diminished. This may go on until, in truth, fatigue suddenly clouds over my thought, confusing the play of ideas, reconstituting the disorder of normal short-term exchanges and the dispersive, restful state of indifference.

Then again, constraint may be at the first level, work may become more noticeable than its effect, the means goes against the end result, and the mind's tension must be nourished by increasingly precarious resources— resources increasingly estranged from the ideal object whose power and action must be maintained at the cost of a fatigue that quickly becomes unbearable. There is indeed a great contrast between two applications of our mind. (50–51)

Not being able to give this text the commentary it deserves, I will merely stress that good disorder does not fatigue; weariness falls upon you. It's a way of ending on a happy note. But the specter of the act that we try to bring on through endless rule- and constraint-making is a fatigue of drying-out and desertification, a fatigue caused by the will and an obstinacy that moves us toward sterility. This is a fatigue effected by rules and perhaps by the breathlessness caused by having to produce an artwork just the same. It is a fatigue caused by being required.

4. Let us pause at this term, *sterility*. In any "this," is it not, at bottom, a question of a banal analogy with the pain of childbirth and with the impatience to give birth.

"This can all be summed up by the following formula: in the production of the artwork, *action comes into contact with the undefinable*" (57; italics in original). Is he stating anything other than that the phallus touches that which lacks it?

And by this touch, assuredly killing the hysterical agitation of renewed beginnings to be forgotten, that of disorders to be misread, of the panic before virtual linkages, a child, too, is engendered: the artwork. As soon as he is born, the child can be subsumed under the rule of knowledge. But at that cost, he will remain misconceived like a child born of inconsistency, as long as he himself has not engendered upon the "consumer" this very same agitation and this very same expectancy of the end of agitation from which the artwork is born.

Besides his *Cahiers* (*Notebooks*),[3] many texts, starting with *La soirée de M. Teste*,[4] demonstrate how this sexual difference (let us call it sexual for the sake of convenience) occupies and undoubtedly preoccupies Valéry's thought. We know his perplexity before femininity and aversion to the possibility of disorder (a male, cognitive term) in his house, the mind.

I shall not develop this point here, but simply state that as much could be said, although in another fashion, of the Kantian preoccupation, the Kantian division between the imagination and reason. With the beautiful, it lies in a division or an emulation, tempered by a marriage [*fiançailles*], and with the sublime, it lies in a conflict brought to the point of rupture where the proliferating network of imaginary possibles becomes shredded and the act or comprehension appears as it truly is in its princely principle: not the rule of knowledge but the law of transcendence and the unknowable, the event itself and the act that is incomparable to any regularity.

I am not particularly beholden to this division of tasks between imaginary and symbolic under the regime of the real, as Lacan would have said, and that Valéry, a bit naively but consistently, calls desire.

I simply state this: "this is art," a cognitively inconsistent sentence, is consistent with regard to the double inconsistency of art (or of writing). There is an "initial" (a poor term) inconsistency in the indetermination of possible linkages that is nevertheless not just hysteria, itself unfelicitously determined in its repetition (here, one would have to explore the area of *unlinking*). And there is a "final" inconsistency of a determinant work-producing event, one that produces it "from time to time," that is, not as an object, but as an occasion, a case, a "this," here and now, the occasion for reiterating the same conflict (which may be sweet or furious) in the said "consumer."

3. REFLECTION

I promised to approach at one point the question of reflection. I lack the moment of reflection, as I always do.

As always, because reflection (which I mean here in the Kantian sense) is of the order of a time in relation to which what we call time, "physical" time, clock time, also called (by antiphrasis, I suppose) "real" time, never ceases being insufficient. The time of reflection, in the wide acception that Kant lends the word (under the rubric of reflecting judgment), is exactly what I have discussed in reference to Valéry under the name of artwork's time.

I repeat that determining an object supposes that we already possess the rule of its signification: the class to which it belongs and the categories of that belonging.

Reflection supposes that we do not possess that rule. Consequently, we do not even possess the object since we are not yet in a position to signify or name it. We can just barely indicate it as "this," as a case or an occasion. This is what Kant says of the object from an aesthetic point of view: it is only occasion.

We do not yet, therefore, possess the rule; we are waiting for it. Actually, in Kantian orthodoxy, it is not the rule of comprehension that we are waiting for, but, where art is concerned, the form imagination might take. But the case (if it may be called such) of reflection being uncertain, expectation and uncontrolled senselessness, is, for this reason, no less pertinent. No less pertinent because it is poorer for the fact that what will serve as act is not even the concept, but the form.

In Kant's *First Critique* there are strange, nearly impenetrable, but decisive pages on the amphibology of the concepts of reflection. I would have liked to lend them some commentary, because they are so enlightening, but I will forgo that wish.

Rather, I would like to focus briefly on the following: reflection is a disposition of the mind by which it judges without concept. To judge, that is, to settle [*trancher*], to decide, to discern: the strength to discern, *Urteilskraft*, is also the strength to bring together, to synthesize. What Valéry calls *act*.

And if this takes place without concept it is because previously, before the advent of a decision, nothing occurs but the senseless flow of every linkage possible—Valéry's "disorder," to which would correspond the comparison with Kant.

We see that this reflection is not a bending of thought back upon itself, but rather a bending within thought of something that seems to not be itself since thought cannot determine it. Yet it is the bending of something that is possibly more "inside" thought than itself.

This further inside is nothing other than feeling, *Empfindung*, or, as we say today, affect. Valéry writes:

A poem on paper is nothing other than a writing subjected to everything one can do to a writing. But among all of its possibilities, there is one and only one that places this text under the conditions where it will take on the strength and form of action. A poem is a discourse demanding and bringing forth a continuous link between the *voice that is* and the *voice that is coming* and *which must come*. And this voice must be such that it imposes itself and inspires the affective state of which the text is the unique verbal expression. Remove the voice and the required voice and all becomes arbitrary, the poem is transformed into a series of signs linked only by the fact that they are traced materially one after the other.[5]

Inspiration of the affective state. I will not insist: we are indeed speaking of the same thing, of a "this" that is in no way a thing, but rather an occasion for a "pure" feeling in the Kantian sense, pure in that it is not motivated by anything. The voice, the double voice, the one that declares that this is beautiful and the one that calls for others to share this feeling-judgment, that voice may also be found in the Kantian analytic.

Again, and to conclude, Valéry: "the works of the mind, poems and others, refer to nothing other than what engenders what engendered them themselves and absolutely nothing else."[6]

A sentence understood clearly as follows: this is art if "this" engenders the pure feeling (disorder, the expectation of its end, and the hope of its transfer to a receiver) from which "this" itself was born.

Such is the resistance of art—a resistance in which all of its consistency consists: determination should never exhaust birth.

Translated by Robert Harvey

12

◆

Prescription

In the Penal Colony[1] will serve as a pretext for exhibiting some of the meanings of the Latin *praescribere*: to write (a name, a title, and so on) at the head of something, to prescribe or appoint, and, in a later form of Latin, to trace an outline in advance, to sketch out. There is also, of course, the meaning of the lower Latin, *praescriptio*, a "limitation," from which derives *"prescription"* in the French civil code, and which designates "the means of acquiring or of freeing oneself, through a certain passage of time, and under the conditions determined by the law." The English "prescription" embraces nearly all of these nuances of meaning. As for German, that language does not confuse the "inquest" [*Vorschrift*], the "decree" [*Verordnung*], the "ordinance" [*Anordnung*], and the *Verjährung*, which is a statute of limitations on a right or obligation.

As always, the violence and simple clarity of Kafka's text require no commentary. If anything, commentary will diminish them—a fact to which I resign myself. My excuse is that I think I can hear, and believe I can make heard, in those pages white with hallucination, the echo of what has been called *the intractable*. I hear them saying that the intractable—that which resists all law—is also an absolute condition of morals. And I think I hear something about the effects of this in politics.

The officer describes to the Western explorer—in French—the machine for execution and how its parts work: the tilting Bed, the box of cogwheels called the Designer, and the Harrow, with its glass needles irrigated by water. The machine writes the sentence on the body of the condemned, recto and verso. Or rather, it cuts it *into* his body until he dies, bloodless. The coup de grace is delivered by a long steel needle (the only one in the apparatus) that pierces his forehead. After which, the bed tips the tortured body into a pit.

The officer describes; the machine inscribes. The officer describes the machine; the machine inscribes the judgment. I'll return to the description . . . let us consider the inscription.

176

The machine executes blindly: the program for the inscription corresponding to the sentence is placed in the box of cogwheels, and it carries it out. This box is what we now term the "dead memory" in a computer, the text of the program being its living memory. Once the program is inserted, one presses the *Enter* key. The machine is blind not because it does not know how to read, but because it can read only the prescriptions inscribed in the language of the former Commandant. Let us say for expedience (too much expedience) that it only reads the prescriptions of the former law. The officer loves the machine because he loves that former law and because the machine is its automaton. This is an artificial intelligence whose memory operates only in the former language. The officer is the servant of this automaton. In his pocket are the papers on which are drawn all of the diagrams corresponding to all of the prescriptions, which in themselves constitute the entirety of the former law. He might be called a maintenance engineer.

Such drawings were termed, in lower Latin, *praescripta*, preinscribed lines; we would say "sketches," lines that direct the execution of something. This is a late (and apparently limited) meaning of *praescribere*—a spatial, and one might say, aesthetic sense of the term. The hand (as one speaks of the hand of the executioner)—here the Harrow—will reproduce the tracings on the body of the condemned. It accomplishes its work according to the model or the template of the lines traced by the former Commandant on the sheet the officer has in his pocket. It executes in the two senses of the word. Latin also gives for this term, "*perimere*." *Perimere* means "to cause to perish" only because it means first of all "to acquire," "to take," or "to buy" . . . completely. The Harrow executes thoroughly and without question, in a peremptory fashion, the reparation of the fault of which the condemned is guilty. The condemned pays with his blood, in full, to the point of its complete drainage. The authority of the forgotten, violated prescription costs him his life.

In this way, I rediscover the initial sense of *praescribere* and *prescriptio*: to write at the head, nearly "to entitle," and to enjoin. The commandment of the former Commandant is a prescriptive sentence. Its form is: do this, do not do that, and so on. It would be appropriate at this point to examine the modalities of the prescription. I will designate all of these modalities with the letter D, which together constitute the spectrum of rights and obligations: obligation, interdiction, the allowed, the tolerated. Insofar as we are subject to these, we are the *destinataire* or addressee—we have obligations. Inasmuch as we can subject others to one of these modalities, we are in the position of *destinateur* or addressor of the prescription—we exert the right to oblige, to interdict, to allow, and so on. As an order deriving from the former law, the prescription is translated aesthetically in the regulating trace, the *praescriptum*, which the machine will follow in order to execute the final *inscriptio*.

I say "aesthetic" for two reasons, one weak, the other strong. The weak reason is that the prescription of the former Commandant must be transcribed on the basis of the words that compose it into lines by which the Designer must abide. We should reflect here on the relation between the letter and the design. Nothing ensures, if we follow Kafka's text, that the writing in use in the penal colony is alphabetical. Indeed there would not even be any need for a transcription if that writing were, so to speak, ideogrammatical, if it were related to the design, like Chinese calligraphy, or the Pharaonic hieroglyph. Thus, the writing is aesthetic in a noble sense of the term. "Noble" because we know, in particular from the Zen Buddhist tradition, that the forming of a sign with a brush dipped in ink requires of the painter-scribe a kind of ascesis, an inner emptying, an elimination of every idiosyncratic passion or intention. This is an aesthetic state of emptiness or absence of everything that is not, let us say, in the spirit of the sign to be inscribed. The body of the scribe must atone for the fault of living, feeling, and willing through a mortification. The required aesthetic is the elimination of what we call aesthetic, the preoccupying influx of the sensible. But this is the path opened by a writing design that is not the one followed by Kafka, so I will pass over it.

The strong, and this time the pertinent, reason for naming the work of the machine "aesthetic" is that its purpose is to make the verbal formulation of the law pass into a corporeal impression. Freud might say: a transcription of word-representations into thing-representations. But here it is a matter of something more than representation, even more than the representation of a thing. It is a matter, in fact, of something other than representation—something other than hallucination, dream, phobia, and so on. If we consult the Freudian catalogue of symptoms, we will find acting-out as a reasonable approximation of what is suffered by the condemned.

The body effects the law, immediately, *in actu*, upon itself—like the hysteric whose wrist is locked, whose nasolabial ridge contracts, or whose stigmata in the hollow of the palms begin to bleed. In his work, Freud observes a favoring of the body in the inscription of the unconscious—a privilege that is called hypochondria. The body (but what are we saying, exactly, with the words, *the body*?) is exposed not only to the obligation of expressing the fault, that is, the unbearable fulfillment of desire, but also to paying for it through suffering. Its most extreme disorder is death. Let me recall here the sequence of impassioned reasons for this argument: the hysterical symptom is found in all neuroses. As is the case with psychosomatization, hypochondria is always associated with melancholia, with a perpetually unresolved loss of a love object. The body accuses itself of this loss, or at least assumes the accusation. It tries to redress the fault of the loss through its suffering and by recalling its perishable nature. Why should this tissue of motifs, this *memento mori* be called "aesthetic"? To be, aesthetically (in the sense of Kant's *First Critique*), is to be-there, here and now, exposed in space-time, and to the space-time of something that touches before any concept or even any representation. This *before* is not known, obviously, because it is there before we are. It is something like birth and infancy (Latin, *in-fans*)—there before we are. The *there* in question is called the body. It is not "I" who am born, who is given birth to. "I" will be born afterwards, with language, precisely upon leaving infancy. My affairs will have been handled and decided before I can answer for them—and once and for all: this infancy, this body, this unconscious remaining there my entire life. When the law comes to me, with the ego and language, it is too late. Things will have already taken a turn. And the turn of the law will not manage to efface the first turn, this first *touch*. Aesthetics has to do with this first touch: the one that touched me when I was not there. This is not the place to develop this negative aesthetics commanding all great art, all writing, and that only reveals itself openly in modern literature and art. Its obligation, its constitutive prescription is to absolve oneself for this insensible touch through the means of the sensible.

The touch is necessarily a fault with regard to the law. It has its place and moment in a savage or alien space and time that are foreign to the law. And to the extent that it maintains itself, persists in the mode of this immemorial space-time, this savagery or this sinful peregrination, it is always there as a potentiality of the body. If the law must both be announced and be obeyed, it must overcome the resistance of this fault or this sinful potentiality constituted at birth (by which I mean a potentiality deriving from the fact that one is born before being born into the law). For the law, the body is in excess. Aesthetics, even the negative aesthetics to which I have referred, cannot suffice to absolve the fault that the body *is* as the space-time of the touch. On the contrary, aesthetics might be said to exacerbate the fault. It repeats, at the very least, the savagery of birth-infancy. This loyalty is the fault of art. But the law must be concerned with this excess of the body.

If the law is to execute itself, it must, like a touch, inscribe itself on the body. The body of which I am speaking can hear nothing of the law; it hears nothing, since it does not belong to the order of the address, to the transmission of *D* in accordance with rights and obligations. Following the requirement of its own cruel aesthetics, the body will have to be *touched*. It will have to be cut into—that is, initially incised. The root of the very late Latin *intaminare* remains *tangere*: "to touch . . . toward and inside." Writing, the holy scripture, will have to be inscribed in the manner of a savage touch upon the body that does not belong to it. This body will be sanctified only by this prescribed inscription of the prescription. This inscription must suppress the body as an outlawed savagery. Only its death can redeem it, atone for it. Redemption requires peremption.

We speak of a "blood debt." But there is blood and blood. *Sanguis*: the blood of life in the arteries and veins; and *cruor*: the blood that is spilled. The first nourishes the flesh. It gives it its hue of blueness, its pinkness, its pallor, its sallowness, its early-morning freshness, the infinite juxtaposition of nuances that drive the painter and the philosopher crazy; an immaterial matter. As for the law, this innocence of the flesh is criminal. It must expiate this fleshly innocence. The blood that flows is called *cruor*. Expiation requires cruelty, *crudelitas* versus *fidelitas*.

The machine of *In the Penal Colony* is the theater of cruelty—the aesthetics of spilled blood demanded by the ethical law when it is enacted. Between the first touch and the second, (which is the last), the touch of the incisive Harrow, the touch of the law, aesthetics changes meaning. We find aesthetics now, placed in the service of the former law, upon and in the tortured body of the condemned man.

The explorer asks the officer: "'Does he [the condemned man] know his sentence [*sein Urteil*]?' 'No,' said the officer." The explorer persists, "'He doesn't know his own sentence [*sein eigenes Urteil*]?'" And here Kafka inserts the stage direction: "'No,' said the officer again, pausing a moment as if to let the explorer elaborate his question" (197). The executor of the law knows that the infant body is ignorant of the law and can know nothing of it (in the sense of an explicit knowledge), unless the law is incised into it to the point where it draws blood. What it *can* know of the law, it can know only in the sense in which *sapere* means *to savor*, to be aesthetically passible, to be *touched*. Indeed, the officer adds, after this silence, "There would be no point in telling him. He'll learn it on his body [*es ihm zu verkünden. Er erfärt es ja auf seinem Leib*]" (197).

The explorer persists: "'But surely he knows that he has been sentenced [*Daß er überhaupt verurteilt wurde, das weiß er doch*]?' 'Nor that either,' said the officer, smiling at the explorer as if expecting him to make further surprising remarks." The explorer, the Westerner (let us remember that he is Western) goes on: "'then he can't know either whether his defense [*Verteidigung*] was effective?'" (197). The response (and once again Kafka's indication regarding the staging or the one): "'He has had no chance [*Gelegenheit*] of putting up a defense,' said the officer, turning his eyes away as if speaking to himself and so sparing the explorer the shame of hearing self-evident matters explained [*dieses ihm selbstverständlichen Dings*]" (197–98). The officer knows that his office, the office of the machine—that is, the necessity for the law to cut into the body to the point where it dies, to execute it in order to execute itself—has its reasons; reasons that are ungraspable to the Westerner. Because the Westerner has forgotten blood;

because he believes that he has already redeemed the body once and for all through some incarnation (Jesus, or Louis XVI), that is, through a law that became flesh at the cost of spilled blood, a *cruor*—but once and for all. Such is the perfunctory attitude of the West regarding the law; such is its nonconfrontation with cruelty. It scarcely wants to know more about cruelty than about the cook's recipe. But you can't make an omelette without breaking some eggs.

The explorer becomes indignant. "'But he must have had some chance [*Gelegenheit*] of defending himself'" (198). And the officer, finally made impatient by the blind nonrecognition which he nevertheless knows and recognizes—the nonrecognition of the crime that *is* the innocent body, the nonrecognition of the fact that, because of this body, the subject of the law and of obligation, the subject *D*, is never obtained—the officer takes the explorer by the arm and shows him the condemned man who salutes in perfect compliance with his superior. Finally, he explains to the explorer:

> "This is how the matter stands. I have been appointed judge in this penal colony. [*Ich bin hier zum Dichter bestellt.*] Despite my youth. For I was the former Commandant's assistant in all penal matters [*in allen Strafsüchen*] and know more about the apparatus than anyone. My guiding principle is this: Guilt is never to be doubted [*Die Schuld ist immer zweifellos*]." (198)

I would willingly make this a "final word." It is, in fact, the word of beginning. The fault is certain—that we have been touched "before" the law touches us. The law can only re-touch us. This re-touching re-touches only if it is peremptory. That is, if it puts an end to the *differend* between the "before" that the body is and the "after," or the law. I emphasize that this is the differend. There is no court that can take up the conflict between the aesthetic and the ethical and decide the matter. A *disputatio* would here be a lie. The body does not argue:

> "'If I had first called the man before me and interrogated him, things would have got into a confused tangle. He would have told lies, and had I exposed these lies he would have backed them up with more lies, and so on and so forth. As it is, I've got him and I won't let him go' [*halte ich ihn und lasse ihn nicht mehr*]" (199).

The differend between the body and the law cannot be converted into a litigation. Only the sacrifice of the body maintains the sanctity of the law. Without deliberation or warranted judgment the sacrificial execution must be repeated automatically each time a criminal birth occurs. The cruelty will be machine-like. The condemned is not saved in another world—he is dumped, dead, into the common grave. It is the law that is affirmed in this manner, and in the world. If the law must execute itself, it will decide the matter upon the body, with the means of the body but against these means. With blood, but blood that will flow and drain out.

What the officer describes is the absolute condition of morals, and its cruelty toward innocence. Innocence is *in all certainty* the sin because it knows nothing of good and evil. It is not *jenseits*, beyond, but on the hither side, *diesseits*. The law prescribes, but not in the sense that it is inscribed in the rubric or the heading. The heading, what comes first, is not the commandment; it is birth or infancy, the aesthetic body. The latter is inscribed so much in advance, on this side, *diesseits*, that the law itself can only inscribe itself by reiterating on the body and in the body an inscription analogous to the one that instituted it. The law is always the body's afterword. It tries to preface the preface that is the *sanguis*. In doing so, it transforms it into a *cruor*, a blood that flows until death—the contrary of a transubstantiation.

I come back now to the *praescripta*, to the sketches that are traced on the former Commandant's papers: the sketches the officer has in his pocket and to which he refers in setting the cogwheels of the Designer in such a way that they will move the Harrow to engrave the words of the law onto the body.

In morals, it is not only a matter of making blood flow. The cruelty must be exhibited. This is its theater, its aesthetics. The body is seized here spatially as the surface into which the letters of the law are cruelly carved. But the time of the body must also be harnessed and touched by the retouching of the Commandment. The law demands the death of a guilty innocence, but it also demands a time of death, and the agony of this innocence.

The officer shows the explorer the papers that bear the *praescripta*, the regulative designs that are traced out by the former Commandant and that serve to program the movements of the Harrow.

> The explorer would have liked to say something appreciative, but all he could see was a labyrinth of lines crossing and re-crossing each other, which covered the paper so thickly that it was difficult to discern the blank spaces between them. (202)

The explorer confesses that he is unable to decipher anything. The officer laughs: "'Yes . . . it's no calligraphy for school children [*es ist keine Schön-schrift für Schuhlkinder*]. It needs to be studied closely'" (202).

This is not a writing to be read, not a writing with which one would teach to read. The child cannot decipher it with his eyes. And yet it is this same indecipherability that will render it decipherable, eminently decipherable, exclusively and peremptorily by the infancy of which I am speaking, the criminal innocence of the body. This is a writing that has no need to be read and will never be. Rather, it is a tracing to be felt, a tracing suffered. What appears to the eyes as a scrambling or scribbling of the line serves the function of extending the ordeal of the body submitted to incision. The officer explains:

"Of course the script can't be a simple one; it's not supposed to kill a man straight off [*Es darf natürlich keine einfache Schrift sein, sie soll janicht so fort töten*], but only after an interval of, on the average, twelve hours; the turning point is reckoned to come at the sixth hour. So there have to be lots and lots of flourishes [*Zieraten*] around the actual script; the script itself runs around the body only in a narrow girdle; the rest of the body is reserved for the embellishments [*Verzierungen*]." (202–3)

The article of the former law to be engraved on the condemned man in the course of the execution attended by the explorer (and Kafka's reader) says, quite briefly in fact, "Honor Thy Superiors! [*Ehre deinen Vorgesetzten*]" (197). If it were a matter of this sole text, the body would be quickly circumscribed with the incision. Would it even die? We could well imagine so. Our executions—those we carry out, we in the West—are in principle expeditious in this way. The former law, on the contrary, requires a time-lag of twelve hours. What is sought from this *post-scriptum*? Why this delay in inscribing itself? Why do the arabesques overlay the text of the law to the point of rendering it undecipherable?

The law requires and awaits another deciphering. The officer describes the agony of the condemned:

"But how quiet he grows at just about the sixth hour! Enlightenment comes to the most dull-witted [*Verstand geht dem Blödesten auf*]. It begins around the eyes. From there it radiates. A moment that might tempt one to get under the Harrow oneself. Nothing more happens [*Es geschiet ja weiter nichts*] than that the man begins to understand the inscription, he purses his mouth as if he were listening. You have seen how difficult it is to decipher the script with one's eyes [*mit dem Augen*]; but our man deciphers it with his wounds [*mit seinen Wunden*]. To be sure, that is a hard task [*Es ist allerdings viel Arbeit*]; he needs six hours to accomplish it." (204)

After which the Harrow runs him "quite through," and he is tossed into the pit.

According to the computation of the Gospel of Mark, Jesus is crucified in the third hour, darkness spreads over the land after the sixth hour, and he dies in the ninth.

Six hours for the wounds to decipher the law, during which, says the officer, "nothing more happens" (204). The agony, properly speaking, the struggle of the body against the law, ceases at the sixth hour; and if nothing more happens, this is because the commandment's retouching, its re-marking, has effaced the initial mark or touch. The immemorial *aisthesis* out of which the innocent body draws its savage resistance to any accusation, or judgment, is broken down, reduced, so to speak. The first six hours are given over, lost perhaps, to resistance, furious resistance, we say, from the Latin *forastica*, from the outside, foreign—resistance whose strength is drawn from outside the law because it comes from something on this side of it, *diesseits*; a torture imposed by what we politely call "moral education." As for sentimental education, there is none. Sentiment is either impolite or dead.

One might say that this delay required by the law for its decipherment is needed not by the law but by the body because it remains hostage to a touch that is blind to all justice. The French law refers to *prescription extinctive* to term a "means of liberation from obligations." This means is determined by two kinds of conditions: first, the conditions determined by the law, which are inscribed here on the papers left to the officer by the former Commandant. But in the terms of *D*, the terms of rights and obligations, as I have said, the prescription is "a means of acquiring or of freeing oneself though a certain passage of time." This prescription is a sentence that derives its authority from a temporal duration. An uninterrupted possession (for a determined period of time) makes something one's property when it is a matter of acquisition. And for the elimination of a debt, uninterrupted service (I suppose this is right: I say "service" for want of a better term), spontaneous subservience, and uninterrupted liability gain absolution for some fault or offense. This meaning of *prescription*, which German translates by *Verjährung*, the superannuation of a crime, can even be applied to the punishment for a crime. We commonly speak of prescription when a deadline has passed and a crime comes under a statute of limitations that annuls the crime and renders the punishment inapplicable.

In the penal colony, at least as the officer wants things, this latter form of prescription can never be involved: the law remains imprescriptible in all cases, that is, always applicable. Every infraction is imprescriptible because it attests to the pre-inscription of an *aisthesis* that is indifferent to *D*, to rights and obligations. And the application of the law always entails the same extinctive prescription: twelve hours of agony in payment for an indubitable offense, that of not having been born *first* to the law but, rather, to and through the *aisthesis*. In the program for inscription placed into the machine, the arabesques are the prescription of this prescription, the commandment of such a term.

Why does the former law prescribe that its execution, its incision on the guilty body, should be delayed in this way? Why not a quick death? Because death is jealous of birth. Or if you will: the law is jealous of the body. Or again: ethics is jealous of aesthetics. The law is jealous because it came second and because *sanguis* did not wait for it in order to circulate "freely."

The body had its time prior to the law, a time when, not being addressed, it did not have to answer. This primary time must also be paid for. In this way, the law's handicap will be eliminated. The law must be an excess of death for the body because the body has the advantage of an excess of birth over the law. The incision of the body by the law must be such that it delays the decision. The gap between decision and incision repeats and annuls the gap between the aesthetic birth and the ethical birth. It repeats it because it maintains the body in the aesthetic through the suffering caused by its wounds. It annuls it because this aesthetic of cruelty has its place and time only on the basis of the ethical.

In the last six hours, the law will have moved into the first place, not only in the way it claims to, but as the body understands it. The body can decipher it only at the cost of spilled blood, and this is the only way in which the law is decipherable. In the eyes of incorporeal spirit—those of the explorer or the new Commandant—it remains indecipherable, like the inexplicable tracings on the papers of the former Commandant. As for the officer who knows how to read these papers and who serves the machine—he also knows that his reading has no significance, no value in regard to the law—it will be necessary—it would have to be necessary—for his body to be flayed by the teeth of the Harrow for him to cease being the overzealous servant of the law and his machine and to become its victim, or better, its instrument [*suppôt*]. To be just it does not suffice to be the officiant of the law: one must suffer from it. This is why the Commandant will lay himself down under the Harrow, as we know, after having set the Designer to the program corresponding to the article of the law he infringes by serving it. And this article says simply: "Be Just."

It must be recognized, then, that the law needs the body, its own dwelling upon the body, as well as the body's resistance to it, in order to inscribe itself, that is, to execute itself. And the law cannot be just without being cruel. If the law does not make blood flow, it is not decipherable and therefore *is* not at all, has no existence. This necessary cruelty is also the homage that the law pays to the body, its way of recognizing a more archaic pre-inscription than its own inscription, and its way of being just toward the *aisthesis* that was not born from it. The way of a jealous justice, which is just because it is jealous.

Latin ascribes the word *praemium* to that part of the spoils that belongs to the god or to the victorious general *before* the victors divide up the whole: a share set aside before the division. The aesthetic infancy of which I am speaking is a portion that does not belong to the division between good and evil. It is set aside from the address *D*. But cutting into this reserved part, the execution of the law stamps it under the name, or the title, of the *praescriptum*, the division. Thus, the body, set aside by its pre-inscription, is in principle placed back under the prescription of the law, obliterated and proscribed. As a *praemium*, it was not meant for *D*. The victor or the god to whom and by whom it was reserved is *aisthesis*. The god or the demon? Indivisible, it was intractable for the prescription of justice. From this difficulty, and with the wrong suffered by this body, arises the question of community and politics.

There is no way to avoid this aporia. The former Commandant and his officiating officer set up what I called the absolute condition of morals in such a way that the reinscription of the intractable under the title (that is, the *praescriptum*) of justice succeeds only by failing. The officer is aware of the aporia. And yet he persists. This is because he admits that justice is unjust with regard to the pre-inscription, the singular body that it seizes. But if it gave up its necessarily torturing inscription by letting itself be intimidated by some *Habeas corpus*, justice, he then thinks, would simply not take place. And it would be unjust in relation to the prescription that is the law. The law prescribes not only *what* must be done, it prescribes *that* it must be done. The sentences *D* that it writes, under the title of *juriscriptio*, demand that they be *enacted*, in the form of a *scriptio in actu*. The act differs from the code by reason of the support of inscription. The law is written on paper, the act of justice in the real. The machine effects the transcription of the one into the other. And the real is necessarily what resists it, innocently, being in no way addressed to it.

The delirious enthusiasm of Kafka's officer expresses this absolutely aporetic condition of morals. The execution of justice, in principle destined to efface an infraction, must automatically entail a wrong, a mortal wrong. The wrong is not occasional in character; it is constitutive of the essence of morals insofar as this essence is *enacted*. And the wrong is not a matter for the law. The law cannot treat it or redress it, because it is based upon it. Once again, this wrong is its condition, as when we speak of a condition of possibility through derealization, and also of the human condition. But in this case, it is an inhuman condition.

This aporia also finds its expression in the order of time, whose pertinence and importance I have tried to demonstrate. I state that the time of agony was required as a compensation for the time of innocence, that is, for the time of the enjoyment of the *praemium* "before" and outside the law of the division. But since it is a matter of enacting the law through the body, this enactment (which is a contradiction, that of justice as a wrong) must manifest itself in the order of time, which is, along with space, the order of the act. This manifestation occurs, however, in a manner that is temporally aporetic, that is, in an impossible torsion of time. I refer here to the first antinomy of the *Third Critique*, recognizing, though I won't develop this any further, that the antinomy is not established on exactly the same contradictory basis as Kafka's. The moment when justice, as an actualization of the law, is inscribed on the body, which it wrongs and even tortures, cannot be *situated*. This moment consists, in fact, in an encounter between the time of an end and a beginning, on the one hand, and on the other, the time that has never begun or finished.

The justice exercised by the machine puts an end to an injustice, the identifiable infraction of which the condemned has become guilty, and, by making him pay for this fault, it absolves him of what was done, preparing him for action that is henceforth freed of this past. In sum, it frees him. Hannah Arendt often commented on this aspect of novelty, of a beginning, even of a birth, entailed by free action, and by the freedom of judgment in particular.

But in Kafka's problematic, this time of a renewal runs up against a time of an entirely different sort, that of the pre-inscription of *aisthesis* as body prior to the law. What I am calling "birth" or "infancy" has nothing to do, at first glance, with the birth entailed by the free act according to Kant or Arendt. In the perspective of reflective reason, the pre-moral, a-moral body is subjected, on the contrary, to the order of an irremediable heteronomy because it is constituted by having been *touched* even before being aware of it, before being able to produce a response to this touch, and having to be responsible for it.

And when I say, "having been touched," I am not even referring to the temporal status of this passibility, which could better be called "intemporal," assuming one collapsed temporality and chronology. But let us say rather that the heteronomy of the body, which is retouched by the Harrow of justice, understands nothing of the succession of cause and effect, and nothing of the extemporaneous temporality wherein arises the causality without cause that is proper to freedom (a causality, that is, which is the effect of nothing). The heteronomy of the body understands nothing of physical time or of ethical time because the *aisthesis* that governs it is neither linked/linking (in the sense of intelligibility) nor unlinked/linking (in the sense of responsibility). The paradox of this body's time—insofar as it is constituted by its non-belonging to itself, its primary disseizure—is that it lacks the modality of any kind of linkage. This is, I think, what Freud meant when he said that "the processes of the system Ucs. are *timeless*."[2] I also think it is poorly stated. These processes are timeless in the sense that time is a chain, in the sense that time links. But time is also stasis.

We say that the pre-intelligible and pre-moral body *was* touched; I reiterate it when I use the prefix *pre-*, and Latin reiterates it with its *praemium*, a pre-purchase, an encumbrance prior to any division. In truth, this preordination to *aisthesis* is aesthetic subordination, and it is not liable to any alteration through the passage of time—it is imprescriptible. I would not even say that it is permanent. Nor primary either, since it is not inscribed in any succession where the secondary would come after it. Let us assume the paradox that when it takes place, there is not yet any time that links.

In the sixth hour, justice passes upon, or into, the tortured body. This is an encounter between the time of redemption and the new beginning with the time of the insistence (or sistence) of the intractable. The officer describes (we arrive now at the description) how the great execution festivities were during the time of the former Commandant. The whole population of the colony was assembled as in a kind of amphitheater on the dunes surrounding the machine; silence reigned and the impassioned interest of the spectators was such that it obliged the officer and his guard to move aside those who wanted to see from up close justice pass over the body of the condemned. "They all knew [says the officer]: Now Justice is being done [*Alle wußten: Jetzt geschieht Gerechtigkeit*]" (209). Nevertheless, the children, according to the wise orders of the Commandant, enjoyed the privilege of being able to come up close. The officer describes the scene to the explorer: "often enough I would be squatting there with a small child in either arm. How we all absorbed the look of transfiguration on the face of the sufferer [*den Ausdruck der Verklärung von dem geänderten Gesicht*], how we bathed our cheeks in the radiance of that justice, achieved at last and fading so quickly [*in den Schein dieser endlich erreichten und sehen vergehenden Gerechtigkeit*]! What times these were, my comrade!" (209)

I shall leave aside for now the question of the little children. One can easily grasp the pertinence, the double pertinence of the privilege accorded to them: infancy of freedom, infancy of the body. And the officer is himself this *bifrons* infant.[3]

The rapture to which the former law has granted them privileged access is *exactly*, that is, it *en-acts*, the moment at which the two infancies merge. Out of this encounter there emanates a ray of light, and this ray is justice itself. The law is written in a writing the body can decipher: in bleeding wounds. This is justice "finally attained," because in this moment the retouching of the body by the stylets of the law obliterates the instant or insistent touch that is its resistant pre-inscription. But it is also justice "already gone," because this re-touching is mortal precisely in that it obliterates. How could an *aisthesis*, or its analogous engraving of the law, be decipherable by what it touches when it is this very touch that constitutes what it touches? The aesthetic body was not a support for inscription of the touch; it is a support for the re-touching, and this suffices to proscribe it. This is why justice fulfills itself only in passing. It *prescribes* itself in the three senses of the word: it is imperative, it has previously transcribed itself through its convolutions in a writing of the body, and it inscribes itself too late to be executable.

But at least the machine, when it was sanctioned in the old days, offered the community the opportunity for the *parousia* of justice. I stated that justice is not situatable. At the site of the desert hills packed with the community waiting for its law, justice cannot be incarnated, it cannot dwell. Justice is a fleeting gleam that passes over the face of the tortured criminal who is finally justified and almost already dead.

Politics enters at this point—that is, the new Commandant. Politics abhors the machine and cruelty. The new Commandant holds public council. Politics deliberates, the new justice provides matter for *disputatio*, for plaintiff and defense, for a trial, for respect of the rights of man even in the condemnation and application of the penalty. The new authority transforms the curious explorer who visits foreign countries into an international expert invited to examine the juridical and penal procedures of the colony's customs and to give his opinion—which can only be very unfavorable. The explorer speaks the language in which the rights of man were written. Women, who were so absolutely absent from the theater of cruelty, are admitted to the affairs of politics. Their delicate handkerchiefs are substituted for the wad of filthy cotton that the dying criminal desperately chews and rechews after a hundred others. As for these handkerchiefs, they wipe away any allusion, stifle any suspicion of allegiance to cruelty. At his death, the former Commandant does not have a right to a consecrated burial. His tomb is hidden under a table in a bar pompously entitled (by the women, I imagine), "Teahouse," and frequented by the workers from the port, "poor, humble people," Kafka writes. The epitaph on the tombstone prophesies despairingly the resurrection of the departed: "Have faith and wait." It indicates that those faithful to the former law "now must be nameless" (226).

These are all signs—each warranting analysis, but which I shall leave unexamined—signs that already the new Commandant and the political order have triumphed, reducing the former to silence, to a clandestine existence, to pseudonymy and to waiting. And thus, signs that the community that gathered together around the machine for the cruel passage of justice has been suppressed. The community now comes together in another manner, through deliberation and tolerance. These are also signs that the Harrow is already out of use, like the papers covered with arabesques, now indecipherable for the new man.

The officer knows all of this, he describes it. And yet he resists, with the resistance of which his body is capable. He asks the explorer to attend the deliberations of the new council and to give no opportunities to the new Commandant, through his responses to the questions that will be asked of him, to officially condemn the former judicial process. He even asks him to cry out or to murmur (that would suffice) his "unshakable conviction" (215) that the procedure is just.

I cannot go into a detailed examination here of this double demand and the officer's hallucinated, anticipatory staging of the episodes of the scene. Nevertheless, it would be essential to follow all the traces of the contradictory, not to say schizophrenic, logic that governs the officer's strategy of persuasion with regard to the explorer. It is all too obvious that the officer doesn't want to know anything about the one to whom he is speaking, though he knows perfectly well who he is. In the excitement of this harangue, even more than in the melancholia of the descriptions, there is a strain of insanity, and above all a dreadful inanity—that of the body that understands that it is forever forgotten by the law.

Seized by the anguish of this prescription, in the sense this time of a peremption due to time (the new, modern time), the officer takes his place on the bed of justice after having dislodged the condemned man. First, he will have set the Designer in such a way that the Harrow should inscribe on his body, with all the required indirection, the prescription of all prescriptions, the law itself: "Be Just [Sei gerecht]." In this manner alone can the law, being enacted, finally reveal itself through a perfect tautology.

For the law to effect the prescription "Be Just," it must engrave itself in the body, like every article of the law. But "Be Just" is a universally valid prescription. It is not normally invoked to punish a specific offense. However, it suits all offenses in that it applies to their essence as an offense, to the "certain offense," which is that of being born "before" the law, outside the law. The impeccable officer is guilty only of this certain offense. By submitting himself to the automatism of the sanction, he will verify one last time the justice of the prescription in relation to his own exemplary case (exemplary precisely because he is exemplary). Such is the tautology: by inscribing upon himself—a purely innocent person—the prescription of justice, he will establish the justice of the prescription. For the commandment and the sanction apply precisely to innocence.

The officer ceases, therefore, to officiate; he subjects himself to the cruel aesthetic of the ethical law. The machine, obviously, understands all of this; it does what is necessary sponte sua. Then, as you know, it breaks down, the box of cogwheels ejects its parts. The officer will be deprived of the agony that his offending body owes to the law. He will also be deprived of the fleeting instant when pure sanctity should radiate from his eyes. The steel needle pierces the skull and kills him, and the broken Harrow holds suspended over the pit a skewered body.

So it would be true that the body is forgotten by the law, true that justice will not have been revealed, true that the new law has already triumphed, a law that has no need of the apparatus of cruelty to act. Adorno will say: true that death itself is dead.

But this is to rush too quickly toward a conclusion. I would end rather with the questions over which the body of the officer remains suspended. Is it true that politics—as it was once enacted and repeated by the Greeks and Romans, then by the Americans and the French two centuries ago—is instituted only at the cost of forgetting the absolute condition of morals, namely, cruelty? Is it true that if the law omits what is absolutely foreign to it, what I have named here the body of *aisthesis* and elsewhere the intractable, it fails to confront the status of its own transcendence and abolishes the support of its effectivity?

Or was that only a delusion, the antimodern, reactionary delusion, as we put it (or as it has been put to us; a delusion with fascist tendencies)? Is the truth of the law not, on the contrary, and as the modern Commandant thinks, that it should be inscribed on paper under the title (*praescriptum*) of an axiom on how to divide—an axiom to which speaking entities (both subject to obligations and holders of rights) will, after deliberation, have agreed? Does not justice consist in the metaprinciple according to which the division applies to everything and must be as nonprejudicial as possible for each and for all? A metaprinciple according to which also, each and all are the sole judges of the division? And must not the good and the bad be understood as what is fitting and unfitting for the interests and expectations of each and all? Are not this good and bad all that is at stake in the question of justice?

Or, finally, must one distinguish between the justices of the new and former Commandants, and maintain both of them, but separately? The one justice appropriate to morals and to its aesthetic of cruelty, the other justice to politics and to its aesthetic of representation? But then, what will be the relation between these two justices? Will it not be—is it not already—the relation between the penitential subject and the citizen? Is this relation itself just?

Translated by Christopher Fynsk

13

◆

Return upon the Return

And then coming back was the worst thing you ever did.

1

How can one be sure that what returns is precisely what had disappeared? Or that what returns not only appears, but is reappearing? Our first gesture would be to challenge reality. What is past is not here, what is here is present. We require a sign—some proof that we are not dreaming—in order to be convinced.

As in a dream, Athena disguises Odysseus as a wandering and miserable old man to make him unrecognizable before he returns to his home in Ithaca. Argos, the dog who has been waiting for him for twenty years, identifies his master (by his smell, I suppose), while the faithful old nurse, Euryclea, identifies him by the scar on his thigh. As for Penelope, expert at deluding suitors, she only decides to trust him when he shows that he knows the secret of the conjugal bed's construction.

Indicators—smell, scar, sexuality—are proofs by the flesh. Only Telemachus takes his father at his word when he says that he is Odysseus. The nominative voice is a sufficient indicator. A son recognizes his father not by his body but by his name.

Several millennia later, here we are, the offspring of the *Odyssey*. We have to believe in the word. Joyce entitled a book *Ulysses*: we are in Ithaca; our father has returned home. From there, Joyce proceeds with his little travel narrative. Confidentially, he will reveal that each of the eighteen sequences of the narrative in fact bears the name of a sequence in the Homeric voyage. An entitled itinerary, the *Odyssey* returns to us in the form of *Ulysses*—or so the work's master assures us.

But how? Some god or goddess has metamorphosed the work to make it unrecognizable. The body of the text bears few indicators that would prove the event of return: no *Odyssey* is perceptible in the *Ulysses* narratives.

As to the name, we sons of Homer cannot trust it. The Greek father's name was *Odusseus*. *Ulysses* is a mere derivative: first from the dialectical Latin, *Olusseus*, and then to the English. The name of the book was deformed by crossing through two cultures, two worlds of names: the Romance world and then classical modern Northern Europe.

Moreover, Joyce's title designates no literary genre, as does the *Odyssey* or the *Aeneid*; these titles designate epic or romanesque cycles. His title indicates nothing of the book's mode of exposition. Some say that this type of title, using the name of the hero, is an old custom (from theater or the novel). But, technically speaking, *Ulysses* is not the name of the book's hero. Rather, it is Bloom, Leopold.

We could say that this is no great transformation: no one is fooled by it. But there is something shifty about it. The title shifts. It does not unravel. It is not a declension of the identity of the *Odyssey*. It evokes it, but in a blurred manner. It makes it equivocal.

Could we say that the journey that Homer traces has served as a model for Joyce and that, at the very least, the *Odyssey* accomplishes a return to *Ulysses* by lending it its compositional structure? We readers, true sons that we are, once in possession of a concordance between Joyce's work and the songs of the Homeric poem, will find it easier to spot the logic of return. But I fear that this ease might also be a trap.

Were we to follow the principle of correspondences, we would never finish counting all the displacements indicating *Ulysses'* divergence from the *Odyssey*. Some of these displacements affect the diegetic universe: namely, reference. Others modify the very story that Homer narrates. And still other displacements (and not the fewest) completely upset the narrative operators lending the *Odyssey* its epic status. I will leave for narratologists the task of counting up these displacements. Their number is such that we would have to wonder how *Ulysses* could ever be recognized as the offspring of the *Odyssey*, especially because the correspondences that we use to designate the episodes in *Ulysses* are only implicit in the text.

Further, the facility that correspondences offer us is an illusory one, for it only reveals to the viewer of classical painting the grid organizing that painting. In the painting, we rediscover the clarity of a *costruzione legittima*, the transparent logic of an ordered spatial and temporal placement. We know, of course, that Joyce employed this ordering not only to make it invisible, but also to unravel it in detail, episode after episode. I am reminded here of something of which we are all aware: his proliferation of the most diverse modes of writing, the heterogeneity of genres and styles, something like a quasi-desperate effort to escape the logic of the artwork in order to render the book inoperative, to prevent it from closing itself into a beautiful totality. The work's construction only serves as a spur for deconstruction. It is not the logic of space-time that is at stake in *Ulysses*, but its paralogisms—paratopisms, parachronisms. While the beautiful classical form closes in upon itself, concludes, and thus makes its return, and while it *is* in itself the return, it is essential that Joycean writing place the cyclical motif under the rule of its disordering and its inconsistency.

Everything is familiar: times of day, places, people encountered, the most insignificant passerby, animals. The adventure is in the language, its proliferation, its dispersion, the transgression of its horizons. *Ulysses* is not the story of a return: the hero has never left. He finds himself at once in the position of an immigrant or a ghost or even a wanderer [*métèque*]. Dubliner though he may be, he does not quite qualify for being *from* Dublin, nor does he manage *to be there*. He does not return: he errs; he is a *flâneur*. He suffers from a breakdown of presence. Each now evokes a once upon a time or another time; each here evokes a there. It is an intermediate state—half-awake, half asleep—which can be likened to the revery of a solitary walker. Everything that is perceived, well-known, too well-known, gives rise to an evocation, to an attentiveness, to a call from elsewhere. Thus Dublin becomes a mere reserve, a depository of day's residues of which the *flâneur*'s daydreaming constitutes itself in order to free him from that city. T. S. Eliot said of Bloom that he "says nothing." In such a *"silent monologue"* all the inner voices call out with no regard for how they might be orchestrated—an orchestration that will become the artwork or the subject.

If the *Odyssey* returns in *Ulysses*, it is in its absence. Ulysses wanders around Ithaca, a place inhabited by its people but deserted—peopled with phantoms. At home, he is not at home. Of King Hamlet, the father's ghost, Dedalus says (in the library episode), that his "speech (his lean unlovely English) is always turned elsewhere, backward" (162). His house is no longer his *oikos*. Thus Hamlet shifts and thus *Ulysses* shifts its gaze toward the *Odyssey*. Hamlet only alluded to the beautiful protective abode and concludes his cycle only in order to direct his speech "elsewhere, backward," according to a space that is not there and a time that is not present.

2

The fact that Ulysses is called *Bloom* is a serious claim to paratopia and to parachronia, to the spatio-temporal breakdown that afflicts the ghost. It is a flagrant trace of the displacement that *Ulysses* imposes upon the *Odyssey* in order to recall it. Bloom the wanderer [*métèque*] par excellence, the converted Jew. A tradition of life and of thought evades the Greek *epos* by a type of being-toward-being that comes from "elsewhere" and from behind, and that is itself largely denied. This is a Ulysses who would shift, through today's Ithaca, toward the land of Canaan and toward a protohistory, without, for all that, returning. The interpolation of the Jewish theme into the Homeric motif, of which there are many occurrences in the Joycean text, should be examined under the title of the return. I will outline some of the characteristics of such an examination.

First, we should recall the parallel suggested by Erich Auerbach, in the first chapter of *Mimesis*,[1] between the Homeric and the Biblical scenes.

At each instant and in every place, the Greek hero *embodies* entirely and expressly his role—the one with which legend enjoins him. His saturation of his own presence to the situation is such that he fulfills his destiny, fills it to completion. He is devoid of sentimentality, by which I mean he has none of the depth, the individual historicity, the unexpected, the "backward," the "else-where" that we moderns attach to affectivity, to the capacity to be affected.

The bard leaves no emotions, situations, or motifs in the shadows, none in reserve. Prosody, the recurrence of stereotypes, and ornamental description render states of the soul and states of fact equally visible. This clarity makes it possible to readily identify voices, references, intentions, and dramatic relations. On the stage thus overexposed, the protagonists are like pure *actants* by which Homeric poetics renders semiotics transparent.

"Homeric style knows only a foreground," writes Auerbach, where the recounting of events unravels a "uniformly illuminated, uniformly objective present," generating a world that "contains nothing but itself." Auerbach points out that "Homeric poems conceal nothing, they contain no teaching and no secret second meaning."[2] They leave no room for interpretation.

To himself as to us, Odysseus is none other than the ever-exposed identity of his role, of his "character." Specifically, he never ages. Athena must disguise him, twenty years after his departure, in order that he be unrecognizable. "Odysseus on his return," notes Auerbach, "is exactly the same as he was when he left Ithaca two decades earlier."[3] His return would provide an example of perfectly identical recurrence, except for the entirely circumstantial modification that the goddess imposes on him.

We moderns, sons of Ulysses, cannot believe that an expedition, an exile, experience in general would not imply some sort of alteration or alienation. Travel stories, *Bildungsromane*, Hegel's *Phenomenology*—all odysseys of consciousness—accustom us to thinking that the spirit only conquers its substance and its final identity, its self-knowledge, by exposing itself to the risky adventure of all its possibilities. We think of the return not as recovered identity of the same with the same, but as the self-identification of the same with the "surveying" [*relève*] of its alterity. At the end of the voyage, Ulysses's truth, for us, is not the same as it was at the moment of departure: the voyage *is* that truth. The truth is in the method, as Hegel said, and the method—the passage through mediations and changes—is in no way extrinsic to self-knowledge (as Athena's metamorphosis of Odysseus is): it *is* self-knowledge.

This amounts to saying that with modernity, what is true ceases to be a place, a dwelling—*domus* or *oikos*—from which some unessential circumstance (external war, the Trojan War) dislodges the master from the house: a place that one would merely need to clean, whose floor need only be washed (by massacring suitors or hanging unfaithful servants) in order to restore intact its cleanliness—a cleanliness that includes the nuptial bed, still resting on its olive stump, the token of an ineradicable self-reference.

In this regard, modernity owes the interiorization of war to Christianity. The return to peace in the house is prevented by an initial exile that drove us out and keeps us from returning. This exile is caused by an altogether internal transgression for which only expiation, the accepted suffering of exile—that is, sacrifice—can bring reparation and allow the return to innocence. The theme of self-sacrifice, of which Christ is the paradigm, subtends the speculative motif of an experience conceived as death and resurrection of the spirit.

Helen's beauty assuredly spreads disorder in Greek houses. Yet that beauty only gives rise to a distant war. Under the name of Eve, woman incarnates the primal figure of sin, the eternal source of the secret war that prohibits the spirit from returning to the house of the father. Yet, in the Christian *geste*,[4] the power of the "surveying" is such that Mary Magdalene, the evil Eve, attends the son in this agony. And thus the prostitute is redeemed. When that pagan-Christian and very Catholic Claudel reads the Homeric *nostos*, he makes sure that Penelope is the symbol of this inner war's conclusion. In his eyes, the olive tree of the conjugal bed, what he calls the "mediator between substance and heaven," is the figuration of the flesh's redemption and the true return.

I am amazed that occasionally some commentator places Molly Bloom and her final "Yes yes" under this pagan-Christian motif of the Virtuous Mother and of shelter regained. Claudel, who was more clear-sighted, returned to Joyce his signed copy of *Ulysses*, labeling it "diabolical." It doesn't matter that Bloom was baptized three times (the same number of times that Peter renounced Jesus), the sacrificial and redemptive dialectic celebrated in the cemetery and the church that he visits remains foreign to him. And we well know that, for Joyce, Rome, every bit as much as London, was the name of Ireland's oppressor.

If there is return in *Ulysses*, that return is no more Christian than it is Greek. I return to Auerbach's parallel. He notes that the text of the Old Testament is a juxtaposition of little stories. Their conjunction requires no more than the *and* that lends order to paratactical time, without distinction between main stories and subordinate ones. These stories touch upon the most ordinary aspects of life. Far from being heroes, the protagonists are petty tribal chiefs or heads of families, shepherds threatened by scarcity, displaced here and there by migrations and by wars in the vast Orient. These brief narrations pass over anything having to do with the decor where the scene unfolds: no descriptions, not even ornamental ones, of persons or sites—just names. Hardly a word is exchanged. The injunctions, the entreaties, the decisions all appear briefly, leaving motives and arguments in obscurity. As in Beckett's theater, silence and a certain indefiniteness suggest that something is at stake that no one, actor or reader, identifies.

Homeric gods deliberate in council and then go out in person to support their protégés while they carry out the plan of strategy imparted to them. Unique and invisible, Yahweh (like Godot) forces, prohibits, promises, makes himself heard without explaining his goals—all this to a people that he holds hostage. "In the Old Testament stories the peace of daily life in the house, in the fields, and among the flocks, is undermined by jealousy over election and the promise of a blessing. . . ."[5]

Auerbach concludes two things concerning this altogether different scenography:

1. On the one hand, it opens onto a demand for realism, a concern for the concrete fact, an exactness stripped of all epic amplification in which he believes the rules of historiography have their source.
2. On the other hand, the enigma surrounding the logic of episodes requires a ceaseless, perhaps interminable effort at interpretation on the part of the reader or the member of the audience—an effort that will engender hermeneutics.

I recall these few observations from Auerbach not because I subscribe to them, nor to discuss them, but because they explain the extent to which the interpolation of the Jewish motif into the return of the Homeric *epos* displaces it. The details of the demonstration need not be reviewed: impenetrability of motifs; attention to the most everyday detail, examined as if under the microscope; the solitude of characters; the difficulty of attributing to individuals the voices as they gossip, discuss, or "monologue"; ruptures in narrative rhythm; propagation of discursive genres and tones . . . while all of this does not derive from Biblical writing alone, none of it belongs to the epic tradition.

Even though polymorphous or metamorphous prose, for example, must be attributed to the modern decomposition of literary languages, and therefore derives only indirectly from Biblical writing, it must nonetheless be linked to it. For this labor of writing inscribes itself in an aesthetic or a counteraesthetic (an an-aesthetic) of the sublime, which, since Longinus, through the Ancient–Modern quarrel and Romanticism, has relentlessly assaulted signifying syntheses. This an-aesthetic not only assaults the rules that establish classical framing (notably spatio-temporal framing) and genres, it assaults the deeper cultural, ideological, and perhaps even ontological syntheses that fix the signifier (scriptural or pictural) into syntactic and semantic groups ranging from the local trope or figure to the broadest finalities on manners of writing or painting. These are the very syntheses that, again and again in ages past, lent their signifying value to the signifier as well as foundation and authority first to poetics and later to the aesthetics of the beautiful.

Now, this anti-synthetic work I have in mind, this work that strives to match the default of representation to which the feeling of the sublime attests, has distant sources in the Biblical text. Longinus, in his *Treatise*, points to this, but still confusedly. It comes to light, however, following Boileau (and notably in the French debate) on the subject of religious eloquence. Recourse to the *"je ne sais quoi"* creates at least the effect of intervention in order to confound "grand style," the "foreground" style, the Greek ideal of beauty and the Roman ideal of eloquence. It opens a breach in the classical wholeness constituted of gods, men, and nature. Through this breach, one begins to perceive a non-world, a desert where a voice calls out in peremptory fashion, saying nothing more than, "Listen."

By the time Joyce wrote *Ulysses*, artists and writers knew (in divergent ways, to be sure) that in a very broad sense the stakes of writing are (as they have always been, but now explicitly) not to create beauty, but rather to bear witness to a liability to that voice that, within man, exceeds man, nature, and their classical concordance.

The aesthetics of a Baudelaire or a Flaubert already prove this. Everything, down to the motif of the city so predominant in *Ulysses*, belongs to the new stakes of writing. It is not enough to consider Bloom as a historian or a sociologist, as the literary counterpart of urbanization in progress. He is also and especially, I believe (with Benjamin), the return of solitude, of the desert, and of inoperativity at the heart of the community. The modern city is the operativity [*œuvre*] in the bosom of which the community and the individual are deprived of their artwork [*œuvre*] by the hegemony of market value. Far from being a free city, Joyce's Dublin is, to use Jean-Luc Nancy's words, an inoperative community.[6] Bloom, the ad salesman, is witness to this painful futility. But his witnessing should not constitute a work in the academic sense; that witnessing is only the muffled mumbling of phrases free-associating "inside" when no one is speaking to you, when you're in the desert. Nor, further, must Joyce be allowed to constitute a work out of Bloom's witnessing. He can only bear witness to the fact that witnessing does not constitute a work—that witnessing is not Greek. *Ulysses* is one of the greatest works devoted to, consecrated to inoperativity. The *Odyssey's* framework returns in it only to be deconstructed and to leave room for the void of interpellation.

Witness the "Aeolus" episode: "We were always loyal to lost causes, professor [MacHugh] said [in the offices of the *Evening Telegraph*]. Success for us is the death of the intellect and of the imagination" (110). The name of this death is England: under its domination, Ireland is doomed not only to palpable misery, but also to the same radical inoperativity as Israel in Egypt. At the college historical society, where assimilation has just been advocated, John F Taylor explains that it is, on the contrary, by preserving and observing the tables of the law "graven," he says, "in the language of the outlaw," by refusing the law of the empire, that the Irish people will, as the Jewish people had done before, succeed in escaping "their house of bondage" (117).

I do not claim that *Ulysses* is the book of the law and the exodus. It is simply written in the writing of the outlaws that were Joseph's sons in Egypt and Parnell's sons in Ireland. In a bastardized [*météquisée*] Ireland situated beyond the pale of Europe, Bloom, the wanderer [*métèque*], is more Irish than the Irish. Being suspicious of his people, Moses looked askance at a people subservient to the idolatry of the false Roman god and to the interests of British power. But Parnell failed to deliver this people. And Bloom, a bad Jew and an ordinary Irishman, is incapable of holy anger. The only thing left in him of Moses' call to rise and leave is a disavowal of what is here, indignity at ordinary life, a cowardly concession of the soul to derisive reality.

"And yet [Moses] died without having entered the land of promise," says J. J. O'Molloy in the same episode. To which Lenehan adds, "And with a great future behind him" (118). The exodus is perhaps a return. It is at least the promise of a return. But this promise remains, and must remain, held as a promise: never realized. Moses, Parnell: dying before fulfillment. The return's future remains hidden in the promise made long ago. The paradox of all ages is what structures the work of an anamnesis: what was announced in the past was that there would be a future to attest to it. Writing is this work of bearing witness to a presence that is not the "foreground" present. Once and for all, presence will have been promised; writing is devoted to not forgetting it.

Speaking to himself in the "Lestrygonians" episode, Bloom says: "Can't bring back time. Like holding water in your hand. Would you go back to then? Just beginning then. Would you? Are you not happy in your home you poor little naughty boy?" (137). The enticing, vulgar interpellation comes from a woman's voice: the quote from a letter Bloom found at the *poste restante* from a correspondant, Martha, answering an obscene solicitation he had sent under the pseudonym, Henry Fleury.

Thus, two things find expression in the lowest of languages and feelings: the sorrow of captivity in Egypt and the misery of a false flight that would be no more than a repetition of the flight Bloom carried out in Molly's company and upon her person. Martha, Molly, the sirens, Bella, Zoe, Flora, Kitty, the girls on the beach—women never assist in the flight from Egypt: they *are* Egypt. Being unhappy at home means being unhappy at *their* home. One must not want or even hope to "repossess" this home of one's own, that is, to return to it. *Home* is not what was promised. Bloom will never again find Penelope. He will lay down, head to feet (the Beckettian position). And he is not the one to whom she will say "yes yes."

Pell-mell, and merely hinted at, these are some indicators for following the cleft or the crack that Jewishness (the Irish condition) creates in the beautiful amphora representing the Homeric voyage.

3

I should address the question of fatherhood insofar as it affects the motif of the return in *Ulysses*. The question of fatherhood or lineage is also that of authority, or of the author, or, as we say, of creation. Under the title of lineage, Joyce lays out his poetics.

I will restrict myself to three observations, all of which concern the motif of return.

To begin with, lineage conforms to the general principle of reversibility. The father is also son of his son, as the son is father of his father. They engender one another. We could say that they are the same individual, self-engendered.

This does not seem to be the case for the *Odyssey*. We do, however, find a trace of this principle in a fact well known to scholars. "Telemachus" is, in addition to Odysseus's voyage, placed prior to it in the narrative order. To complete this collage, Telemachus, who leaves for Ithaca in Song 4, only arrives there in Song 15, just shortly before his father. The son's adventures are like a pre-image of his father's.

Joyce respects this disposition in the composition of *Ulysses*. When Dedalus first meets Bloom at the brothel, only in the fifteenth episode, the question to be posed is whether, when this return of the son to the father and of the father to the son occurs, the father recognizes himself in the son, as if he were himself the son, and vice-versa. This is apparently the case in the *Odyssey*.

In *Ulysses*, the encounter, as we know, concludes with a separation. I would even venture to say that it begins with this separation. In the end, Bloom settles back into his home, while Dedalus leaves it. The lineage appears shattered, impossible. The son does not re-create his father. But it is precisely by this failure of identification that the true principle of generation is made clear. The authentic lineage requires the rupture, the interruption of the link between father and son.

Let me address the *mise-en-scène* of this rupture. In the Ithaca episode, Dedalus has just refused Bloom's hospitality, and they leave together, saying goodbye. Bloom heads off first with his candle, followed by Dedalus, diaconal hat on his head and rod of ash in hand (two props of the exodus introduced in the third episode, "Proteus") (40). Question: "With what intonation *secreto* of what commemorative psalm?" Answer: "The 113th, *modus peregrinus: In exitu Israel de Egypto: domus Jacob de populo barbaro*" (573). Commemoration, secret, peregrination or pilgrimage, exodus— this text is that of the Vulgate Bible. In the Torah, the rabbinical translation of Psalm 114 reads: "When Israel came out of Egypt, / the House of Jacob from a foreign nation."

Note, obviously, the resurgence of the wandering Jew at the precise moment of non-return. If the son rejects the father, the father also persists in returning toward the flesh of his house, toward his wife and carnal generation, that is, toward the Egypt of representations.

I refer to only two indicators of this movement in the second part of Bloom's journey: to the fact that his meeting with Dedalus alters the figure of the father and that it renders it alien to the son.

At the moment that Dedalus finds Bloom, in the brothel, Bloom is in the process of reclaiming the potato (Irish misery, once more) from Zoe. He carries this potato in his pocket and had given it to her upon entering, like a fetish. He reclaims it in these terms: "It is nothing, but still, a relic of poor mamma. There is a memory attached to it. I should like to have it." To which Stephen replies: "To have or not to have that is the question" (453).

To possess the memory of the wife and the house, to have it back. The son comes upon the father engaged in the imaginary dimension of this return— that of nostalgia. The scene of domestic *jouissance* and its appropriation, where this movement is completed, unfolds sumptuously in the Ithacan episode. The lady daydreams upstairs in the tepidness of intimate flesh and underwear. Downstairs, in the kitchen, her husband totes up all the petty modern (or postmodern) interests of a semi-skilled worker: puttering, minor patents, astronomy-made-easy, subway eroticism, playing the horses, moonlighting to supplement the budget, gardening, obtaining credit, seeking petty distinction. Already in the "Eumaeus" episode, we are reminded that Parnell has failed to free Ireland because of a woman. As soon as they offer themselves, flesh and incarnation, by their furor, cause writing and exodus to fail. Once one is satisfied, exaltàtion fails also, because it requires accounting. These are two meanings of the French word *jouissance*. We also learn that Bloom has been thrice baptized: Protestant, English, and Egyptian.

A complementary indicator of the necessary separation between father and son can be found in the son's story. From the beginning of "Telemachus," Dedalus is en route for, or rather, is rehashing, an irremissible inner exodus. I only mention one example (out of thousands) of distancing within apparent presence. Dedalus has sent Mulligan a telegram. Mulligan reads it aloud joyfully in front of the library debating club, which Dedalus himself has just met up with ("Scylla and Charybdis"): *"The sentimentalist is he who would enjoy without incurring the immense debtorship for a thing done.* Signed: Dedalus" (164).

This inscription from afar, this telegraphy (Does "Telemachus" mean "the end of battle" or "battle at a distance"?) recalls the indignity of all sentimentality: getting something for nothing. To assume that one is free from debt because one has paid the "returned" object through *jouissance.* But the debt is enormous, prohibiting the completion of this return that is *jouissance.* Through this, the flow of "sentimentality" that inundates Bloom, having returned from Ithaca, finds itself distanced.

A second observation. The thesis of fatherhood or true lineage is expounded, in this same library and primarily through Stephen's words, regarding the case of Shakespeare's identification with Hamlet. Elsinore is a failed Ithaca. The suitor has conquered Penelope, and Ulysses (the king) has been murdered. Penelope has been unfaithful like Helen. The father can only return to the son in absence, through his voice, which recalls the debt. You must revenge me, reestablish me, that is, engender me anew. Dedalus holds (without sustaining it) the thesis that Shakespeare was this absent, humiliated, cuckolded father, that he always played the dead king at the Globe, and that his wife, Anne, was, like the queen, a whore, a Molly.

In the end, there is no consubstantial fatherhood, except in the mystical sense that is also the highest degree of uncertainty concerning lineage. "Fatherhood, in the sense of conscious begetting, is unknown to man" (170). And further, "in the economy of heaven, foretold by Hamlet, there are no more marriages, glorified man, an androgynous angel, being a wife unto himself" (175). In the domestic economy, incest rages along all lines of kinship, except the father-son lineage. "They are sundered by a bodily shame. . . . What links them in nature? An instant of blind rut" (170–71). What links them separates them: the complusion to copulate, woman, the "agenbite of inwit."

> Fatherhood . . . is a mystical estate, an apostolic succession, from only begetter to only begotten. On that mystery and not on the madonna which the cunning Italian intellect flung to the mob of Europe the church is founded and founded irremovably because founded, like the world, macro and microcosm, upon the void. Upon incertitude, upon unlikelihood. . . . Paternity may be a legal fiction. (170)

Lineage, or more precisely, true paternization, is only the transmission of what I have termed *calling.* There is no carnal lineage between males: the feminine house is useless, even harmful to it. At Shakespeare's birth, "[a] star, a daystar, a firedrake, rose" (172). It is the star William follows upon leaving Stratford and the "arms" of his future. "A star by night, Stephen said. A pillar of the cloud by day" (173). Once again the theme of the wandering Jew. Shakespeare answers the call that comes to him from the desert. In fleeing from the incestuous and lascivious mother, Egypt, he also flees from the pretenders to carnal fatherhood. One leaves *here*, one goes over there, backward, elsewhere, toward the true past that is still to come.

A final remark on the question of fatherhood as unfulfilled return. What is said of the father and son must also be understood with regard to the writer and reader. The reader engenders the author, and the author is the reader of his reader. But there is also a flesh interposed between them that impedes a pure genealogy: language, the whore that language is. It can represent, say, and make love to everything. It is the Egypt of writing.

Language is like water, a kind of great profligate carnal sea that offers itself to everything, infiltrates everywhere, redoubles and represents everything. Joyce's writing, plunged in this water, tries to defer the effect of representation and ductility, to hold back the insidious tide. In the catechism recited at Ithaca, Bloom's elegy to water takes on the dimension of an inundation. Bloom surrenders himself to the immersion. But he is careful not to inform Stephen of his adoration and his drowning. The reason: "The incompatibility of aquacity with the erratic originality of genius" (550).

One must necessarily give in to language when one writes, but one cannot give in to it either. The defeat, which consists in the trust one puts into language, must necessarily be continuously defeated in its turn; the trust must remain suspended. "I believe, O Lord, help my unbelief. That is, help me to believe or help me to unbelieve? Who helps to believe? *Egomen*. Who to unbelieve? Other chap" (176). What says yes to the permanent yes of woman-language is the Ego. As for the "other chap" (who tells him no, no, that's not it, you haven't got it, arise and leave), I hear in him the shattering voice that calls. ("To chap" is also "to split," "to cleave." And a "chap" is a "peddler," the traveling salesman.)

Literary genealogy responds to the same demand and runs into the same aporia as lineage. How, if one writes, is it possible not to say yes to the sea of language? Genius consists in inscribing within it what it cannot espouse. One thing that cannot be done with water is to part it. Joyce-Dedalus lacerates language. It closes up again immediately under his flamboyant style.

I return to the catechism of the Ithaca episode. Question: "For what creature was the door of egress a door of ingress?" Answer: "For a cat" (573).

This is thus a final return, accompanied by this she-cat [*chatte*], a return upon and of sexual difference. An argumentative genre.

On the one hand, since the father is son of the son and the son father of the father, *male* is what engenders itself without sexual intercourse. Or, rather, only engenders itself, in truth, according to the voice, which is male. From oneself, through the sole obeyance to the injunction, issues nothing (fire and storm cloud) to hear, that is, nothing to write. With regard to carnal fatherhood, the Lord, blessed be His name, can very well pull some Isaac from the withered belly of an old woman and make of him a gift to his old man. But there will nonetheless come a day when the voice will come to reclaim him, if not by sacrifice, at least by *ageda*, by binding or alliance. This is a warning that males, the Ulysses's and the Abrahams, would be mistaken to expect any revenue from what their wives claim to offer them. Bloom has lost his son Rudy. And Stephen has rebuffed the final wishes of his dying mother. The sexual generation is only the occasion for sin, for forgetting memory's debt. This memory is that nothing returns, that everything is an advent. This is what anamnesis means: a thinking, a struggle backwards, of which the work of writing consists. And this is endless. A peregrination without return.

But, on the other hand, there is the she-cat [*chatte*] (it is, as we know, a term of endearment the French give to the female sexual organ), which is the passage through which the father enters and out of which emerges his son. The pussy objects that it is, in the male-to-male lineage, the obligatory threshold, the inevitable path for the transmission of the seed. It argues that if the Lord has created us sexed, sectioned and separated, and if he holds the power to reunite us according to the fire in our loins, it is not only to test us, but to expose the mystery of his ways. In particular, that the self-engenderment, of which sexuality is the sole heavenly guardian, resides (oh so palpably!) *ad portas mulieris*.

We see the argument. It is that of the Virgin Mother and the prostituted saint.

Now, what relation can this *disputatio* on sex have with the return and the return upon the return? That relation in which the things are not properly ordered: first, the adequation of the father-son, of voice and writing; second, the passage through the woman, the feminine passage, the concession and *jouissance*. No, it is the contrary, or, rather, not even the contrary: it is not even the same order returned on the same time line, it is the initial definitive disorganization of that so-called time line, which is only time consciousness.

The question *Ulysses* poses in return is not even whether one can step twice in the same stream, which is a pardonable uneasiness of consciousness faced with chronological succession (that succession forcing consciousness to forever defer its actualization, so that it must always catch up with itself, so that it must hold back at every step of its advance along the time line).

Ulysses poses another question altogether: Is not sexual difference the same as ontological difference? Is it not from sexual difference that the temporalizing separation of consciousness with itself is engendered? And from it that the unconscious as extra-memorial past is formed?—a past that does not last as past and that one cannot have back, that is, an inappropriable past. Is it not this immemorial that calls out? And is it not writing that attempts, desperately, to formulate an answer to this remainder to which the soul is held hostage?

Objection: Why would sexual difference occupy this eminent position in engendering when it has been established that, according to Joyce-Dedalus, true generation, fecundity, and propagation owe nothing to it and that it is carried out in the father-son identity?

Answer: It is readily demonstrable that the idea of male self-engendering—autochthony of warriors in the Greek version, the voice's injunction ("call") in the Hebrew version—only betrays (translates and disguises) the irreparable preeminence of sexual difference.

Argument: Homeric males go off to war to seek an unfaithful woman and Odysseus would simply have no need to return had he not taken part in this expedition. By this consecution, and also because the whore lies dormant in the matron, Helen takes precedence over Penelope. As for the Jews, their book recounts the fact that original sin (the offense of claiming to equal and substitute for divine transcendence: the voice) is the doing of a woman. By this consecution, and here because the she-devil lies awake in the wife, Eve takes precedence over Sarah. As proof, the laughter that overcomes the old woman when her belated pregnancy is announced: this is the same offense that Eve committed against the Lord. Another name for Israel is "it will laugh."

Concession: To be sure, this return that the *Odyssey* is attempts to form the scar of difference, and this exodus that the Pentateuch recounts attempts to free itself from it.

Conclusion: Both attempts bear within them the admission of an initial and recurrent servitude. This is why an originary position, before any mediation, as perennial source, must be granted to sexual difference. It is not because Joyce is overly obsessed, obeying some realist scruple or bent on shocking us, that there is so much sex in *Ulysses*. Rather, it is because the writing of Homeric return—even returned via the Biblical exodus—cannot fail to come up against that difference, that more ancient, intimate obstacle that is opposed to return, to crash into it and ceaselessly return to it.

In returning upon and against the event of sexual difference (a difference that has no site, no representation, one that engenders uncontrollable anxiety, but whose ductile force ceaselessly immerses this anxiety and impotence), and in reinscribing this event in language. Joyce's writing announces the irreparability of the offense and the impossibility of return. The writer can only bear witness to his magnetic attraction at the level of language. For it is not enough to take this anxiety linked to the irremissible hidden separation as the object of a discourse (as I myself am doing here). To truly bear witness to it, one must make language anxious.

There is an eternal undoing of the spirit. We cannot avenge it. By avenging it, we repeat it, as Hamlet does. It is not situated in a temporality of successions. This anxiety, this obsession for pleasure, this horror, always begins again. This is what supports parataxis, the return of the *and*; this is what interferes with any return.

I shall end. Dedalus presents Shakespeare's initial undoing in these terms:

"Belief in himself has been untimely killed. He was overborne in a cornfield first (a ryefield, I should say) and he will never be a victor in his own eyes after nor play victoriously the game of laugh and lie down. Assumed dongiovannism will not save him. No later undoing will undo the first undoing. The tusk of the boar has wounded him there where love lies ableeding. If the shrew is worsted yet there remains to her woman's invisible weapon. There is, I feel in the words, some goad of the flesh driving him into a new passion, a darker shadow of the first, darkening even his own understanding of himself. A like fate awaits him and the two rages commingle in a whirlpool. . . . The soul has been before stricken mortally, a poison poured in the porch of a sleeping ear" (161).

Stephen slips this message to King Hamlet: "The poisoning and the beast with two backs that urged it King Hamlet's ghost could not know of were he not endowed with knowledge by his creator" (162).

Suppose that the creator reveals nothing to us of this poisoning. And suppose that, because the creator does not exist or, at least, does not speak, the voice having silenced itself, we take an entire lifetime to learn that we were not murdered but engendered by this poisoning of the flesh.

It is then that Dedalus adds these words that will have served to return me upon the return, to return it and to attempt (with Joyce) to turn myself away from it: "That is why the speech [Hamlet's, Shakespeare's, Joyce's] is always turned elsewhere, backward" (162). Words that Dedalus comments upon as follows: "Ravisher and ravished, what he would but would not" (162); in other words, the very designation of the work of inoperativity. With this one last joke: "He goes back, weary of the creation he has piled up to hide him from himself, an old dog licking an old sore. But, because loss is his gain, he passes on towards eternity in undiminished personality" (162). *Dog* is the re-turned truth of *God*, yet no writing can prevent *Dog* from returning, in its turn, into *God*. Return, nonetheless, of inoperativity. Amen.

Translated by Robert Harvey and Mark S. Roberts

Notes

◆

INTRODUCTION

1. Lyotard's first book, *La Phénoménologie* (1954), was published in translation in 1991 (see under "1954" in the Bibliography). The translation of his second, and perhaps most important work, *Discours, figure* (1971) is forthcoming. *La Condition postmoderne* (1979), however, was the first to be translated, in 1984. The anthologies in question are *Driftworks* (1984) and *The Lyotard Reader* (1989).
2. A selection of these articles is now collected, with an introduction by Mohammed Ramdani, in Jean-François Lyotard, *La Guerre des Algériens: Écrits, 1956–1963* (Paris: Galilée, 1989).
3. Other notable members of "Socialisme ou barbarie" were Cornelius Castoriadis and Claude Lefort. For Lyotard's history of the group, see his "Memorial of Marxism: For Pierre Souyri" in *Peregrinations: Law, Form, Event* (1988), 45–75.
4. Page 90 in this book.

CHAPTER 1. THE PSYCHOANALYTIC APPROACH TO ARTISTIC AND LITERARY EXPRESSION

1. In this connection, see the following linguists' research: for the structuralist school, Ivan Fónagy, "Le Langage poétique: Forme et fonction," *Diogène* 51 (1965), and "Der Ausdruck als Inhalt," *Dichtung und Mathematik* (1965); for the school of semiotics, Tzvetan Todorov, "Les Anomalies sémantiques," *Langages* 1 (1966). Here we see the buildup of a concept—that of transgression— that is the anticoncept of structuralism just as expression ("style") is antiliterature ("antiwriting"); cf. Roland Barthes, *Writing Degree Zero* (New York: Hill and Wang, 1967). This falls squarely in the "logic" of desire, itself antilogical.
2. Gilbert Lascault derives from this set of problems the same methodological difficulty as we encounter here: "to constitute a theoretical discourse that goes beyond the metaphors of aesthetics without disregarding them." I agree with him that "psychoanalysis makes it possible to define this project." Gilbert Lascault, "Esthétique et psychanalyse," in *La Psychanalyse* (Paris: Denoël "Le Point de la question," 1969), 272.
3. Sigmund Freud, "The Unconscious" (1915), in *The Standard Edition of the Complete Psychological Writings of Sigmund Freud*, ed. by James Strachey (London: Hogarth Press, 1953–74), vol. 14, 167. Henceforth all references to

Freud's writings will be to the *Standard Edition*, which will be referred to as, for example, *SE* 14, 167.

4. See Anton Ehrenzweig, *The Psychoanalysis of Artistic Vision and Hearing: An Introduction to a Theory of Unconscious Perception* (London: Routledge and Kegan Paul, 1953); "Une Nouvelle Approche psychanalytique de l'esthétique," in André Berge et al., *Entretiens sur l'art et la psychanalyse* (Paris–La Haye: Mouton, 1968). Cf. Jean-François Lyotard, "Le Travail du rêve ne pense pas," *Revue d'esthétique* 21 (1968): 26–61.

5. Sigmund Freud, *The Interpretation of Dreams* (1900), *SE* 4–5; chapter 7.

6. Here I am using (with a different vocabulary) Ehrenzweig's research. He characterizes this figure as *Gestalt-free* and *thing-free*, liberated from good form and from thing-bound realism.

7. Here it would be possible to discuss form as expounded by Vladimir Propp in his *Morphology of the Folktale* (Bloomington: Indiana University Research Center in Anthropology, Folklore, and Linguistics, Publication 10, 1958, 1968), and as contested by strict structuralism: cf. Claude Lévi-Strauss, "La Structure et la forme," *Cahiers de l'Institut de science économique appliquée* 99 (1960).

8. Sigmund Freud, *Inhibitions, Symptoms, and Anxiety* (1926), *SE* 20, 87.

9. Sigmund Freud, "Project for a Scientific Psychology" (1895), *SE* 1; *The Interpretation of Dreams*, chapter 7; "Formulations on the Two Principles of Mental Functioning" (1911), *SE* 12.

10. Emotional space, that is, the support of literary or visual space, is constituted on the basis of this withdrawal of the signifier; such is the thesis maintained by Pierre Kaufmann in his remarkable book, *L'Expérience émotionelle de l'espace* (Paris: Vrin, 1967); the close correspondence between Kaufmann's book and Jacques Lacan's reading of Freud will be apparent. See also Kaufmann's contributions in Berge et al., *Entretiens, passim*. Cf. Jean Laplanche, *Hölderlin et la question du père* (Paris: Presses Universitaires de France, 1961). An easily available summary of Lacan's interpretation may be found in "The Seminar on 'The Purloined Letter'" (1957), useful as an example of the whole of the work of this French psychoanalyst (who himself placed it at the beginning of his *Ecrits* [Paris: Seuil, 1966] with supplements), and at the same time decisive with regard to our problem since it bears on a literary work, Edgar Allan Poe's tale, "The Purloined Letter." Far from saying that literature should be treated as a field for interpretation, as a symptom, it produces a representation-text that shows that "the unconscious means that man is inhabited by the signifier" (35). It is vain to put it aside, to *purloin* it; it will always reach its destination, as "The Purloined Letter" instructs us.

11. See Sigmund Freud, *Delusions and Dreams in Jensen's "Gradiva"* (1907), *SE* 9; "Creative Writers and Daydreaming" (1908), *SE* 9; *Leonardo Da Vinci and a Memory of His Childhood* (1910), *SE* 11; "Formulations . . . ," (1911).

12. Freud, "Formulations," para. 6.

13. Freud, "Creative Writers," 153.

14. Freud, "Formulations," para. 6.

15. Freud, "Creative Writers," 153.

16. Paul Ricoeur, *Freud and Philosophy* (New Haven: Yale University Press, 1970). Originating in this same question of external inwardness, of unreal reality, but still in line with the Freudian approach, is the theory of the transitional object formulated by D. W. Winnicott in his "Transitional Objects and Transitional Phenomena: A Study of the First Not-Me Possession," *International Journal of*

Psychoanalysis 34, no. 2 (1955). An artistic or literary object would seem to play the same role as a transitional object (thumb, "blankie," teddy bear, later toys): while preceding the reality test, it would not be an internal object in Klein's sense of the word either. In connection with this object, an adult never asks a child "Did you think of it yourself?" or "Where did you get that idea?" They are held together by a sort of convention of illusion. André Green (see note 36) applies this concept to the nature of tragedy.

17. Freud, "Creative Writers."
18. Herbert Marcuse, *Eros and Civilization: A Philosophical Inquiry into Freud* (Boston: Beacon Press, 1955); see in particular part 2.
19. On this question, see Melanie Klein, "Infantile Anxiety Situations Reflected in a Work of Art and the Creative Impulse" (1929), in *Contributions to Psychoanalysis* (London: Hogarth Press, 1948); E. H. Gombrich, in "Psychoanalysis and the History of Art," *International Journal of Psychoanalysis* 35, no. 4 (1954), stresses this aspect by comparing in particular nudes of Academic French art with Picasso's *Demoiselles d'Avignon*; with a distortion glass the aesthetic image of the former is "improved"; from this he concludes that "ugliness" restores the onlooker to activity, whereas the best of official art makes him revert to passivity.
20. "Une Nouvelle Approche psychanalytique de l'esthétique" in Berge, et al., *Entretiens*, 90.
21. See Freud, *Leonardo Da Vinci*; "The Uncanny" (1919), *SE* 17; Freud's writings on Hamlet and Oedipus collected by Jean Starobinski in the preface to the French translation (Paris: Gallimard, 1967) of Ernest Jones, *Hamlet and Oedipus* (London: Hogarth Press, 1949).
22. Maurice Blanchot, *L'Espace littéraire* (Paris: Gallimard, 1955).
23. See note 18, and Susan Isaacs, "The Nature and Function of Phantasy," in *Developments in Psychoanalysis* (London: Hogarth Press, 1952). Mauron's theory of creation has developed in the same direction: cf. "L'Art et la psychanalyse," *Psyché* 63 (1952); *Introduction à la psychanalyse de Mallarmé* (Neuchâtel: La Baconnière, 1950); *Des Métaphores obsédantes au mythe personnel: Introduction à la psychocritique* (Paris: Corti, 1963).
24. "*Wo Es war, soll Ich werden*" (Where Id was, there Ego shall be) are the last words of the third of Freud's *New Introductory Lectures on Psychoanalysis* (1932), *SE* 22, 80. Freud himself had given a fair idea of the measure of success that may be expected from this "*sollen*" by writing, in "A Metapsychological Supplement to the Theory of Dreams" (1915), *SE* 14, that in themselves the unconscious processes are unknowable.
25. The thesis of such reversibility is maintained by Ernst Kris, *Psychoanalytic Explorations in Art* (New York: Schocken, 1952), particularly in chapter 1, "Approaches to Art," for example: "The relationship familiar in dreamwork is reversed: we are justified in speaking of the Ego's control of the primary process . . . the capacity of gaining easy access to Id material. . . . The most general, one might say the only general hypothesis advanced in this respect came from Freud, who speaks of a certain 'flexibility of repression' in the artist" (25). (Freud's book in question is the *Introductory Lectures on Psychoanalysis* [1917], *SE* 15–16). Another example from Kris: "In states of inspiration it leads to active elaboration in creation. The process is dominated by the Ego and put to its own purposes—for sublimation in creative activity" (302).
   In the *Introductory Lectures*, Freud does not use the term *flexibility*, but

Lockerheit, "laxity" or "laxism," in repressions that normally put an end to conflict. He associates this laxity with the capacity to sublimate. Yet neither one nor the other allows us to suspect that the Ego should dominate the process of "creation," let alone control the primary process. Kris compares artistic production with scientific thinking (298); this goes quite against Freud's consistently maintained differentiation between knowledge and expression; flexibility of repression would bring the artist closer to the pervert than to the scientist. This thesis by Kris appears also in E. P. Mosse, "Psychological Mechanisms in Art Production," *The Psychoanalytic Review* 38 (1951) and in Mauron, *Des Métaphores*, from which I have borrowed the expression "reversible regression" (234). Everything becomes clear when Mauron describes the moment of the backward look in the following terms: "He takes Eurydice back from Hell only to lose her again through a mistake which is curiously reminiscent of that made by Lot's wife." And even more plainly: "Poetry is here conceived as an attempt at a synthesis of different elements—the conscience and two alien universes: the external and the unconscious. . . . This effort should be made by another agency. I have called it the 'Orphic ego'" (221).

As for Kris, he defines sublimation under two characteristics: displacement to a socially acceptable aim and "neutralization" of libidinal energy. He conceives of this neutralization as a "liaison of energy" (26ff.). But Freud had always taught that such a liaison constitutes not a neutralization of the primary process, but of the secondary process. How then to reconcile it with "flexibility of repression" and in general with visual or poetic creation, which cannot occur without transgression of the secondary order? In his approach to sublimation, Freud always related it to *Lockerheit* (laxity) of repression: compare the text of the *Introductory Lectures* with that of "The Ego and the Id" (1923), *SE* 19, in which sublimation is once again considered in relation to the existence of an unbound quantity of energy, displaceable (*verschiebbare*) and endowed with *Lockerheit*. A few lines before the passage quoted from the *Introductory Lectures*, Freud wrote, in connection with the decisive character of the quantitative factor in resistance to the neurosis: "All depends on the *quantity* of untapped libido that a person is able to hold in abeyance [*in Schwebe*] and the proportion of his libido that he is able to direct away from sexual purposes towards sublimation" (389). It is clear that, far from depending on the control of the Ego over the Id, sublimation derives from the floating nature of energy, therefore from the distress of the Ego.

26. See Paula Heimann, "A Contribution to the Problem of Sublimation and Its Relation to the Process of Internalization," *International Journal of Psychoanalysis* 33, no. 1 (1942). After an acting-out, the subject (a woman painter) compulsively produced a painting in a Victorian style that was quite the opposite of her usual genre.

27. Joanna Field, *On Not Being Able to Paint* (London: W. Heinemann, 1950); W. R. D. Fairbairn, "Critical Notice on J. Field, *On Not Being, etc.* . . . ," *British Journal of Medical Psychology* 33, no. 2 (1950); D. W. Winnicot, "Critical Notice on J. Field," ibid., 23.

28. On this subject see Maurice Blanchot's preface, entitled "La Folie par excellence," to the French translation (Paris: Minuit, 1953) of Karl Jaspers, *Strindberg and Van Gogh*, trans. by Oskar Grunow and David Woloshin (Tucson: University of Arizona Press, 1977). It seems to me that this study suffers from making too many concessions to the idea of "the dialectic of mental aberration,"

of the "mediation" of the poet between the excesses of (unconscious) desire and the common measure. See also Jacques Derrida, "La Parole soufflée," in *Writing and Difference*, trans. by Alan Bass (Chicago: University of Chicago Press, 1978).

29. It will be necessary to compare the encounter of psychoanalysis with art to the ridiculous dialogue of a "blind analyst suffering from logorrhea" with a "deaf and dumb" aesthetician, as did Gilbert Lascault ("Pour une psychanalyse du visible," in Bernard Teyssedre et al., *Les Sciences humaines et l'oeuvre d'art* [Bruxelles: La Connaissance, 1969]).

30. Charles Mauron, "Note sur la structure de l'inconscient chez Van Gogh," *Psyché* 75, 76, and 77–78 (1953).

31. Daniel E. Schneider, *The Psychoanalyst and the Artist* (New York: International Universities Press, 1954), 230. The author has no fear in concluding his study of Van Gogh with these words: "Nothing is so obscene as self-torture which almost always flows from the sick distrust that underlies pathologic self-love." But "obscene" is not in the Freudian vocabulary.

32. Marthe Robert, "Vincent Van Gogh, le génie et son double," *Preuves* 204 (1968).

33. On this subject see the recent clarification by H. Marinow, "Der malende Schizophrene und der schizophrene Maler," *Zeitschrift für Psychotherapie und medizinische Psychologie* (Nov. 1967); there is no psycho-pathological art (*Volmat*), but there is a psycho-pathology of art (a schizophrenic painter) and a psycho-pathology of pictorial activity (a schizophrenic who paints). Schneider attempts to establish in certain paintings by Chagall a relationship between the subject pictured and a presumed aggressive compulsion against male authority (*The Psychoanalyst and the Artist*, 197–205). But this relationship is established in an unmediated way, the strictly pictorial properties being neglected in proportion to their abstraction in relation to the traumatic scene in Schneider's hypothesis. The analysis focuses on the subject of the picture; Schneider finds it more difficult to relate to the agressive compulsion in the palette and color scale used by Chagall. Finally, it fails to account for the spatial organization itself, other than to say that it is of the dream type (condensation and juxtaposition of heterogeneous elements; see 197).

34. See, on the importance of transgression, Gilbert Lascault, "L'Art contemporain et la 'vieille taupe,'" *Art et contestation* (Bruxelles: La Connaissance, 1968). The reversing is ignored, for example, in the classical study by Marie Bonaparte on Edgar Allan Poe: "Both [the dream and art] in fact, act as safety valves to humanity's over-repressed instincts. . . . Thus, works of art, like dreams, reveal themselves as phantom presences which tower over our lives, with one foot in the past and one in the present" ("Poe and the Function of Literature," in William Philips, ed., *Art and Psychoanalysis* [New York: Criterion Books, 1957], 83 and 86). Bonaparte in particular states that the artist is subject to compulsive repetition just like anyone else. I acknowledge that he is subject to it, but not in the same manner. Bonaparte's interpretation is based on the "compulsion" theory of artworks. The remark also applies to Didier Anzieu's attempt at a psychoanalytical reading of Robbe-Grillet's novels ("Le Discours de l'obsessionnel dans les romans de Robbe-Grillet," *Les Temps modernes* 233, 608–37 [1965]). In an article appearing in the same issue of *Les Temps modernes*, "L'Oeuvre et l'analyste," Bernard Pingaud pinpoints the essential, maintaining that even if the written work actually addresses itself to its reader as to an impersonation of the psychoanalyst, then the "writing appears to be the opposite

(and the refusal) of the cure," because it sets speech in "a place beyond space, a moment outside time, where no one speaks to anyone else any more"—a place in which one recognizes the representational scene. "Instead of disarming fantasies and obsessions by bringing them forth to the light of consciousness," Pingaud adds, "writing seeks to maintain their force intact, to use their wealth to its own benefit" (638).

35. Here, I follow Jean Starobinski (see note 21); cf. Jean Starobinski, "Psychanalyse et critique littéraire," *Preuves* 181 (1966). There are also some thoughts on the function of truth in the theater in an article by O. Mannoni, "Le Théâtre du point de vue de l'imaginaire": "The theater is perhaps not so much an illusion as the reduction of an illusion. By evoking them, after having incited them, the stage puts back in their place (in other words, concentrates on the scene of the dream) the classic, imaginary fear and pity" (in *Clés pour l'imaginaire* [Paris: Seuil, 1969], 215). Marthe Robert, in "Raconter des histoires" (*L'Éphémère* 13 [1970], 77), takes up a similar viewpoint on the relationship between the genre of the novel and what Freud has called the "family romances of neurotics" (Sigmund Freud, "Family Romances" [1909], *SE* 9, 235ff.): "It may be said that that romance of the origins, the romance of neurotics, not only reveals the psychological origins of the *genre* . . . but is the *genre* itself."

36. Particularly in André Green, *Un Oeil en trop: Le Complexe d'Oedipe dans la trajédie* (Paris: Minuit, 1969), we find the bridge between the function of truth in theatrical representation (examined principally in connection with the *Oresteia* and Sophocles' Theban plays, in other words, the dramatization of parental relations) and the thesis of the withdrawal of the signifier, formulated by Lacan (*Ecrits*, 1966), that bears out Pierre Kaufmann's work referred to in note 10. Here, in condensed form, is the formula of this conjunction: "Briefly, it is because the problem of the relationship to the Other manifests itself as representation that the drama appears in its turn as a representation of that very relationship to the Other" (98). This should be understood as follows: the relationship to the Other, that is, to the parents in the Oedipal triangle, is always *representation* in the sense of its hallucinatory form: the lack of the signifier constitutes the space of desire where the representation opens. What is represented is always the relationship to the Other, the relationship of kinship as the place where disseizure occurs, since it is in the latter that the wish represents what is absent. Green (268ff.) rightly stresses the element of separation and alienation: the tragedy in no way provides a spectacle of reconciliation, but rather that of non-recognition: "The chief signifier . . . is the death instinct." He also praises Hölderlin for having considered the presentation of the tragic as the unbearable coupling of "God-and-man" purified by their unlimited separation (Hölderlin, *Remarques sur Oedipe*, trans. by François Fédier [Paris, Union Générale d'Editions, 1965], 63). The only reservation to be made would concern Green's identification of dream-work with the work of tragedy, or the identification of instinctual representative with theatrical representation. Here he ignores the function of the double inversion inherent in an artwork; yet, as we have seen, he is perfectly able to situate its inversion of content (that is, the absence of the progenitor opens a space for disseizure and alienation) and receptacle (that is, the space of alienation, of representation, opens itself to the lack of the signifier). In this connection see "Jewish Oedipus" (1970) [pp. 27–40 here—Eds.].

37. The reason I have not mentioned the works of Gaston Bachelard or of Jean-Paul Sartre in this survey is that the only thing they have borrowed from

psychoanalysis is its name (a borrowing whose meaning has yet to be inter-preted). In both cases, this represents an effort by philosophies of consciousness to avoid the dimension of the unconscious. An idea of the difference between existential psychoanalysis and psychoanalysis proper may be gathered from the closing words of Sartre's *Baudelaire* (1947): "The free choice made by man of himself is absolutely identical with what is called his fate." Sartre expounds on what he means by existential psychoanalysis in *Being and Nothingness* (1943). *The Words* (1964) is probably the most "Freudian" of Sartre's books.

As for Bachelard, he himself finally dropped the word "psychoanalysis" (explicitly in *Poetics of Space* [1964]), which he had previously used in an anti-Freudian sense, even though—or, rather, inasmuch as—in *The Psychoanaly-sis of Fire* (1964), the question of "sexuality" assumed some prominence. On this subject, see the issue of *L'Arc* (1970) devoted to Bachelard. The same remark applies to "Bachelardian" literary criticism: cf. Heinz-Dieter Weber and Michel Guiomar.

CHAPTER 2. ON A FIGURE OF DISCOURSE

1. You will have no trouble recognizing here some of the points made by Philippe Hamon on illegibility as well as those made on the Anaphora and the Other by Per Åg Brandt. [Since there is no record available of the proceedings at the above-mentioned symposium, we assume that Hamon and Brandt were, like Lyotard, also participants.—Eds.]
2. See Emile Benveniste, *Problems in General Linguistics*, trans. by Mary Elizabeth Meek (Coral Gables, FL: University of Miami Press, 1971), 195–239 and *passim*.
3. Gérard Genette, *Figures II* (Paris: Seuil, 1969), 66. [See *Figures of Literary Discourse*, trans. by Alan Sheridan (New York: Columbia University Press, 1982) for selections from *Figures I–III*.—Eds.]
4. *Le Monde* (27–28 February 1972), 7.
5. An analysis intended to show how this very "simple" text corroborates the libidinal function of a language-like apparatus that serves to equate the figure-discourse and the figure-narrative is presented in my article, "Petite Economie libidinale d'un dispositif narratif: La Régie Renault raconte le meurtre de Pierre Overney," in *Des dispositifs pulsionnels* (Paris: Christian Bourgois, 1980), 171–214.
6. Emmanuel Levinas, *Quatre Lectures talmudiques* (Paris: Minuit, 1968), 104–5, 107.
7. Josef Breuer and Sigmund Freud, *Studies on Hysteria* (1895), *SE* 2, 280–81.
8. Jacques Lacan, *Ecrits* (Paris: Seuil, 1966), 616.
9. Ibid., 629.
10. Ibid., 617.
11. Sigmund Freud, "Observations on Transference-Love" (1915), *SE* 12, 166.
12. Ibid., 165.
13. Ibid., 169.
14. Ibid., 170.
15. Sigmund Freud, *Psychoanalytic Notes upon an Autobiographical Account of a Case of Paranoia (Dementia Paranoides)* (1911), *SE* 12, 78–79.
16. Ibid., 79.

CHAPTER 3. JEWISH OEDIPUS

1. André Green, "Prologue: The Psycho-Analytic Reading of Tragedy," in *The Tragic Effect: The Oedipus Complex in Tragedy*, trans. by Alan Sheridan (Cambridge: Cambridge University Press, 1979); "La Lecture psychanalytique des tragiques," prologue to *Un Oeil en trop: Le complexe d'Oedipe dans la tragédie* (Paris: Minuit, 1969), 41.
2. Jean Laplanche, "Interpréter (avec) Freud," in *Freud* (Paris: L'Arc [34], 1968), 39.
3. Green, *Un Oeil en trop*, 282.
4. Ibid., 286–87.
5. [This preface is, of course, to be found in the French translation: Ernest Jones, *Hamlet et Oedipe*, trans. by Anne-Marie Le Gall (Paris: Gallimard, 1967).— Eds.]
6. Ibid., xxxvi.
7. Ibid., xxxv ff.
8. Ibid., xxxvi.
9. I would differ with André Green on a precise point: it seems to me that he does not accord the *reversal of spaces* its true place, which is that of theater and, in general, art (Green, *Un Oeil en trop*, 280ff.). His model of double reversal (12ff.), borrowed from the theories of narcissism and masochism, fails to account for the truth function of representation.
10. Theodor Reik, *Listening with the Third Ear: The Inner Experience of a Psychoanalyst* (New York: Farrar, Straus, Giroux, 1983).
11. Quotes for *Hamlet* taken from *Shakespeare Tragedies*, ed. by W. J. Craig (London: Oxford University Press, 1912).
12. Rudolf Bultmann, *Primitive Christianity in Its Contemporary Setting*, trans. by R. H. Fuller (Cleveland: World Publishing Co., 1956).
13. Emmanuel Levinas, *Quatre Lectures talmudiques* (Paris: Minuit, 1968), 130.
14. Emmanuel Levinas, "Humanisme et anarchie," *Revue internationale de philosophie* 85–86 (1968), 335.
15. Ibid., 336.
16. Levinas, *Quatre Lectures*, 82–83.
17. Ibid., 73, 19.
18. Ibid., 73–74.
19. Ibid., 78.
20. Sigmund Freud, "Creative Writers and Daydreaming" (1908), *SE* 9, 141–53.
21. Levinas, *Quatre Lectures*, 68.
22. Ibid., 106, 107, 104–5.
23. Ibid., 103.
24. Emmanuel Levinas, *Totality and Infinity*, trans. by Alphonso Lingis (Pittsburgh: Duquesne University Press, 1969).
25. Levinas, "Humanisme et anarchie," 333–34.
26. Sigmund Freud, *Moses and Monotheism* (1939), *SE* 23, 89.
27. Against Freud's construction in *Moses and Monotheism*, it could be shown that this figure corresponds to the mode of rejecting foreclosure rather than that of repression.
28. Sigmund Freud, "Recommendations to Physicians Practising Psychoanalysis" (1912), *SE* 12, 118.
29. Sigmund Freud, *Psychoanalysis and Faith: The Letters of Sigmund Freud and Oskar Pfister* [9 October 1918] (New York: Basic Books, 1963).

CHAPTER 4. "A FEW WORDS TO SING"

["A few words to sing" comes from the libretto to Luciano Berio's *Sequenza III: Per voce femminile* (London: Universal Editions, 1968). The words are from a poem by Markus Kutter—Eds.]

1. Sigmund Freud, *The Interpretation of Dreams* (1900), *SE* 4–5, 277–508.
2. Sigmund Freud, "The Unconscious" (1915), *SE* 14, 186–87.
3. [The term *free jazz* refers to the works of Cecil Taylor, Albert Ayler, Pharaoh Sanders, Don Cherry, and, most importantly, Ornette Coleman, who, in 1960, recorded *Free Jazz*. This improvisational music is characterized by the absence of tonality and predetermined chord sequence and by the abandonment of more traditional jazz structures. The works of these musicians is sometimes referred to by the terms *improvisational jazz*, *avant-garde jazz*, *action jazz*, or the *New Thing*. See *The New Grove Dictionary of Jazz*, vol. 1, ed. by Barry Kernfield (New York: Macmillan Press, 1988).—Trans.]
4. Jean-Jacques Rousseau, *Essay on the Origin of Languages* (with Johann Gottfried Herder's *Essay on the Origin of Languages*), trans. by John H. Moran and Alexander Gode (Chicago: University of Chicago Press, 1966), 9.
5. Rousseau, *Essay*, 15.
6. [The American singer, Cathy Berberian (1928–1983), was married to Berio from 1950 to 1966, and her "vocal virtuosity, darting, witty intelligence, and vivid presence" inspired several of Berio's works, *Circles*, *Sequenza III*, *Visage*, and *Recital I*. Other composers who have written works for her include Stravinsky, Henze, and Hauberstock-Ramati. Her own compositions include *Stripsody* for solo voice (1966) and *Moriscat(h)y* for piano (1971). See *The New Grove Dictionary of Music and Musicians*, vol. 2, ed. by Stanley Sadie (New York: Macmillan Press, 1980).—Trans.]
7. Rousseau, *Essay*, 16.
8. [Italian opera was introduced into France during the second half of the seventeenth century. Italian opera, especially that called *opera serie*, developed in Naples at the beginning of the eighteenth century, possessed a very rigid form and was characterized by scrupulous balance between recitation and aria. Its subject matter was always classical legends and history. Thus it tended toward grandeur and pomposity. The influence of Italian opera on French productions provoked a great deal of debate and even led to the formation of "warring" factions. It eventually led to what is now a familiar polarization in French operatic history between *tragédie lyrique* and *opéra comique*. In *opéra comique*, music played a subsidiary, though essential, role to spoken dialogue. It consisted of farces and satires and used common and well-known street songs. See *The Concise Oxford Dictionary of Opera*, ed. by Harold Rosenthal and John Warrach (New York: Oxford University Press, 1979).—Trans.]
9. Rousseau, *Essay*, 15.

CHAPTER 5. ON THE STRENGTH OF THE WEAK

[An essay under the same title appeared in *Semiotext(e)* 3, no. 2 (1978): 204–14. The essays are entirely different, apart from the titles.—Eds.]

1. In this regard, one must read Carl Prantl's *Geschichte der Logik im Abendlande* (Graz: Akademische Druck-U. Verlagsamtalt, 1855) and A. J. Festugière on

Antisthenes in *Revue des sciences philosophiques et théologiques* 21 (1932), or the small note by Jules Tricot in Aristotle's *Metaphysics* (Paris: Vrin, 1991), 1024b 33: "Aristotle rarely speaks about Antisthenes and without kindness, perhaps because Antisthenes was *nothos* (foreign born) and recruited his clientele from the common people."

CHAPTER 6. HUMOR IN SEMIOTHEOLOGY

1. Louis Marin, *La Critique du discours: Sur la "Logique de Port-Royal" et les "Pensées" de Pascal* (Paris: Minuit, 1975).
2. Ibid., 283.
3. Ibid., 194.
4. Louis Marin, *Etudes sémiologiques* (Paris: Klincksieck, 1971); *Sémiotique de la Passion* (Paris: Aubier Montaigne, 1971); *Utopiques* (Paris: Minuit, 1973); and three articles that are essential to my point here, published in Claude Chabrol and Louis Marin, *Le Récit évangélique* (Paris: Aubier Montaigne, 1974).
5. Blaise Pascal, *Pascal's Pensées*, trans. by W. F. Trotter (New York: E. P. Dutton, 1932), [684].
6. Marin, *La Critique du discours*, 141, 142.
7. Ibid., 33.
8. Ibid., 55.
9. Ibid., 56.
10. [*The Oxford English Dictionary* gives "'one who audits accounts.' The designation of various functionaries under the Byzantine emperors; applied . . . to a high official corresponding to the 'chancellor' of Western kingdoms." —Trans.]
11. Marin, *La Critique du discours*, 57, 48.
12. Ibid., 57, 57.
13. I need not state what these themes owe to Gilles Deleuze, *Présentation de Sacher-Masoch: Le froid et le cruel* (Paris: Minuit, 1967); *Sacher-Masoch: An Interpretation*, trans. by John McNeill (London: Faber, 1971).
14. Blaise Pascal, *Lettre à Mlle. de Roannez*, no. 4, Brunschvicg.
15. *Pensées*, trans. by Trotter, [788].
16. Marin, *La Critique du discours*, 117.
17. Blaise Pascal, *Pascal's Pensées*, trans. by Martin Turnell (New York: Harper and Brothers, 1962), [155] 113.
18. *Pensées*, trans. Trotter, [114].
19. Blaise Pascal, *Pensées: The Provincial Letters*, trans. by Thomas M'Crie (New York: Random House, 1941), 471.
20. Pierre Klossowski, *Le Baphomet* (Paris: Mercure de France, 1965); *The Baphomet*, trans. by Sophie Hawkes and Stephen Sartarelli (Hygiene, CO: Eridanos Press, 1988).
21. To judge by his most recent work, Louis Marin, in any case, seems to be moving in that direction. See his lecture on utopia (Cerisy, August 1975), which indicates his departure from *Utopiques* and his complicity with the humor in Ernst Bloch's *Traces*. See also his analysis of *Puss in Boots* (Urbino, July 1975), in which a funny and cruel logic of efficient ruse is admirably laid out.
22. *Pensées*, trans. Trotter, 282.
23. Marin, *La Critique du discours*, 131.
24. Ibid., 346; Marin is commenting here on a passage from the *Logic*.

25. Ibid., 358–59.
26. Ibid., 400ff.
27. Ibid., 142.

CHAPTER 7. FUTILITY IN REVOLUTION

1. Jules Michelet, *Histoire de la Révolution française: La Terreur* (Paris: Calmann-Lévy, 1899); *History of the French Revolution*, trans. by Keith Botsford (Wynnewood, PA: Kolokol Press, 1973).
2. Jules Michelet, "Le Tyran," preface to the 1869 edition of *La Terreur*.
3. Louis Marin, *La Critique du discours: sur la "Logique de Port-Royal" et les "Pensées" de Pascal* (Paris: Minuit, 1975). ·
4. See Gilbert Lascault, *Le Monstre dans l'art occidental: Un Problème esthétique* (Paris: Klincksieck, 1973).
5. Michelet, *Histoire*, 412.
6. Pierre Klossowski, *Le Baphomet* (Paris: Mercure de France, 1965), 155; *The Baphomet*, trans. by Sophie Hawkes and Stephen Sartarelli (Hygiene, CO: Eridanos Press, 1988).
7. Pierre Klossowski, *Origines culturelles et mythiques d'un certain comportement des dames romaines* (Montpellier: Fata Morgana, 1968), 61.
8. Klossowski, *Origines culturelles*, 61.
9. [Latin philologist—Trans.]
10. Daniel Guérin, *La Lutte de classes sous la Première République: 1793–1797*, vol. 1 (Paris: Gallimard, 1968), 306–7; *Class Struggle in the First French Republic: Bourgeois and Bras Nus, 1793–1795*, trans. by Ian Patterson (London: Pluto Press, 1977) [abridged translation, slightly modified by editors].
    The reader may easily surmise what my approach owes to Guérin's work. I wish to make clear, however, that the criticisms leveled here against the (Trotskyist) position of his discourse on the French Revolution do not modify in the least the importance of his book for me nor the long-lasting esteem I have for his work in general. Nor lastly do they alter the friendship that binds us—we only truly argue with those closest to us.
11. Guérin, *La Lutte de classes*, 338.
12. Michelet, *Histoire*, 419.
13. Ibid., 422.
14. See note 2.
15. See Jean-Marc Blanchard, *De la théorie à la pratique: notes sur les débuts de l'éloquence révolutionnaire* (Paris, 1970).
16. Robespierre, *Discours et rapports à la Convention* (Paris: Union Générale d'Editions, 1965), 228–34.
17. Guérin, *La Lutte de classes*, 296.
18. Ibid., 305–6.
19. Ibid., 333ff.
20. Ibid., 337–39.
21. Maurice Agulhon, "Esquisse pour une archéologie de la République: L'Allégorie civique féminine," *Annales, Economies, Sociétés, Civilisation* (January–February) (1973), 5–34.
22. D. A. F. de Sade, "Français encore un effort si vous voulez être républicains," in *La Philosophie dans le boudoir*, in *Oeuvres complètes du Marquis de Sade*, vol. 3 (Paris: Jean-Jacques Pauvert, 1986), 490–544.

23. Pierre Klossowski, "Sade et Fourier," *Topique* 4–5 (1970), 79–98.
24. Mona Ozouf, *La Fête révolutionnaire (1789–1799)* (Paris: Gallimard, 1976); *Festivals and the French Revolution*, trans. by Alan Sheridan (Cambridge, MA: Harvard University Press, 1988).
25. Ibid., 37.
26. Ozouf, *Festivals*, chapter 4.
27. Ibid., 330.
28. Ibid., 331.
29. Ibid., 340.
30. Ibid., 123–24.
31. *Le Moniteur*, 28, no. 420; cited in Guérin, *La Lutte de classes*, 308.
32. *Le Moniteur*, 28, no. 479; cited in Guérin, *La Lutte de classes*, 308–9.
33. Dommanget, cited in Guérin, *La Lutte de classes*, 311. Stephens also reckons that "in some places the worship of Reason showed a tendency to degenerate into something not unlike saturnalia." Winifred Stephens, *Women of the French Revolution* (London: Chapman and Hall, 1922), 226.
34. Jean-Marc Blanchard, "Le Théâtre patriote et la sémiotique révolutionnaire," *Annales de la Révolution française* (1970): 89–94.
35. See Dommanget, "Sylvain Maréchal [1750–1803], l'égalitaire, l'"homme sans dieu,'" *Spartacus* (1950), 258ff. [An 1877 edition gives the play's longer, descriptive title, "Le Jugement dernier des rois: prophétie . . . jouée sur le théâtre de la république au mois vendémiaire et jours suivants."—Eds.] The play was re-edited by Daniel Hamiche, *Le Théâtre et la Révolution (La Lutte de classes au théâtre en 1789 et en 1793)* (Paris: Union Générale d'Editions, 1973).
36. Lesson 28 in *Premières Leçons du fils aîné d'un roi* [A king's eldest son's first lessons], 1788.
37. *Dame Nature à la barre de l'Assemblée Nationale*, 30–31.
38. *La Feuille de Salut public*, 18 October 1793.
39. Michelet, *Histoire*, 427.
40. Cited in Guérin, *La Lutte de classes*, 463.
41. Albert Soboul, *Les Sans-culottes parisiens en l'an II* (Paris: Seuil, 1968), 229.
42. See Soboul, *Les Sans-culottes parisiens*, 230ff.
43. Stephens, *Women of the French Revolution*, 253.
44. Ibid., 267–68; see Guérin, *La Lutte de classes*, 271–78. [For the sake of comparison with Lyotard's paraphrase, Stephen's remark on the impact of the Committee's arguments concerning sexual relations reads: "They reached down to the fundamental principles of relations between the sexes. They were a prelude to the laws, which, from that day to this, have determined those relations throughout the country" (267).—Trans.]
45. Cited in Guérin, *La Lutte de classes*, 277.
46. See Hermann Weiss, *Kostümkunde* (Stuttgart, 1860); Mary Houston, *Ancient Greek, Roman, and Byzantine Costume* (London, 1920); Erhard Klepper, *Costume in Antiquity* (New York: C. N. Potter, 1964).
47. Cited in Dommanget, "Sylvain Maréchal," 194.
48. Ibid., 192–93.
49. Michelet, *History*, trans. by Botsford, 7: 40.
50. Ibid.
51. Sylvain Maréchal in *Les Révolutions de Paris (dédiées à la nation et au district des Petits Augustins)* ([Paris]: Prudhomme, 1789–1794), 215 (23–30 brumaire an II).
52. Stephens, *Women of the French Revolution*, 269.

53. Cited (and very much in agreement with this sentiment) by Jean Robiquet, *La Vie quotidienne au temps de la Révolution* (Paris: Hachette, 1938), 67.
54. Cited in Soboul, *Les Sans-culottes parisiens*, 215.
55. See Agulhon, "Esquisse."
56. Gustave Flaubert, *L'Éducation sentimentale*, in *Oeuvres* (Paris: Gallimard, 1951–52), 321.
57. Leo Spitzer, "A propos de la *Vie de Marianne*," *Romanic Review* 44 (1953): 122; cited by Georges May, *Le Dilemme du roman au XVIIIe siècle* (New Haven: Yale University Press, 1963), 242.

CHAPTER 8. RETORTION IN THEOPOLITICS

1. Ernst Bloch, *Spuren* (Frankfurt-am-Main: Suhrkamp, 1959), 159.
2. Ernst Bloch, *Subjekt-Objekt: Erläuterungen zu Hegel* (Frankfurt-am-Main: Suhrkamp, 1972), 512.
3. Ernst Bloch, *La Philosophie de la Renaissance* (Paris: Payot, 1974), 87.
4. Bloch, *Subjekt-Objeckt*, 515.
5. Ibid.
6. Bloch, *La Philosophie*, 90–91.
7. Martin Buber, *Les Récits hassidiques* (Paris: Plon, 1963), 209.
8. Ernst Bloch, *Thomas Münzer als Theologe der Revolution* (Berlin: Aufbau-Verlag, 1960). [Lyotard quotes from the French translation, *Thomas Münzer* (Paris: Julliard, 1964), 143; his stress—Eds.]
9. Ibid., 178–80.
10. Bloch, *Spuren*, 104–6.
11. Ernst Bloch, *Geist der Utopie* (Frankfurt: Suhrkamp Taschenbücher, 1973), 240; from a translation by Anne-Marie Lang and Catherine Piron-Audard.
12. Bloch, *Thomas Münzer*, trans., 234; see also the important note by Maurice de Gandillac at this page.
13. Ibid., 247.
14. Bloch, *Geist der Utopie*, 238ff.
15. Bloch, *Thomas Münzer*, trans., 50.
16. Cited by Henri Strohl, *Luther, sa vie et sa pensée* (Strasbourg: Oberlin, 1953), 259, 269, 279; himself quoted by Dmitri Merejkovski, *Luther* (Paris: Gallimard, 1949), 178–79.
17. Bloch, *Thomas Münzer*, trans., 50.
18. Ibid., 249; Philipp Melanchthon, however, attributes this statement to Münzer.
19. Ibid., 217ff.
20. Ibid., 125.
21. Ibid., 116ff.
22. Ibid., 219.
23. Ibid., 252.

CHAPTER 9. FALSE FLIGHTS IN LITERATURE

1. Michel Butor, *Mobile: Étude pour une représentation des Etats-Unis* (Paris: Gallimard, 1962); *Mobile: Study for a Representation of the United States*, trans.

by Richard Howard (New York: Simon and Schuster, 1963).

2. Blaise Cendrars, *La Prose du Transsibérien et la Petite Jeanne de France* (Paris: Editions des Hommes Nouveaux, 1913); [in English in *Selected Writings of Blaise Cendrars*, trans. by Walter Albert (New York: New Directions, 1962). The French original was illustrated by Sonia Delaunay—Trans.]

3. [In English in the French original—Trans.]

4. Georges Charbonnier, *Entretiens avec Michel Butor* (Paris: Gallimard, 1967), 27.

5. Ibid., 69.

6. Ibid., 37.

7. Ibid., 43.

8. Ibid.

9. Michel Vachey, "L'Espace indien," in Georges Raillard, ed., *Butor* (Paris: Union Générale d'Editions "10/18," 1974), 112. [*Butor* consists of the texts offered at the 1973 colloquium at Cerisy-la-Salle entitled "Approches de Michel Butor." "False Flights in Literature" is a revised version of the paper Lyotard gave there, which was published in the 1974 volume under the title "The Cut Confession" (124–46)—Trans.]

10. Charbonnier, *Entretiens*, 72.

11. Michel Butor, *Intervalle: Anecdote en expansion* (Paris: Gallimard, 1973), 90.

12. Ibid., 90–91.

13. Ibid., 157.

14. Charbonnier, *Entretiens*, 59.

15. Michel Butor, *6.810.000 Litres d'eau par seconde, étude stéréophonique* (Paris: Gallimard, 1965); *Niagara*, trans. by Elinor S. Miller (Chicago: Regnery, 1969).

16. Michel Butor, *Passage de Milan* (Paris: Minuit, 1954).

17. Charbonnier, *Entretiens*, 86–87.

18. Michel Butor, *Le Génie du lieu* (Paris: Grasset, 1958), 164–65; *The Spirit of Mediterranean Places*, trans. by Lydia Davis (Marlboro, VT: Marlboro Press, 1986), 116–17. [Very slight alterations made on this translation—Trans.]

19. Ibid., 114–15.

20. *Aleph* 1 (1967) 54–55.

21. See Charbonnier, *Entretiens*.

22. *Include* is a very bad word. Butor has an even worse one: *integrate* (Michel Butor, "L'opéra, c'est-à-dire le théâtre").

23. [The theme of "English weather/time" refers to Butor's *L'Emploi du temps* (Paris: Minuit, 1956); "a train to Rome" constitutes the narrative time of *La Modification* (Paris: Minuit, 1957). These works are in English in *"Passing Time" and "A Change of Heart": Two Novels*, trans. by Jean Stewart (New York: Simon and Schuster, 1969). *Mobile* is the "grid of America"—Trans.]

24. Butor, *Mobile*, (French edition), 131.

25. Charbonnier, *Entretiens*, 69–70.

26. Michel Butor, *Illustrations III* (Paris: Gallimard, 1973), 92.

27. Ibid., 76.

28. Charbonnier, *Entretiens*, 161, 55.

29. Ibid., 117.

30. "Maquereau, *makelare*: faire, faire des affaires." [In slang, *maquereau*, or its shortened form, *mac*, means a pimp; *grand Mac* is the expression used in Lyotard's original French. Jean Genet often used this expression, especially in his prose writings.—Trans.]

CHAPTER 10. THE SURVIVOR

1. Elias Canetti, *Crowds and Power*, trans. by Carol Stewart (New York: Farrar, Straus, Giroux, 1973).
2. Hannah Arendt, *The Human Condition* (Chicago: University of Chicago Press, 1958), 246–57.
3. Ibid., 246–47.
4. Hannah Arendt, "Die Verborgene Tradition," in *Sechs Essays* (Heidelberg: Lambert Schneider, 1948), 81–111; "The Jew as Pariah: A Hidden Tradition," in *The Jew as Pariah: Jewish Identity and Politics in the Modern Age*, ed. by Ron H. Feldman (New York: Grove Press, 1978), 67–90.
5. Hannah Arendt, *The Origins of Totalitarianism* (New York: Harcourt Brace, 1973).
6. Arendt, *The Jew as Pariah*, 85.
7. Ibid., 71.
8. Hannah Arendt, "We Refugees," in *The Jew as Pariah*, 55–66.
9. Rolf Hochhuth, *Der Stellvertreter* (Reinbek bei Hamburg: Rowohlt, 1963); *The Deputy*, trans. by Richard and Clara Winston (New York: Grove Press, 1964).
10. Hannah Arendt, *Eichmann in Jerusalem: A Report on the Banality of Evil* (New York: Viking Press, 1963).
11. Arendt, *The Jew as Pariah*, 66.
12. Ibid., 64.
13. Hannah Arendt, *Rahel Varnhagen: The Life of a Jewess*, trans. by Richard and Clara Winston (London: Published for the Institute by the East and West Library, 1958).
14. Arendt, *Eichmann in Jerusalem*, 256.
15. Ibid., 305.
16. Hannah Arendt, *Between Past and Future: Six Exercises in Political Thought* (New York: Viking Press, 1968).
17. Arendt, *Between Past and Future*, 1968 edition, 132.
18. Ibid., 336.
19. Arendt, *Origins of Totalitarianism*, 223.
20. Ibid., 337, 338.
21. Ibid., 463, 465, 465.
22. Arendt, *Between Past and Future*, 1968 edition, 188.
23. Ibid., 7.
24. Arendt, *Origins of Totalitarianism*, 224ff.

CHAPTER 11. ON WHAT IS "ART"

1. [Cf. Jean-François Lyotard, *The Differend: Phrases in Dispute*, trans. by Georges Van Den Abbeele (Minneapolis: University of Minnesota Press, 1988.—Trans.]
2. Paul Valéry, *Introduction à la poétique* (Paris: Gallimard, 1938), 38–39; italics in original. The volume contains two texts: "De l'Enseignement de la Poétique au Collège de France" (February 1937), an outline of the course Valéry gave beginning in December 1937, and "Première Leçon," the inaugural lecture of that course, given on 10 December 1937. Unless otherwise noted, all references are to this work.

3. Paul Valéry, *Cahiers* (Paris: Gallimard, 1987).
4. Paul Valéry, *La Soirée de Monsieur Teste* (Paris: Nouvelle Revue Française, 1927).
5. Paul Valéry, *Introduction à la poétique*, 40–41.
6. Ibid., 42.

CHAPTER 12. PRESCRIPTION

1. Franz Kafka, *In der Strafkolonie*; "In the Penal Colony," in *The Penal Colony: Stories and Short Pieces*, trans. by Willa Muir and Edwin Muir (New York: Schocken Books, 1948), 191–227. All references are to this translation.
2. Sigmund Freud, "The Unconscious" (1915), *SE* 14, 187.
3. [*bifrons*: "with double forehead or countenance, epithet of Janus, Vergil," *Cassell's New Latin Dictionary* (New York: Funk and Wagnalls, 1959).—Eds.]

CHAPTER 13. RETURN UPON THE RETURN

Lecture delivered at the Eleventh International James Joyce Symposium in Venice, June 1988. *Ulysses* page references are to the "corrected" edition: James Joyce, *Ulysses*, ed. by Hans Walter Gabler with Wolfhard Steppe and Claus Melchior (New York: Random House, 1986).
1. Erich Auerbach, *Mimesis: The Representation of Reality in Western Literature*, trans. by Willard R. Trask (Princeton, NJ: Princeton University Press, 1953). The chapter on the *Odyssey* is entitled "Odysseus' Scar" (3–23).
2. Ibid., 7, 13.
3. Ibid., 17.
4. [Lyotard uses this word to designate *chansons de geste*, medieval Biblical chronicles in verse. The genre is akin to the passion play.—Trans.]
5. Auerbach, *Mimesis*, 22. [To alleviate any ambiguity between Lyotard's use of this quote and Auerbach's meaning, we have decided to furnish more of the sentence than appeared in the original French.—Trans.]
6. Cf. Jean-Luc Nancy, *The Inoperative Community*, trans. by Peter Connor, Lisa Garbus, Michael Holland, and Simona Sawhney (Minneapolis: University of Minnesota Press, 1990).

Bibliography

———◆———

The following works have been of great help in compiling this bibliography: Eddie Yeghiayan, "Checklist of Writings by and about Jean-François Lyotard: A Selected Bibliography," in *Peregrinations: Law, Form, Event* (New York: Columbia University Press, 1988); the bibliography compiled by Geoff Bennington in his *Lyotard: Writing the Event* (New York: Columbia University Press, 1988); and Joan Nordquist, *Jean-François Lyotard: A Bibliography* (Santa Cruz, CA: Reference and Research Services, 1991). Other bibliographies that should also be mentioned are *Lyotard* (Paris: L'Arc [64], 1976): 87–88; and "Jean-François Lyotard: A Partial Bibliography," *Camera Obscura* 12 (1984): 107–9.

BOOKS AND ARTICLES BY JEAN-FRANÇOIS LYOTARD

For a given year, all books are listed first, then articles. (Lyotard's many articles published in *Socialisme ou barbarie* have not been listed: for a selection of those texts, see *La Guerre des Algériens* [1989]; for a bibliographic checklist, see *Peregrinations* [1988].)

1948

"La Culpabilité allemande." Review of Karl Jaspers, *Die Schulfrage: Ein Beitrag zur deutschen Frage. L'Age nouveau* 28 (1948): 90–94.

"Nés en 1925." *Les Temps modernes* 3, no. 32 (1948): 2052–57.

"Rencontre avec la jeunesse allemande." *L'Age nouveau* 24 (1948): 62–66.

1949

"Texte." *Imprudence* 3 (1949): 78–82.

1952

Review of Elliot Jaques, *The Changing Culture of a Factory. Cahiers internationaux de sociologie* 12 (1952): 179–81.

223

1954

La Phénoménologie. Paris: Presses Universitaires de France, 1954, 1956, 1959, 1961, 1964, 1967, 1969, 1976, 1982, 1986. *Phenomenology.* Trans. by Brian Beakley. Albany: State University of New York Press, 1991.

1957

"Note sur le marxisme." In Alfred Weber et Denis Huisman, eds. *Tableau de la philosophie contemporaine,* 55–61. Vol. 3 of *Histoire de la philosophie européenne de 1850 à 1957.* Paris: Fischbacher, 1957.

1963

"Algeria." *International Socialism* 13 (1963): 21–26. Trans. by Ian Birchall.

1965

"Les Indiens ne cueillent pas les fleurs." *Annales E. S. C.* 20, no. 1 (1965): 62–83.

1966

"Les Formes de l'action." *Cahiers de philosophie* 2–3 (1966): 13–25.

1967

Review of André Jacob, *Temps et langage.* *L'Homme et la société* 5 (1967): 220–24.

1968

"Préambule à une charte." *Esprit* 36, no. 373 (1968): 21–25.

"Le Travail du rêve ne pense pas." *Revue d'esthétique* 21 (1968): 26–61. "The Dream-Work Does Not Think." *Oxford Literary Review* 6, no. 1 (1983): 3–34. Trans. by Mary Lydon.

1969

"A la place de l'homme, l'expression." Review of Mikel Dufrenne, *Pour l'homme.* *Esprit* 7–8: 383 (1969): 155–78.

"Un Marx non marxiste." *Le Monde* 7530 (30–31 March 1969): 15.

1970

"L'Eau prend le ciel: Proposition de collage pour figurer le déni bachelardien." In *Bachelard.* Paris: L'Arc (42), 1970: 38–54.

"Espace plastique et espace politique." *Revue d'esthétique* 23, nos. 3–4 (1970): 255–77. With Dominique Avron and Bruno Lemenuel. "Plastic Space and Political Space." *Boundary 2* 14, no. 1–2 (1985): 211–30. Trans. by Mark S. Roberts.

"Nanterre: Ici, maintenant." *Les Temps modernes* 26, no. 285 (1970): 1665.

"Note sur la fonction critique de l'oeuvre." *Revue d'esthétique* 23, no. 3–4 (1970): 400–14. "Notes on the Critical Function of the Work of Art." In *Driftworks* (1984): 69–83. Trans. by Susan Hanson.

"Oedipe juif." *Critique* 26, no. 277 (1970): 530–45. "Jewish Oedipus." *Genre* 10, no. 3 (1977): 395–411. Trans. by Susan Hanson.

1971

Discours, figure. Paris: Klincksieck, 1971. *Discourse, Figure*. Trans. by Mary Lydon. Cambridge, MA: Harvard University Press, forthcoming.

"'A Few Words to Sing': *Sequenza III* de Berio." *Musique en jen* 2 (1971): 30–44. Written with Dominique Avron.

1972

"Capitalisme énergumène." *Critique* 28, no. 306 (1972): 923–56. "Energumen Capitalism." *Semiotext(e)* 2, no. 3 (1977): 11–26. Trans. by James Leigh.

"Plusieurs silences." *Musique en jeu* 9 (1972): 64–76. "Several Silences." In *Driftworks* (1984): 91–110. Trans. by Joseph Maier.

"Psychanalyse et peinture." In *Encyclopaedia universalis*. Paris: Encyclopaedia Universalis, 1972, 13: 745–50.

1973

Dérive à partir de Marx et Freud. Paris: Union Générale d'Editions, 1973. *Driftworks*. New York: Semiotext(e); Columbia University Press, 1984. (Selection of essays from original).

Des Dispositifs pulsionnels. Paris: Union Générale d'Editions, 1973. Reedited Paris: Christian Bourgois, 1980.

"L'Acinéma: Le nihilisme des mouvements convenus." *Revue d'esthétique* 26, nos. 2–4 (1973): 357–69. "Acinema." *Wide Angle* 2, no. 3 (1978): 52–59. Trans. by Paisley N. Livingston with Jean-François Lyotard.

"Contribution des tableaux de Jacques Monory à l'intelligence de l'économie politique libidinale du capital dans son rapport avec le dispositif pictural." In Bernard Lamarche-Vadel, ed., *Nouvelles Figurations, 1960/1973*, 154–238. Paris: Union Générale d'Editions, 1973.

"Le Corps vénal: Les Filles machines folles de Lindner." *L'Art vivant* 41 (1973): 8–9.

"En attendant Guiffrey." *L'Art vivant* 39 (1973): 6–7.

"Esquisse d'une économie de l'hyperréalisme." *L'Art vivant* 36 (1973): 9–12.

"Notes sur le retour et le Kapital" and "Discussion." In Pierre Boudot et al., *Nietzsche aujourd'hui*, 1: 141–57, 175–90. Paris: Union Générale d'Editions, 1973. "Notes on the Return and Kapital." *Semiotext(e)* 3, no. 1 (1978): 44–53. Trans. by Roger McKeon.

"La Peinture comme dispositif libidinal." *Documents de travail et pré-publications*, Centro Internazionale de Semiotica e di linguistica, Università di Urbino (Series F[23]): 1–31.

1974

Economie libidinale. Paris: Minuit, 1974.

"Adorno as the Devil." *Telos* 19 (1974): 128–37. Trans. by Robert Hurley.

"Ante diem rationis." In Boris Eizykman, ed., *Science-fiction et capitalisme: Critique de la position de désir de la science*, 225–43. Tours: Mame (Collection "Repères"; Sciences humaines, idéologies, no. 9), 1974.

"Biblioclastes." *L'Art vivant* 47 (1974): 9–12.

"Coïtus reservatus." *Critique* 30, no. 320 (1974): 3–13. Review of Robert Van Gulik, *La Vie sexuelle dans la Chine ancienne*.

"La Confession coupée." In Georges Raillard, ed., *Butor*, 124–69. Paris: Union Générale d'Editions, 1974.

"Par-delà la représentation," Introduction to Anton Ehrenzweig, *L'Ordre caché de l'art: Essai sur la psychologie de l'imagination artistique*. Paris: Gallimard, 1974. "Beyond Representation." *Human Context* 7, no. 3 (1975): 495–502. Trans. by Jonathan Culler.

1975

Le Mur du Pacifique. Paris: Christian Bourgois, 1975. Reedited Paris: Galilée, 1979. *Pacific Wall.* Trans. by Bruce Boone. Venice, CA: Lapis Press, 1990.

"A propos du département de psychanalyse de Vincennes." *Les Temps modernes* 30, no. 342 (1975): 862–63. With Gilles Deleuze.

"Considérations préliminaires à une histoire païenne: Notes sur la déchristianisation." In *Vers une esthéthique sans entrave: Mélanges offerts à Mikel Dufrenne*, 255–87. Paris: Union Générale d'Editions, 1975.

"De l'Apathie théorique." *Critique* 31, no. 333 (1975): 254–65.

"For a Pseudo-Theory." *Yale French Studies* 52 (1975): 115–27. Trans. by Moshe Ron.

"In cui si considerano certe pareti come gli elementi potenzialmente celibi di alcune macchine semplici." In Marc Le Bot et al., *Le Macchine Celibi/The Bachelor Machines: Texts*, 98–108. New York: Rizzoli, 1975.

"Marcel Duchamp ou le grand sophiste." Review of Jean Clair, *Marcel Duchamp ou le grand fictif: Essai de mythanalyse du grand verre. L'Art vivant* 56 (1975) 34–35.

"Que le signe est hostie, et l'inverse; et comment s'en débarrasser." Review of Louis Marin, *La Critique du discours. Critique* 30, no. 342 (1975): 1111–26.

1976

Sur cinq peintures de René Guiffrey. Paris: Galerie Stevenson and Palluel, 1976.

"L'Incorporéité de l'Allemagne." *Quel corps?* 6 (1976): 44–47.

"Une lettre de M. Jean-François Lyotard." *Le Nouvel Observateur* 596 (1976): 3.

"Petite mise en perspective de la décadence et de quelques combats minoritaires à y mener." In Dominique Grisoni, ed., *Politiques de la philosophie*, 121–53. Paris: Grasset, 1976.

"Puissance des traces, ou contribution de Bloch à une histoire païenne." In Gérard Raulet, ed., *Utopie-Marxisme selon Ernst Bloch: Un système de l'inconstructible: Hommages à Ernst Bloch sur son 90eme anniversaire*, 57–67. Paris: Payot, 1976.

"Sur la force des faibles." In *Lyotard*, 4–12 Paris: L'Arc (64) 1976. "On the Strength of the Weak." *Semiotext(e)* 3, no. 2 (1978): 204–14. Trans. by Roger McKeon.

"The Tooth, the Palm." *SubStance* 15 (1976): 105–10. Trans. by Anne Knap and Michel Benamou. "Gift of Organs." In *Driftworks* (1984): 85–89. Trans. by Richard Lockwood.

1977

Instructions païennes. Paris: Galilée, 1977.

Récits tremblants. Paris: Galilée, 1977.

Rudiments païens: Genre dissertatif. Paris: Union Générale d'Editions, 1977.

Les Transformateurs Duchamp. Paris: Galilée, 1977. *Duchamp's Transformers: A Book.* Trans. by Ian McLeod. Venice, CA: Lapis Press, 1990.

"Inventaire du dernier nu." In Jean Clair, ed., *Marcel Duchamp: Abécédaire: Approches critiques*, v. 3: 86–109. Paris: Centre Georges Pompidou, 1977.

"Leçon sur la condition secrète des langues. Genre didactique." *Erres* 3–4 (1977): 69–74.

"The Unconscious as Mise-en-Scène." In Michel Benamou and Charles Caramello, eds., *Performance in Postmodern Culture*, 87–98. Madison, WI: Coda Press, 1977. Trans. by Joseph Maier.

1978

"L'Autre dans les énoncés prescriptifs et le problème de l'autonomie." In Christian Delacampagne, ed., *En Marge: L'Occident et ses "autres,"* 237–56. Paris: Aubier Montaigne, 1978.

"L'Endurance et la profession." *Critique* 34, no. 369 (1978): 198–205. "Endurance and the Profession." *Yale French Studies* 63 (1982): 72–77. Trans. by Christophe Gallier, Steven Ungar, and Barbara Johnson.

"Gorgias." *Art Press International* 20 (1978): 25.

"Notes préliminaires sur le pragmatique des oeuvres (en particulier de Daniel Buren)." *Critique* 34, no. 378 (1978): 1075–85. "Preliminary Notes on the Pragmatic of Works: Daniel Buren." *October* 10 (1979): 59–67. Trans. by Thomas Repensek.

"One of the Things at Stake in Women's Struggles." *SubStance* 20 (1978): 9–17; *Wedge* 6 (1984): 24–29. Trans. by Deborah J. Clarke, Winifred Woodhull, and John Mowitt. From *Rudiments païens* (1977).

1979

Au juste: Conversations. Paris: Christian Bourgois, 1979. With Jean-Loup Thébaud. *Just Gaming.* Trans. by Wlad Godzich. Minneapolis: University of Minnesota Press, 1985.

La Condition postmoderne: Rapport sur le savoir. Paris: Minuit, 1979. *The Postmodern Condition: A Report on Knowledge.* Trans. by Geoff Bennington and Brian Massumi. Minneapolis: University of Minnesota Press, 1984. Contains "Answering the Question: What Is Postmodernism?" Trans. by Régis Durand, 71–82.

"La Micrologie de Lascault, ou la grandeur du petit." Review of Gilbert Lascault, *Voyage d'automne et d'hiver. La Quinzaine littéraire* 302 (1979): 8–9.

"L'Opera come propria prammatica" and "Discussione." In Egidio Mucci and Pier Luigi Tazzi, eds., *Teoria e pratiche della critica d'arte,* 88–98, 98–109. Milano: Feltrinelli, 1979. Trans. by Egidio Mucci and Daniela De Agostini.

"Petites ruminations sur le commentaire d'art." *Opus International* 70–71 (1979): 16–17.

"The Psychoanalytic Approach." In Mikel Dufrenne, ed., *Main Trends in Aesthetics and the Sciences of Art,* 134–49. New York: Holmes and Meier, 1979.

"That Part of Cinema Called Television: An Assessment of Television." *Framework* 11 (1979): 37–39.

1980

La Partie de peinture. Illustrated by Henri Maccheroni. Cannes: Editions Maryse Candela, 1980.

Sur la constitution du temps par la couleur dans les oeuvres récentes d'Albert Aymé. Paris: Editions Traversière, 1980.

"Deux Métamorphoses du séduisant au cinéma." In Maurice Olender and Jacques Sojcher, eds., *La Séduction*, 93–100. Paris: Aubier Montaigne, 1980.

"Logique de Levinas." In François Laruelle, ed., *Textes pour Emmanuel Levinas*, 127–50. Paris: Jean-Marie Place, 1980. "Levinas' Logic." In Richard A. Cohen, ed., *Face to Face with Levinas*, 117–58. Albany: State University of New York Press, 1986. Trans. by Ian McLeod.

"Tromeur." *La Quinzaine littéraire* 327 (1980): 20–21.

1981

Daniel Buren, les couleurs, sculptures, les formes, peintures. Paris: Centre Georges Pompidou, 1981. With Benjamin H. D. Buchloh and Jean-Hubert Martin.

La Ligne. Paris: Adami Catalogue, Galerie Maeght, 1981.

Monory. Ciels: Nébuleuses et galaxies: Les Confins d'un dandysme. Paris: Galerie Maeght [Derrière le miroir, 244], 1981.

"Analyzing Speculative Discourse as Language Game." *Oxford Literary Review* 4, no. 3 (1981): 59–67. Trans. by Geoff Bennington.

"Discussions, ou: Phraser 'après Auschwitz.'" In Philippe Lacoue Labarthe and Jean-Luc Nancy, eds. *Les Fins de l'homme: A partir du travail de Jacques Derrida*, 283–310. Paris: Galilée, 1981. "Discussions, or Phrasing 'after Auschwitz.'" *Working Paper* 2: 1–32. Milwaukee: Center for Twentieth Century Studies, University of Wisconsin, 1986. Trans. by Georges Van Den Abbeele.

"Edipo o Don Giovanni? Legittimazione, giustizia e scambio ineguale." *Aut Aut* 182–83 (1981): 87–103. With Rossella Prezzo.

"Essai d'analyse du dispositif spéculatif." *Degrés* 9 (1981): 26–27. "Analyzing Speculative Discourse as Language Game." *Oxford Literary Review* 4, no. 3 (1981): 59–67. Trans. by Geoff Bennington.

"Introduction à une étude du politique selon Kant." In Luc Ferry et al., *Rejouer le politique: Travaux du Centre de recherches philosophiques sur le politique*, 91–134. Paris: Galilée, 1981.

"Making the Invisible Seen, or: Against Realism." In *Daniel Buren, Les Couleurs, sculptures: Les formes, peintures.* Paris: Centre Georges Pompidou, 1981.

"La Performance et la phrase chez Daniel Buren." In Chantal Pontbriand, ed., *Performance, Text(e)s & Documents*, 66–69, 224. Montréal: Parachute, 1981.

"La Philosophie et la peinture à l'ère de leur expérimentation: Contribution à une idée de la postmodernité." *Rivista di Estètica* 21, no. 9 (1981): 3–15. "Philosophy and Painting in the Age of their Experimentation: Contribution to an Idea of Postmodernity." *Camera Obscura* 12 (1984): 110–25. Trans. by Maria Minich Brewer and Daniel Brewer.

"Regole e paradossi." *Alfabeta* 3, no. 24 (1981): 3. Trans. by Maurizio Ferraris.

"Theory as Art: A Pragmatic Point of View." In Wendy Steiner, ed., *Image and Code*, 71-77. Ann Arbor: University of Michigan Press, 1981. Trans. by Robert Vollrath.

"Use Me." *Semiotext(e)* 4, no. 1 (1981): 82–85. Trans. by Michel Feher and Tom Gora.

"The Works and Writings and Daniel Buren: An Introduction to the Philosophy of Contemporary Art." *Artforum* 19, no. 6 (1981): 56–64. Trans. by Lisa Leibmann.

1982

Monogrammes/Loin du doux. Paris: Catalogue Barchello, Galerie de dessin, 1982.

Le Travail et l'écrit chez Daniel Buren: Une Introduction à la philosophie des arts contemporains. Limoges: NDLR, 1982.

"Presenting the Unpresentable: The Sublime." *Artforum* 20, no. 8 (1982): 64–69. Trans. by Lisa Liebmann.

"Règles et paradoxes et appendice svelte." *Babylone* 1 (1982–83): 67–80. "Rules and Paradoxes and Svelte Appendix." *Cultural Critique* 5 (1986–87): 209–19. Trans. by Brian Massumi. See "Regole e paradossi" (1981).

"Réponse à la question: Qu'est-ce que le postmoderne?" *Critique* 38, no. 419 (1982): 1979. "Answering the Question: What Is Postmodernism?" In Ihab Hassan and Sally Hassan, eds., *Innovation/Renovation: New Perspectives on the Humanities*, 329–41. Madison: University of Wisconsin Press, 1983. Trans. by Régis Durand. Reprinted in *The Postmodern Condition* (1984).

1983

Le Différend. Paris: Minuit, 1983. *The Differend: Phrases in Dispute*. Trans. by George Van Den Abbeele. Minneapolis: University of Minnesota Press, 1988.

L'Histoire de Ruth. Paris: Le Castor Astral, 1983. With Ruth Francken.

"L'Archipel et le signe (sur la pensée kantienne de l'historico-politique)." In *Recherches sur la philosophie et le langage*, 107–28. Paris: Vrin, 1983.

"Dinge machen, von denen wir nicht wissen, was sie sind. Ein Gespräch." *Information Philosophie* 3 (1983): 10–13; 4 (1983): 26–29.

"Il dissidio. 'Le Différend': Scheda di lettura." *Alfabeta* 5, no. 55 (1983): 19. Trans. by Maurizio Ferraris.

"Fiscourse Digure: The Utopia behind the Scenes of the Phantasy." *Theatre Journal* 35, no. 3 (1983): 333–57. Trans. by Mary Lydon.

"The Insistence of Pragmatics." *Mississipi Review* 33 (1983): 65–92. With Jean-Loup Thébaud.

"On dirait qu'une ligne . . ." Preface to *Adami: Peintures récentes*. Paris: Galerie

Maeght, 1983. "It's As If a Line . . ." *Contemporary Literature* 29, no. 3 (1988): 457–82. Trans. by Mary Lydon.

"Presentations." In Alan Montefiore, ed., *Philosophy in France Today*, 116–35. London: Cambridge University Press, 1983. Trans. by Kathleen McLaughlin.

"La Quantité du silence." *Aléa* 4 (1983): 55–63.

"Un Succès de Sartre." *Critique* 39, no. 430 (1983): 177–89. Review of Denis Hollier, *Politique de la prose: Sartre en l'an quarante.*

1984

L'Assassinat de l'expérience par la peinture, Monory. Talence: Le Castor Astral, 1984.

La Peinture du sacré à l'ère postmoderne. Paris: Centre Georges Pompidou, 1984.

Tombeau de l'intellectuel et autres papiers. Paris: Galilée, 1984.

"Le Concubinage du savoir et de l'Etat." *Le Monde* 12, 264 (1984): xv.

"The *Différend*, the Referent and the Proper Name." *Diacritics*, 14, no. 3 (1984): 3–15. Trans. by Georges Van Den Abbeele.

"Das Erhabene und die Avantgarde." *Merkur* 38, no. 2 (1984): 151–64; *Kunstforum International* 7 (1984): 121–28. Trans. by Heike Rutke and Clemens-Carl Härle. "The Sublime and the Avant-Garde." *Artforum* 22, no. 8 (1984): 36–43. Trans. by Lisa Liebmann.

"Figure forclose." *L'Ecrit du Temps* "Questions de Judaïsme" 5 (1984): 63–105.

"Les Immatériaux." *Parachute* 36 (1984): 43–48.

"L'Instant, Newman." In Michel Baudson, ed., *L'Art et le temps: Regards sur la quatrième dimension*, 99–105. Paris: Albin Michel, 1984.

"Longitude 180° W or E." In *Arakawa* (Mostra Padiglione d'arte contemporanea 19 gennaio-20 febbraio 1984). Milano: Padiglione d'arte contemporanea, 1984. Trans. by Maurizio Ferraris and Mary Ann Caws.

"La Peinture du secret à l'ère postmoderne, Baruchello." *Traverses* 30–31 (1984): 95–101.

"Ruth Francken, les portraits." *Opus International* 92 (1984): 44–45.

"Le Seuil de l'histoire." *Digraphe* 33 (1984): 10–56; 34 (1984): 36–74.

"The Unconscious, History, and Phrases: Notes on [Fredric Jameson,] *The Political Unconscious.*" *New Orleans Review* 11, no. 1 (1984): 73–79. Trans. by Michael Clark.

1985

L'Art des confins: Mélanges offerts à Maurice de Gandillac. Paris: Presses Universitaires de France, 1985. Coeditor, with Annie Cazenave. Includes "La Philosophie et la peinture à l'ère de leur expérimentation," 465–77.

"Les Immatériaux." Art and Text 17 (1985): 8–10, 45–57.

Traitement de textes: Cartes et brouillons de Michel Butor. Gourdon: Dominique Bedou, 1985. With Michel Butor et al. Includes "Sites et récits de sites," 9–14.

"Entretien sur la finalité de l'éducation." Le Monde de l'éducation (April 1985): 19–21.

"Histoire universelle et différences culturelles." Critique 41, no. 456 (1985): 559–68.

"Judicieux dans le différend." In Jean-François Lyotard, ed., La Faculté de juger, 195–236. Paris: Minuit, 1985. "Judiciousness in Dispute, or Kant after Marx." In Murray Krieger, ed., The Aims of Representation: Subject/Text/History, 23–67. New York: Columbia University Press, 1987. Trans. by Cecile Lindsay.

"Par-dessus le pathos." Colóquio-Artes 64 (1985): 24–25.

"Retour au postmoderne." Magazine littéraire 225 (1985): 43.

"Le sublime, à présent." Po&sie 34 (1985): 97–116.

"The Sublime and the Avant-Garde." Paragraph 6 (1985): 1–18. With Geoff Bennington, Lisa Liebmann, and Marian Hobson.

"The Tensor." Oxford Literary Review 7, nos. 1–2 (1985): 25–40. Trans. by Sean Hand.

1986

L'Enthousiasme: La Critique kantienne de l'histoire. Paris: Galilée, 1986.

Le Postmoderne expliqué aux enfants: correspondance, 1982–1985. Paris: Galilée, 1986.

"Le Cours philosophique." In La Grève des philosophes: Ecole et philosophie, 34–40. Paris: Editions Osiris, 1986.

"Defining the Postmodern," "A Response to Philippe Lacoue-Labarthe," "Complexity and the Sublime," "A Response to Kenneth Frampton," and "Brief Reflections on Popular Culture." In Lisa Appignanesi, ed., Postmodernism, 6–7; 8; 10–12; 30–31, 58. London: Institute of Contemporary Arts Publications, 1986. Trans. by Geoff Bennington.

"Gespräch." In R. Rotzer, ed., Französische Philosophen im Gespräch, 101–18. Munich: Boer, 1986.

"Grundlagenkrise." Neue Hefte für Philosophie 26 (1986): 1–33.

"L'Obédience." Inharmoniques 1 (1986): 106–17. Trans. by J. Wagner.

"Quelque chose comme: 'Communication . . . sans communication.'" In Robert Allezand, ed., Art et Communication, 10–17. Paris: Editions Osiris, 1986.

1987

Que peindre? Adami, Arakawa, Buren. Paris: Editions de la Différence, 1987.

"Notes on Legitimation." *Oxford Literary Review* 9, nos. 1–2 (1987): 106–18. Trans. by Cecile Lindsay.

"The Postmodern Condition." In Kenneth Baynes, James Bohman, and Thomas McCarthy, eds., *After Philosophy: End or Transformation?* 67–94. Cambridge, MA: MIT Press, 1987.

"Re-writing Modernity." *SubStance* 54 [16: 3] (1987): 3–16. "Réécrire la modernité." *Cahiers de Philosophie* 5 (1988): 193–203.

"Sensus Communis." *Le Cahier* [du Collège International de Philosophie] 3 (1987): 67–87. *Paragraph* 11, no. 1 (1988): 1–23. Trans. by Marian Hobson and Geoff Bennington.

"The Sign of History." In Derek Attridge, Geoff Bennington, and Robert Young, eds., *Poststructuralism and the Question of History*, 162–80. Cambridge, New York: Cambridge University Press, 1987. Trans. by Geoff Bennington.

1988

Heidegger et "les juifs." Paris: Galilée, 1988. *Heidegger and "the jews."* Minneapolis: University of Minnesota Press, 1990. Trans. by Andreas Michel and Mark S. Roberts.

L'Inhumain: Causeries sur le temps. Paris: Galilée, 1988. *Inhuman: Reflections on Time.* Trans. by Geoff Bennington and Rachel Bowlby. London: Polity Press, 1991.

Peregrinations: Law, Form, Event. New York: Columbia University Press, 1988 (with David Carroll). *Pérégrinations: Loi, forme, événement.* Paris: Galilée, 1990.

"A l'insu." In Nicole Loraux, Jean-Luc Einaudi, Jean-François Lyotard, and Maurice Olender, eds., *Politiques de l'oubli*, 37–44. Paris: Seuil [Le Genre humain, 18], 1988.

"*Domus* et la Mégapole." *Po&sie* 44 (1988): 93–102.

"L'intérêt du sublime." In Michel Deguy, ed., *Du Sublime*, 149–77 Paris: Belin, 1988.

"Retour sur le retour." *L'Ecrit du temps* 19 (1988): 3–17.

"Scapeland." *Revue des Sciences Humaines* 80, no. 209 (1988): 39–48.

"The Subject in the Status of Birth." *Topoi* 7, no. 2 (1988): 161–73. Trans. by Marian Hobson.

"Le Survivant." In Miguel Abensour et al., eds., *Ontologie et politique: Actes du colloque Hannah Arendt*, 257–76. Paris: Tierce, 1988.

"Le Temps aujourd'hui." *Critique* 493–94 (1988): 563–78. "Time Today." *The*

Oxford Literary Review 11, nos. 1–2 (1989): 3–20. Trans. by Geoff Bennington and Rachel Bowlby.

"Vertiginous Sexuality: Schreber's Commerce with God." In David B. Allison et al., eds., *Psychosis and Sexual Identity*, 143–54. Albany: State University of New York Press, 1988. Trans. by David B. Allison and Mark S. Roberts.

1989

La Guerre des Algériens: Écrits, 1956–1963. Paris: Galilée, 1989.

The Lyotard Reader, ed. by Andrew Benjamin. Cambridge, MA: Blackwell, 1989.

"Can Thought Go on without a Body?" *Discourse* 11, no. 1 (1988/89): 74–87. Trans. by Bruce Boone and Lee Hildreth.

"Emma." *Nouvelle Revue de psychanalyse* 39 (1989): 43–70.

"Sans Appel." *Journal of Philosophy and the Visual Arts* 1 (1989): 8–18. Trans. by David Macey. "Sans Appel." *Artstudio* 18 (Paris: Daniel Templon, 1990), 36pp. + illus.

"Der/Das Überlebende," *Heidelberger Jahrbücher* 33 (1989): 39–60. Trans. by Christine Pries.

1990

"After the Sublime: The State of Aesthetics." In David Carroll, ed., *The States of "Theory": History, Art, and Critical Discourse*, 297–304. New York: Columbia University Press, 1990.

"L'Europe, les juifs et le livre." *Esprit* 162 (1990): 113–16.

"L'Inarticulé, ou le différend même." In Michel Meyer and Alain Lempereur, eds., *Figures et conflits rhétoriques*, 201–7. Brussels: Université de Bruxelles, 1990.

"Mainmise." *Autres temps* 25 (1990): 16–26.

"Matter and Time." *Journal of Philosophy and the Visual Arts* 2 (1990): 12–16. Trans. by Geoff Bennington.

"Notes du traducteur." *Revue philosophique française* 115, no. 2 (1990): 285–92.

"Les Voix d'une voix." *Nouvelle Revue de psychanalyse* 42 (1990): 199–215.

1991

La Face des choses. Catalogue de l'exposition Lapouge, Hôtel de Ville du Havre. Fécamp: La Bénédictine, 1991.

Leçons sur l'analytique du sublime. Paris: Galilée, 1991.

Lectures d'enfance. Paris: Galilée, 1991.

Die Mauer, der Golf und die Söhne: Eine Fabel. Vienna: Passagen, 1991.

"Aller et retour." In John Rajchman and Cornel West, eds., *La Pensée américaine contemporaine*, 5–30. Paris: Presses Universitaires de France, 1991.

"Anamnèse." *Hors Cadre* 9 (1991): 107–15.

La Brûlure du silence. Catalogue de l'exposition Ruth Francken. Metz: Musée des Beaux Arts, 1991.

"Critical Reflections." *Artforum* 29, no. 8 (1991): 92–93. Trans. by W. G. J. Niesluchowski.

"Foreword after the Words." In Joseph Kosuth, *Art after Philosophy and After: Collected Writings, 1966–1990,* Ed. by Gabriele Guercio, xv–xviii. Cambridge, MA: MIT Press, 1991.

"Mémorial immémorial." Film project. The Hague: Visual Arts National Office, 1991.

"La Prescription," *Rue Descartes* (Collège International de Philosophie) 1, no. 2 (1991): 239–54; "The Prescription," *L'Esprit Créateur* 31, no. 1 (1991): 15–32. Trans. by Christopher Fynsk.

"La Réflexion dans l'esthétique kantienne." *Revue Internationale de Philosophie* (Brussels) 44, no. 3[175] (1991): 507–51.

"Ticket to a New Decor (Millennium)." *Harper's Magazine* 276 (28 June 1991): 26.

FORTHCOMING

André Malraux: Une biographie. Paris: Grasset, 1994.

Le geste d'Appel sous commentaire. Paris: Galilée, 1992.

Leçon de ténèbres: "Like the paintings of a blind man" (Sam Francis). Trans. by Geoff Bennington. Los Angeles, CA: Lapis Press, forthcoming.

Lyotard [collective work]. Paris: Seuil, forthcoming.

Supplément au "Différend." Paris: Galilée, forthcoming.

"D'un Trait d'union," *Rue Descartes* (Collège International de Philosophie), forthcoming.

"Libidinal Economy in Sade and Klossowski." In David B. Allison, Mark S. Roberts, and Allen S. Weiss, eds., *Sade Beyond Measure: Categories of Reading.* Cambridge: Cambridge University Press, forthcoming. Trans. by David B. Allison and Mark S. Roberts.

INTERVIEWS OF JEAN-FRANÇOIS LYOTARD

"Sur la théorie." *VH 101* 1 (1970): 55–65. With Brigitte Devismes.

"En finir avec l'illusion de la politique." *La Quinzaine littéraire* 140 (1972): 18–19. With Gilbert Lascault.

"L'Important, ce sont les 'intensités,' pas le sens." *La Quinzaine littéraire* 201 (1975): 5–6. With Christian Descamps.

"Un Barbare parle du socialisme." *Le Nouvel Observateur* 584 (1976): 52–53. With Bernard-Henri Lévy.

"Narrations incommensurables. Réponses à des questions de Patrick de Haas." *Art Press International* 13 (1977): 19.

"Jean-François Lyotard: De la fonction critique à la transformation." *Parachute* 11 (1978): 4–9. With Jean Papineau.

"Jean-François Lyotard dans la société 'post-moderne.'" *Le Monde* 10,795 (1979): 16.

"Conversazione con Lyotard." *Filmcritica* 30, no. 300 (1979): 426–29. With Gianfranco Baruchello.

"Le Jeu de l'informatique et du savoir." *Dialectiques* 29 (1980): 3–12. With Yannick Blanc.

"*Il Dissidio*, Conversazione di Jean-François Lyotard con Paolo Fabbri e Maurizio Ferraris." *Alfabeta* 5, no. 55 (1983): 20–22.

"La Déflexion des grands récits: Entretien avec Jean-François Lyotard." *Intervention* 7 (1983/84): 48–58. With Etienne Tassin.

"On Theory: An Interview," *Driftworks* (1984): 19–33. With Brigitte Devismes. Edited and translated by Roger McKeon.

"Le Design au-delà de l'esthétique: 'Passage du témoin' de Jean-François Lyotard à François Burkhardt." *Le Monde* 12,372 (4–5 November 1984): xi.

"Interview: Jean-François Lyotard." *Diacritics* 14, no. 3 (1984): 16–21. With Georges Van Den Abbeele.

"Langage, temps, travail." *Change International* 2 (1984): 42–47. With Giairo Daghini.

"Plaidoyer pour la métaphysique: 'Passage de témoin' de Jacques Derrida à Jean-François Lyotard." *Le Monde* 12,366 (28–29 October 1984): ix.

"Un collòquio con Lyotard." *Domus* 662 (1985): 64. With Giuliano Nicolo.

"A Conversation with Jean-François Lyotard." *Flash Art* 121 (1985): 32–39. With Bernard Blistène.

"Discussion entre Jean-François Lyotard et Richard Rorty." *Critique* 41, no. 456 (1985): 581–84.

"Les Immatériaux." *Du: Zeitschrift für Kunst und Kultur* 6 (1985): 106–7. With Marie-Louise Syring and Clemens-Carl Härle.

"Les Petits récits de chrysalide: Entretien Jean-François Lyotard–Elie Theofilakis." In Elie Theofilakis, ed., *Modernes et après? "Les Immatériaux,"* 4–14. Paris: Autrement, 1985.

"La Police de la pensée." *L'Autre journal* 10 (1985): 27–34. With Jacob Rogozinski.

"Quand un philosophe s'expose." *Sciences et Avenir* 485 (1985): 86–88. With Cécile Lestienne.

"A propos du *Différend.*" *Cahiers de philosophie* (Lille) 5 (1988): 35–62. Collective interview introduced by Christine Buci-Glucksman.

"An interview with Jean-François Lyotard." *Theory, Culture, and Society* 5, nos. 2–3 (1988): 277–309. With Willem van Reijen and Dick Veerman.

"Les lumières, le sublime." *Cahiers de Philosophie* (Lille) 5 (1988): 63–98. With Willem van Reijen and Dick Veerman.

"El laberinto de los inmateriales: Entrevista con Jean-François Lyotard." *Quimera* 46–47 (n.d.): 23–29.

"Entretien avec Jean-François Lyotard." In *Les Métamorphoses Butor*, 59–73. Sainte Foy, Québec: Le Griffon d'argile, 1991. With Mireille Calle.

"Jean-François Lyotard: La Ruine du marxisme peut atteindre Hegel." *Le Figaro littéraire* (30 September 1991): 6. With Lucile Laveggi.

BOOKS ABOUT JEAN-FRANÇOIS LYOTARD

Attridge, Derek, Geoff Bennington, and Robert Young, eds. *Post-Structuralism and the Question of History.* New York: Cambridge University Press, 1987.

Bennington, Geoff. *Lyotard: Writing the Event.* New York: Columbia University Press, 1988.

Boulad-Ayoub, Josiane, ed. *Le Discours de la représentation.* Montréal: Université du Québec, 1989.

Carroll, David. *Paraesthetics: Foucault, Lyotard, Derrida.* New York: Methuen, 1987.

Clément, Catherine and Gilbert Lascault, eds. *Lyotard.* Paris: L'Arc [64], 1976.

Dasenbrock, Reed Way, ed. *Redrawing the Lines: Analytic Philosophy, Deconstruction, and Literary Theory.* Minneapolis: University of Minnesota Press, 1989.

Dews, Peter. *The Logics of Disintegration: Post-Structuralist Thought and the Claims of Critical Theory.* London: Verso, 1987.

Frank, Manfred. *What Is Neostructuralism?* Trans. by Sabine Wilke and Richard Gray. Minneapolis: University of Minnesota Press, 1989.

Gribal, Francis, Jacob Rogozinski, et al. *Témoigner du différend, quand phraser ne se peut: Autour de Jean-François Lyotard.* Paris: Osiris, 1989.

Jean-François Lyotard. Special issue of *Diacritics* (14, no. 3 [1984]).

Kauffman, Lane, ed. *Passages, Genres, Differends: Jean-François Lyotard.* Special issue of *L'Esprit créateur* (31, no. 1 [1991]).

Murphy, John W. *Postmodern Social Analysis and Criticism.* Westport, CT: Greenwood Press, 1989.

Pefanis, Julia. *Heterology and the Postmodern: Bataille, Baudrillard, Lyotard.* Durham, NC: Duke University Press, 1991.

Readings, Bill. *Introducing Lyotard: Art and Politics*. London: Routledge, 1991.

Reise-Schäffer, Walter. *Lyotard: Zur Einführung*. Hamburg: Junius Verlag, 1988.

Roberts, Mark S. *Jean-François Lyotard: Toward a Libidinal Aesthetics*. Ph.D. dissertation, State University of New York, Stony Brook, 1987.

Sarup, Madan. *An Introductory Guide to Post-Structuralism and Postmodernism*. Athens: University of Georgia Press, 1989.

Veerman, Dick, et al., eds. *Postmodernism*. Special issue of *Theory, Culture, and Society* (5, nos. 2–3 [1988]).
——, eds. *Jean-François Lyotard: Réécrire la modernité*. Special issue of *Cahiers de philosophie* (Lille) (5 [1988]).

ARTICLES ABOUT JEAN-FRANÇOIS LYOTARD

Altieri, Charles. "Judgment and Justice under Postmodern Conditions, or How Lyotard Helps Us Read Rawls as a Postmodern Thinker." In Reed Way Dasenbrock, ed., *Redrawing the Lines*, 61–91. Minneapolis: University of Minnesota Press, 1989.

Badiou, Alain. "Custos, Quid Noctis?" *Critique* 450 (1984): 851–63.

Beardslee, William A. "Christ in the Postmodern Age: Reflections Inspired by Lyotard." In David Ray Griffin, ed., *Varieties of Postmodern Theology*, 63–80. Albany: SUNY Press, 1989.

Beardsworth, Richard. "Just Attempts at Justice." *Paragraph* 10 (1987): 103–8.

Benhabib, Seyla. "Epistemologies of Postmodernism: A Rejoinder to Jean-François Lyotard." *New German Critique* 33 (1984): 103–26.

Bennington, Geoff. "August: Double Justice." *Diacritics* 14, no. 3 (1984): 64–71.

——. "Complexity without Contradiction in Architecture." *AA Files* 15 (1987): 15–18.

——. "Lyotard: From Discourse and Figure to Experimentation and Event." *Paragraph* 6 (1985): 19–27.

——. "Not Yet." *Diacritics* 12, no. 3 (1982): 23–32.

Birringer, J. "Overexposure: 'Les immatériaux.'" *Performing Arts Journal* 10, no. 2 (1986): 6–11.

Blanchard, Marc. "Never Say Why?" *Diacritics* 9, no. 2 (1979): 17–29.

Bourriand, Nicolas. "Anti-Thinkers in the 1980's." *Flash Art* 142 (1988): 83–85.

Boyne, Roy, and Scott Lash. "Communicative Rationality and Desire." *Telos* 61 (1984): 152–58.

Brunkhorst, Hauke. "Adorno, Heidegger, and Postmodernity." *Philosophy and Social Criticism* 14 (1988): 411–24.

Butor, Michel. "Le Début d'un voyage." *Le Monde* 9351 (7 February 1975): 20.

Cacciavillani, Giovanni. "J.-F. Lyotard e le macchine desideranti." *Aut Aut* 175–76 (1980): 123–45.

Calinescu, Matei. "Marxism as a Work of Art: Poststructuralist Readings of Marx." *Stanford French Review* 3, no. 1 (1979): 131–35.

———. "Postmodernism and Some Paradoxes of Periodization." In Douwe Fokkema and Hans Bertens, eds., *Approaching Postmodernism*, 239–54. Philadelphia, PA: John Benjamins, 1986.

Carravetta, Peter. "Jean-François Lyotard: The Discourse of Modernity and the Idea of Language." In Peter Carravetta, *Prefaces to the Diaphora: Rhetorics, Allegory, and the Interpretation of Modernity*, 191–212. West Lafayette, IN: Purdue University Press, 1991.

Carroll, David. "Aesthetic Antagonism. Lyotard." *Paraesthetics: Foucault, Lyotard, Derrida*, 23–52. New York: Methuen, 1987.

———. "Narrative, Heterogeneity, and the Question of the Political: Bakhtin and Lyotard." In Murray Krieger, ed., *The Aims of Representation: Subject/Text/History*, 69–106. New York: Columbia University Press, 1987.

———. "Rephrasing the Political with Kant and Lyotard: From Aesthetic to Political Judgments." *Diacritics* 14, no. 3 (1984): 74–88.

Clark, Timothy. "French Heidegger and an English Poet: Charles Tomlison's *Poem* and the Status of Heideggerian *Dichtung*." *Man and World* 20 (1987): 305–25.

Corcoran, Paul. "Godot Is Waiting Too: Endings in Thought and History." *Theory and Society* 18, no. 4 (1988): 495–529.

Defontaine, Bernard, and Jeanne Defontaine-Ouazana. "La Figure dans le langage, l'art et la représentation politique." *Annales E. S. C.* 28, no. 1 (1973): 125–41.

Delannoi, Gilles. "Jean-François Lyotard: *Le Différend*." *Esprit* 91–92 (1984): 182–83.

Descamps, Christian. "Jean-François Lyotard." In *Entretiens avec Le Monde*, 149–57. Vol. 1: *Philosophies*. Paris: La Découverte/*Le Monde*, 1984.

Descombes, Vincent. "The End of Time." *Modern French Philosophy*, 168–90. New York: Cambridge University Press, 1981.

Dews, Peter. "Jean-François Lyotard: From Perception to Desire." *Logics of Disintegration: Post-Structuralist Thought and the Claims of Critical Theory*, 109–43. London: University of Toronto Press, 1987.

———. "The Letter and the Line: Discourse and Its Other in Lyotard." *Diacritics* 14, no. 3 (1984): 40–49.

Droit, Roger-Pol. "Lyotard et la politique de Kant." *Le Monde* 13,012 (29 November 1986): 24.

Dufrenne, Mikel. "The Imaginary" and "Painting, Forever." In *In the Presence of the Sensuous: Essays in Aesthetics*, 39–67, 139–55. Atlantic Highlands, NJ: Humanities Press International, Inc., 1987.

Eagleton, Terry. "Awakening from Modernity." *Times Literary Supplement* 4377 (20 February 1987): 194.

―――. "Capitalism, Modernism, and Postmodernism." *New Left Review* 152 (1985): 60–73.

Enaudeau, Michel. "Mais nul discours ne possède son objet." *Revue d'esthétique* 25, no. 3 (1972): 356–62.

Formenti, Carlo. "La macchina, il cyborg, il manna, l'immaginario scientifico di Lyotard." *Aut Aut* 179–80 (1980): 63–83.

Fraser, Nancy, and Linda Nicholson. "Social Criticism without Philosophy: An Encounter between Feminism and Postmodernism." In Andrew Ross, ed., *Universal Abandon? The Politics of Postmodernism*, 83–104. Minneapolis: University of Minnesota Press, 1988.

Fritzman, J. M., "Lyotard's Paralogy and Rorty's Pluralism: Their Differences and Pedagogical Implications." *Educational Theory* 40, no. 3 (1990): 371–80.

Gattinara, Enrico Cartelli. "Jean-François Lyotard: L'Enthousiasme." In Karl Lowith, ed., *Scetticismo e storia*, 145–48. Firenze: La Nuova Italia Editrice, 1988.

Geiman, Kevin. "Lyotard's Kantian Socialism." *Philosophy and Social Criticism* 16, no. 1 (1990): 23–27.

Gervais, Richard. "D'un recours kantien de Lyotard." In Josiane Boulad-Ayoub, ed., *Le Discours de la représentation*, 79–98. Montréal: Université du Québec, 1989.

Grisoni, Dominique-Antoine. "Le Regard de Jean-François Lyotard: Retour au postmoderne." *Magazine Littéraire* 225 (1985): 43.

Harney, Maurita. "The Philosophy of Technology Review of Works by P. Durbin and F. Rapp, J. D. Bolter, D. Ihde, J.-F. Lyotard, F. Rapp, and S. Turkle." *Australasian Journal of Philosophy* 63 (1985): 520–32.

Honneth, Axel. "Der Affekt gegen das Allgemeine: Zu Lyotards Konzept der Postmoderne." *Merkur* 38, no. 8 (1984): 893–902.

Hurley, Robert. "Introduction to Lyotard." *Telos* 19 (1974): 124–26.

Ingram, David. "Legitimacy and the Postmodern Condition: The Political Thought of Jean-François Lyotard." *Praxis International* 7 (1987–88): 286–305.

―――. "The Postmodern Kantianism of Arendt and Lyotard." *The Review of Metaphysics* 42 (1988): 51–77.

Jameson, Fredric. "Foreword." In Jean-François Lyotard, *The Postmodern Condition: A Report on Knowledge*, vii–xxi. Trans. Geoff Bennington and Brian Massumi. Minneapolis: University of Minnesota Press, 1984.

Jones, Steven Jeffrey. "Pluralism, Agnostics, and the Postmodern Condition." In Werner Leinfellner, ed., *The Tasks of Contemporary Philosophy*, 475–79. Vienna: Holder-Pichler, 1986.

Jouffroy, Alain. "Lyotard, le deleuzisme et la peinture." *Opus International* 48 (1974): 93–94.

Kamper, Dietmar. "After Modernism: Outlines of an Aesthetics of Posthistory." *Theory, Culture, and Society* 7, no. 1 (1990): 107–18.

Keane, John. "The Modern Democratic Revolution: Reflections on Jean-François Lyotard's *La Condition postmoderne.*" *Chicago Review* 35, no. 4 (1987): 4–19.

Kearney, Richard. "The Crisis of the Post-Modern Image." *Philosophy* 21 (1987): 113–22.

Kiernan, Suzanne. "Jean-François Lyotard's *The Postmodern Condition* and G. B. Vico's *De Nostri Temporis Studiorum Ratione.*" *New Vico Studies* 4 (1986): 101–12.

Kiziltan, Mustapha, William Bain, and Anita Canizares. "Postmodern Conditions: Rethinking Public Education." *Educational Theory* 40, no. 3 (1990): 351–69.

Klatt, Gudrun. "Moderne und Postmoderne im Streit zwischen Jean-François Lyotard und Jürgen Habermas." *Weimarer Beiträge* 35, no. 2 (1989): 271–92.

Lacoue-Labarthe, Philippe. "A Jean-François Lyotard: Où en étions-nous?" In Philippe Lacoue-Labarthe, ed., *L'Imitation des modernes*, 257–85. Paris: Galilée, 1986.

————. "Talks." *Diacritics* 14, no. 3 (1984): 24–37.

Laermans, Rudi. "Desirologie—of het mislukte afscheid." *Krisis* 2, no. 4 (1981–82): 5–16.

Lash, Scott. "Postmodernity and Desire." *Theory and Society* 14, no. 1 (1985): 1–33.

Lea, Kenneth. "In the Most Highly Developed Societies: Lyotard and Postmodernism." *The Oxford Literary Review* 9, nos. 1–2 (1987): 86–104.

Leo, John R. "Postmodernity, Narratives, Sexual Politics: Reflections on Jean-François Lyotard." *The Centennial Review* 32, no. 4 (1988): 336–50.

Lingis, Alphonso. "A New Philosophical Interpretation of the Libido." *SubStance* 25 [8, no. 4] (1980): 87–97.

Linker, Kate. "A Reflection on Post-Modernism: Jean-François Lyotard's 'Les Immatériaux'." *Artforum* 24, no. 1 (1985): 104–5.

Lipovetsky, Gilles. "Travail, désir." *Critique* 29, no. 314 (1973): 615–35.
Massey, Irving. "The Effortless in Art and Ethics: Meditations on 'The Frog King, or Iron Henry.'" *Georgia Review* 37, no. 3 (1983): 640–58.

May, Todd. "Is Post-Structuralist Political Theory Anarchist?" *Philosophy and Social Criticism* 15, no. 2 (1989): 167–82.

Merrell, Floyd. "The Heyday of Master Narratives: Reflections on Flybottles and Fallibilism." *Semiotica* 72, nos. 1–2 (1988): 125–57.

Miguel, André. "Pour une nouvelle critique picturale." *Clés pour les Arts* 37 (1973): 28–29.

Misgeld, Dieter. "Modernity and Social Science: Habermas and Rorty." *Philosophy and Social Criticism* 11, no. 4 (1986): 355–72.

Montefiore, Alan. "Philosophical Survey: Philosophy in France." *Philosophy* 30 (1955): 167–70.

Morris, Meaghan. "Postmodernity and Lyotard's Sublime." *Art and Text* 16 (1984/85): 44–67.

Murray, Patrick, and Jeanne Schuler. "Post-Marxism in a French Context." *History of European Ideas* 9 (1988): 321–34.

Nicholls, Peter. "Divergences: Modernism, Postmodernism, Jameson, and Lyotard." *Critical Quarterly* 33, no. 3 (1991): 1–18.

Nicholson, Carol. "Postmodernism, Feminism, and Education: The Need for Solidarity." *Educational Theory* 39 (1989): 197–205.

Paden, Roger. "Lyotard, Postmodernism, and the Crisis in Higher Education." *International Studies in Philosophy* 19, no. 1 (1987): 53–58.

Peters, Michael. "Techno-Science, Rationality, and the University: Lyotard on the 'Postmodern Condition.'" *Educational Theory* 39 (1989): 93–105.

Peterson, Eric. "On the Boundaries of Postmodern Aesthetics." *Text and Performance Quarterly* 9, no. 2 (1989): 165–69.

Rabate, Jean-Michel. "'Rien n'aura eu lieu que le lieu': Mallarmé and Postmodernism." In David Wood, ed., *Writing the Future*, 37–54. London: Routledge, 1990.

Rajchman, John. "The Postmodern Museum." *Art in America* 73, no. 10 (1985): 110–20.

Rapaport, Herman. "Lyotard, Jean-François: Le Différend." *SubStance* 15, no. 1 (1986): 82–86.

Raulet, Gérard. "La Fin de la 'raison dans l'histoire.'" *Dialogue* 22 (1983): 631–46.

Redding, Paul. "Habermas, Lyotard, Wittgenstein: Philosophy at the Limits of Modernity." *Thesis Eleven* 14 (1986): 9–25.

Restany, D. "The Immaterial: Designs by Jean-François Lyotard." *Domus* 662 (1985): 60.

Roberts, Mark S. "Jean-François Lyotard: La Condition postmoderne." *Man and World* 16, no. 2 (1983): 161–65.

———. "Philosophies of Desire: Lyotard, Deleuze, and Guattari." *Contemporary French Civilization*, forthcoming.

———. "Review of Heidegger et 'les juifs.'" *Art and Text* 32 (1989): 121–24.

Ronell, Avital. "The Differends of Man." *Diacritics* 19, nos. 3–4 (1989): 63–64.

Rorty, Richard. "Le Cosmopolitisme sans émancipation: En Réponse à Jean-François Lyotard." *Critique* 41, no. 456 (1985): 569–80.

———. "Habermas and Lyotard on Post-modernity." *Praxis International* 4 (1984): 32–44.

———. "Habermas, Lyotard et la postmodernité." *Critique* 40, no. 442 (1984): 181–97.

Rowe, John Carlos. "Modern Art and the Invention of Postmodern Capital." *American Quarterly* 39, no. 1 (1987): 155–73.

Ruthrof, Horst. "Discourse and Metaphysics." *Philosophy Today* 33, no. 2 (1989): 130–43.

Sassower, R., and C.P. Ogaz. "Philosophical Hierarchies and Lyotard's Dichotomies." *Philosophy Today* 35, no. 2 (1991): 153–61.

Sève, Lucien. "Concepts d'une exposition," *Pensée* 246 (1985): 3–19.

Sim, Stuart. "Lyotard and the Politics of Antifoundationalism." *Radical Philosophy* 44 (1986): 8–13.

———. "'Svelte Discourse' and the Philosophy of Caution." *Radical Philosophy* 49 (1988): 31–36.

Steele, Meili. "Lyotard's Politics of the Sentence." *Cultural Critique* 16 (1990): 193–214.

Still, Judith. "Reacting to 'Lyotard.'" *Paragraph* 12, no. 3 (1989): 239–48.

Suchin, Peter. "Postmodernism and the 'Postmodern Debate in Britain': An Introduction." *Variant* 4 (1987/88): 31–35.

Thébaud, Jean-Loup. "La Chair et l'infini: J. -F. Lyotard et Merleau-Ponty." *Esprit* 6 (1982): 158–62.

Thévoz, Michel. "Lyotard pyromane." *Le Monde* 9352 (7 February 1975): 20.

Turdiman, Richard. "Deconstructing Memory: On Representing the Past and Theorizing Culture in France since the Revolution." *Diacritics* 15, no. 4 (1985): 13–36.

Turim, Maureen. "Desire in Art and Politics: The Theories of Jean-François Lyotard." *Camera Obscura* 12 (1984): 91–125. Trans. by Maria Minich Brewer and Daniel Brewer.

Vachey, Michel. "Lyotard et les labyrinthes." *L'Art vivant* 55 (1975): 21.

Van Den Abbeele, Georges, "Up against the Wall: The Stage of Judgment." *Diacritics* 14, no. 3 (1984): 90–98.

Van Reijen, Willem. "Philosophical-Political Polytheism: Habermas versus Lyotard." *Theory, Culture, and Society* 7, no. 4 (1990): 95–103.

Watson, Stephen H. "The Adventures of the Narrative: Lyotard and the Passage of the Phantasm." In Hugh J. Silverman, ed., *Philosophy and Non-Philosophy since*

Merleau-Ponty, 174–90. London: Routledge, 1988.

———. "Jürgen Habermas and Jean-François Lyotard: Post-Modernism and the Crisis of Rationality." *Philosophy and Social Criticism* 10, no. 2 (1984): 1–24.

Weber, Alexander. "Lyotard's Combative Theory of Discourse." *Telos* 83 (1990): 141–50.

Wellmer, Albrecht. "On the Dialectic of Modernism and Postmodernism." *Praxis International* 4, no. 4 (1985): 337–62.

Welsch, Wolfgang. "Heterogenität, Widerstreit, Vernuft: Zu Jean-François Lyotards philosophischer Konzeption von Postmoderne." *Philosophische Rundschau* 34 (1987): 161–86.

———. "Postmoderne und Postmetaphysik: Eine Konfrontation von Lyotard und Heidegger." *Philosophisches Jahrbuch* 92, no. 1 (1985): 116–22.

White, Stephen K. "Justice and the Postmodern Problematic." *Praxis International* 7 (1987–88): 306–19.

Williams, Bernard. "Leviathan and the Post-Modern." *History of European Ideas* 10 (1989): 569–76.

Index

Abraham, 122, 204
Acting-out, 35, 178, 210n. 26. *See also* Agieren
Adam, 82
Adorno, Theodor, 136, 159, 190
Advent, 133
Affects, 51, 174–75; circulation of, 12, 48, 53, 71; gift of, 23; language of, 52–55; signs of, 75; sonority of, 49
Agieren, 37–39. *See also* Acting-out
Agony, time of, 186
Agulhon, Maurice, 98
Aisthesis, 183–85, 187–88, 191
Algerian War, xiii
Alienation, 48
Amar, Jean-Baptiste, 109
Amazon, 110
Amplification, figure of, 63
Anaclisis of art and illness, 5–7
Anamnesis, 39, 199, 204
Ancient-Modern quarrel, 197
Anti-art, 48
Antigone, 149
Antiquity, chthonic cults of, 98
Anti-Semitism, 154
Antisthenes, 68, 84–85
Anzieu, Didier, 211n. 34
Apollo, 40, 58
Apparatus (work), 15, 74; abstraction, 127; discursive, 19, 62, 66; language, 12; language-like, 17, 213n. 5; libidinal, 16–20; political, 12; psychical (machine), 13–15, 46; psychoanalytic, 19–24
Arendt, Hannah, 144, 148, 149–63;

Between Past and Future, 156–57, 160; *Eichmann in Jerusalem*, 153, 155, 157, 161; *The Human Condition*, 150–52, 153; *The Jew as Pariah*, 153; *The Origins of Totalitarianism*, 152, 156, 158–59, 161; *Rahel Varnhagen*, 154; "Die Verborgene Tradition", 152–53, 154; "We Refugees", 153–55; notion of beginning, 187
Aristotelianism, 64, 68
Aristotle, 10, 62, 63, 120, 165; *Metaphysics*, 84; *Rhetoric*, 63
Arnauld, Antoine, 76, 83
Art: creation and, 5–6; double inconsistency of, 173; function of, 5, 41; illness and, 5–8, 11, 69, 211nn. 31, 33; modern, 10, 73, 164, 179
Artaud, Antonin, 7, 136
Articulation, 54–57
Articuli, 42, 58
Artists, work of, 7
Artwork, 168–70, 172–74, 193; expression of drives, 11; technology of, 136; time of, 173
Athens, 101
Atomism, 108
Auerbach, Erich: *Mimesis*, 195–97
Augustine, Saint, 119, 124, 146
Augustinianism, 122
Aulard, F.-A., 100
Auschwitz, 159

Bacchanalia, 113
Bach, Johann Sebastian: *Musical*

Offering, cannons in, 135
Bachelard, Gaston, 47, 212–13n. 37
Baudelaire, Charles, 5; aesthetics of, 191
Beautiful, category of the, 5–6, 155, 198
Beckett, Samuel: *Waiting for Godot*, 197; "Beckettian position," 200
Being, flight of, 128
Benjamin, Walter, 146, 153, 198
Benveniste, Emile, 18; *linguistic time*, 42; *"modes of utterance"*, 16
Berberian, Cathy, 53, 215n. 6
Berio, Luciano, xvi, 42–46, 48–59; *Circles*, 51, 215n. 6; *Recital I*, 215n. 6; *Sequenza III*, 43–46, 50–57, 215n. 6; *Sequenza VII*, 56; *Sinfonia*, 57; *Visage*, 48–49, 50, 58, 215n. 6
Berlin, 137
Bible, 33–34, 121–22, 198; Judaic reading of, 75; Mark, Gospel of, 83; New Testament, 33; Old Testament (Talmud), 20, 33, 196–97; Parables, 119; Psalm 114, 201; Revelation, Book of, 34, 122
Biblioclasm, 125, 138
Binding. *See* Libido
Birth, 146–47, 148, 149–53, 154–58, 160–63, 172–73, 175, 179, 182, 184–85, 187; debt of, 149, 153, 158, 161–62, 184; event of, 155; excess of, 185. *See also* Infancy
Blanchot, Maurice, 5
Bloch, Ernst, xvii, 100, 115–24; *Thomas Münzer*, 118–24; hasidism of, 115
Blood, 177; *cruor*, 180, 181, 182, 185; *sanguis*, 180, 182, 184
Blücher, Heinrich, 162
Body, 14, 23, 63, 122, 127, 160, 178, 179, 182–88, 190, 206; criminal innocence of, 182, 184; expressive power of, 48, 51–53, 64, 68–69, 74; heteronomy of, 187; incision of, 183, 185, 188; infancy of, 188; narrative of, 89; political, xv; recognition by, 192; redemption by, 181; social, 99, 104, 106, 108, 110, 111, 114, 123; suffering, 128, 131; text as, xvi; time of, 185, 187; volume of, 125; weak, 68–70

Boehme, Jacob, 116–17
Boileau, Nicolas, 198
Boissy d'Anglas, François Antoine, comte de, 94
Boltanski, Marc, 131
Bonaparte, Marie, 211n. 34
Bonapartism, 95, 96. *See also* Napoleon I
Book: material support of, 126; perversion of, 125, 126, 129
Borges, Jorge Luis, 140
Bouin de Marigny, Jean-Fortune, 113
Brecht, Bertolt, 79; aesthetic of distanciation, 111
Breton, André, 136
Breuer, Josef, 20
Brissotins, 98
Brittany, 137
Brutus, 98, 108, 137; historians as, 93–94
Bultmann, Rudolf, 32
Butor, Michel, 125–26, 128–42; *Illustrations III*, 139–40; *Intervalle*, 132–33, 142; *Mobile*, xvi, 125, 137–38, 142; *Niagara*, 128, 133, 137; *Passage de Milan*, 133–34, 135–36, 137: Angèle's death in, 133–34, 135, 137, 138

Caesar, 98, 99, 130, 137, 138, 139, 140, 142; *Commentaries*, 137; body of, 141; politicians as, 93–94. *See also* Butor, Michel
Caesarism, 100, 140
Cage, John, xvi, 125; *A Year from Monday*, 125; *Mural Plus Rain Forest*, 139; *Silence*, 125
Calligraphy, 16, 49, 178
Canetti, Elias, 149
Capital, 119, 120; circulation of, 48, 66; discourse of, 48; Marxist critique of, 77–78, 79
Capitalism, 58, 97; discourse of, 59; exchange value in, 47–48, 66; force of labor in, 14
Carneades, 65
Carnegie, Andrew, 131
Castoriadis, Cornelius, 207n. 3
Cat, female (she-cat), 203–4
Catharsis, 4–5, 10, 106

Cathexis, 3, 26; mobility of, 7
Catholics, 100
Celan, Paul, 153
Cendrars, Blaise: *Prose of the Trans-Siberian*, 125
Cézanne, Paul, 10, 47; paintings of Mont Sainte-Victoire, 28
Chalier, Catherine, 159
Chaplin, Charles: as "suspect", 152
Charbonnier, Georges, 128–30, 133
Charlier, Louis-Joseph, 109
Chaumette, Pierre-Gaspard, 94–96, 106, 107, 109, 112
Chénier, Marie-Joseph, 102, 111
Childhood, children, 149–56, 160–62, 172–73. *See also* Infancy
Chomsky, Noam: noun phrase, 165
Christian Caesarism, 92
Christianity, 35, 39
Cicero, 65, 66
Cities, 135, 137
Claudel, Paul, 196
Clemenceau, Georges, 157
Clement of Alexandria, 124
Cleopatra, 141
Clootz, Jean-Baptiste, comte de, 95
Collage-montage, 126, 137; book, 127; bricolage-découpage-collage, 136
Complexification (entropy), 147–48, 151, 159–60, 162–63
Condensation, 5, 15, 27, 41, 53–54
Consistency, 164, 167, 169–73
Cora, 5
Corax: eloquence and, 62–63
Corinthians, 119
Crates, 64, 68
Criticism, literary and art, 168
Critique, xv, 41, 42, 46–48, 124, 136–37
Cruelty, 185; aesthetics of, 191; theater of, 180, 182, 189
Culioli, Antoine, 17
Cummings, e. e., 51
Cynicism, 148
Cynics, 64, 68, 71, 72, 82, 84

Dada, 47
Danton, Georges-Jacques, 87, 94
Dartigoeyte, Pierre-Arnaud, 94
David, Louis, 102
Day's residues, 27, 194

Death, 6, 70, 87–89, 105–8, 131, 134, 137, 138, 147, 148, 149–50, 151, 153, 155, 156, 157, 159–61, 172, 190, 196, 199; disorder, 178; event of, 129; excess of, 185; jealous of birth, 184; stay of, 144; time of, 182–83
Death instinct, 13, 15, 31, 48, 87, 89–90
Debt: payment (fulfillment) of, 37, 202
Decadence, 70
Dechristianization movement, 90, 93–100; antireligious fervor in, 91. *See also* Republic, First
Deconstruction, 5, 7, 9, 28, 42, 49, 51, 55–59, 194, 198; accelerated, 31, 46
Découpage, 49, 50, 55, 57, 131, 137, 157. *See also* Collage-montage
Deictics, 69, 88, 165–67, 169
Delaunay, Sonia, 125
Deleuze, Gilles, 216n. 13
Descartes, René, 146
Desexualization, 93
Desire, 91, 157, 173; advent of, 10; capitalism and, 47; fate of, 32; figure of, 38; fulfillment of, 13, 31, 38, 41, 178; logic of, 207n. 1; meanings in Freud, 13; philosophy of, 74; scandal of, 37; space of, 10–11, 212n. 36; subject of, 127; theology of, 85–86; to know or to see, 40; trace of, 27, 48–49; unfulfillment of, 32, 38
Dialectics, 63
Diderot, Denis, xv; Rameau's nephew, 55
Differend: between body and law, 181
Diogenes Laertes, 64, 68–70
Dionysus, 58, 99, 124
Diotimes, 86
Discourse, 18–19, 22, 23, 27, 28, 32, 40, 48–50, 65–66, 69, 82, 86, 213n. 5; anxiety in, 51; arts of, 63; cognitive, 157; communicative, 41–46; critique of, 75, 81; decadence of, 73; figure of, 22, 25; historically compared to painting and literature, 16–17; representative theory of, 76; system of, 121; theoretical, 126; weak, 64; work on, 50–59
Displacement, 5, 14, 23, 27, 36, 41, 48, 49, 57–58, 69, 93, 105, 126, 137, 193, 194, 210n. 25

Disputatio, 65, 189
Disruption: metaphor of, 93–94, 105
Disseizure, 9, 11, 25, 29, 32–34, 40,
    137, 142, 171, 212n. 36; space of, 28
Dissimulation, 91, 115, 118, 121
Dog, 206
Dommanget, Jean-Baptiste, 103
Dream, 29, 41; theory of, 13
Dream-thought, 27
Dream-work, 10, 212n. 36
Dublin, 198
Duchamp, Marcel: "The Large Glass",
    167
Dufrenne, Mikel: notion of poetic
    language, xiv
Dürer, Albrecht, 16

Economy: libidinal, 12, 21, 24;
    political, 21, 24
Ego, 6, 11, 23, 26, 34, 85, 107, 122,
    130, 203; gratification of, 6;
    identification of, 117
Egypt, 134, 137–38, 139, 141, 199, 200,
    201, 203
Ehrenzweig, Anton, 5; psychoanalytic
    theory of art, 3
Eichmann, Adolph, 155, 161
Eliot, T. S., 194
Empire, 65, 123, 128–29, 134, 140;
    luminous, 131, 134. *See also* Rome
Energy: discharge of, 23, 56; errant,
    15; libidinal, 19, 22, 104
Engels, Friedrich, 123
Enlightenment, xiv
Enragées, 87, 95. *See also* Sansculottes
Epicureanism, 107
Epicurus, 108
Eros, 33, 71, 86, 87–89, 90, 147; birth
    of, 70
Ethics jealous of aesthetics, 184
Euathlos, 65–66
Eubulides, 66–68; Liar's Paradox,
    66–67
Eucharist, 81, 88; eucharistic utterance,
    73–77, 85
Eurydice, 5–7, 28
Eusebius of Caesarea, 124
Eve, 196, 205
Event, 15, 59, 84, 90, 118, 145, 147,

151–53, 172; libidinal, 18; musical,
    46–47, 56
Exile, 196
Exodus, 199, 201–2, 205
Expression: pictorial, 2, 6; concept of,
    2; literary, 2, 6

Faibusch, Rabbi (Phoebus Apollo), 153
Fairbairn, William, 7
Faith, discourse of, 24–25
Fantasm, 13
Fantasy: exteriorization of, 11; figural
    space of, 29, 31; primal, 28
Fatherhood, 200–205
Fechner, Gustav Theodor, 147
Femininity, 93, 108, 111–14, 173;
    emergence of in male political
    society, 70; humor of, 70. *See also*
    Women
Field, Joanna, 7
Fielding, Henry: *Tom Jones*, 108
Figuration, 5; relationship to discourse,
    58
Figure, 4–11, 15–16, 32, 35, 50, 54, 66,
    153, 213n. 5; event of, 31; expression
    of, 49, 58; order of, 57; primacy of,
    3; replication in, 31; space of, 51;
    work of, 41–46
Film: discourse of, 42
Final Solution. *See* Reich, Third
Flaubert, Gustave, 113; aesthetics of,
    198
Flavius Philostratus, 71
Fliess, Wilhelm, 29, 32
Flight, 135–39, 141–42, 199. *See also*
    Libidinal: scanning
Foreclosure, 157, 214n. 27
Forestier, Henri, 94
Fouché, Joseph, 107, 110
Fourier, Charles, 99, 129, 138, 140–41
Francastel, Pierre, 47
Franklin, Benjamin, 111
Fratres Arvales, 110
Free association, 11, 28, 40, 57, 171,
    198
Freedom of speech, 88
Free jazz, 47, 56, 215n. 3
Frege, Gottlob, 165
Freud, Sigmund, xiv, xvii, 2–5, 10,

12–15, 20–24, 25–26, 27, 29–32,
34–36, 39–40, 87, 90, 92, 107, 121,
144, 157, 161, 208n. 10, 209n. 25,
211n. 31; *Beyond the Pleasure
Principle* (1920), 12, 147; *Civilization
and Its Discontents* (1930), 13;
"Creative Writers and Daydreaming"
(1908), 32; *Ego and the Id* (1923),
21–23, 210n. 25; "Family Romances"
(1909), 212n. 35; "Formulations on
Two Principles of Mental
Functioning" (1911), 32; "Instincts
and Their Vicissitudes" (1915), 27;
The Interpretation of Dreams (1900),
13–14, 57; *Introductory Lectures on
Psychoanalysis* (1917), 209–10n. 25;
*Jokes and Their Relation to the
Unconscious* (1912), 3, 46; "A
Metapsychological Supplement to the
Theory of Dreams" (1917), 209n. 24;
Moses and Monotheism (1939), 4,
34–35, 214n. 27; *New Introductory
Lectures on Psychoanalysis* (1932),
209n. 24; "Observations on
Transference-Love" (1915), 22;
"Project for a Scientific Psychology"
(1887 [1950]), 10, 13, 27;
"Psychoanalytic Notes on an
Autobiographical Account of a Case
of Paranoia (Dementia Paranoides)"
(1911), 26; "Recommendations to
Physicians Practising
Psychoanalysis" (1912), 36; *Studies
on Hysteria* (1895), 20; *Totem and
Taboo* (1913), 35; "The
Unconscious" (1915), 14, 31; Anna
O., 20; language of knowledge in,
27; libido theory of, xii; on split
between primary and secondary
processes, 59; on the unconscious,
41–42; truth-work in, 27, 29–32;
Wolf Man, 138
Furet, François, xvii

Gaea, 98
Game, 4
Genette, Gérard, 17
God, 19–20, 23–25, 32, 75, 83–86, 99,
115, 118, 121, 122, 141, 142, 197,

206; concealment of, 81; laughter of,
82; ruse of, 79
Gojowczyk, Humbertus, 125, 139
Gorgias, 62, 64, 119
Gossec, François-Joseph, 102, 111
Gouges, Olympe de, 108
Green, André, 25, 27–29, 209n. 16,
212n. 36, 214n. 9
Grock [Adrien Wettach], 52
Guérin, Daniel, 217n. 10

Hades, 5
Hallucination, 4, 7
Headlessness (acephalous), 108, 131–32
Hébertists, 95, 96
Hegel, G. W. F., 20, 78, 81, 144–45,
146, 148; *Phenomenology of Spirit*,
144, 195; *Philosophy of Right*, 79;
Realphilosophie I, 130; dialectic of,
89, 116; master-slave relationship in,
71, 107; "place of meaning", 75;
sublation [*Aufhebung*], 141, 144,
145; totality, 90
Heidegger, Martin, 146, 157; notion of
being-been, 145
Heine, Heinrich: *Melodies*,
"Schlemihl" in, 152, 153
Helmholtz, H. L. F. von, 27
Hermeneutics, 124
Herold, Jacques: "great transparency",
139
Hieroglyph, 178
Himmler, Heinrich, 158
Hipparchia, 63–65, 68
History: Jacobin, 93; discourse of, 91,
94, 97, 118; libidinal, 90–92, 94, 118;
pagan, 92–93; "princely", 89–91
Hitler, Adolph, 157, 159. *See also*
Reich, Third
Hochhuth, Rolf: *The Deputy*, 153
Hölderlin, Friedrich, 7, 31, 212n. 36
Homer: *Odyssey*, 192–93, 195–96, 200,
202, 205; poetics of, 195
Hope, 166–69, 124, 151, 152
Horace, 72
Hugo, Victor, 168
Humor, 83, 118–19; and ordinary
people, 80–81; and ruse, 81
Hungarian Councils, 162

Husserl, Edmund, 18, 119; *Retention*, 145
Hysteria, 25

Id, 6, 130
Identification, 30–31, 35, 37
Imperative mood (grammar), 20
In actu, 166, 169–70, 174, 178, 186, 188, 190–91
Incest, 36, 202–3
Inconsistency, 64, 164–69, 173, 194
Infancy, infant [*infans*], 163, 179, 182–83, 187, 188. *See also* Childhood, children
Informal address, 113
Instrument [*suppôt*], 125–29, 130–31, 138, 185
Intensification, 106
Intensities, 7, 15, 18, 21, 90, 108, 118, 120, 126, 133, 135, 139; cathectic, 41–42; desire of, 14, 12; great conductive skin of anonymous, 123, 140–42; politics of, 123; semiotics of, 121; waste and, 92, 99
Interpretation. *See* Metalanguage
Intractable, 176, 186, 191; time of the insistence of, 188
Investment, 15
Ireland, 196; people of, 199; condition of, 200
Irony, 83; and the great, 80–81
Isaac, 204
Israel, 140; name of, 205; people of, 23–25, 117–18, 201
Italian Communist party, 124

Jacob, 19, 117–18, 201
Jacobins, Jacobinism, 79, 88, 91, 101, 108, 110, 112–14, 124; against womens' movements, 112–14; assemblies, 93, 94; "eye" of, 90–91; history, 97; mind, 108
Jakobson, Roman, 126
Jansenism, 73, 78; Marxist reading of, 75
Jealousy, 118
Jeanmaire, Henri, 24
Jesus Christ, 20, 33, 75, 77–78, 80, 81, 116, 130, 181, 196; birth of, 150–53; crucifixion of, 183; word of, 85

Jewish ethics (*kerygma*), 32, 40
Jews, 32–35, 154–55, 199, 200, 205; anamnesis and, 39; atheist, 40; wandering, 194, 199, 201, 203
Job, 117
Jones, Ernest: *Hamlet and Oedipus*, 29, 35
Joseph: sons of, 199
Josephus: *The Jewish War*, 155
Jotapata, 155
Jouissance, 5, 15, 25, 92, 113, 127, 128, 130, 133, 134, 135, 137, 201–2, 204; banker of, 142; suspension of, 23
Joyce, James: *Ulysses*, 193–206; concordance of correspondences with *Odyssey*, 193; Homeric motifs in, 193–95; Jewish theme in, 197; poetics of, 200; writing of, 10, 193–94, 203
Judaism, 19–20, 23–25, 124; ethics, 32; faith in, 19; hasidic, 115, 116–18
Judeo-Christian piety, 124
Judgment, 41, 47, 74, 76, 84, 149, 154–55, 159–63, 171, 173, 175, 181, 184; freedom of, 187
July 1936, 92
Jünger, Ernst, 159
Jung, Carl, 98

Kafka, Franz, 137; *The Castle*, 152, 160–61; "In the Penal Colony", xvi, 176–91; melancholia in work of, 163
Kagel, Mauricio, xvi, 127
Kant, Immanuel, 145, 146, 164–65, 173, 187; *Critique of Judgment*, 151, 162, 175; "Analytic of Aesthetic Judgment", 154–55; Antinomy of Reason, 151; first antinomy of, 186; *Critique of Practical Reason*, 151; *Critique of Pure Reason*, 174, 179; aesthetic point of view, 174; beautiful, 173, 175; division between imagination and reason, 173; reason, 91; *sensus communis*, 162; sublime, 173
Kaufmann, Pierre, xiv, xvii, 9, 208n. 10, 212n. 36
Kierkegaard, Søren, 34
Kirili, Alain, 16
Klein, Melanie: school of, 5–6, 8

Klossowski, Pierre, 92, 125–27, 130, 142; *Les Lois de l'hospitalité (Roberte ce soir)*: Roberte's skin, 125–27, 129, 134–35; *The Baphomet*, 83
Korea, 137
Kraus, Gerhard, 8
Kripke, Saul: "rigid designators", 166
Kris, Ernst, 209–10n. 25
Kunika, 68–70
Kutter, Markus, 50–51

Lacan, Jacques, 12, 86, 89, 173, 208n. 10, 212n. 36; on paranoia, 26; on the unconscious, 21, 79
Laclos, Choderlos de: *Les Liaisons dangereuses*, 108
Lacombe, Rose, 96, 109
Lamartine, Alphonse de, 168
Language, 2, 16, 21, 46–48, 59; articulated, 48; as code, 15; as game, 89; as whore, 203; communicative, 49–51; initiation to, xvi; philanthropic banker of, 131; power of, 62; scientific consideration of, 15; surfaces of, 63
Laplanche, Jean, 28
Lascault, Gilbert, 208n. 2, 211n. 29
Laughter, 52–53, 64, 68, 81–83, 84–85, 92, 100, 103, 104, 121–22, 205; language of clown, 52; pagan, 105. *See also* Grock
Law, 25, 65, 66, 70, 71, 85, 138, 150, 154, 159, 176–77, 178–91, 199; ethical, 180; homage to body, 185; inscription of, xvi, 176–77, 179–80, 182–83, 184, 187; jealousy of, 184–85; need for body, 185; "touch" of, 179, 180, 184, 187, 188
Lazare, Bernard: character of the "pariah" in, 152, 154
Leclerc, Victor-Emmanuel, 96, 106
Lefort, Claude, 207n. 3
Lemenuel, Bruno, 125
Leninism, 124; word in, 79
Leonardo da Vinci, 4, 16
Lequinio, Joseph-Marie, 107
Leuterbreuver, Christophe: *The Cut Confession*, 127–29, 132, 133, 138, 141
Levinas, Emmanuel, 20, 32–34, 131

Lévi-Strauss, Claude, 208n. 7
Leyde, Jean de, 124
Lhote, André, xiv, xvii
Liberalia, 113
Liberalism, 124
Libertinage, 74, 108
Libidinal: band, 132; body, 137; duplicity, 138; energy, 127, 210n. 25; events, 128; experimentation, 126; intensities, 12, 137; jealousy, 117; language, 19; locus, 137; object, 126; politics, 140; scanning, 99, 130, 137; surface, 141
Libido: binding of, 16–17; energy of, 17; formations of, 48
Life instinct, 87
Literature: modern, 47, 179
London, 137, 196
Loneliness, 161, 163
Longinus: *Treatise on the Sublime*, 197–98
Louis XIV, 78
Louis XVI, 98, 112, 181
Ludi scoenici ("playing out scenes"), 92–93, 98–99, 106, 111–12
Lutherian resignation, 121
Luther, Martin, 118, 121, 123, 124
Lyotard, Jean-François, xii–xvii; *The Differend*, 165

Machiavellianism, 90
Mâcon, Council of, 109
Mahler, Gustav: *Symphony No. 2*, 57
Mallarmé, Stéphane, 9–10, 47
Mannoni, Octave, 212n. 35
Maoism, 124
Marcuse, Herbert, 5
Maréchal, Sylvain, 110; *Le Jugement dernier des rois*, 105–6
Marianne, 98
Marianne, La (Republican secret society [post-1851]), 114
Marie-Antoinette: execution of, 105
Marin, Louis, 216n. 21; *Critique of Discourse*, xvii, 73–79, 81–82, 85–86, 88; on "logothete", 77–78
Marivaux, Pierre Carlet de Chamblain de: *La Vie de Marianne*, 114
Marxism, 76–78, 79, 115, 123
Marx, Karl, xiv; on comical repetition

in history, 106; on Jesus Christ, 77–78; political economics of, xii, 97
Mary Magdalene, 196
Mary, Virgin, 204
Masochism, 214n. 9
Master, 115; relationship to slave, 25
Mathiez, A., 100
Mauron, Charles, 8–9; psychocriticism, 8
Maury, Jean-Siffrein, 105
May '68, xii, 72, 92, 120, 123
Meaning, withdrawal of, 9
Megarians, 64, 65, 66, 69, 71, 84
Melancholia, 146–50, 163, 178, 190
Memory: debt of, 204
Mercantilism, 78
Méricourt, Théroigne de, 108–9
Merleau-Ponty, Maurice: phenomenology, xiii–xiv
Metalanguage, 2, 14, 82, 84–85
Metrocles, 68
Michelangelo [Buonarroti]: *Moses*, 4
Michelet, Jules: *Histoire de la Révolution française*, 87–88, 90, 93, 94–96, 98, 111
Millenarism, 115
Mimesis, 69
Minerva, 110
Minerva's owl, 145, 146
Minorities, xv, 64–65, 83, 101
Mise en scène, xv, 93
Möbius strip, 89, 137
Mondrian, Piet, 127, 137; rectangles of, 135
Montaigne, Michel de, 82
Montesquieu, Charles de Secondat, baron de, 111
Moses, 19, 23–25, 34–35, 39, 124, 199
Mount Sinai, 32
Mourning, 6, 11, 144, 146; narcissism of, 144
Mülhausen, 123
Münster, 122, 124
Münzer, Thomas, 115, 118, 119–22, 124; Anabaptist movement of, 120
Music, xvi, 127; as discourse, 42–46; electronic, 47, 57; language and, 46–48, 50; modern, 15–16, 46–47; space of, 47; writing and, 54–57

Name, recognition by, 192–93
Nancy, Jean-Luc: notion of inoperativity, 193, 198, 206
Napoleon I, 141; empire of, 100, 106
Napoleon III: coup d'état of, 114
Narcissism, 214n. 9
Narratives, 18; historical, 16
Nazism, 154, 162. See also Reich, Third
Nero, 155
Neumann, Erich, 98
Neurosis, 39, 40, 48
Nicole, Pierre, 76, 83
Nietzsche, Friedrich, 5, 13, 65, 71, 74, 76, 84, 85, 122, 130; *Ecce Homo*, 69–70; paganism of, 92; will to power, 14
Nihilism, 96–98, 115, 119–20, 147, 148
Nijinsky, Vatslav Fomitch: madness of, 135
Nominal definitions (nominalism), 83–85
Nonae Caprotinae, 110
Nonsense, 22, 27, 82, 174; traces of, 100
Normandy, 159

Obsession, 7
Onomatopoeia, 49–50
Opéra Comique, 113
Orpheus, 5–7
Overney, Pierre, 17–18
Ozouf, Mona: *Festivals and the French Revolution*, xvii, 100–102

Paganism, 93, 96–98, 116, 124, 133
Painting: abstract, 127; *costruzione legittima* in, 193; modern, 15–16, 47; plastic support of, 47
Paris, 135–36, 137, 139
Parnell, Charles Stewart, 199; and women, 201
Parousia of justice, 189
Parricide, 36
Parthenon, 169
Pascal, Blaise, xvii, 75, 81, 82, 83–86, 148; "De l'esprit géométrique", 83, 80; "Lettres provinciales", 82; *Pensées*, 73, 75, 80, 81, 82; "Sur la condition des grands", 80; critique

in, 73–74, 76, 78, 80; joy in, 163
Paul, Saint, 119
Peretz, Isaac Leib, 115, 117
Performance art, 166
Perversion, 133–34, 141–42. *See also*
  Book
Peter, Saint, 196
Pfister, Pastor, 40
Phallus, 172
Phoenix, 71
Phrygian cap, 98, 110
Picasso, Pablo, 10, 209n. 19
Pingaud, Bernard, 211n. 34
Pius XII, 153
Plato, 34, 62, 63, 67–68, 70–72, 79;
  Republic, 79
Platonism, 124; "Platonic Socratism",
  64
Playing out scenes. *See Ludi scoenici*
Pleasure principle, 3–4, 23, 42
Poe, Edgar Allen, 208n. 10, 211n. 34
Politics, 189, 191; cleavage with
  culture, 105; desire in, 89–90;
  discourse of, 91; function of, 41
Poros, 70–72
Port Royal *Logic*, xvii, 73–74, 76–78,
  83, 85; representative model in,
  73–74
Pousseur, Henri, xvi, 55, 127, 139
Poverty, 69, 118–19, 149. *See also*
  Women
Power: circuit of, 78
Primal scene, 133
Primary mobility, 48
Primary process, 3–4, 7, 10, 32, 40, 41,
  46, 47, 48, 55, 210n. 25; trace of, 42;
  reconciliation with secondary, 57–59
Probability, 62–63
Propp, Vladimir, 208n. 7
Protagoras, 62–63, 64, 65–66, 67–68,
  71–72, 124; humor of, 66
Proust, Marcel, 157; *Remembrance of
  Things Past*, xvi, 137
Psychical reality, 3–4, 42
Psychoanalysis, 2, 121; cure, 12;
  difference from science, 25; evenly
  suspended (free-floating) attention
  ("third ear"), 11, 28, 31, 40, 121. *See
  also* Freud, Sigmund
Psychosis, 48

Pyrrho, 82

Quinet, Edgar, 94

Rabelais, François, 65, 122
Raphael of Belz, Rabbi, 115
Reality principle, 4
Recognition. *See* Sophocles: *Oedipus
  Rex*; Shakespeare: *Hamlet*
Redemption, 128, 130, 131, 133, 151,
  180, 196; time of 188
Reich, Third, 137; Final Solution,
  153–54
Reik, Theodor, 31
Renault Corporation, 17–18
Repetition of the same, 133
Representation, 13, 201; aesthetic of,
  191; limit of, 31, 198; plastic, 42;
  truth function of, 214n. 9;
  unconscious, 29, 41
Repression, 9, 48, 214n. 27
Republic, First, 87–91, 93–114;
  monstrous body of, 87–89, 93, 102,
  112; Chamber of Representatives,
  104; Commune 94, 95, 104–5, 111,
  112; Convention, 102, 104–5, 109;
  Cordeliers, 109; Festival of Reason,
  102, 104–5, 106, 110–12; Festival of
  the Supreme Being, 102; Committee
  of Public Safety, 95, 103; Committee
  of General Security, 109; Mountain,
  94, 95, 108; Valmy, battle of, 106;
  Vendée, 106. *See also* Terror;
  Women
Responsibility, 23
Restif de la Bretonne, Nicolas, 99
Return, 117–18, 205; event of, 192;
  impossibility of, 206; logic of, 193;
  proof of, 192; unfulfillment of, 203
Ricoeur, Paul, 4
Rimbaud, Arthur, 7
Robert, Marthe, 8, 212n. 35
Robespierre, Maximilien Marie Isidore
  de, 88, 94, 96, 104, 106, 107–8;
  vagueness in speeches of, 90–91
Robespierrism, 87, 95
Rochefort, Henri, 107
Romanticism, 197
Rome, 101, 106, 110, 113, 119, 138,
  141, 196; empire, 131; gods of

ancient imperial Catholic, 92, 99, 131; libidinal body of, 92; pagan, 107
Romme, Charles-Gilbert, 95
Roth, Dieter, 125, 139
Rothko, Mark, 127, 139, 137
Rousseau, Jean-Jacques, xv, 109, 111–12; *Essay on the Origin of Language*, 49–50, 54, 57–58; exclusion of women from social body, 114
Rousset, David, 163
Roux, Jacques, 96, 103
Royalists, 112, 114
Rubicon, 137
Ruse, 63, 70, 74, 78–81, 117; reason and, 79, 116
Russell, Bertrand, 66–67, 165
Ryjik, Kyril, 137

Sade, D. A. F. de, 99, 125–26; *Philosophy in the Bedroom*, 99, 126; as sansculotte philosopher, 107; Sadian experimentation, 125
Saint-Germain-des-Prés church, 103
Saint-Just, Louis-Antoine de, 87
Sansculottes, 88, 113; as ethnologists, 104; paganism of, 94, 108; parodic games of, xv, 93, 102, 104–7; sections of Paris, 97–99, 103–5, 106, 109, 112, 113. *See also Enragées*
Sarah, 205
Sartre, Jean-Paul, 212–13n. 37
Scene, 3, 9, 10, 13, 18, 21, 28–29, 35, 38, 39, 47, 157, 190
Scenography, 78–79, 95
Schizophrenia, 7
Schnebel, Dieter: *Atemstücke*, 139
Schneider, Daniel E., 8, 211nn. 31, 33
Schoenberg, Arnold, 47, 136, 139; serial composition technique of, 56, 135
Schreber, Daniel Paul, 26
Science, 25, 30, 47, 63, 74, 116–17, 167; discourse of, 15; operative criterion of, 15
Secondary: process, 5, 9, 32, 41, 48, 54, 57; revision, 41, 49; space, 40
Semantics, 51
Semiology, 8

Semiotics, 73; representation and, 74
Sentence [law], 176–77, 180, 184; ignorance of, 180
Sexual difference, 204–5
Shakespeare, Anne, 202
Shakespeare, William, 31, 202; *Hamlet*, 10–11, 29–30, 31–33, 35–40, 194, 202–3, 206; displacement in, 35; Hamlet as hysteric, 32; neurosis in, 10, 29; oedipal figure in, 38; parricide and incest in, 38–39; unfulfillment of desire in, 35; *Julius Caesar*, 137, tragedy, 10, 35
Shoah, 154–55
Signs: circulation of, 48
Simulacrum, 49–50
Sin, 20, 33, 86, 127, 128, 131–33, 141–42, 179, 182, 196, 204, 205
Skepticism, 107
Soboul, Albert, xvii
"Socialisme ou barbarie", xiii, xiv, 207n. 3
Socrates, 62, 71–72, 84, 86, 152
Sophists, 64, 65–66, 71, 72, 82, 84–85, 119; as nomads, 64
Sophocles, 10, 30–31, 212n. 36; *Oedipus Rex*, 10–11, 29–33, 35–36, 39; errancy in, 30; incest in, 30; non-recognition, 30–31; parricide in, 30; unconscious desire in, 10
Space: artistic, 10; figural, 30–31, 38; linguistic, 27
Sparta, 101
Spartacus movement, 162
Spectacle, economy of, 93
Spitzer, Leo, 114
Stalingrad, 159
Stalinist church, 124
Starobinski, Jean, xvii, 10, 29–32, 40, 212n. 35
Statute of limitations [*prescription extinctive*; *Verjährung*], 176, 184
Steinberg, Saul: pseudowriting of, 49
Stephens, Winifred, 109
Stockhausen, Karlheinz: *Momente*, 52
Stoicism, 107
Stoics, 65, 69
Structuralism, 207n. 1, 208n. 7
Stübner, Markus, 121

Sublimation, 11, 40, 47, 110, 209n. 25
Sublime, category of the, 155, 197–98
Symptom, 11, 39
Syntax, 50–51

Talmud. *See* Bible: Old Testament
Temptation, 131–33
Tensions, 116–17
Tensor, 117, 121, 139; prophetic sign as, 122
Terror, 5, 87–88, 106, 158–59; Jacobin, 94, 96
Tertullian, 82, 120, 124
Theater: empire of, 75; end of, 40; interior, 13, 28, 31 (*see also* Unconscious); of the Other, 74; political, 105–8; semiotic, 74–75, 78–79; truth in, 212nn. 35, 36, 214n. 9
Théâtre de la République, 105
Theory: limit of, 31
Thingness, 6
Time, 173; torsion of, 186
Tisias, 62
Tokyo: public transportation in, 139; Nikkei Index, 159
Torah, 33–34
Torsion, 24–26, 63
Totalitarianism, 156–58, 159–60, 162–63
Trace, 3–4, 9, 27–28, 32–33, 42, 55, 121–22, 135, 142, 146, 182; event of, 30; sect of, 122–24
Tradition, 149, 153–54, 156, 160–62, 194
Tragedy as art, 10
Transference, 22
Transgression, 7, 10, 47, 51, 52, 194, 196, 207n. 1, 211n. 34; space of, 31
Translaboration, 23
Transubstantiation, 73, 182
Trotskyism, 79, 96, 124, 217n. 10
Truth, 6–7, 25, 29, 32, 36, 51, 62, 63, 67, 68, 71–72, 73, 75, 81, 84, 89, 107, 147–48, 161, 165, 195; figures of, 28; Greek function of, 40; in literature and art, 11; ruse of, 81–83; urge or desire for, 7, 87
Tübingen, 115
Tudor, David: *Mural Plus Rain Forest*, 139

Ugliness, 5
Unconscious, 3, 5, 21, 24, 27, 29–31, 39, 51, 55, 57, 135, 178–79, 187, 205, 208n. 10; as work, 41–42; atemporality of, 53, 99; eruption of, 7; figure of, 6, 9; space of, 11
Unfulfillment, 5, 32–33, 37–39
United States, 137; busing of schoolchildren in, 162

Vachey, Michel, 125, 127, 130, 138, 139
Valéry, Paul, 164, 173; *Cahiers*, 173; *Introduction to Poetics*, 168–72, 174–75; 221n. 2; *La Soirée de M. Teste*, 173; conceptualization of disorder, 164, 171–74
Van Gogh, Vincent, 3, 7; letters to Theo, 3; supposed epilepsy of, 8
Varlet, Jean-François, 96
Varro, Marcus Terentius: theatrical theology of, 92, 102, 124
Venus de Milo, 167
Vergniaud, Pierre-Victurnien, 87
Vernant, Jean-Pierre, 24
Vernet, Carle, xv
Versailles, 112
Vidal-Naquet, Pierre, 24
Vienna, 137
Virgil: *Aeneid*, 193
Voltaire (François-Marie Arouet), 111

Wagner, Richard, 47
Wall Street, 159
Washington, 137, 138, 139
Weak force, 62–72, 81, 118, 120
Webern, Anton von, 47
Will, philosophy of, 74
Wish, 3–4, 6, 13; fulfillment of, 4–5
Witness, witnessing, to bear witness, 71, 146, 148, 152–53, 161, 164, 198, 201
Wittenberg, 121
Wittgenstein, Ludwig: philosophy of language of, xiii
Women, 189, 199–205; Republican Revolutionary Women's Club, 109, 112; as poverty in the master's discourse, 71; exclusion from performative political function, 93,

111–14; repression of, 108–11; revolutionaries passion for, 87, 98; voice of, 199

Word representations, 178
Writing, support for, 125

Xeniades, 69

Yahweh. *See* God
Yehiel Mikhal, Rabbi, 117

Zen Buddhism, 178
Zeno's Paradox, 69
Zlothso, 117
Zwickau, prophets of, 121–22